Greenhill Books

THE ART OF
WAR IN SPAIN
The Conquest of Granada
1481–1492

THE ART OF WAR IN SPAIN

The Conquest of Granada
1481-1492

WILLIAM H. PRESCOTT
EDITED BY ALBERT D. MCJOYNT

Greenhill Books, London
Stackpole Books, Pennsylvania

The Art of War in Spain
first published 1995 by Greenhill Books
Lionel Leventhal Limited, Park House, 1 Russell Gardens
London NW11 9NN
and
Stackpole Books, 5067 Ritter Road, Mechanicsburg, PA 17055, USA

© Albert D. McJoynt, 1995

British Library Cataloguing in Publication Data
Prescott, William H.
Art of War in Spain: Conquest of Granada, 1481–92
I. Title   II. McJoynt, Albert D.
946.03

ISBN 1–85367–193–2

Library of Congress Cataloging-in-Publication Data
Prescott, William Hickling, 1796–1859
The art of war in Spain: the conquest of Granada, 1481–1492
by W.H. Prescott: with new material by Albert D. McJoynt
p.   cm.
Based on seven chapters of the author's previously published work:
A History of the reign of Ferdinand and Isabella. 3rd ed.
New York: J.B. Alden, 1841, with extensive new material added.
Includes bibliographical references and index.
ISBN 1–85367–193–2
1. Granada (Kingdom)—History—Spanish Conquest, 1476–1492.
2. Spain—History, Military.   3. Military art and science—Spain—History.
I. McJoynt, Albert D.   II. Prescott, William Hickling, 1796–1859.
History of the reign of Ferdinand and Isabella.   III. Title.
DP123.P74   1995
946'.8203—dc20
94-47614

Typeset by DP Photosetting, Aylesbury, Bucks
Printed and bound in Great Britain by
Butler & Tanner Limited, Frome and London

CONTENTS

MAPS, CHARTS AND ILLUSTRATIONS

ACKNOWLEDGEMENTS

As the editor of this work I owe much to the support and encouragement of many individuals.

I am very grateful to professors Paul Stewart and Weston Cook, Jr. for thoughtfully reviewing early drafts of the editorial text and patiently addressing my many questions. Their vast knowledge of the late medieval Spanish and Maghribi military systems respectively was invaluable in providing a synthesis of current knowledge on the 1481–92 War of Granada. I am indebted to John Sloan and Curt C. Johnson, who reviewed draft material pertaining to the broader aspects of Western military history, and who made available the Xenophon Group's database on military history for use in the notes and Glossary.

I am also very grateful for the assistance of Phyllis Cassler and staff of the Van Noy Library, Fort Belvoir, Virginia. Their diligent professionalism permitted my access to many books of limited availability in the United States, and tested the inter-library loan system to its limits. Certainly my gratitude extends to the many libraries that cooperated and responded as part of the OCLC network. Recognition is due to José Paláu who assisted me in performing follow-up research in Spain, and to Donald J. LaRocca of The Metropolitan Museum of Art, Arms and Armour Section, New York, who reviewed and commented upon armament portions of the draft text. I owe much to the many individuals who so graciously assisted me at various museums in Spain and at academic libraries in the United States. An indispensable contribution has been provided by Kate Ryle, who studiously read several drafts, and proposed numerous constructive changes to the text.

In particular, I am most appreciative for the support, encouragement and vital assistance provided by Barbara, my wife and companion in the pursuit of the study of history.

Albert D. McJoynt
Mount Vernon, Virginia
1995

PREFACE

G ranada was the scene of one of the most spectacular and pivotal wars in history. Moorish Granada's fall was the culmination of a broad struggle between two cultures, and its conclusion not only settled the cultural fate of a large portion of Europe, but established the basis for the discovery of the Americas. With the conquest in January, 1492, of the last stronghold of Islamic Spain, the Spanish 'Catholic Sovereigns', Isabella and Ferdinand, were able to launch the momentous voyage of Columbus, and to pursue a world empire with a revitalized military force.

Accounts of the conquest of Granada have been written in many languages, but none has surpassed the English-language versions by two great American authors of the early nineteenth century. In the way of narrative storytelling, little can be added to Washington Irving's *Chronicle of the Conquest of Granada* (first published in 1829) or to the methodically researched *History of the Reign of Ferdinand and Isabella the Catholic* (first published in 1837) by the historian William H. Prescott. Both men made use of material available in the Spanish archives of their day. While neither Prescott nor Irving attempted to describe the war with an emphasis on military history, the former's work provides an excellent foundation for such a description. It is, therefore, the purpose of this present book to focus on the appropriate sections of Prescott's magnificent study and to add comments based upon observations and findings that have surfaced since Prescott's day.

Prescott's detailed study of the war, incidental to his broader topic, produced a valuable account that has well served English and American scholars of military history. Only a few French and Spanish scholars seem to have gone directly to the primary sources used by Prescott. Recently, some American scholars have shown renewed interest in the war, but the general public does not enjoy easy access to their works, which are ensconced in various professional journals and unpublished manuscripts. Furthermore, the popular military history surveys, which are the most readily available to the general reading public, tend to skip over the conquest of Granada as they leap from the Hundred Years' War (concluded in 1453) to the Italian Wars that began at the very end of the fifteenth century. In so doing, the survey histories create a gap of awareness, passing over facts that are critical to understanding the development of European warfare. This issue is addressed, with other military aspects of the conquest of Granada, in the Introduction.

Prescott's unabridged text, which provides the fundamental framework of this book, is taken from his *History of the Reign of Ferdinand and Isabella*, Volume I, First Part, Chapters VIII to XV, inclusive. Excluding one short chapter on the Inquisition, these sections form Chapters One to Seven of this book.

All of Prescott's valuable notes are included in this work. Editor's additions are contained within square brackets, followed with the expression '– ED'. Editorially added dates of battles and significant events, and alternative spellings, are presented within brackets, without the expression '– ED'. Several other editorial conventions used in this book are noted in the editorial commentary on Prescott and his work found at the end of this book.

Added editorial sections to this book are: this Preface, the two-part Introduction, commentary on Prescott and his sources, and various graphics. A short Glossary should assist a reader who is not familiar with several expressions and some military terms addressed in this book. The objective is to provide an appreciation of the conquest of Granada as an important episode in the emergence of early modern warfare – specifically in the areas of developing standing armies, adopting gunpowder weapons, and planning logistical support for sustained year-long campaigns.

Part I of the Introduction places the War of Granada in context of the broader era of European warfare during the late fifteenth century. The need for such a section emerged in the course of researching the military aspects of the conquest, and as a consequence of many informal discussions with military historians as to the significant role the war had in the art of warfare in Europe. Part II of the Introduction summarizes *La Reconquista*, the Christian Reconquest of the Iberian Peninsula, and briefly reviews the struggle that established Ferdinand and Isabella as sovereigns. Both parts of the Introduction provide background knowledge which is essential to an understanding of the military and historic significance of the War of Granada.

In the first of Prescott's chapters, the civilization of the Spanish Muslims is described. This was necessary in the context of his broader work, *History of the Reign of Ferdinand and Isabella*. Prescott describes the Spanish Umayyad dynasty up to the end of the tenth century and then passes to Nasrid Granada in the late thirteenth century. The risk of duplication in Part II of the Introduction and Chapter I is minor. Each part reviews the pre-Granadan War Iberian history from a different perspective. Prescott's chapter portrays the Spanish Muslim scene. The Introduction canvasses the continuous and fluctuating pattern of almost eight hundred years of the *Reconquista*, which is crucial in examining the War of Granada. The Introduction also provides a brief overview of the Castilian War of Succession (1474–79), a topic which occupied a considerable part of Prescott's original work, but is not included in this book.

The five-hundred-year anniversary, in 1992, of the surrender of Granada, inspired the editor's review of this extraordinary military enterprise. Many histories present the War of Granada as a distant event, peripheral to European warfare of the fifteenth century. In fact, Granada was the dramatic final curtain of the *Reconquista*, successfully reclaiming the first European Christian land conquered by the Muslims. The War of Granada concluded the nearly millennium-long struggle between two cultures for the control of the Iberian Peninsula.

In comparison with the many wars which receive more attention in popular literature, few can claim such portentous features as the War of Granada. The conquest of Granada ensured the solidification of the united rule of Castile and Aragón in Spain. This unification was on uncertain ground at the beginning and during half of the war; it is doubtful that the union would have survived and Spain have emerged to become the world-power that it did if there had not been a military victory over the Moors' Nasrid kingdom. The victory led to the direct sponsoring of Columbus' voyage, which had been repeatedly postponed during and due to the war. It was a war that had to be won before Columbus could sail to the New World.

Albert D. McJoynt

INTRODUCTION, PART I

MILITARY ASPECTS OF THE WAR FOR THE CONQUEST OF GRANADA

I LATE FIFTEENTH-CENTURY EUROPEAN WARFARE

An understanding of the major historical trends of Western European warfare during the fifteenth century is essential if the War of Granada is to be seen in context. Most of the influential trends in Western European medieval warfare had been initiated by the middle of the fifteenth century, and were to converge in Italy at the end of that century to form a new epoch in the development of warfare.[1]

This initial section of the Introduction on late fifteenth-century warfare gives disproportionately more attention to Western European aspects of warfare than to the dramatic developments which were occurring in Eastern Europe and the major Muslim realms of the Ottomans and Mamluks [Mamelukes] during the same time-frame. The reasons for this imbalance are twofold. Firstly, the Castilian army became a key element in the evolution of Western European warfare. Secondly, the Muslim Hispano-Maghribi system in the Granadan War had departed significantly from the military patterns that emerged in robust fifteenth-century eastern Islamic societies. By the end of the century, eastern Muslim military might had crushed the decayed Byzantine Empire, threatened most of the Eastern European states and challenged the Italian naval presence in the eastern Mediterranean. In the West, European military power gained unquestioned supremacy with the conquest of Granada and incursions into the rim of North Africa. Attention given in the Introduction to Muslim warfare is limited to the impact other Muslim military powers had on the strategic balance during the war, and, more specifically, to the influence of Muslim military traditions on the Nasrid military system. The Spanish Muslim military was a distinct blend of Euro-Islamic, but more particularly Hispano-Maghribi, influences unique to the southern Iberian Peninsula region of Andalus in the late fifteenth century.[2] Specific aspects of the Castilian and Granadan military are addressed later in the Introduction.

The late fifteenth century was an era when changes in tactics and weapons transformed European warfare from its feudal customs. For the most part, these changes were extrapolations of trends already in motion by the middle of the century. As they evolved, the impact of some trends became more pronounced, while others fell by the wayside. The military trends can be traced in two general areas: technological (influencing new weapon capabilities) and organizational (tactical and administrative). During the latter part of the fifteenth century these trends were interwoven in various engagements and influenced the outcome of battles, campaigns and wars. Since many of the developments interacted, it would be difficult to declare any one development to have been singularly decisive.

By the mid fifteenth century, European warfare was undergoing two fundamental changes. One was the increasing vulnerability of the formidable castle-strongholds which had developed since the Crusades of the twelfth century. The other was the decreasing dominance of heavily armoured men-at-arms due to newly emerging infantry tactics. While such changes were the result of a mixture of weapons technology and tactics, there were also organizational changes affecting the fate of the traditional military structure. Feudal military levies were being replaced by professional combatants who participated in sustained campaigns as mercenaries or as regularly paid warriors of a dynastic kingdom or small city-state. France, under Charles VII, went further than most in establishing a standing army, supported by a state tax system and with direct allegiance to the sovereign.

In general, the dominant status of infantry, which had been gaining strength during the fourteenth century, was reinforced in the fifteenth century. There were two principal infantry tactical schemes, each associated with a different weapon system. These were the Swiss pikemen, in well disciplined phalanx formation, and the English longbow infantry-archers, who delivered devastating missile fire at an attacking opponent. Such infantry configurations stood out distinctively from the normal feudal infantries of lightly armed forces which fought with various pole arms, spears and swords.

Throughout the fifteenth century almost every European army adopted gunpowder weapons. The effectiveness of the new technology developed slowly, and was achieved by both improvements in manufacture and better understanding of its employment. Gunpowder weapons achieved significant and undeniable success in siege operations by the late fifteenth century. Increasing emphasis on gunpowder weapons enhanced confidence in their use in the late fifteenth century, and enabled the growth of large and lethal infantry formations in the early sixteenth century.

The evolution of these influential trends in warfare, while not present in every case, is recognizable in a comprehensive examination of the Hundred Years' War (1337–1453) between England and France, and in the various Swiss

Wars for Independence from Austria (1315–88), continuing with the Swiss–Burgundian Wars (1476–77). These wars established the reputations of the English longbow and the Swiss pike phalanx.

There were also other important military events which had peripheral impact on Western Europe. The Hussite Wars (1419–34), in which gunpowder weapons played an important part, may have indirectly promoted the spread of these weapons in Eastern Europe and Germany.[3] The Ottoman–Turkish wars with Eastern European states introduced one form of light cavalry, but the most noticeable impact of these wars was the employment of impressive artillery (particularly in the size of some of the guns) in the 1453 Siege of Constantinople.

Some major European military trends that proved to be pivotal during the last half of the century receive scant attention in many surveys of warfare. In particular, these trends were manifest in the reconquests of French Normandy (1450) and Guyenne [Aquitaine] (1451–53) in the last period of the Hundred Years' War, and the final phase of the *Reconquista* of Christian Spain (1481–92). This is not the place to analyze why these subjects are slighted in so many military history studies available in English. It might be noted that these reconquests do not fit easily into established concepts, or support theories about late medieval warfare that some authors consider important. One factor common to these reconquests is the predominant employment of gunpowder artillery in highly developed, aggressive siege campaigns. Many military historians are unenthusiastic about siege warfare, preferring to concentrate on open-field battles. As for the final *Reconquista*, it is evident that neither the English longbow nor the Swiss pike phalanx was a significant element of the War of Granada; though it should be noted that some longbowmen supposedly accompanied the English volunteer Edward Woodville ('Lord Scales'), and Ferdinand and Isabella invited a small Swiss contingent. The military engagements of the war did not seem to require these particular tactical techniques.

For the most part, these late medieval warfare developments converged in the 'Great Italian Wars' – the label used frequently by Charles Oman for the conflicts that began with the invasion by the French King, Charles VIII, of Italy in 1494.[4] For the purpose of this Introduction it is not necessary to address the full scope of these wars. To evaluate the War of Granada, it is only necessary to consider the performance of the first two Spanish expeditions (1495–96 and 1500–04) in the Italian Wars. Charles VIII's seizure of Naples led Ferdinand the Catholic to deploy the first Spanish military expedition (May 1495) under *el Gran Capitán* ('The Great Captain'), Gonzalo Fernández de Córdoba, involving many veterans of the War of Granada.[5] Its composition is noted by Paul Stewart: 5,000 infantry and 600 light cavalry (*jinetes*). The Spanish did not bring artillery and relied on obtaining heavy cavalry from the *condottieri* of their Italian allies.[6] Charles VIII's successor, Louis XII of France, again invaded northern Italy, only to be confronted by a second Spanish expedition under 'The Great Captain' and suffer a disastrous military defeat. The climactic Battle of Cerignola (26 April 1503) was one of the first engagements where the Swiss pike formation, in the French service, was decisively stopped by Spanish hand-guns and small cannon.

The leading military contingents of the Italian Wars were the French, Italian, Swiss, German, and Spanish. The wars opened with French and Italian armies opposing one another, but soon evolved into a struggle between French and Spanish armies, the latter becoming part of the armies of the Austrian– Habsburg Empire. German and Swiss contingents fought with either side, the Germans eventually aligning themselves with the Austrian–Spanish Habsburg Empire. The Swiss became a dominant mercenary infantry component of the French field forces.

With remarkable unanimity, military historians acknowledge that the Spanish army emerged from the Italian Wars as the superior military force in the world at that time. Almost as remarkable is the number of writers of military surveys of the period, and of the Italian Wars, in particular, who fail to examine the Spanish military experience, the decade-long War of Granada, out of which this army grew.[7] This is, of course, the 'gap of awareness' cited earlier in the Preface.

As a result of ignoring the developments immediately influencing the army that would be victorious in the Italian Wars, many writers conclude that the Spanish came to these wars with a 'blank slate' of experience. They imply that the Spanish army in the Italian Wars merely copied their adversaries and, somehow, managed to put everything together more successfully than the people they imitated. It should be apparent that the War of Granada (1481–92) needs to be examined for a proper perspective of the development of European warfare that preceded and influenced the initial course of the Italian Wars.[8]

II THE WAR OF GRANADA IN THE CONTEXT OF WEST EUROPEAN WARFARE

A. THE COMBAT ARMS

Whereas in twentieth-century military terminology 'combat arms' would include a large number of technically diverse military functions, fifteenth-century armies were limited to the 'combat arms' of cavalry, infantry and artillery of the land armies. Naval and joint operations between land and naval forces are covered separately.

(1) Cavalry

Heavy Cavalry

The armies of the Christian Spanish kingdoms had a heavy cavalry tradition that was considerably influenced by French and Italian medieval weaponry and

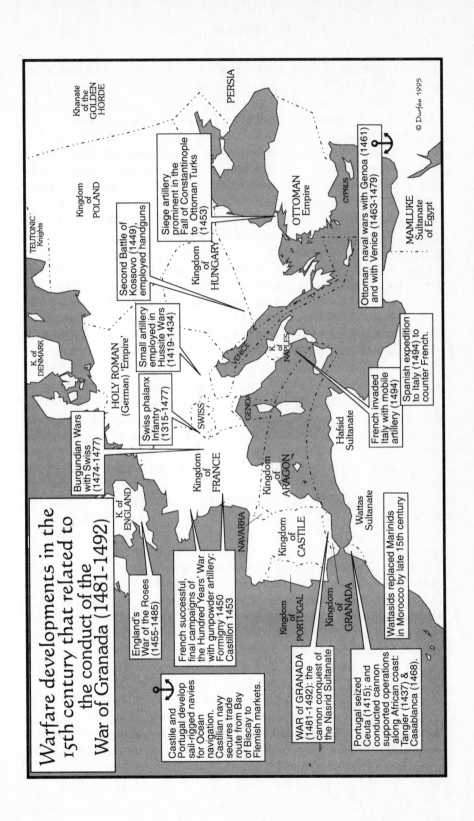

Warfare developments in the
15th century that related to
the conduct of the
War of Granada (1481-1492)

© Durfee 1995

Khanate
of the
GOLDEN
HORDE

PERSIA

TEUTONIC
Knights

Kingdom
of
POLAND

K. of
DENMARK

HOLY ROMAN
(German) 'Empire'

OTTOMAN
Empire

CYPRUS

MAMLUKE
Sultanate
of Egypt

Siege artillery
prominent in the
Fall of Constantinople
to Ottoman Turks
(1453)

Second Battle of
Kossovo (1449),
employed handguns

Kingdom
of
HUNGARY

Ottoman naval wars with Genoa (1461)
and with Venice (1463-1479)

Small artillery
employed in
Hussite Wars
(1419-1434)

VENICE

K. of
NAPLES

GENOA

Swiss phalanx
Infantry
(1315-1477)

SWISS

Spanish expedition
to Italy (1494) to
counter French.

Burgundian Wars
with Swiss
(1474-1477)

Kingdom
of
FRANCE

French invaded
Italy with mobile
artillery (1494)

Hafsid
Sultanate

K. of
ENGLAND

Kingdom
of
ARAGON

Wattas
Sultanate

England's
War of the Roses
(1455-1485)

NAVARRA

Kingdom
of
CASTILE

French successful,
final campaigns of
the Hundred Years' War
with gunpowder artillery:
Formigny 1450
Castillon 1453

Wattasids replaced Marinids
in Morocco by late 15th century

Kingdom
of
PORTUGAL

Kingdom
of
GRANADA

Castile and
Portugal develop
sail-rigged navies
for Ocean
navigation.
Castilian navy
secures trade
route from Bay
of Biscay to
Flemish markets.

WAR of GRANADA
(1481-1492): the
cannon conquest of
the Nasrid Sultanate

Portugal seized
Ceuta (1415); and
conducted cannon
supported operations
along African coast:
Tangier (1437) &
Casablanca (1468).

tactics. French influences on military organization went back to the late twelfth and early thirteenth centuries, when Philippe II, 'le Auguste', and later Louis IX, extended French power into Southern France, conquering most of Aquitaine and Toulouse. Occasionally, French knights participated in the campaigns of the *Reconquista*. The influence remained strong in Castile and Catalonia until the early fifteenth century; long-established Italian contacts were broadened by Aragón's expansion into the Mediterranean.[9] Italy was well into its Renaissance as a fountain of culture on a par with that of the Muslim world, and was famous in particular for some of the very finest armour and weapons used in Europe.[10]

The demise of the feudal heavy cavalry's dominance was a result of two newly structured infantry techniques that emerged during the fourteenth century. One was based upon the disciplined tactical formation of the Swiss phalanx armed with a large portion of long pikes. The other was based upon the unique firepower capabilities of the English longbow. The foregoing statement cannot stand without recognition of the remarkable tactical employment of early gunpowder weapons and war-wagons in the East-Central European Hussite Wars (1419–34). The Taborite army of Jan Žižka demonstrated that early fifteenth-century handguns and small artillery, employed in a well chosen tactical defensive position, could defeat the traditional European heavy cavalry attack. However, the Hussite wagon-fortress and artillery did not directly spawn any European military tradition outside its limited area. Their wars have no verifiable link to developments in Western European warfare, but some indirect influences can be surmised. Except for the difference in the type of missile used, the Hussite tactical scheme is closely related to that of the English longbow.

The Flemish pole-armed infantry victory over mounted French knights at the Battle of Courtrai (11 July 1302) is sometimes considered to have signalled the demise of the feudal mounted men-at-arms. However, a subsequent series of reverse outcomes, involving much the same forces (at the battles of Mons-en-Pevele, 18 Aug 1304, Cassel, 23 August 1328, and Roosebeke, 27 Nov 1382) indicates otherwise. The first sustained defeats – where there were no reverse outcomes when the same general type of forces fought again – of feudal cavalry were inflicted by the Swiss pole-armed infantry. These began with the battles against the Austrian Emperor at Morgarten (15 November 1315), Laupen (21 June 1339), and Sempach (9 July 1386). In the fifteenth century the Swiss repeatedly defeated the last real vestiges of the French-styled heavily armed cavalry of Duke of Burgundy, Charles 'the Rash'.[11]

Charles's Burgundian army was an impressive mix of almost every known arm: crossbow and longbow missile-men, pole-armed infantry, and fledgling attempts at field artillery. His personal attention to structuring his army went beyond almost every reform that had been adopted by the French under Charles

VII at the end of the Hundred Years' War. It is hard to criticize the detailed attention Charles paid to the structuring and the equipping of his army. However, as a commander he over-emphasized his Franco-Burgundian heavy cavalry and failed to integrate his formidable assets into a cohesive military force. He thereby delivered his magnificent military resources into the hands of his Swiss opponents in a series of battles that are covered later in the discussion of infantry.

The longbow's reputation was established with the victory of the English King Edward III over the heavily armed French men-at-arms at the Battle of Crécy (26 Aug 1346) in the opening phase of the Hundred Years' War.[12] After a string of similar victories at the battles of Poitiers (19 Sep 1356), Agincourt (25 Oct 1415) and Verneuil (1424), the English longbow shared the status, along with the Swiss pike phalanx, of one of the two primary tactical methods that brought an end to the dominance of heavy cavalry on the Western European battlefields.

A fundamental weakness of the feudal cavalry system was that it lacked an organizational structure by which commanders could respond to events and direct tactical movements in the course of the battle. Cavalry hosts formed three or more *batailles* ('battles') before an engagement. The 'battles' were tactical groupings of men-at-arms,[13] composed of smaller groupings of *routes* (Fr.) or *cuadrillas* (Sp.), referred to as 'squadrons' in some later writings.[14] The *routes* or *cuadrillas* were led by a knight [*chevalier* (Fr.), *caballero* (Sp.)] with a *pennon* (pennant). The principal tactical concept was to prevail as a shock force. However, the 'shock' could only be achieved with the first on-rush of the heavily armed cavalry. Unless the opponents were overcome by the attack, a *mêlée* generally followed the initial charge. During the *mêlées*, the men-at-arms tended to fight in small groups, gathering around the leading knight's pennon. At this point, there was no way an overall commander could control the tactical situation.[15]

Despite its loss of dominance, heavy cavalry remained important. As Malcolm Vale observes in *War and Chivalry*, cavalry was usually needed to deliver a true victory on the battlefield.[16] Cavalry was always part of the English tactical system, even though the longbow infantry received the acclaim. At Poitiers (1356), for instance, the final mounted charge by 'The Black Prince' Edward, son of Edward III, may have been the decisive moment. Though seldom having a cavalry of their own, the Swiss victories were aided by allied cavalry. At Morat (1476) the pursuit was led by mounted nobles of Lorraine; and at Nancy (1477), Campbasso's Italian cavalry cut off the Burgundian retreat. Vale concludes that, 'to see Burgundian power meeting its end solely through defeat at the hands of urban leagues and Swiss infantry is to distort the pattern of military events between 1474 and 1477'.[17]

The Castilian men-at-arms did not fare any better than the French when confronted with English longbow tactics. Spanish men-at-arms were decisively defeated when confronted by English, diverted from the Hundred Years' War, at the battles of Nájera [Navarette] (1367) and Aljubarrota (1385). However, mounted men-at-arms (*caballeros armados*) remained a significant factor when Christian Spanish forces fought one another. It was with the French-style heavy cavalry that Enríque of Trastámara defeated Pedro I (now without his English allies) at the Battle of Montiel (1369), and Ferdinand led heavy cavalry in a two-hour attack that routed the men-at-arms of the Portuguese and Castilian rebels at the Battle of Toro (1476), securing Isabella's claim to the Castilian crown.

The *caballeros armados* of the Christian Spanish kingdoms were most responsible for the landmark victories in the *Reconquista* prior to the War of Granada. Victories over larger Muslim forces at the battles of Las Navas de Tolosa (1212), Salado (1340), and Higueruela (1431) sustained the Spanish appreciation for the shock value offered by the European heavy cavalry over the lighter Berber cavalry in open field engagements. Many of these victories depended on the staunch Christian infantry which routinely drove off the Muslim infantry, and then firmly held against assaults of usually more numerous swarms of Muslim cavalry.

Though the Castilian heavy cavalry played its role in the *Reconquista* and the internal wars of the Christian dynasties in Spain, the massive mountain ranges of Granada constrained its usefulness. In the War of Granada, the Castilian heavy cavalry encountered some initially jarring reverses, the most notable being the March 1483 'rout' of the Christian men-at-arms in the deep defiles of the Ajarquía range. The heavy cavalry's role became restricted primarily to protecting the Castilian artillery during siege operations from Granadan relief forces or sorties from the besieged fortresses, and escorting raids to devastate the agricultural fields of the main Nasrid fortress-towns.

Light Cavalry

Lightly armed horse-mounted warriors were not part of the normal European armies, except at the 'frontiers' with Muslim dominions where swift moving and agile cavalry was generally very popular. The Iberian Peninsula was one of those warfare frontiers (the other being Eastern Europe). The Spanish *jinete*, armed with a few javelins and a small leather shield, typified the Spanish light cavalry arm for centuries. The *jinete* technique was introduced from North Africa and contrasted with European cavalry traditions. Though the mainstay of the armed forays (*cavalgadas*) that prevailed almost continuously on the Christian–Muslim frontiers of the Iberian Peninsula, the *jinetes* were employed with the heavy cavalry in the major battles of the *Reconquista* mentioned earlier. There was not a great difference between the Christian and the Muslim light cavalries of Spain, and there were Christian Spanish campaigns that sometimes included a contingent of Spanish Muslim *jinetes*.

Jinetes deployed with Gonzalo de Córdoba's first expedition to Italy in 1495. The Spanish commander found that his Italian allies had a similar resource, the *stradiots*, light cavalry of Albanian origin and originally introduced into Italy by the Venetians. As the roles of *jinetes* and *stradiots* were inherently similar, the Spanish commanders were well prepared to make maximum use of them. These light cavalry forces contributed substantially to reconnaissance missions, disruption of enemy logistics, and pursuit of a disorganized enemy. 'The Great Captain's' skilful use of light cavalry is not always sufficiently recognized, as compared to the dramatic battles between different infantries and heavy cavalry, in many summary histories of the Italian Wars. Spanish successful employment of light cavalry in Italy is understandable in light of the predominant part played by *jinetes* in the War of Granada.

The circumstances of Gonzalo de Córdoba's defeat at the First Battle of Seminara (1495) is sometimes misinterpreted as the result of poor performance by the Spanish *jinetes*. Research suggests that the defeat had more to do with a misunderstanding on the part of Gonzalo's Italian allies than with the Spanish cavalry's performance.[18] In 'The Great Captain's' successful Siege of Atella (1496), it was his skilful employment of both *jinetes* and *stradiots* that sustained the blockade and forced the surrender of the French under Montpensier.[19]

Cavalry, both heavy and light, continued to have a valuable role on the European battlefields at the end of the fifteenth century. In fact, both heavy shock and light, swift-moving mounted forces would remain well into the next century, long after either the longbow or the Swiss pike. The Spanish military leaders' balanced acceptance of both types of cavalry is probably best exhibited by the carvings of the War of Granada in the Cathedral of Toledo. In the various scenes, Ferdinand the Catholic wears the battle dress of either a *caballero armado* or a *jinete*.

(2) Infantry

Some of the milestone battles of the late medieval infantries have already been cited in the discussion of the diminishing role of heavy cavalry. After their fourteenth-century victories over the Austrian knights, the Swiss began to campaign outside their mountainous homelands. In the first half of the fifteenth century, the Swiss incurred only two setbacks. Their defeat by dismounted men-at-arms of the Milanese *condottieri* at the Battle of Arbedo (30 June 1422) persuaded the Swiss to place more emphasis on the pike rather than the halberd as their principal weapon. They made their defeat by a much larger force of French men-at-arms at Jacobs-en-Birs (24 September 1444) so costly for the victors that the Swiss reputation remained undiminished. The Swiss infantry continued to improve its tactical configuration for tactical effectiveness in open battles away from their familiar mountains. The Swiss even adopted the use of some firearms and small cannon. Their phalanx increased the number and the length of their pike weapons, so as to better engage heavy cavalry on open battlefields. In the last half of the fifteenth century, the Swiss continued their triumphant infantry system with a string of spectacular victories over Charles 'the Rash', Duke of Burgundy, at the battles of Héricourt (13 November 1474), Grandson (2 March 1476), Morat [Murten] (22 June 1476), and Nancy (5 January 1477). Following their victories over the well equipped (and theoretically impressive) forces of Charles 'the Rash', the Swiss went on to deliver another decisive victory over the Austrian Emperor at the Battle of Dornach (22 July 1499).[20]

The Swiss technique involved more than just pole weapons used by a resolute infantry. It comprised a well disciplined and drilled formation that was able to execute an attack while maintaining a menacing 'hedgehog' thicket of pikes. The Swiss were aware of their formation's vulnerability to missile fire. To counter the threat, they stressed rapid movement through such deadly hail, to engage their opponents in close quarters as quickly as possible. The Swiss pike-phalanx was never tested against the English longbow, under an English commander.[21] A few examples of Burgundian archers having success against Flemish pole-armed infantry is no fairer an example than would be the Swiss successes against Charles 'the Rash's' small contingents of longbowmen.[22] By the end of the fifteenth century, the Swiss had no reason to suspect that their real missile nemesis would be the slow-firing handguns.[23]

Unlike the English use of longbowmen, whose training took many years and began at a young age, the Swiss pike formation could be imitated in other societies. Maximilian I raised a Flemish near-equivalent to the Swiss infantry to protect his Burgundian holdings from the French.[24] Needing a force to serve his broader empire, Maximilian began, in 1482, recruiting men from the German Rhineland to train in the Swiss-like tactics. They acquired the name 'landsknechts' sometime between 1486 and 1495, and were employed successfully in campaigns in Italy (1487) and Hungary (1491–92). During the Swiss–Swabian War of 1499, Maximilian's landsknechts suffered terribly against the Swiss, most dramatically at the Battle of Dornach (22 July 1499). Although some writers dwell on the early ancestry of the landsknechts, they made their most noticeable impact in battles after the end of the century.[25]

The English archer and spear infantry technique (supported with dismounted and mounted men-at-arms) required the enemy to attack, as the archers launched their deadly fire from a static position. The defensive nature of the tactic had its limitations. The enemy could avoid attacking the English long-bow formation and thereby frustrate the overall goal of the campaign. This partly explains the discouraging English accomplishments during the 'Du

Guesclin War' (1369–96) phase in the Hundred Years' War.[26] Though the English conducted three grand *chevauchées* (raiding expeditions) during the period, they lost most of their gains in France won from the battles of Crécy and Poitiers. This highlighted the inadequacy of the English tactical system for campaigns of conquest when pitted against adversaries like Charles V of France and his skilful constable, Du Guesclin. The lesson would be lost by the later French leaders who played into the hands of the English at Agincourt (25 Oct 1415). As the Hundred Years' War progressed, gunpowder technology introduced an alternative missile system to the English longbow, and a system more responsive than the crossbow to fundamental social and economic changes that came to influence medieval warfare.[27]

The longbow's attributes, examined as a weapon alone and not in context of the required skilled archers, suggested that it would reign for a long time on the battlefields of Europe. Its rate-of-fire gave it a significant advantage over the contemporary infantry missile weapons, the crossbow and the early handgun. The most skilled longbowmen could usually equal the range and usually the penetrating power of the crossbow, but the crossbow was more reliably consistent in its performance when used by the average bowman, the more available resource to the medieval armies. Crossbows, especially the most effective steel ones with necessary equipment to span their bow-strings, were expensive, and their rate-of-fire was not much better than that of the handguns. Handguns were an awkward weapon at the beginning of the fifteenth century and, with the exception of the Hussites, no tactical concept included their explicit employment. Until the middle of the century, their employment was largely improvised on the battlefield and often indistinguishable from the use of small cannon.

Only once was the longbow tactic tested against gunpowder missile artillery during the Hundred Years' War. This was at the Battle of Formigny (15 April 1450), where French culverins fired upon English crossbowmen positions. Both artillery and the longbow were commonly employed in the battles of the English War of the Roses (1455–85), but clearly with no change in emphasis from previous English tactics. There is no instance of these two missile systems fighting in isolation of other arms anywhere in Europe. What is evident, even in the awkward early stages of small 'field' artillery and handguns at the end of the fifteenth century, is that gunpowder missile weapons could influence the conduct of the battle. Prior to the Italian Wars, the Hundred Years' War battles of Formigny and Castillon (17 July 1453) foretold the effectiveness of the gunpowder missile's contribution to 'combined arms' in field engagements.[28]

The Spanish witnessed the English longbow tactic against medieval heavy cavalry at the battles of Nájera [Navarette] (1367) and Aljubarrota (1385), as mentioned earlier in the heavy cavalry section. Though these battles receive considerable attention from historians, they did not greatly influence Spanish infantry warfare. One of the main reasons for this was that there was no way the English archers could be replicated in the Spanish environment. The English longbow capability was virtually impossible to create outside the English society. Only on a few occasions were English longbowmen exported as mercenaries in any effective quantity. The English *condottiere*, John Hawkwood, used them early in his ventures in Italy, beginning in 1364. Charles 'the Rash' did not seem to have enough longbowmen in his battles with the Swiss. Indeed, longbowmen appeared to be in short supply for overseas expeditions even by the English at the end of the Hundred Years' War.

At the end of the fifteenth century, continental European armies wishing to develop an indigenous infantry missile component had only the crossbow and the handgun between which to choose. Considering the handgun's disadvantage for night fighting (a lit match was always needed) and general awkwardness in aiming, it is interesting that the handgun slowly began to increase in numbers more than the crossbow. The steel crossbow was at its technical zenith. On the other hand, gunpowder improved (in explosive power, availability and convenience of use), and handguns benefited in range and penetrating power, as well as in ability to support use in large numbers. With the development of the matchlock system, the handgun could be aimed much like the crossbow. Unfortunately there does not appear to be a recorded field test comparison of the two weapons, nor contemporary documents arguing the technical merits of the handgun over the crossbow.

In contrast to their European neighbours, the Spanish military had an eclectic military tradition. They were not attached to a 'preferred weapon' linked with a particular tactical technique. This was especially true of the infantry, whose leaders were free to exploit the handgun with an effort to make the best of its shortcomings. Furthermore, the Spanish infantry had adapted to siege operations, which demanded the utmost in close-fighting skills. The siege-experience contributed to the Spanish infantrymen's closer familiarity with gunpowder weapons at a crucial period in the development of that technology.

The reason for the adoption of the handgun in Spain may be the lower cost of manufacture, which had to be considered when equipping a large army of infantry with no previous training in a weapon system. During the War of Granada, the Catholic Sovereigns faced what late twentieth-century military establishments would consider a 'cost-effective' decision as Castile struggled to rapidly construct a large army for conquest. Another factor was that handgun infantry weapons benefited from the drive by royal establishments to improve technology (gunpowder and metallurgy) primarily for more effective siege artillery pieces.

The *dismounted* man-at-arms receives substantial attention in military histories examining infantry of the fifteenth century. Hans Delbrück makes an important point when he emphasizes that merely fighting on foot does not make an infantry. There were many occasions throughout the medieval era when the feudal man-at-arms, who had horses and could perform as cavalry, fought on foot. In some of the socially stratified armies there was a reluctance on the part of nobles, who possessed horses and were trained to fight mounted, to dismount and fight among peasants or common militia. This reluctance was not necessarily snobbery and had some valid military reason. Often, a dismounted medieval knight, encumbered with heavy metal protective suit, became just a less mobile combatant at a disadvantage with a more simply clothed and agile infantryman, no matter the social rank or professional training. Sometimes there was a sound basis for dismounting the men-at-arms, as when the English did so to support their archers. However, when French knights, who were essentially heavy cavalry, dismounted and executed frontal assaults on foot, the gesture was meaningless. They were not inspiring a force of infantry at their side, but merely placing their own fighting skills at a disadvantage. Like the English knights who stood in support of their archers, the Spanish men-at-arms were accustomed to fight dismounted. They thus provided a valuable source for professional leadership as the Spanish army of the Catholic Sovereigns expanded its infantry and artillery forces during the War of Granada. Delbrück also stresses that a good infantry possesses a state of mind for combat – a 'warriorhood'. Interestingly, the Spanish infantry tradition was bred on frontier warfare which well honed its 'warriorhood'.[29] The Spanish warrior of the late fifteenth century had the spirit that was derived from continuous, hard warfare.

Even before the War of Granada, the Spanish infantry tradition was known outside the Iberian Peninsula. Spaniards provided a 'number of the leading infantry captains in the papal army' by the mid fifteenth century.[30] Their presence in Italy coincided with the increasing introduction of firearms to the battlefield.

When the Italian Wars brought the leading infantries of continental Europe into confrontation at the end of the fifteenth and beginning of the sixteenth centuries, the Spanish demonstrated their readiness to incorporate what they needed from the Swiss tactical system, without mimicking blindly as did the German *landsknechts*. Indeed, the *landsknechts*, as they eventually fought in the Spanish–Habsburg coalition armies of the wars, learned from the Spanish the value of the firearm missiles. The Swiss never seemed to develop their use of firearms beyond performing a harassing role, forward of the main pike phalanx and in an attempt to disrupt the opponent's formation. What is interesting, here, is that German and Swiss (along with Flemish, Italian, and French) gun manufacturing industries appeared to be more advanced than any in Spain at the time.

Writings on the Italian Wars usually allude to the impressive performance of the Spanish 'sword-and-buckler' technique against the Swiss pike. Since such close-combat with sword and small shield had long been fundamental to warfare, the significance is not that a new technique or weapon was introduced but rather that a high degree of proficiency was displayed by the Spanish.[31] This can be traced in the frequent references to the combat required of the Castilian *escaladores* (scalers of the fortress walls) in the War of Granada. Such close-combat had limited use for a pole weapon, and this is emphasized by the depictions of the combatants with swords and shields in the carvings on the choir stalls of the Cathedral in Toledo.[32] As will be addressed later in this Introduction, when describing the Castilian force structure in the Granadan War, the basic 'spear-and-shield men' (*lanza y escudo*) of the Spanish Catholic Sovereigns' infantry were required to have a dagger or sword.

The famous infantries of the fifteenth century, the longbow and the Swiss pike, though perceiving themselves at their peak of glory, faced dilemmas at the end of the fifteenth century. Neither the longbow nor the Swiss pike served one of the most pressing military challenges at the time: the siege of fortified strongholds. Siege warfare, not mere battlefield victories alone, was required for conquest. Otherwise, wars degenerated into a series of raids.

The fifteenth-century infantry with a future was the Spanish infantry, not because it possessed one of the famous infantry techniques of the era, but because it had the fundamental preparation to be an aggressive and flexible force. More than any other European infantry of the period, it was embracing the individual missile weapon system of the future (albeit probably more for economic than tactical reasons). The Spanish infantry would be known for being the first real gunpowder infantry – Hussites remaining a special exception – in the mainstream of European warfare.

B. GUNPOWDER WEAPONS

(1) Artillery

Gunpowder introduced a genuinely new dimension to European warfare during the fifteenth century. The gunpowder weapon was one of the first major technological introductions that significantly influenced military tactics, strategies and organization within the timespan of recorded history. The medieval accounts of the early employment of gunpowder weapons in Europe provide some interesting analogies to the twentieth-century emergence of aircraft and electronics. Similarities are reflected in the initial slow rate of growth and then a spurt of activity as the technology matures, a confusion of designs and terms, the role of the 'civilian' manager to assist the professional military in application, and the stress on administering increased logistical demands and costs.

The latter facet is one which requires the highest governmental supervision in order to marshal the assets needed to develop and to exploit the potential of the new technology. In the late fifteenth century, sovereigns had to have resources, in terms of money and individual skills within their armies, to possess an artillery train of conquest. Acquisition costs and logistical support for a viable siege artillery train were beyond the means of the feudal lord, or even of a small country. Several states had some attractively decorated and skilfully made cannon, some of which were of the highest technical design of the time. These attractive and technically interesting pieces were merely collections compared with the siege artillery trains of France, Spain and the Ottoman Empire at the end of the fifteenth century.

In the late fifteenth century, gunpowder bombards and cannon were the weapons of conquest – or 'reconquest' in the cases of France and Spain. The sovereigns who spent large sums to acquire the resources were seeking to conquer the heretofore formidable fortresses constructed during the early and mid medieval period. This aspect is often obscured by the almost immediate response of emplacing artillery as part of fortress defences, a reaction to the initiative of artillery in the besieging role.

Gunpowder artillery is a controversial topic, especially as it pertains to Europe in the late fifteenth and sixteenth centuries. Some writers dismiss its importance, while others consider it to be the focal point of the technological revolution in warfare.[33] Some of the best works on gunpowder technology emphasize its value in sixteenth-century naval warfare.[34]

Two very fine and greatly needed articles appeared in 1993, in successive issues of *Journal of Military History* [*JMH*].[35] In his 'The Cannon Conquest of Nasrid Spain and the End of the Reconquista', Weston F. Cook Jr. makes the convincing case that 'Gunpowder firepower and artillery siege operations won the Granadan war, and other factors in the Spanish victory were actually secondary and derivative'. In doing so, Cook draws extensively upon the primary Spanish and Muslim chroniclers, as well as considering the latest research of several scholars. It is only natural that Cook recognized that the War of Granada resembled more the Valois eviction of the English from France than it did the earlier campaigns of the *Reconquista*.[36] Clifford J. Rogers' 'Military Revolution of the Hundred Years' War', provides considerable detail of the 'revolutionary' technical changes in manufacture of guns, projectiles and gunpowder in the first half of the fifteenth century, which permitted the effective performance of artillery in the latter half of the century.[37]

As mutually supporting as these *JMH* articles are, they reflect two distinct views taken by writers on the development of artillery. One view emphasizes technology, and generally perceives battlefield results to be directly a consequence of invention and weapon improvements. The other view, expressed by Cook, discerns the principal importance to be the manner in which new weaponry is employed. Military historians who regard technology as secondary appreciate that the gunpowder weapon, like the bow and pike, was nothing exceptional until it was incorporated into a tactical scheme and employed with conviction by knowledgeable commanders.

In the late fifteenth century, those who directed the most successful artillery operations were not the traditional military commanders. The new technology required the vision and confidence to perceive how to assemble, to place, and to direct the cannon for the best effect. Further attention had to be given to maintain the guns, and to ensure a suitable and safe rate-of-fire. Some of this knowledge was understandably foreign to the old managers of siege-machines.[38] What experience there was with non-gunpowder siege-machines was not necessarily relevant. Admittedly, there were some transferable aspects, and both systems were used in the sieges during the War of Granada. Some of the differences were important. For example, the older method of the *trébuchet*, the popular counterweight throwing-engine of medieval warfare, was used to hurl objects *over* the walls and into the fortress. As Henry V discovered during his Siege of Harfleur (1415), his cannon had more effect if aimed directly *at* the walls.[39] After 1420, gunpowder artillery became increasingly effective in destroying fortress walls and making the besieged vulnerable to infantry assault.[40]

Undoubtedly, improved manufacturing of cannon and gunpowder revolu-tionized the power of artillery by the mid fifteenth century.[41] However, beyond the mere technical means, effective military performance required men who understood how to apply that power, such as the French and Spanish Masters of Artillery of the late fifteenth century 'reconquests' (Jean Bureau and Francisco Ramírez de Madrid, respectively), who were well praised by the chroniclers of the time. To appreciate the role individuals played in the artillery revolution of the fifteenth century, one might consider the interplay between prophets, field commanders and technology in the more recent and better documented examples of new technologies introduced to warfare: submarines, mechaniza-tion of land forces, the array of air weapons, and various electronic-assisted weaponry.

Siege Artillery

Spain had considerable experience with gunpowder siege artillery prior to the fifteenth century. Ismail I (1314–25), the Nasrid sultan, is reported to have captured Huéscar (1324) and Baza (1325) with gunpowder artillery.[42] There are however expurgators of such early claims of gunpowder weapons appearing on the Iberian Peninsula. Some authors assert that it is improbable that the Muslims had cannon at the 1342 Siege of Alicante. In her carefully focused survey, *Arms and Armour in Spain*, Ada Bruhn Hoffmeyer finds it 'difficult to deny', given obvious awareness of such weapons at the time. There is more certainty towards the end of the fourteenth century that gunpowder artillery was appearing alongside the traditional siege machines. The reference to the Spanish Muslims' use of cannon against the Castilian army of King Alfonso XI at the Siege of Algeciras (1342) is one of the more reliable.[43]

In spite of the Spanish Muslims' early use of gunpowder artillery, they did not advance it technologically or pursue its incorporation into their military strategic or tactical schemes. For whatever reasons, the Islamic powers during the late fourteenth and early fifteenth centuries left the technological improvements of gunpowder weapons to the initiative of the Western Christian dominions. At the beginning of the fifteenth century, the Christian Spanish were able to capture the imposing fortress-castle of Zahara (1407).[44] The Granadans surrendered after witnessing the damage wrought by the first few cannon balls.[45] Cook observes that artillery was not a decisive part of warfare in the Iberian Peninsula prior to the War of Granada, at least not compared with the prominence of artillery in France during the last phase of the Hundred Years' War.[46]

Artillery development during the Hundred Years' War (1337–1457), particularly during the last phase, was important both for the technological as well as for the operational employment of gunpowder weapons in warfare.[47] There is no doubt that the French artillery reconquests of the early 1450s were the model for Ferdinand the Catholic's bold commitment to a siege-artillery offensive in the War of Granada.

The Siege of Harfleur (1415) by King Henry V of England witnessed an impressive use of gunpowder artillery for that time. However, the city surrendered due to starvation. Rogers contrasts advancements in artillery by comparing the three-month English siege in 1415 with the French sixteen-day bombardment that retook Harfleur in 1449. The transformation was not an aberration. The French went on to take one hundred English strongpoints in their 1450 reconquest of Normandy, many of which had required long sieges by the English.[48] The successful Siege of Pontoise (1441) conducted by the great French artillerist/engineer, Jean Bureau, is as good as any event to mark the turning point where the French siege artillery began to dictate the final course of the Hundred Years' War.[49]

The Siege of Constantinople (1453) had more emotional impact on Western Europeans than significance for military warfare.[50] The Ottoman Turkish Sultan, Muhammad II, assembled an impressive array of large pieces which effectively blasted breaches in the walls of the city.[51] However, the Ottomans' over-rated large guns were not as effective as their ones of regular calibre. Nor did the Ottomans exhibit any later originality in the advancements of gunpowder weapons.

The most significant use of artillery in Spain, prior to the War of Granada, was during the Portuguese–Castilian War (1474–79), which was in part a Castilian civil war, to secure the Castilian throne for Isabella I. Ferdinand's brother managed the Siege of the Castle of Burgos (14 Jun 1475). It was effectively a blockade, and the castle surrendered due to attrition after four months.[52]

At the beginning of the War of Granada, Spain did not have an indigenous gunpowder artillery capability sufficient to furnish the siege train Ferdinand envisioned for his strategy. However, the Catholic Sovereigns were fortunate in having the leading artillery communities in close proximity, and Ferdinand was able to take advantage of the considerable number of French and Burgundian veteran gunners from the recent wars.[53]

Technologically, the Spanish artillery used in the War of Granada may not have been of the very latest design; this is apparent in comparison with descriptions and pictures of a few more advanced cast bronze pieces made in Austria, Italy, Flanders, and France at the time. For the sake of expediency and economy, Ferdinand made good use of the forged-iron, hooped-ringed *bombardas*, *pasavolantes* (*culverin*-type cannon), and *pedreros* (mortars) not much different from those used in the later part of the Hundred Years' War. Many still shot stone balls, although cast-iron shot was becoming common. To be effective, the siege guns had to be brought close to the fortress walls.[54] The gunners were exposed to the handgun and archery fire from the defending fortress. Gun emplacements were protected by large movable shields, as well as by supporting handgunners and crossbowmen delivering suppressive-fire against the defenders.

Ferdinand followed the French and Burgundian example and appointed a Master of Artillery, and a Frenchman was made the first commander of the new Castilian artillery.[55] In 1482, a Castilian, Francisco Ramírez y Ramírez (?–1501) was placed in the highest administrative authority over the acquisition and management of the artillery trains. Ramírez was made a member of the king's *Casa Real* (Royal Household), and, at the same time, the artillery was formed as a standing military organization, responsible directly to king.

The War of Granada was primarily a war of sieges with gunpowder artillery, and the main events are dramatically related by Prescott. Results of current scholarship lead to a clearer understanding and appreciation of the enormous undertaking of the Catholic Sovereigns. Ferdinand must be commended for his high-command decision to pursue the strategy of a series of dynamic artillery siege campaigns. It is apparent that the scope of Ferdinand's success would not have been possible had the means of gunpowder technology not been available, but equally it is true that such potential could not have been manifested had it not been for Ferdinand's adoption of a cannon-driven grand strategy, and for the abilities of the Catholic Sovereigns to organize the creation and support of such a large investment of resources.

Field Cannon

Oddly, many authors on the subject of early gunpowder artillery omit the battles where cannon first affected the development of the battle.[56] In the last phase of the Hundred Years' War, two significant field engagements took place during the siege-dominated campaigns to reconquer Normandy and Acquitaine. Fortunately for the English reader, the battles of Formigny (1450) and Castillon (1453) are addressed to a fair extent by Charles Oman and Alfred H. Burne.[57] Both authorities leave no doubt that they were field battles, not merely the turning of siege guns about in another direction. There appears to be no research on whether the battles of Formigny and Castillon influenced subsequent warfare tactics. Without more research, it can only be conjecture that the incidents influenced the developments under the French monarchs Charles VII and Louis XI, along with their cousin, Charles 'the Rash' of Burgundy, that resulted in the first true field artillery train which accompanied Charles VIII, of France, when he launched into Italy in 1494.

Spain's experience with cannon in the field was typical of most in Europe at the time. The overspill events of the Hundred Years' War [Nájera (1367) and Aljubarrota (1385)] introduced European artillery technology and employment conventions into Spain, but nothing promising came from the use of cannon in the field. It should be noted that Muslim auxiliaries served the Spanish Christians in these engagements. At these early dates, any guns brought onto the field had to be medium to light weight. The smaller cannon of the late fifteenth century were breech-loaded and had multiple breech pieces that permitted repeated firing during the engagement, although the rate-of-fire could not have been as fast as for the hand-held, or -supported, guns which were used much like field artillery.

The War of Granada had no notable occasion to place cannon in the field. There were a few occasions where *ribaulds*, or *ribadoquines* (possibly the multi-small-barrelled type), were used. These were anti-personnel weapons, gun barrels bound together and fired simultaneously. Oman traces their initial introduction into European warfare around the end of the fourteenth century.[58] An early Spanish chronicler reports that the fire of *ribadoquines* broke up a Muslim army poised to attack the Christian camp at Vélez Málaga in the 1478 campaign.[59] Many writers on the War of Granada mention the Granadans making a sortie (the small Battle of Zubia) before the fortress of Granada in 1491. In this incident, the Granadans are reported to have towed out a couple of light pieces, presumed to be *ribadoquines*. It is doubtful that such multi-barrelled guns could have been fired more than once during the engagement due to the time it took to reload.

The following brief overview is based primarily on an array of artillery categories that the Spanish military historian Jorge Vigón described in his *Historia de la artillera Española*. Other data is from Paul J. Stewart, Jr.'s doctorate dissertation, *The Army of the Catholic Kings: Spanish Military Organization and Administration in the Reign of Ferdinand and Isabella, 1474–1516*. The labels given to the various categories of artillery are somewhat arbitrary generalizations. Fifteenth-century gunpowder weapons were made by individual artisans and requested by different institutions. Not until the sixteenth century were there records that categorized the various artillery pieces. Contemporary accounts and military men followed their separate conventions in terminology when referring to the pieces.

Nomenclature and Varieties of Gunpowder Artillery Pieces (*boca de fuego*) [grouped according to Vigón[60]]

HEAVY PIECES THAT FIRED STONE SHOT

lombarda (or *bombarda*) in Spanish, but *bombard* in French and English.
Appeared during the late fourteenth century, barrel length ten to twelve times its diameter. Wide diameter at mouth, cone-shaped, fired 2 lb to 70 lb stone or metal projectiles. Other versions: *lombarda grande, media*, or *pequeña*. Bronze or iron. Cast in two parts: barrel and smaller chamber. Approximate weights: gun 9,500 lb, shot 70 lb. Maximum range of about 2,000 metres.

lombarda trabuquera
Became the *mortero* or *pedrero*; barrel lengths varied from one to three times the diameter; usually cone-shaped, wide mouth, shot stone. Akin to the modern mortar.

bombardeta
Appeared during fourteenth century; was of smaller diameter and greater barrel length, eventually sixty times the diameter.

HEAVY PIECES THAT FIRED CAST-IRON SHOT

pasavolantes
Appeared around 1469, 15 to 20 cm in diameter and 14 to 16 times the diameter in length. At the end of the fifteenth century they narrowed to 10 cm in diameter and lengthened to sixty times their diameter. Approximate weights: gun 10,000 lb, shot 8 lb. Approximate range 5,000 yards. References by Spanish writers to *serpentinas* (*serpentines*) appear to be in this category.

MEDIUM-WEIGHT PIECES, FIRED CAST-IRON SHOT

cerbatanas
Longer than *lombarda*, between 2 and 7 cm in diameter and 25 to 40 times

the diameter in length; appeared a little before the middle of fifteenth century, with troops of Alfonso V; 2 to 7 cm diameter, 40 times the diameter in length. Approximate weights: gun 5,700 lb, shot 4 lb; approximate range 4,000 yards.

culebrinas

Larger than the *cerbatana*, appears to be a derivative at the turn of the century. In general, the Spanish *cerbatanas* and *culebrinas* were comparable to the *veuglaries* and *cannons* mentioned in French and English texts relating to warfare of the period.

MEDIUM TO SMALL PIECES THAT FIRED CAST-IRON SHOT

falconetes (or *falcon* in most French and English texts)
Lighter and more easily transported pieces, 5 to 7 cm in diameter. Approximate weights: gun 2,400 lb, shot 2.5 lb. Approximate range 3,000 yards.

SMALL BORE AND SHORT PIECES THAT FIRED SMALL BULLETS OF IRON OR LEAD

ribadoquines (or *ribaudequins* in most French and English texts)
Introduced late fifteenth century, 2 to 7 cm diameter and 20 to 30 times the diameter in length; divided into *grand*, *medios* and *pequeños*; the *grand* very close to the *cerbatanas*; the *medias ribadoquines* was also called *mosqetes de orejas*. Very long (4,000 cm) and usually less than 5 cm in diameter, these are believed to have led to the musket (of the early sixteenth century) as did other semi-portable weapons: *espingardon y mosquetón, esmeriles, espingardas, sacbuches* and *lagartijas*. Between the *lombardeta* and the *cerbatana*, with a length of 20 to 30 times the diameter, one fifteenth-century piece in *Museo del Ejército*, Madrid, has a 3 cm diameter. Approximate weights: gun 800 lbs, shot 1.25 lbs. Approximate range 2,454 yards. At times, a *ribadoquin* was the term for a gun system with the barrels clustered and mounted on a wheeled cart (also called '*organos*', 'organ-guns'). These were attempts at rapid and mass-fire as well as for portability.

To summarize, gunpowder artillery was the 'hi-tech' of European warfare at the time of the War of Granada. Technological improvements in gun manufacture and gunpowder did not really separate armies' artillery capabilities as much as did the methods of employment. Employment of gunpowder artillery was considerably influenced by the perceived need for artillery to alter the military status in respect to their 'national' or dynastic goals. Armies which were comfortable with their military systems at the beginning of the century hardly foresaw a need to change. The Swiss were not desperate for conquest, and seemed content with being a mercenary infantry arm; Austria and some small Italian and Flemish states possessed the technology – and even exported it. A sense of urgency was required for a state to acquire and to maintain an artillery train of conquest, which involved tremendous logistics in transportation and positioning of weapons. France and Spain were so motivated. Burgundy inherited the French tradition, but squandered it with poor leadership. The English, captivated by their magnificent longbow, did not appreciate the potential for improvements in artillery and firearms.[61] The English were more motivated to keep abreast of seapower capabilities and quickly followed Portugal, Spain and France in placing cannon on their ocean-going sail ships. In the area of cannon-armed warships, and particularly in naval gunnery, the English would be in the forefront of the naval powers of the following centuries.[62]

Like the Ottomans, Spain did not immediately develop special field artillery. The War of Granada did not call for the Spanish to promote the employment of artillery in the field. Initiative in this area was almost solely pursued by the French, demonstrated by Charles VIII's artillery train that invaded Italy in 1494.[63] However, as the Italian Wars developed, Spanish hand-held firearms proved to be an equally, if not sometimes more, effective gunpowder weapon than cannon on the battlefield. Many military writers consider hand-held firearms of the late medieval era as an extension of artillery. Though they had a definite role as 'light artillery', hand-held guns were evolving in the late fifteenth century as an important infantry missile weapon.

(2) Handguns (Firearms)

Handguns, or firearms, appear with the earliest depictions of cannon and are frequently referenced. There are some very early examples of small gun-barrels attached to long wooden shafts which were obviously manned by an individual. The early handguns needed support by driving one end of the shaft into the ground, clamping the shaft under the arm, or resting the shaft on the shoulder. Handguns took considerable time to reload and the gunners fired from fortress ramparts or from behind shields (as was the tradition for bowmen) when on the battlefield. Gunners firing from fortress positions usually had assistants loading other weapons for the next firing. The use of a hand-held match distracted the gunner's aiming, and this led to the very earliest handgunners having an assistant to place the lit match, or hot coal, to the gun's touchhole. In order to be more effective, some of the early firearms were enlarged until they were unmanageable unless supported on walls or special supports.

Many references in French, Italian, and Spanish early histories join the terms for one of the lighter cannon to the word for 'hand', such as the Spanish *cañones de mano y culebrinas de mano*. The expressions reflect the obvious first steps towards providing a gunpowder missile system for the individual combatant, and concurrently there was an incentive to make the larger weapons more usable in the field. There were clear associations of the early handguns with the crossbow, and references to a number of *ballestas de trueno* (suggesting 'cross-bows that made thunderclaps') in Aragón appeared as early as 1374. Castilian records at the end of fourteenth century mention the Muslims using '*trueno de mano*' (handguns) at the Battle of Egea (1391), and the chronicler of Enríque III of Castile described their *fuégo muerto* (deadly fire).[64] Late medieval firearms eventually acquired their own distinctive names: the *espingarda* was mentioned in 1449, in Toledo; the *escopeta* (of Italian origin) appeared at the end of the fifteenth and early sixteenth century.[65]

The *culverin*, a popular term in the late medieval era, was often used with imprecision by early chroniclers. The term '*culverin*', or probably with more accuracy the term *couleuvrine*, was used generally to mean a handgun, or 'portable' small cannon by contemporary chroniclers of French and Burgundian wars.[66] A little later, the *culverin* appeared to take the place of '*bombard*' as a category of medium size cannon, similar to the *pasavolante* and *cerbatana* mentioned in the earlier coverage of artillery pieces. The reference to the hand-held *culverin*, or *couleuvrine*, faded. The confusion is not far from that created by the word 'gun' in twentieth-century English. Unless placed in context, the casual (non-military) use could suggest either a hand-held weapon or an artillery piece.

Handguns became suitable as an infantry weapon when they could be held and fired by just one man. This occurred around the middle of the fifteenth century with the introduction of the *arquebus*, *espingarda* or *escopeta*, to cite but a few of the many separate terms used by early chroniclers. The term most broadly used by historians is '*arquebus*' (or *harquebus*). The term was derived from German *Hakenbüchse* (gun with a hook), which referred to the protruding stem that appeared on early handguns.[67] The hook shape was used either to insert into a rest-arm or was laid over a wall or some other support to minimize gun recoil. The configuration of the *arquebus* changed frequently during the fifteenth century, a period of aggressive experimentation and important progress in the evolution of the handgun. By the late fifteenth century the hook was no longer on the *arquebuse*, and it was sufficiently light enough not to require a rest.[68] The *arquebus* at the end of the fifteenth century was distinctive for its 'matchlock' device which allowed the gunner to concentrate on aiming as he moved a lever which mechanically aligned the lit match to the touchhole in the bore of the gun.

Matchlock systems evolved throughout the late fifteenth century in many variations, which have rusted away and left little archaeological evidence. Most of what is known is from brief written references and contemporary artworks. Early matchlocks were a simple S- or Z-shaped bar, called a '*serpentine*'. The *serpentine* was attached to the side of the gunstock, pivoted in the middle and had a lighted match clamped on the upper end. The shooter lowered the bar to bring the lit match into contact with the touchhole, or powder in a pan near the touchhole. The lit match contacting the powder in the pan produced a flash sufficient to ignite the powder charge behind the bullet. The *serpentine* was part of, or indirectly connected to, a trigger, which was a long lever that the shooter's hand squeezed in towards the stock as he aimed. For protection, the trigger-linkage mechanism (crafted much as the workings of a chest- or door-lock) was usually covered with a metal plate.[69] The matchlock permitted improvements in the shape of the gun stocks. Not surprisingly, the manner of firing was similar to that which was evolving for the crossbow.[70]

Michael Mallett remarks that it was a long evolution as the 'arquebus began to replace the hand-gun as the main hand firearm after 1470'.[71] However, it was widely noted that the Spanish were well ahead of even Italy in the use of handguns by the end of the century. Vigón reports that the *espingarda* was mentioned in 1449 in Toledo, and that the Italian *escopeta* appeared at the end of the fifteenth and beginning of the sixteenth century.[72] If this is so, references to a 'Spanish *escopeta*' before the War of Granada must be referring to the *espingarda*.

By 1470 *arquebusiers* were already appearing alongside crossbowmen, and their numbers increased as the century wore on. At the time of the War of Granada, handguns began replacing a large number of crossbows in many European armies. Why did this happen? There were some obviously inherent drawbacks to the *arquebus*. Loading the powder and then the ball was awkward, the lit match was a disadvantage at night, and it was more susceptible to the weather than bow weapons. For accuracy or fast rate-of-fire, the fifteenth-century *arquebus*, or *espingarda*, could not compare with the longbow, and was probably not quite equal yet to the crossbow.[73] What kept the early *arquebus* in the fray was probably its low manufacturing cost and the relative ease with which unskilled infantry could be acquainted with its use.[74] Its principal advantage was to equip a rapidly expanding infantry army.

Interestingly, the Ottomans and French, both in the forefront of siege artillery, did not lead in acquiring firearms in the fifteenth century.[75] Of the early artillery powers, the Spanish are distinctive for having been ahead in adopting the handgun, and particularly their form of the *arquebus*, the *espingarda*. Their chroniclers called men who fired them *espingarderos*.[76] Oman points out that the Escorial painting of the Battle of Higueruela (1431), shows handgunners as skirmishers in a *mêlée* with *jinetes*.[77]

Like all versions of the *arquebus*, the *espingarda* was continuously undergoing experimentation and evolution in design. Miguel Ladero Quesada identifies two general types of *espingarda*: those with early simple serpentine-lever triggering devices, the *llanas* (plain) type, and the other version, *de llave* (with gun-lock), which was a more advanced matchlock.[78] It appears that the handgun had by 1481 passed beyond the awkward, hand-held, match-lighting phase. In fact, the carvings on the choir stalls of the Cathedral of Toledo show many *espingarderos* shooting alongside the crossbowmen. The *espingardas* are being fired and aimed from the shoulder by the Castilian infantrymen.

In the War of Granada, firearms were used by both Spanish Muslims and Christians. The two sides used them as fire support weapons in sieges to clear the defenders from the walls. In defensive positions, they were directed toward the attackers. The Muslims found them particularly suitable in mountain ambushes. Like the crossbow, the early *espingardas* were a useful harassment weapon. No scheme of controlled fire was adopted for it. To compensate for its slow rate-of-fire (powder and shot had to be rammed down the barrel for each firing) it was best employed in large numbers. It thus provided reasonable fire support alongside artillery to suppress opposing fire on the artillerymen or to discourage the repair of damaged walls.

The War of Granada was definitely the launching-pad for the Spanish army's preference for firearms. For economical reasons as much as for tactical purposes, the Catholic Sovereigns armed a large portion of their new levies of untrained infantrymen. The King established quotas for towns to furnish armed *espingarderos* for the *Santa Hermandad* and militia forces.[79] As the war progressed, Spanish infantrymen acquired a familiarity and a confidence in the firearm. The incentive was there to make the best of the weapon. There were obvious improvements that could be made. The Italians may have led in advancing the design improvements and craftsmanship of firearms, in the Italian Wars, which were soon to follow the conquest of Granada, but it was the Spanish who demonstrated dominant proficiency in their employment.[80]

In the following century, Spanish determination would develop the handgun to surpass the crossbow as an effective infantry missile weapon. The longbow would long excel over contending infantry missile weapons in any 'proving-ground test', but the weapon's ever diminishing role on the European battle-fields was evident even before the end of the fifteenth century. The English longbow was expensive to manufacture and was impossible to support with the requisite skilled archers in the numbers required for the new continental European wars.

C. COMBINED ARMS

Charles Oman quite rightly noted that by the end of fifteenth century cavalry remained important 'in combination with missile-bearing infantry and artillery'.[81] As already mentioned, the English longbow, the Swiss phalanx, and French 'field' cannon victories necessitated the coordinated employment of other arms.

The concept did not escape the notice of good field commanders, and the principle was not foreign to the best paradigms of feudal warfare. Conditions of the late fifteenth century made the need for balanced field forces more important as tactics were restructured – largely due to the introduction of gunpowder weapons – and as disciplined formations of infantry played more prominently on the battlefield. A thorough understanding of coordinated employment of the combined arms was one of the distinguishing features in Gonzalo de Córboda's greatest contribution to tactics of the Italian wars.[82]

D. ORGANIZATION FOR WAR

The Catholic Sovereigns faced three great organizational issues concerning their war against the Nasrid kingdom. One was to control the feudal nobles and their independent armies. This was necessary as much for their own security against rebellious nobles, as for effectively prosecuting the war against the Spanish Muslims. Another was to create a 'standing army', much as the French King Charles VII had done in the last phase of the Hundred Years' War. A third organizational challenge was to administer the acquisition and disposition of the tremendous amount of men and materiel to be used in the massive campaigns of the War of Granada.

The approach toward supplanting the nobles took two forms. One was to appoint senior administrators to special jurisdictions and special missions for the crown.[83] This by-passed the feudal convention of ruling through regional nobles, who often had inherited their authority. The other method, which subtly undercut the martial influence of feudal aristocracy, was for the Catholic Sovereigns to appoint captains to command the newly raised military units and the various contingents of mixed forces in the campaigns. Furthermore, the strong papal endorsement of the Catholic Sovereigns' crusade helped to elicit the cooperation not only of other Christian states but also of the powerful Spanish nobles and Holy Military Orders.

In creating a standing army Ferdinand adopted the general thrust, but not the detail, of the system by which the French King, Charles VII created the *compagnies d'ordonnance*. The goals were the same: royal command and control over all the forces, and standardization (mainly for economy, but it did contribute to military efficiency) of the combatant components in a standing army.

Isabella devoted tremendous energy and resourcefulness to managing the logistics of the war effort. The new strategy necessitated devising innovative administrative arrangements and seeking the best advisors. Her initiatives contributed considerably to the creation of a royal state bureaucracy that was to prove itself in the later, crucial undertakings of African expeditions, overseas expansion to the New World, and the wars in Italy. Her role was essential to maintain a large army in the field under the command of her husband, Ferdinand. Rarely can it be expected that the field commander can, or should, address such vast logistical functions.[84]

The influence of artillery on the new state organization has to be noted. The raising of a large artillery for sustained siege warfare required a strong central government to find money and to solicit skills in manufacture and operation of the latest technology. Clifford J. Rogers, in analyzing the technological aspects of warfare in the Hundred Years' War, states that central governments of large states could acquire and maintain large siege trains, but smaller states could not.[85] He further acknowledges that '. . . the process by which France and Spain became unified nation-states owed much to the Artillery Revolution'.[86]

The standing army is often misunderstood. Michael Mallett (*Mercenaries and Their Master: Warfare in Renaissance Italy*) stresses the 'standing armies' of the Italian states evolved before Charles VII of France began to create his *compagnies d'ordonnance* in 1439. Oman points out that the French reforms took a few years to evolve and that Charles VII did not have the 'first real standing army' until after 1444.[87] Those who prefer the Italian claim to the first standing armies stress that the *condotta*, the agreement the *condottieri* made with the states, were 'long-term' contracts. However, this misses the point. The distinguishing feature of the French and Spanish standing armies was their development of a 'permanent' chain-of-command directly from the sovereigns to the military units. It was not a long-term purchase of the combatants' service through a 'provider and manager'. In assuming responsibility to provide a regular subsidy to these permanent forces, the French and Spanish sovereigns eventually acquired control over the configuration of the units and appointment of commanders. This led to more standardization and developed state bureaucratic structure to manage large armies. No doubt the Italians and French were addressing the common issue at the same time, and both had legitimate influence on Spanish initiatives. However, Spain's needs and procedures were more akin to those of France, in that both were large states that sought armies of reconquest and were compelled to construct large siege-artillery trains.

The Spanish military did not restructure itself during the War of Granada as it did for the later Italian Wars. However, the Catholic Sovereigns did initiate new arrangements in command and control and promoted acquisition of new gunpowder weapons. These initiatives set in motion many structural reforms in the Spanish army which took place immediately after the war, and prepared the Spanish to engage more tradition-bound, formidable Western armies in the Italian Wars. 'The army in the wars of the Holy League in Italy had its beginnings in the Granada wars.'[88]

E. NAVAL ASPECTS AND JOINT OPERATIONS

Except for the exemplary joint (naval and land forces) operations at the siege of Málaga (1487) and general acknowledgement of the effective blockade of the Granadan sea coast, little detail has been related about the broader naval actions of the War of Granada. An appreciation of the War of Granada should recognize two factors which relate to the naval aspects of the war: firstly, there was the inherent joint nature of galley naval operations which prevailed in the Mediterranean from ancient times through the fifteenth century. Secondly, the nature of the blockade of Muslim Andalus was very much part of a larger strategic naval struggle in the Mediterranean.

(1) The Ships

The late fifteenth century was an era before the great sailing ships and independent naval operations with distinct sea-fighting tactics. Though round hulled, two- to three-masted sailing ships participated in some Mediterranean naval engagements of the late fifteenth century, such ships were at a disadvantage against the manoeuvrable oar-powered galleys until effective shipboard guns were acquired early in the following century.[89] Under mainly the Portuguese flag, square-sail rigged *caravels* were venturing into the Atlantic in exploration of new trade routes around Africa. They were also found to be more seaworthy than galleys in the Atlantic waters of Northern Europe. The Atlantic fleets of Northern Europe were mostly round hulled, square-rigged sailing vessels: *cogs* and *carracks*. The ship-to-ship fighting capabilities of the sail ships were not much different from those of galleys at the end of the fifteenth century. The unique fighting advantages of large sailing warships would not be realized until the sixteenth century, when they could be provided with large numbers of cast-iron cannon.

Until well into the seventeenth century, the dominant combatant ships in the Mediterranean were galleys. The galley was tied to littoral operations by the nature of its configuration. A galley did not have the space for provisions for the large number of crewmen, nor did it have the rigging and hull design that permitted deep ocean voyages. They had one to two masts, rigged with lateen (triangular) sails, though their primary propulsion was by oars. The galley designs varied from a large *galleass*, which had three sail masts, to the small *galliot*, with less than twenty one-man oars. The larger vessels were expensive and were not as plentiful in the Mediterranean as they would be in the sixteenth century for their ability to mount many cannon along the sides. The galliot had excellent speed for corsair tactics and was especially popular with the smaller Hispano-Maghribi Muslim navies.

(2) Galley Warfare

Usually war galleys were commanded by noblemen or warrior captains who were equally at home directing land battles. Galley naval combat was much like fighting a land battle, though there were unique features in crewing and manoeuvring such ships. Late medieval galley engagements no longer emphasized the ancient tactics of ramming. The re-enforced prows were used mostly to break the oars of the enemy ship, leaving it helpless to manoeuvre. The engagement proceeded with missile fire as archers and hand-gunners in their elevated platforms ('castles') shot down upon the enemy 'marine' troops and oarsmen. Hook lines were thrown to grapple the ships together, allowing the ship-borne troops to decide the issue with hand-to-hand fighting. The missile fire was delivered by the various means used in land warfare, though crossbows were considered the most effective. Since the thirteenth century, gunpowder weapons had been added to galleys. Two or three small cannon could be placed at the bow. Rail-guns and handgunners were placed with the archers and crossbowmen on the 'castle' structures, at the stern of the galleys. By the mid fifteenth century almost all Mediterranean galleys were equipped with a few light cannon.[90]

Mediterranean naval operations fell into two general categories in the medieval era. One style was that of corsair, or privateer actions. These would be single ships, or possibly a small squadron, that deployed on independent raids of coastal towns or attacks of merchant ships. Their reward was usually the booty they acquired. They were considered pirates by their victims, but many operated under the authorization of some sovereign who allowed them safe-haven ports. The other category was fleet operations which were commanded by a sovereign-appointed naval leader and had missions which were usually part of a military siege, amphibious landing or defensive operation against such attacks. Fleets were usually made up of allies, as few sovereigns maintained a large standing naval force. Building and maintaining standing naval fleets was too expensive, and contracting self-supporting corsairs for special campaigns was the most feasible course, unless there were a need to protect a vital maritime economy.

A lively description of naval galley action during the fifteenth century can be found in Gutierre Díez de Games' romanticized account of a Castilian knight, Pero Niño, Count of Buelna, who as a commander of a galley conducted corsair (privateer) naval operations in the late fourteenth-century Western Mediterranean. In *El Victorial: Crónica de don Pero Niño*, Díez de Games, who was Pero Niño's lieutenant, graphically relates some of the tactics employed during naval raids against Muslim ports in the Mediterranean and, later, against English coastal towns during the Hundred Years' War around 1370–80.[91]

(3) Joint Warfare Aspects

Up through the medieval period there was usually a comprehensive military perception that is important to note in understanding late medieval warfare. The nature of the leadership emphasized the near seamless divide between land and naval warfare at the time. Up to the twentieth century, there were only two mediums of warfare: land and water. Until the seventeenth century, land operations, though often very dependent upon naval support, dominated most wars and campaigns. Joint operations in medieval warfare were rarely obstructed by rivalries between land and naval warfare specialists as they would be in later eras. When there were problems or differences they were usually between two prideful commanders, a phenomenon shared with land operations and all time periods. The naval role in the conquest of Granada illustrates the nature of joint warfare in late fifteenth-century Europe.

The naval blockade of al-Andalus was fundamental to the overall strategic balance of military power during the ten-year War of Granada. From the earliest times, the control of the narrow stretch of the Mediterranean between North Africa and the Iberian Peninsula was as important as control of the English Channel.[92] Both were 'water bridges' that either permitted or deterred invasion. For most of the Medieval period, this Mediterranean water path was open to the Berber hosts to enter the Iberian Peninsula. Rarely, until the thirteenth century, were there significant attempts to launch raids in the other direction. Castilian galleys made a brief attack on Salé, Morocco, in 1260 and Louis IX (1226–70) of France failed in his 1270 assault on Tunis. A major contest for the Strait was begun under Alfonso X (1252–84), but when he attempted a siege of Algeciras in 1279 his Castilian fleet was driven from its blockade mission by a North African Marinid fleet. The Granadan fleet, supported by some Maghribi ships, won a 1325 victory over a Castilian force. The Castilian fleet, reinforced with some Aragonese ships, was destroyed later off Gibraltar in 1340 by a Marinid force.[93] The recovery of the Castilian navy and the balance of the naval power between the Maghrib and the Iberian Peninsula during the late fifteenth century is part of a much larger scene.

Besides enforcing a blockade, other forms of naval support to land armies were: sea transport and resupply, off-shore firepower in support of amphibious landings or coastal operations, and denial to the enemy of their naval support. Underpinning such naval assistance was the ability to prevail in ship-to-ship combat. While there is a paucity of recorded specifics on sea actions directly tied to the War of Granada, there is much to be noted in the broader arena of contemporary naval affairs that explains the overall Mediterranean naval balance affecting the war.

(4) Strategic Naval Considerations in the Mediterranean: Christian and Muslim Navies

Iberian Peninsula Christian Naval Power

The nature of the geography and the course of the *Reconquista* influenced the naval development in the medieval Christian kingdoms of the Iberian Peninsula. Castile's north Cantabrian coast was necessary for access to the Atlantic and vital for its wool trade with Europe. Castile did not have a southern port until the capture of Sevilla (1248) nor a Mediterranean port until the capture of Gibraltar in 1462. By the fifteenth century, Castile's southern boundary represented the principal Christian frontier with the Muslim Andalus. This essentially placed Castile as the prime participant in the *Reconquista*, and encouraged both Aragón and Portugal to look outward toward their extensive coastlines for expansion.

After failure in 1309 to capture the Granadan port of Almería, Aragón delegated the *Reconquista* second to expanding its realm eastward, which meant becoming a maritime power in the Mediterranean. Aragón created a formidable naval capability. The Catalan navy was instrumental in defeating the Angevin fleets in 1283 and 1284 in the Aragonese conquest of Naples. Aragón had bombards on its galleys as early as 1359.[94] Though they were in contention with one another, Aragonese and Genoese navies cooperated with Castile in the capture of Algeciras in 1344. Aragón conquered Sardinia from Genoa in 1353. In the fourteenth century, Aragón was an empire. During Alfonso the Magnanimous' time it stretched as far as Greece, though a defeat by the Genoese at the naval Battle of Ponzain (1435) marked the limits of the Aragonese naval expansion into the middle Mediterranean.[95] Aragón conducted much of its own Mediterranean maritime trade, while the Genoese generally served southern Castile. The fifteenth-century Aragón navy was the strongest of the Iberian Peninsula kingdoms east of the Strait of Gibraltar. Early in the century, Barcelona's economy deteriorated due to a loss in trade and many Catalan ships resorted to piracy; their principal victims were Granadan and Maghribi coastal towns and merchant ships.[96] The War of Granada only intensified this activity and cloaked it with a nobler mantle.

In the early fifteenth century, Portugal's naval prowess asserted itself around the north-western coasts of Africa and the Atlantic. Launching continuous attacks against western Morocco, the Portuguese captured Ceuta [Sabta] in 1415 and occupied the Madeira Islands, off the coast of western Africa in 1420. At this time, the Portuguese were placing gunpowder cannon on their caravel sailing ships. These, as well as other evolving configurations of sailing vessels, were useful in the Mediterranean as artillery platforms in naval engagements.[97] The wider hulls of such ships and removal of oarsmen permitted mounting guns along the ships' sides. Sail masts supported 'nests' that served as high shooting platforms for bowmen and handgunners. The sails of the Mediterranean caravels were generally lateen (triangular), which adapted better to coastal navigation and rapid shifts of the wind. Atlantic caravels generally used square sails, which were favoured by the stronger winds of the open seas. Portugal was the preeminent naval power in the Atlantic. North European maritime states in the Low Lands and England were certainly emerging, but the Atlantic was the stage for Portugal's golden age of naval expeditions.

Portugal probably contested more with Castile than with any other

Christian naval power in the late fifteenth century. The Treaty of Alcacovas (1479), concluded at the end of the Portuguese–Castilian War (1474–79), put a temporary end to their competition. The terms conveniently served the short-term goals of each country: Castile was allowed claim to the Canary Islands and Portugal obtained exclusive naval operational rights over the Maghribi coast.[98]

An impressive aspect of the Portuguese naval assaults against Moroccan coastal towns is the use of ship-to-shore bombardment in support of the landing or land operations. Portuguese ship guns were used to support landing and successful seizure of Qasr-s-Saghir in 1458. Naval guns assisted the Portuguese capture of Arzila, and provided covering fire for the subsequent march along the coast to take Tangier in 1471.[99] The accounts are not clear whether these gun-supported amphibious and land operations benefited by more fire support provided by the larger sailing ships. Certainly the predominant portion of the Portuguese fleets in the Mediterranean were galleys. Portuguese joint naval operations set an obvious precedent for the Spanish Christians when the Nasrid port cities, especially Málaga, had to be attacked in the War of Granada.

With Genoese assistance, Alfonso X of Castile constructed a fleet and appointed an admiral (*adelantado de la mar*, or in some accounts: *almirante mayor de la mar*). Before the middle of the fourteenth century a small fleet of galleys (*galeras*) operated from Sevilla.[100] The fledgling Castilian navy was dealt a severe reverse with the 1340 defeat off Gibraltar. The immediate military consequence of this loss was offset by Alfonso X's defeat of the Muslim land force, along with its Granadan allies, at the Battle of Salado of the same year. A Genoese naval force defeated the Granadan fleet in 1343 which ensured Castile's naval blockade and capture of Algeciras in 1344. Castile rebuilt its navy with resolve and acquired sufficient strength in the Strait to discourage any further invasions from North Africa.[101] By the end of the fourteenth century, Castilian naval prowess had grown sufficiently to intercede in the Hundred Years' War on behalf of France. Castilian naval forces were primarily credited with the French victory over the English fleet off La Rochelle on 23 June 1372.[102] Castilian naval actions followed with raids on coastal towns in English-occupied France and in England. A combined Castilian–French fleet from Harfleur burned Winchelsea (1380) [Les-Espagnols-sur-Mer] and Gravesend. The death of Enríque II (1379) and Charles V (1380) seemed to end this period of Castilian–French naval cooperation. The energetic involvement of Castile in the English Channel was more than Enríque II (of Trastámara) merely repaying French help in gaining his crown. Castile wanted to secure its control over the Bay of Biscay and protect its wool trade with the markets of Flanders.[103]

Castile signed a truce with England in 1402 which, for a time, essentially withdrew Castile from the French and English Hundred Years' War.[104] It was an opportunity for Castile's navy to venture out further into the Atlantic to conquer the Canary Islands in 1402–04, which they successfully defended from later Portuguese expeditions against their claim in 1425, 1450 and 1453. The Castilian office of *almirante* became hereditary in 1405, in the Enríquez family.[105] The Castilian navy again ventured in to the English Channel in 1419 and by 1420, pushed aside the Hanseatic League's domination of trade in the Channel and established Castile's 'historic link to Flanders, altering the Low-lands ties to England and France.'[106]

Promoting the growth of a robust Castilian navy was a deliberate initiative of the Catholic Sovereigns. As with most of the naval powers of the time, there was no large standing royal fleet, and emergencies were met by hiring indivi-dual corsairs or armed merchant ships. The sovereigns encouraged shipbuilding with financial rewards and promises of advantageous trade allocations.[107] A measurement of Castile's powerful naval position during the war is the fact that the Catholic Sovereigns were able to support several overseas ventures: in 1480, a large number of Castilian ships joined with navies from other Christian states in the Mediterranean to help the Knights of St. John at Rhodes, besieged by the Ottomans; in 1481, seventy Castilian ships deployed in another combined Christian fleet that expelled the Turks from Otranto in southeastern Italy; and in 1489, the Catholic Sovereigns despatched the first of two naval expeditions that transported Castilian soldiers to Brittany to support English-backed rebels in the 'Mad War' (1488–91) against the French monarch. These latter deployments were made even though the large Nasrid seaports of Málaga and Almería were still not reduced.

During a critical phase in the War of Granada, the Catholic Sovereigns organized the Aragonese and Castilian naval resources in to one effective armada.[108] This initiative proved vital in subduing the strong Granadan coastal fortresses. At Málaga (1487–88), the Castilian and Aragonese naval forces provided a floating artillery base to assist in the siege. The Castilian–Aragonese navies transported part of the artillery train and resupplied the overland expeditions once they neared the coast. Coordinated naval and land operations were a fundamental trademark of Ferdinand's grand strategy even after the War of Granada, as the Spanish ventured against North African ports and into the Italian Wars.[109]

Italian Maritime States

Genoa and Venice possessed the strongest Christian navies in the Mediterra-nean during the late medieval era. These Italian states perceived their fortunes in maritime frontiers and they were in the forefront of shipbuilding innovation. Their naval emphasis was on galley warships which were most manoeuvrable in the fickle winds of the Mediterranean. Small sailing ships, like the carrack, were used for carrying cargo. Genoa and Venice often clashed, but by the middle of the fifteenth century it appears an accommodation had been made. They usually stood together against Muslim forces and generally began to separate their geographic focus. Genoa stressed the western end of the Mediterranean while Venice contented in the eastern part. Genoa cooperated with the navies of the Iberian Peninsula, making use of the ports as Genoese merchant ships travelled to north European markets. Genoese ships accompanied Castilian naval forces in some of the campaigns to northern Europe and close ties between Castilian and Genoese navies continued into the late fifteenth century.[110] In the last part of the fifteenth century, Venice was left to oppose the growing Ottoman naval threat and fought desperately to protect its ports and islands off the Aegean and Adriatic.

Eastern Mediterranean Naval Power

The dominant Muslim naval force in the Mediterranean of the fifteenth century emerged from the Ottoman Empire.[111] Though initially a land power, the Ottomans employed seamen from their conquered lands to challenge the naval position of the Genoese and Venetians in the Black Sea and the Eastern Mediterranean. A defeat in 1416 of his Turkish fleet off Gallipoli by the Venetians forced Muhammad I (1413–21) to seek temporary peace as he improved his naval structure. In their next war with Venice (1425–30) the Ottomans captured coastal cities in Albania, and in another war (1463–79) they acquired most of the Venetian ports in Albania. Intermittent Turkish–Venetian naval warfare for control of the Aegean continued until the successful conquest of Constantinople in 1453. In 1480, the Ottoman Sultan seized Otranto, Italy, and launched a siege of Rhodes. A combined fleet of Christian galleys successfully thwarted the attack on Rhodes and compelled the Ottomans to withdraw from Otranto. The death of the sultan in 1481 caused the Ottomans to discontinue their siege of the island fortress.

   The Ottomans were preoccupied with settling a dynastic dispute as well as warring with and defeating the Mamluk provinces in Syria. The distractions of the new Ottoman Sultan, Bayazid II (1481–1512), were sufficient and long enough to dissuade any aid to the Granadans during their 1481–92 struggle. By 1495 the Ottoman sultan was recruiting corsair commanders from their *ghazis* territories.[112] The result of this effort was seen in the first and second battles of Lepanto (1499 and 1500), both of which were Turkish naval victories over Venetians and led to the conquest of many Venetian coastal possessions in the Aegean and Ionian seas.[113] It is only an interesting aside to wonder how the War of Granada would have been affected had there not been a hiatus in the emergence of the Ottoman naval might during 1481 to 1492.

Western Mediterranean Naval Power

At the western end of the Mediterranean, the North African kingdoms did not maintain their once creditable naval force, and in the late fifteenth century they were at a disadvantage against the naval forces of the adjacent Christian kingdoms.[114] Western Muslim naval power at this time had not reached the height of the earlier caliphate counterpart, and the Berber Almohads had little concern for it. The evidence of sea encounters would suggest that the Marinids of Morocco had a credible naval force, and, with some ships from Tlemcen, were probably the main allied component involved in defeating Castilian naval forces in 1325 and 1340. Spanish–Maghribi naval power was insufficient to prevent Castile's seizure of the important Granadan port cities of Tarifa (1340) and Algeciras (1344), made possible by a coalition of Genoese, Aragonese and Castilian ships.

The real nemesis to Maghribi naval power was Portugal, which had probably the most advanced coordinated maritime policy at the time and had particularly targeted the best Maghribi naval facilities. The North African coast was increasingly subject to Portuguese and Spanish attacks during the early fifteenth century. The biggest blow to both Maghribi and Nasrid naval posture was the Portuguese conquest of Ceuta in 1415. In 1437, at Tangier the Portuguese were severely repulsed. The Portuguese seizure of Qasr-s-Saghir (1458) probably contributed to a dynastic war between the Marinids and Wattasids which lasted from 1458 until 1472.[115] Moroccan naval power was eroded during this war, which the Marinids eventually lost. The raids of Maghribi corsairs (*qarasin*) were irregular and lacked a strategic focus.[116] The Portuguese sacked and temporarily destroyed a Muslim 'pirate' base at Casablanca in 1468. By the late fifteenth century Maghribi ports were vulnerable, and Wattas rulers cowered.[117]

The Umayyad Caliphate of Córdoba had maritime control of the whole western Mediterranean littoral. The medieval chronicles do not give as much attention to naval affairs as they do to land warfare following the fall of the caliphate. The evolving naval balance in the western Mediterranean has to be gleaned from scattered references. Christian accounts mixed the terms 'Saracens' and 'Moors' when referring to Muslim naval actions in the Mediterranean and it is difficult to ascertain whether references of naval battles are to the Nasrids or their Maghribi allies.[118] There is no doubt that the Spanish Muslim maritime superiority in the Mediterranean declined under the Almohads, during the late twelfth century.[119] The Italian states (particularly the Genoese) and the Portuguese came to be the powerful navies in the western Mediterranean by the thirteenth century. By the mid fourteenth century, Castilian and Aragonese naval forces were able to harass the Granadan littoral.[120]

The Spanish Muslims relied substantially upon the naval prowess of their Maghribi allies. The Nasrid fleet never fully recovered from its 1342 defeat by the Genoese, and when the Marinid dynasty began to weaken in the late fourteenth century, the Granadan coast was increasingly subject to Aragonese corsair attacks. These attacks were more like pirate raids and not part of any military campaign. The Nasrids constructed numerous watch towers (*talia* in Arabic, *atalays* in Spanish) along the coasts to signal the appearance and to report the movements of corsair raiders. These lookouts alerted town militia and Granadan regional garrison troops to gather and challenge a threatening raid.[121]

The Spanish Muslim chroniclers give some information on the theoretical composition of the naval squadrons (*ustul*) or fleet (*huddam al-ustul*) at the apogee of Nasrid power. The commander of the naval force was the *qaid al-bahr* or *qaid al-ustul*, and in common with the Christians, was a noble. The ships were both sail and galley; their commanders had the title of *rais*.[122] Fleet battles were rare and most naval combat was between small flotillas or individual ships. Like the land warfare, raiding of port or merchant ships was the general practice. The Hispano-Maghribi corsairs (*harariq* or *qarasin*) employed the small, fast galliot (*qarib*). Their naval operations were similar to, but lacked prowess of those of the Ottoman sea *ghazis*, in the eastern Mediterranean.[123]

The fundamental naval strategy in the Mediterranean was to gain control of the important ports. At the onset of the War of Granada the great western Muslim ports of Ceuta, Algeciras, and Gibraltar had been lost to Portugal and Castile. This left the Nasrid kingdom in 1480 with Marbella, Almería, Almuñecar, and Málaga. None of these could be taken easily from a direct seaborne attack. They had to be taken primarily by land campaigns. Marbella was taken soon after its major supporting big city, Ronda, fell to siege in 1485. Málaga, with its impressive Gebalfaro fortress, was the port with the most imposing landward defences. When Málaga fell to the Spanish Christians in 1488 after a long, difficult siege, the remaining port cities were sufficiently intimidated. Almería and Almuñecar surrendered without being besieged in 1489. Even before they fell, the Nasrid ports were practically useless after the summer of 1484 when the Aragonese fleet began a relentless presence along the Granadan littoral and effected a complete blockade of Málaga during the 1487–88 siege.[124]

(5) Final Analysis

In the War of Granada, the Catholic Sovereigns displayed a discerning grasp of coordinated, joint land-army and naval operations in pursuing their strategy.[125] It was essential to deflect the traditional source of aid to the Spanish Muslims from their North African brethren. Since 1086 in the *Reconquista*, one of the most important impediments to united Christian Spain's military power was the intervention of Berber armies from Africa.[126] With the vast resources of Castilian, Aragonese, and Genoese navies, Ferdinand ensured that Granada was cut off from relief by the sea. Throughout the War of Granada, the Catholic Sovereigns' naval patrols maintained uninterrupted control of the waters between North Africa and the Iberian Peninsula.[127] Strategic maritime factors were important. Venetian land and naval forces and wars with eastern Mamluk provinces had retarded the encroachment of the growing Ottoman navy. Portugal's independent aggression against the North African coast happily coincided with the Castilian naval strategy in the conquest of Granada.

F. COALITION ASPECTS

Throughout the *Reconquista* it was evident that the Christian kingdoms had to ally themselves to achieve the celebrated victories of Las Navas de Tolosa (1212) and Salado (30 Oct 1340) when the Spanish Muslims were bolstered by Berber forces from North Africa. At least three times, the Muslim kingdoms of Andalus sought major military support from their Berber kin in North Africa. In the final struggle for Granada, they were unable to obtain it. To the misfortune of the Nasrid kingdom at the time of the War of Granada, no Muslim state could offer significant assistance. The traditional source, the Muslim kingdoms at the western end of the Mediterranean, in North Africa, were beset by internal strife as well as Portuguese aggression. At the same time, the powerful Ottoman and Mamluk dynasties to the east were warring among themselves and too distracted to make the effort.

In the strategic sphere, the imbalance of allied support was significant in the outcome of the War of Granada. Though considerable credit is due to the diplomacy of the Catholic Sovereigns, it must be recognized that there were many other factors in their favour. Ironically, the dramatic impact of the fall of Constantinople (1453) renewed the crusading ethos of Western Europe, which elicited even French and Portuguese support behind the efforts of the Catholic Sovereigns.

There were some qualifications to the support Ferdinand and Isabella received from their Christian allies. At the outset of the war, French assistance was forthcoming, particularly in assisting the development of the Spanish gunpowder artillery establishment. However, there was still tension between France and Aragón over the provinces of Rosellon (Roussillon to the French) and Cerdaña (Cedagne) and the Kingdom of Naples. This led to a more permanent realignment in the historic relationship between France and Castile during the reign of the Catholic Sovereigns.

The French–Aragonese contention festered and became almost a personal rivalry between Louis XI of France and Ferdinand the Catholic – who was

Ferdinand V of Castile as well as Ferdinand II of Aragón. The long amicable association between France and Castile quickly deteriorated and was replaced with an English–Spanish affiliation. There were moments during the War for Granada when Ferdinand was tempted to interrupt his campaigning, and take to the field against the French. The most effective response Ferdinand could attempt (as Prescott notes in chapter six of this work) was to try to keep the French king distracted in other areas. The Catholic Sovereigns despatched expeditions to aid English-supported Breton factions fighting Anne de Beaujeu (the French regent for young Charles VIII) in the 'Mad War' (1488–91) for the dukedom of Brittany. A thousand Spanish were casualties at the Battle of St. Aubin, in 1488. Two thousand more Spaniards were sent in the spring of 1489. Though the French king prevailed in Brittany, it is arguable that Ferdinand achieved his goal of diminishing French initiatives along Aragón's northern borders.

III STRUCTURE OF FORCES

A. CASTILIAN[128]

The structure of the Catholic Sovereigns' military forces during the War of Granada was essentially that of a medieval army with several modifications unique to Spain, and to Castile in particular. The combat specialties were: infantrymen (*peones*), cavalrymen (*caballeria*), and artillery personnel (*artilleros*). The infantry consisted of spearmen (*lanceros*), crossbowmen (*ballesteros*) and handgunners (*espingarderos*). The combatants were acquired by various sources which brought them to serve in campaigns as members of separate armies, neither standardized nor always compatible, led by Spanish noblemen, Masters of Military Orders (*Ordenes Militares*), *alcaides* of town militias (*milicias concejiles*), and *capitáns* (captains) of an establishment unique to Castile, the *Santa Hermandad* ('Holy Brotherhood').

The foregoing organizational sources were augmented by individuals. One such category was the 'lesser' nobility, who did not have the resources to provide their own armies. Such nobles reported individually to serve the sovereign and were referred to as *vasallos del rey* (vassals of the king), and encompassed *caballeros* (knights) and *hidalgos* (who held their rank due to past honours conveyed to the family). Another category of the vassals was the *acostamiento*, who fought for either pay or land rights. Quite often the individuals in the last two categories volunteered. However, they were recruited by the crown in 1487 for the large expedition against Málaga.[129] *Combatientes extranjeros* (foreign volunteers) also played their part, as the war became celebrated as a holy crusade and drew considerable talent from Europe. Prescott refers to the Englishman Edward Woodville (erroneously titled 'Lord Scales' by several authors), who brought his own small force, and recent research by Spanish historians has provided more evidence of the impact of the Swiss contingent.[130] A further source of combatants were *los Homicianos* (pardoned criminals), who began to be used late in the war, although a precedent for this existed as far back as Alfonso XI of Castile (1312–50).[131]

The following is a brief description of forces of the Catholic Sovereigns grouped according to their source:

Nobles

The great nobles generally had their own armed contingents whom they led on raids or brought with them when summoned by the sovereign. The Andalusian nobles of the frontier with Granada enjoyed considerable independence in wars with the Spanish Muslims prior to 1482, when King Ferdinand decided to take command of the relief of Alhama. While the nobility remained a dominant part of the Catholic Sovereigns' overall army in the war, the nobles slowly lost control to the King over the direction of their forces. Paul Stewart notes that by 'sending lieutenants in charge of their troops in the later years [of the war] the nobility virtually abdicated command over their own troops. And when they did come they found themselves in protected positions serving almost as auxiliary troops to the royal forces.'[132] The war bolstered the long-held goal of the Crown to diminish the military independence of the nobles.

Military Orders

The Holy Military Orders of Alcántara, Calatrava, Santiago and Montesa also enjoyed substantial power and influence. The leaders of the orders were usually members of the great noble families in Spain: 'The Master of Santiago was one of the six most important men in the government of Castile under the Catholic Kings', and Ferdinand was to assume this title in 1499.[133] The War of Granada provided the conditions by which Ferdinand gradually appropriated controlling influence over the Spanish Military Orders, and before the end of his reign he had gained authority by taking on such roles as head of the Royal Council of the Military Orders (*Real Consejo de las Ordenes Militares*). The composition of the forces of the Military Orders, like that of the nobles' armies, was mostly cavalry.

Town Militias

The *milicias concejiles* were a traditional source for infantry forces. They were originally led by local town leaders and varied in composition. To make such units more effective, Ferdinand appointed his own captains (*capitáns*) over the militias, but was never comfortable with the non-standard mix of combatant

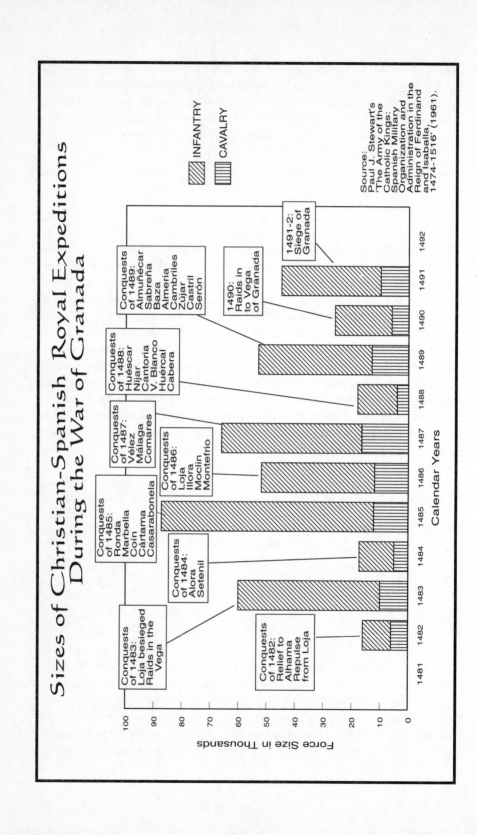

Sizes of Christian-Spanish Royal Expeditions During the War of Granada

INFANTRY

CAVALRY

Conquests of 1483: Loja besieged Raids in the Vega

Conquests of 1485: Ronda Marbella Coín Cártama Casarabonela

Conquests of 1487: Vélez Málaga Comares

Conquests of 1488: Huéscar Níjar Cantoria V. Blanco Huércal Cabera

Conquests of 1489: Almuñécar Sabreña Baza Almería Cambriles Zújar Castril Serón

Conquests of 1486: Loja Illora Moclín Montefrío

Conquests of 1484: Alora Setenil

Conquests of 1482: Relief to Alhama Repulse from Loja

1490: Raids in to Vega of Granada

1491-2: Siege of Granada

Force Size in Thousands

100 90 80 70 60 50 40 30 20 10 0

1481 1482 1483 1484 1485 1486 1487 1488 1489 1490 1491 1492

Calendar Years

Source: Paul J. Stewart's 'The Army of the Catholic Kings: Spanish Military Organization and Administration in the Reign of Ferdinand and Isabella, 1474-1516' (1961).

skills. Those from frontier towns had abundant experience in the type of warfare to be encountered in Granada. As the Sovereigns placed more emphasis on the townships' support of the *Hermandad*, separate municipal military forces began to play a smaller role.[134] Later in the war, the town militias served mostly as sources for *repartos*, men of lesser military skills, who were useful to enlarge the expeditions that raided the vega of Granada.

Hermandad

Isabella revived the institution of the *Hermandad* in April 1476, as the *Santa Hermandad*, in response to a challenge to her power by some of the nobles. The institution had originally been formed in the late thirteenth century as a means by which urban areas in Castile could band together in military 'brotherhoods' to deal with crises and for mutual protection. They had been suppressed during the reign of Enríque IV, possibly due to pressure from the nobility, who were sometimes the common threat to the towns.[135] The original intent of the Catholic Sovereigns in reviving the institution was 'to bring order among their noblemen and to harness national power to royal use'.[136] Every town in Castile was to contribute men and money, through a special tax, for the *Hermandad*. Ecclesiastical authorities promoted local support for the institution. Initial requirements were for a town to maintain one light horseman for each 100 inhabitants and one man-at-arms for each 150 inhabitants; the militia force was apportioned to be two-thirds horse and one-third foot. When the *Hermandad* was fully established in 1476, Ferdinand's brother was appointed its captain-general.[137]

The Catholic Sovereigns found excuses to extend the institution, originally created for a limited period, despite protests from the towns. The duration of war against Granada gave the sovereigns an opportunity not only to strengthen their hold on the *Hermandad* but to influence the structure of the combatant units to the particular needs of the war. In 1485, a royal *cédula* (decree) organized the *Hermandad* infantry component under a central Royal command, and a simple 'uniform' for the soldiers was prescribed. The act transformed the purpose of the *Santa Hermandad* from local protection to serve a broader national purpose.[138] Though the *Hermandad* expanded from Castile into Galicia (1481) and Aragón (1488), its role in these regions was mainly to maintain local order. Royal-directed modifications of the *Santa Hermandad* continued throughout the war, and by 1488 it 'might be called the first regular infantry of the reign'.[139]

In 1488, the *Hermandad* began to be consolidated under royal authority and was no longer a collection of forces provided by separate municipalities, though the townships continued to support the force with men and money. The entire *Santa Hermandad* was divided into twelve captaincies (*capitanías*), each under a captain (*capitán*).[140] Each *capitanía* was subdivided into twenty-four squadrons (*escuadras* or *cuadrillas*). The *cuadrillas* were commanded by *cuadrilleros*. Towns paid the men, but the Sovereigns paid the commanders.[141]

To facilitate planning, Ferdinand tried to standardize the *capitanías* of the *Hermandad* in 1488. At first, the companies contained 834 men (800 combatants).[142] By 1492, the *Hermandad* units were usually 50-man and 100-man *capitanías*. The *Hermandad* did not last long as an institution following the War of Granada. However, it set the direction for Ferdinand's life-long pursuit of an army organization to serve an empire.

Royal Artillery

A royal *cedula*, dated 10 Jan 1489, using funds of the *Hermandad*, established a regular artillery organization with permanent personnel.[143] Ferdinand appointed a Master of Artillery (*mariscal*) who was elevated to the *Casa Real* (palace household) and given a staff. Gunners (*cañoneros* or *lombarderos*) were assigned to each large cannon. Their crew chiefs and assistants were identified as *tiradores* and *ayudantes*. Common crewmen were *gastadores*. When the Catholic Sovereigns came to power, there were four artillerymen in the Castilian army; by 1480, there were seventeen; and in 1482, there were sixty-five.[144]

The nature of siege artillery warfare required a much larger number of men than just those who manned the pieces. Even before the age of gunpowder, siege operations were tremendous feats of engineering. There had always been a requirement for diggers, masons, carpenters, and many other specialized craftsmen. With gunpowder artillery, there were added needs for ironworkers and stone-cutters. The records of the large siege expeditions show thousands of carts needed to carry weapons and material from the large *casas del artillería* (artillery parks, or manufacturing centres for particular types of artillery) at the towns of Ecija, Baza, Medina del Campo, and Córdoba. The building and improving of roads, necessary to transport artillery, and the construction of besieging machines and positions were all under the responsibility of the Master of Artillery.

Royal Bodyguard

Paul Stewart states that there was no official royal Castilian bodyguard during the War of Granada. A *Guardas Viejas* (Old Guard) existed in earlier times and was re-established by the Sovereigns in 1493.[145] Ferdinand and Isabella had armed courtiers and usually travelled with armed escorts. Many of these courtiers were lightly armed when performing their stately functions, but were equipped as men-at-arms when travelling with the Sovereigns. They had the appearance of a royal bodyguard. These courtiers/men-at-arms showed great loyalty to Isabella and Ferdinand, and many of them were appointed the *capitáns* of the *Hermandad* and of various other armed contingents during military expeditions. When established in 1493, the *Guardas Viejas* of Castile had twenty-five companies of 100 horse each, all under a captain-general.[146] With the end of the Granadan conquest and the phaseout of the *Hermandad*, the *Guardas Viejas* became the focus of Ferdinand's military reforms.

Military Formation

Once assembled, the Spanish forces were formed into *batallas* ('battles'), in the tradition of medieval European armies, to undertake expeditions of the sieges or raids. The forces of the nobles and of the Military Orders were mostly cavalry and compatible enough to be grouped together in the same *batallas*. The remaining forces were considered the *Las Tropas Reales* ('The Royal Troops') and were generally gathered into *batallas* separate from the nobles.

The composition of some of the major expeditions in the War of Granada is described in Miguel Angel Ladero Quesada's *Castilla y la Conquista del Reino de Granada*.[147] A review of this data shows that there was no fixed number of *batallas*. *Batallas* were made up of ten *cuadrillas* of fifty men each, led by *cuadrilleros*. Five 500-man *batallas* could be grouped to form a 'division' of 2,500 men. Such groupings were theoretical schemes and served as rough guides in forming an expedition.[148] Quesada's figures, taken from various pay and muster rolls of different townships, show some interesting trends, but no fixed standards as to the composition of the expeditions.

A 1483 expedition had the traditional medieval structure of a *vanguardia* (the foremost *batalla*), under the Master of Santiago, with over 1,000 *jinetes* and almost 2,000 *peones*. Before the *vanguardia* was a small *batalla* (*delantera*) of almost 200 *jinetes* and 300 *peones*. Behind the *vanguardia* were two 'wings'. The right wing had almost 600 *jinetes*, 1,000 *peones*, and 120 *hombres de armas*. The left wing had over 400 *jinetes*, 400 *peones*, and 40 *hombres de armas*. Three other *batallas* were led by great nobles: the Duke of Nájera had almost 1,000 *jinetes*; the Duke of Alburquerque had 675 *jinetes*, 600 *peones*, and 110 *hombres de armas*; and the Count of Cabra had 550 *jinetes*. The *batalla* of the king had a little over 1,000 *jinetes*. This *batalla* had two wings: the right with 550 *jinetes* and 5,000 *peones*; and the left with 750 *jinetes* and 5,000 *peones*. The *rezaga* (rearward *batalla*) had 725 *jinetes*, over 2,000 *peones*, and 120 *hombres de armas*. The artillery, with 10 *jinetes* and 10 *peones*, and baggage followed in separate groupings.

In a 1487 expedition, the records reflect only '*lanzas*' (of cavalry) and *peones*. The *delantera* had 250 '*lanzas*' and 450 *peones*. The *vanguardia* had 1,200 '*lanzas*' and 11,000 *peones*. The *vanguardia* had two wings, each with a little over 200 '*lanzas*'. There were nine *batallas* led by noblemen, with a total of 4,500 '*lanzas*' and 3,000 *peones*. The royal *batalla* had 1,800 *lanzas* and 6,000 *peones*. The royal *batalla* had two wings: the right with 600 '*lanzas*' and 5,000 *peones*; and the left with 500 '*lanzas*' and 3,500 *peones*. The *batalla* with the *Guión Real* (Royal Standard) had 700 *lanzas* and 1,000 *peones*. The *rezaga* had 650 '*lanzas*' and 3,500 *peones*. The artillery now had 2,000 '*lanzas*' and 7,600 *peones*, over 3,000 of whom were really engineers and general craftsmen.

The trend seen is almost a complete reduction of *hombres de armas*, as such for heavy cavalry, and a dramatic surge in the size of the artillery train. There are a variety of expressions to classify the fighting men. Some interesting terms used are distinctions between '*sençillas*' and '*dobladas*' (indicating 'simply' or 'heavily' armed) under the category of '*lanzas*'.[149] It is most likely that the difference distinguished lightly armed *jinetes* and the heavier armed *hombres de armas*. There are some men identified as *lanza y escudo* (lance/spear and buckler). Those without a *lanza* were to possess a *ballesta* or *espingarda* (crossbow or handgun). All *peones* were to be armed with *casquete* (simple steel helmet), *escudo, puñal y espada* (dagger and sword).[150] It is evident that the 'sword and buckler' was a part of every Castilian infantryman's technique. The method was obviously a regular part of the sieges and mountain skirmishes in the War of Granada.

B. NASRID

The few Spanish Muslim chronicles that exist which tell of the War of Granada do not describe Nasrid forces with the detail that is recorded about the armies of the Christian Spanish. There did not remain a kingdom to record its story, and many of the contemporary Nasrid documents were destroyed or transported to North Africa. Some of what is known of the Nasrid military is derived from works of Muslim scholars of later eras who abridged the writings of the Granadan writers. To some degree, information about the Granadan forces can be inferred from the chronicles of the Spanish Christians.[151] Though the Christian accounts are suspect in many ways, they provide convincing evidence of the formidable challenge of the Granadan military. Prescott's narrative of the Conquest of Granada certainly conveys the Granadan military prowess better than a mere static description of its structure. Nevertheless, an overview of the structure helps the narrative.

The Nasrid military was not an isolated establishment, being at one of the crossroads of the Muslim and European civilizations. Though the Cordoban Caliphate had long disappeared by the onset of the final War of Granada, the military and administrative terms remain like ghosts of past grandeur. For centuries Arabic military and bureaucratic terms (*e.g. alferes mor* for army commander, *alcalde* for governor of a castle or fortified city) were used in the Spanish Christian domains, gradually being changed during the fourteenth century. The Nasrid military system was not completely engulfed by influences from other Muslim realms. It had considerable contact, both as adversary and as sometime ally, with its neighbouring European Christian states.

It would appear that there was little innovation on the Granadan side, at a time when dramatic change in warfare was occurring to the north and east of al-Andalus. The Spanish Muslims had become complacent with traditional force structure patterns partly inherited from the old Caliphate, and partly influenced by changes introduced during temporary occupation by the vigorously militant Almoravids and Almohads. By the fifteenth century, there was really nothing left of the caliphal era military tradition except concepts of organization. A nostalgic sense of inherent elite status prevailed among the unconquered Spanish Muslims, permitting an easy rationalization of the slow erosion of the Muslim domains. However, concepts did adjust to the pragmatic realities of more limited resources of the Granadan kingdom and its special environment. Changes were implemented gradually and were not recognized as a revolution in military posture. The late caliphal era had adopted a strategic concept of regional defences to cope with the long standing – but slowly retreating – frontier with the Spanish Christians. Upon the fall of the Caliphate, the small Spanish Muslim kingdoms sought military assistance from North African Muslims, who had been colonies of the previous Cordoban realm. In two cases, this led to major invasions and conquest by their Muslim saviours. The incursions of the militant Almoravids and Almohads briefly interrupted the overall trend of the *Reconquista* and also fused the Nasrid military posture with a broader Hispano-Maghribi system. The Granadan military had two components: a main regular army under the Nasrid king and a contingent of foreign (mostly North African) 'volunteers'.

Nasrid Regular Army

Western Muslim armies of the late medieval era were separated conceptually into two broad categories: *al-furu* and *al-usul*. The *furu* were assortments of lesser skilled and generally non-permanent armies who were employed as skirmishers. These were separate from the *usul*, the main body.[152] Though much of the warfare in the Iberian Peninsula was in the form of expeditions, none seem to have required the formal administrative structure described by the late medieval Muslim chronicler and reported in E. Lévi-Provençal's *Histoire de l'Espagne musulmane*. Ferdinand Lot, in *L'Art Militaire et les Armées au Moyen Age en Europe et dans le Proche Orient*, cautions that this structure was theoretical and that the terms were not always used.[153] However, the administrative structure furnishes a basis for understanding the general relationship of ranks and units that surface in various Muslim narratives. It also highlights a distinctive preference of the Muslim armies – at least in the Western regions – to organize in units of five.

Theoretical structure of the Granadan Army

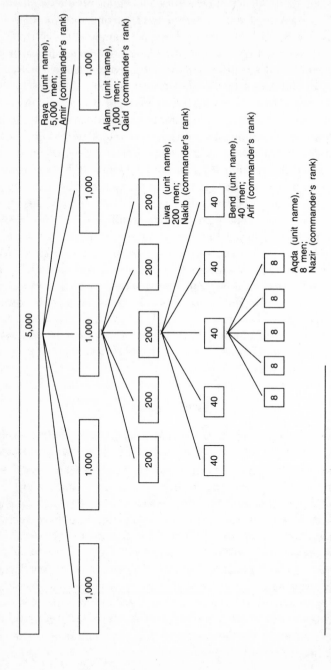

Raya (unit name),
5,000 men;
Amir (commander's rank)

Alam (unit name),
1,000 men;
Qaid (commander's rank)

Liwa (unit name),
200 men;
Nakib (commander's rank)

Bend (unit name),
40 men;
Arif (commander's rank)

Aqda (unit name),
8 men;
Nazir (commander's rank)

Source: Weston F. Cook's *The Hundred Years War for Moroco* (1994),
as adapted from Louis Mercier's translation of Ibn Hudhyal.

To describe the disposition of a Muslim army in the field, one needs to address another theoretical scheme, known as the *'tabiya'* (essentially the *usul*), which was established late in the Umayyad period. Weston Cook describes the force being divided into five main divisions, called *khamis*. Each division consisted of men of the same tribe, or otherwise known to each other. This was similar to practices of the European 'battle' field formations. The pattern of five seems to be distinctly emphasized, the components of the forces corresponding closely with European medieval military practice. The five *khami* parts (*akhmas*, pl) of the *tabiya* were: the centre (*qalb*) where the commanding amir and his personal bodyguard were also located; the left (*maysara*) wing (*jina*); and the right wing (*maymana jina*). In front was the van (*al-muqaddam*). A rearguard (*saqa*) followed with baggage and siege train. Separate from the main five-*khami* formation that made up the *tabiya*, were light-armed troops (*mujarrada*), scouts (*talia*), and a vanguard (*jalishiya*).[154]

In a set-piece battle, facing the enemy, the *tabiya* formed on-line, in elongated ranks (*masaff* or *masafafa*), cavalry troops and infantry in rectangular groupings side-by-side.[155] In front of the army ranks were lightly armed, usually irregular or militia, skirmishers (*furu*) to act as a screen for the main body. Conde de Clonard's *Historia orgánica de la armas de infantería y caballería españolas desde la creación del ejército permanente hasta el día*, contains a diagram of the opposing Castilian and Nasrid forces at the Battle of Higueruela [known also as Andaraxemel or Sierra Elvira] (1431), which reflects the Muslim disposition just described. The purpose of the Muslim battle formation was to execute two principal types of tactical manoeuvres. One offensive manoeuvre was to advance *en masse*, either to envelop or to overwhelm the opponent, with a large, concentrated force. The other manoeuvre was to launch attacks and then withdraw in an effort to disrupt the opponent's formation, possibly luring the enemy into a disorganized advance.[156] The latter scheme was a common tactic (*al-karr wa 'l-farr*) of Granadan and Maghribi forces, as Prescott's narrative recounts. Ferdinand the Catholic was seriously routed by this stratagem in his first encounter with the wily Granadan military leader, Ali Atar, at Loja (1482).[157]

An instructive way to look at the Nasrid military structure for the War of Granada is to view the kingdom's strategic defensive arrangements in the last quarter of the fifteenth century. By the mid fourteenth century, Granada had fully adopted a strategic defensive orientation.[158] The Granadan military forces were postured to serve territorial defensive regions that incorporated a series of fortified towns and castles. These strongholds were situated in vast, rugged mountain ranges, which severely restricted an invader's line of approach and offered numerous locations to ambush hostile incursions. A system of mountain watch towers linked the many fortresses.

Much of the Nasrid fortress system had been well established under

Muhammad II at the end of the thirteenth century, and it remained one of the most formidable of the mid fifteenth century.[159] The fortresses of al-Andalus were influenced by the Almohad stone and brick architecture. Most often, an outer wall, which conformed to the surrounding mountain precipices, complemented with commanding towers, completely encircled the town. Within the town, perched on the highest ground, would be another wall around the main *alcazaba*. Rectangular towers and horseshoe-shaped portals were distinctive characteristics of the structures. Access past the initial gates was via labyrinthine paths, which were channelled by high walls and dominated by towers. The commanding defensive structures were completed by a network of mutually supporting military contingents that mobilized most of the kingdom's rural and urban populace. At the time of the War of Granada, a few Nasrid fortresses had emplacements for gunpowder artillery. Should the outer defensive positions fail, the *qaid* and his most select troops withdrew to the *alcazaba*. Often this last strongpoint was not taken, and many a siege expedition had to be content with looting the town and then withdrawing. When such defensive citadels were taken, it was more often than not due to treachery or tactical stealth. Besieging an *alcazaba* directly was usually not considered worth the costs of lives of the besiegers in the typical medieval expedition, which must be recognized as separate from a 'crusade' for reconquest.[160] Geography further endowed the Nasrid kingdom with a vast coastline and some of the best fortified ports in the Mediterranean, the historic point of entry for the critical military succour from Muslim allies. Granada had reason to be confident in this terrain-based system of fortress strongholds which had protected the Amirate for so long.

The Granadan defensive system could be briefly described as a 'triad' of fortresses, rugged mountains, and armies of both local and mobile forces. While each point of this triad was important, a cohesive and efficiently directed mobile army was essential glue to hold the system together. Nasrid defensive strategy did not anticipate the rapid progression of highly organized Castilian offensive, with a logistically well supported gunpowder artillery train. Even against such a new onslaught, successful defensive measures might have been possible if there had been cohesion between the garrisons and the regional forces.

The Nasrid defensive zones – the precise boundaries do not appear to have been delineated – each had a military establishment managed by an army council (*diwan al-jaysh*), as part of a central government (*makhzan*). At the head of each was an *amir*, who commanded a main force of 4,000 to 7,000 horsemen and a standing army of 10,000.[161] There were three *makhzan* provincial garrisons: Ronda (Arabic: Runda); Málaga (Malah); and Gaudix (Wadi Ash). A provincial army, a *jund*, of 1,000 men, was commanded by a *rais*. These forces included town guilds (*ramat*), quasi-military groups that practised with crossbow and arquebus, and religious 'brotherhoods' (*murabit*). Certain large cities were designed as regional commands (*shiya khassa*), commanded by a royal *qaid*. These forces included Christian mercenaries and converts. For the most part, cities were defended by militia and *ramat* forces; rural areas relied upon the *murabit*.[162]

The military strongholds in Granada were commanded by provincial governors who had considerable independence from the overall *amir* (sultan, or king) of Granada. This arrangement was similar to the conditions of the Christian-held territories in Andalusia in 1481. Though not so well identified in .Prescott's narrative, which relied heavily on Christian Spanish sources, there were powerful provincial noble families in Granada, such as the families of Ibn al-Sarraj (Abencerrajes), Mufarrij, Ibn al-Barr, and the Banu Ashqilula.[163] Some historians refer to the Granadan noble families as 'clans' or 'tribes', but they appear to be on par with the Guzmáns (Duke of Medina Sidonia) and families of Ponce de León (Duke of Cádiz), Count of Cabra, and other Castilian *grandees*.

Like their Christian opponents, the Nasrid army leaders were mostly noblemen. Many contemporary accounts relate how the Granadan military leaders were similar to their Spanish Christian counterparts. The Granadan warrior leaders were knights (*faris*), and espoused traditions of chivalry in combat. They preferred to be mounted warriors, eagerly responded to personal challenges and duels, and appeared to show respect to an enemy of equal social status. Prescott's narrative places considerable emphasis on this. In doing so, Prescott is probably influenced by his main sources, who were Christian writers imbued with a nostalgic sentiment of knightly conduct. It is apparent that for the most of the ten-year war, the behaviour of noble warriors – the knights – was hardly different from that practised in Western Europe. Though there were lapses in chivalrous conduct of both Christian and Muslims in the war, this aristocratic, warrior-class attitude appeared to be one of the features that distinguished the Nasrid leaders from their Maghribi allies.

African Volunteers

Military auxiliary contingents from North Africa were a vital, strategic reserve to brace the main Granadan defensive system. These forces were valuable not so much for shoring up any deficiency in Granadan manpower, but rather for the vigorous warriors that the harsher North African environment produced, as evidenced by their series of successful invasions since the downfall of the Cordoban Caliphate. The Nasrid rulers had become accustomed to working with the Marinids, who had replaced the Almohads as the dominant power in western North Africa.[164] The Marinids, while not as powerful a community as the previous Maghrib Almoravids or Almohads, did acquire a foothold on the Iberian Peninsula until their defeat at the Battle of Salado [or Tarifa] (January,

1340). Like their Berber predecessors, the Marinids were a dangerous ally for the Spanish Muslims. The often more spartan rulers of the Maghribi kingdoms looked down upon the aristocrats of al-Andalus, whom they regarded as decadent and pretentiously over-proud of their ancient Arab lineage, and contaminated from prolonged contact with Christian Europeans.

Sometimes the military assistance from North African domains took the form of strong expeditions under aggressive and ambitious Berber leaders. Historians refer to these Maghribi military contingents variously as 'mercenaries' and 'Volunteers of the Faith'. The indirect evidence is that both kinds existed. For a time, an overall Berber nobleman commanded the North African contingents, and he was technically a member of the Nasrid king's military staff with considerable political power. The arrogant independence of such commanders led to several incidents, even rebellions against the Nasrid rulers. In 1372, Muhammad V appointed his own commander over the African forces.[165]

The North African forces consisted of small standing armies (*dawia*) of a regional *qaid* or *amir* (terms usually interchangeable in the Maghribi societies) and substantially expanded by tribal (*jaysh*) units. These Maghribi armies often served as mercenaries to the Nasrid king as well as other monarchs. One of the contingents clearly identified in the War of Granada was the *ghumara* (or *gomeres*), negro troops from the Maghrib. They came from the *Gomera* Berber tribe and had long been known as formidable mountain fighters in mountains of Andalus.[166] The early Spanish chroniclers reported that some *ghumara* carried firearms and used them to ambush the forces of Ferdinand the Catholic in the hills around Ronda. The best veterans formed cavalry units called *ghuzat* under the *shaykh al-ghuzat al-maghariba* ('Chief of the Maghrib Warriors').[167]

Cavalry

In general, Muslim cavalries of the Medieval era preferred to engage in a more agile fighting style than did European cavalries. Unless they heavily outnumbered their opponent, the Muslim forces normally did not attempt to overpower an enemy with a direct assault or the shock of a heavy cavalry charge. Rather Muslim military tactics sought to probe for weakness, and to sap the opponent's strength with a system of harrying attacks and withdrawals. The initial encounters began with a launch of missiles, javelins (*amdas*) or arrows. Closing with the enemy was delayed until an opportunity to exploit an advantage was perceived. What was common between the Granadan–Maghribi and most medieval Christian cavalries of the era was that their branch was the most prestigious of the armies. There was a trend for the Spanish Muslims to adopt some of the metal body protection and weapons of the Christian armed knights. However, this trend subsided by the fourteenth century.[168]

The much cited Christian victories at the battles of Las Navas de Tolosa

(1212) and Salado (1340), encourage perceptions of an inevitable dominance of European heavy cavalry forces over the lighter Muslim cavalry. However, there are many Muslim victories intermingled with the Spanish Christian ones, the battles of Ecija (May 1275), Moclin (1280), the Vega (12 May 1319), to name but a few.[169] During much of the fourteenth century, internal wars among the Christians allowed the Granadans considerable opportunity to regain some of their towns.

The early fifteenth century saw the renewal of the Castilian *Reconquista*. Defeats at the Battle of Higueruela [Andaraxemel], (1431) and Battle of Alporchones (1452) reflected a comparative advantage for the Spanish Castilian heavy cavalry.[170] Granadan forces no longer appeared willing to engage in open battles that gave an advantage to heavily armed cavalry. By the late fifteenth century, the Granadan army did not appear to have a distinct 'heavy cavalry'. The nature of Granadan warfare had evolved so that it favoured the strengths of the Spanish Muslim light cavalry, which fought *jinete* style. Taking advantage of the constricted terrain of Granada's mountainous passes, Prince Abul Hacen's light cavalry defeated expeditions of the Christian Andalusian lords Rodrigo Ponce de León near Estepa (April 1461) and Miguel Lucas de Iranzo at Arenas (July 1461). This is the same Abul Hacen [Abu 'l-Hasan] who, as later Nasrid King, would launch the War of Granada by supporting the seizure of Zahara in 1481.

The Granadan light cavalry, derived largely from Muslim and Maghribi military heritage, became the dominant non-siege type of warfare in the Granadan war. The javelin-throwing *jinete* light cavalry was particularly adaptable to the Granadan environment and tactical requirements of warfare in southern Spain. As mentioned earlier, it was adopted even by the Christian *caballeros* of Andalusia. Iberian Christian–Muslim frontier warfare during the fourteenth and fifteenth centuries emphasized light cavalry and infantry. Operations were often long-distance raids (*razzia, ghazu, saraya*) launched by local military governors and nobles with large regional authority. It might be well to distinguish the typical Iberian frontier raid from the slower moving *cavalgadas (fonsado* Spanish) executed by European 'hosts' in the French–English Hundred Years' War, and major monarch-led '*huestes*' in the Iberian wars to acquire Algeciras (1275, 1309, 1344, 1350), Tarifa (1292), and Gibraltar (1309–10). The Maghribi light cavalry style was modified in the Iberian environment. Both Spanish Christian and Muslim *jinetes* wore slightly more body protection than the North African tribal cavalries. Climate, as well as preferred tactics, may have influenced the lack of heavier armament. The *jinetes* wore leather and quilted fabric clothing, simple metal or thick leather helmets, and possibly short chain-mail coats and mail coifs. They were armed with lances, javelins, swords, and carried shields. Granadan cavalry leaders appear to have had a distinctive Granadan '*espada jinéta*' sword that is displayed in several modern museums and is consistently shown with contemporary images of Nasrid noblemen. These swords had a straight, long blade, with a highly decorative handle and uniquely shaped guard. They were worn with a baudrier (over-the-shoulder sling). There is no convincing evidence that the Granadan–Maghribi warriors had scimitars, or highly curve-bladed swords during the War of Granada. The typical western Muslims' sword was the very slightly curve-bladed *saif*.[171]

As combatants, the Granadan cavalry, on a one-to-one basis, compared favourably with the Castilian knights. Narratives describe individual Muslim knights having weapons and protective clothing on a par with that of their Christian opponents. A good portion of Granadans seem to have aspired to the image of an armed mounted knight. Armour was acquired by the wealthy Nasrid nobles; no doubt some was captured, but they were able to purchase plate metal suits made in Italy. The fitted plate metal suits probably were worn in the many tournaments, events for show and training, which the Muslims took to as enthusiastically as did the Christians. However, full metal suits were rare in the battles of the War of Granada. The carvings in the Cathedral of Toledo show even the Christians wearing only part of their plate metal body protection when configured *a la brida*. The *a la jenete (jinéta)* style of cavalry reflected the dominant cavalry fighting in the war. Chronicles give accounts of Granadan knights challenging their Castilian counterparts, similarly attired, and engaging in duels before the walls of besieged fortresses. The Castilians did not exhibit any particular advantage in these one-to-one encounters and Ferdinand the Catholic discouraged the events.

Distinction must be made between those who fought mounted, and those who merely rode on an expedition and in combat fought dismounted. The concept of foot soldiers riding animals to participate in long-distance campaigns dates at least back to ancient Greece, and was prevalent in many of the campaigns of the Hundred Years' War. The concept is especially valuable for deployment of missile infantrymen, and one which the conditions in al-Andalus allowed the Granadans to exploit. The crossbowmen and handgunners who subjected the Castilian expedition to numerous devastating ambushes in the dramatic rout of Ajarquía (1483), and on many other less noted occasions, were such 'dragoon'-type troops. Though the terms dragoon did not emerge until the following century, with the further development of the handgun, the Granadan War foretold the value of the concept. Such troops were not trained, equipped, nor mounted to fight like cavalry. The nature of the expeditions and raids, that required traversing long mountainous routes, led to many soldiers riding an animal to battle, but dismounting to fight. As a rule, most of the non-cavalry rode donkeys or low-breed horses. There are reports that some of the Granadans fired their crossbows and handguns from horseback. In both cases, these would be much more demanding accomplishments than firing the traditional small simple or composite bow. Simple or composite bows were usually part of the Muslim cavalrymen's weapons. At this time, the only effective horse-archers, using composite bows, were in the eastern Muslim armies. Like the English longbow, the archer's skill took years to develop. There is no record of a significant horse-archer presence in the Nasrid forces.

Infantry

As with most medieval armies, the Nasrid foot soldiers in the War of Granada were generally of the lower social classes and were mostly under the direction of a nobleman. There were two general categories of Granadan foot soldiers: the trained warriors who were experienced with the use of spears, javelins, swords and bow-weapons; and the civilian militia. The first category consisted of native Granadans and North African volunteers; these made up most of the troops that deployed on expeditions along with the cavalry. The second category consisted of combatants obtained from the urban populations, the size of which had swelled by the migration of many rural dwellers who had evacuated fallen Muslim towns and sought safety behind the town-fortress walls from the ravages of Castilian raids. To some extent the civilian augmentation was valuable for fortress defensive operations. Handgunners and crossbowmen needed assistance in reloading their weapons, fortress structures damaged by the besieging artillery required continuous repairs, crews for defensive artillery machines were augmented by townspeople, and in some cases counter-mines needed digging. The Granadan city militia were more than just labourers; many had limited combatant roles which were particularly suited to fortress defence. Many large towns had a *ramat*; these were 'civilian quasi-militia clubs devoted to crossbow or arquebuse marksmanship', which could be formidable when positioned along walls and in bastion towers.[172] Accounts of the war confirm that the key Muslim strongholds, such as Loja, Málaga, Baza and Granada, were defended by resolute 'community armies' as well as a core of professional warriors. The large reserve of manpower in the Nasrid main fortress cities was one of the major challenges to the Castilian conquest. Such personnel strength should have ensured the security of these Granadan strongholds against the typical medieval siege without large gunpowder artillery trains or resources to conduct a long investment. The negative side of a large population within a besieged fortress was that it strained the food and water resources under long sieges.

For most of the *Reconquista*, the Spanish Muslim and Maghribi infantries had not prevailed well against the Castilian or Aragonese foot soldiers in close hand-to-hand combat in open battlefields. In the late fifteenth century the Hispano-Maghribi infantry adhered to traditional Muslim infantry tactics that were similar to those of their cavalries. The technique can be effective when executed by inherently mobile cavalry, but there are limits when attempted by less mobile foot soldiers. Hispano-Maghribi infantry were generally preceded by small engagements, in which the foot soldiers often worked in concert with cavalry, to probe and to lure the enemy into a vulnerable position. The attack and retreat (al-karr wa 'l-farr) method did not work well against the disciplined Castilian and Aragonese infantries, which were exceptionally effective in close fighting with swords and spears. Unlike the contemporary infantries of eastern Muslims, such as the Ottomans, the Spanish Muslims did not succeed in forming infantry contingents which specialized in close formation combat with swords and spears, or with massed archers. The Spanish Muslim infantries preferred to engage the enemy at a distance, and emphasized missile weapons: javelins, slings, arrows from straight or composite bows and bolts from crossbows. However, they never adopted the massed archery Janissary corps that the Ottomans so effectively employed in the eastern Islamic regions. Though composite bows were used by the Hispano-Maghribi armies, their emphasis was on the crossbow – a weapon more adaptable to individual marksmanship than to mass firepower.

The Granadans' stress on crossbows and handguns led to their reputed skill as individual marksmen in both, which is begrudgingly attested by contemporary Spanish chroniclers. These weapons were suited to mountain ambushes and returning fire from fortress walls and towers. The absence of administrative records prevents comparing the amount of crossbows to those of handguns in their force. However, from Christian accounts and the few contemporary depictions of combat, it appears that the Granadans did not have nearly the volume of handguns that the Castilians possessed. This should not be surprising, since the extensive acquisition of gunpowder weapons by the Castilians was a major innovation by the Catholic Sovereigns in constructing their forces. Given the known commonality of many of the Granadan and Castilian individual weapons, it is reasonable to assume that the Granadan *midfa* or *kabus* (arquebus?) and *kisi akkara* (crossbow) were technically equal to the *espingarda* and *ballesta* of the Castilians.[173]

Handguns were reviewed earlier in the section on gunpowder weapons, but some mention is necessary of the crossbow. The crossbow was an ancient weapon that had a re-birth around the eleventh century. The crossbow was evidently not well known by the early Muslim forces when used by Christian armies in the First Crusade to the Holy Land. Since the Western forces were represented by a large number of French, the crossbow was described initially by the Muslims as a 'French bow' (*gaws ifrangiyya*).[174] The crossbow was a popular weapon of the Granadan infantry by the late fifteenth century. The crossbow's introduction into Granada probably reflects a European influence, very likely introduced by the Genoese who actively traded with the Spanish Muslims.[175]

The medieval crossbow had advanced upon the early wood crossbows with better composite and eventually, by the early fifteenth century, steel bows. The steel crossbows had 'power levels that no organic material of the time could equal'.[176] The heavier and most powerful hand-held crossbows were made of steel and required mechanical devices, just as were needed for the strongest composite bows, to span them. Such devices were usually detachable winch-and-pulley, hand-wound mechanisms called a 'windlass', or attached ratchet-cranks (*cranequins*) to draw back the very strong steel bows.[177] There was also a 'goat's foot' lever device, which may not have been as good for the steel bows as it was for the composite bow. Crossbows were carried by some mounted troops and most likely were fired from a stationary position or with the archer dismounted.[178] Lighter bows could be spanned with a simple belt hook and foot stirrup. A stirrup fixed to the front of the crossbow allowed the bowman's foot to steady, or push away, as the bowstring was being pulled backwards to engage the notch. The notch held the bowstring in a drawn position, keeping the bow in tension until tripped by a trigger, thereby releasing the bolt. The strong commitment to the crossbow may account for the fact that the Granadans adapted more quickly to handguns than they had to gunpowder artillery by the time of the War of Granada. As a hand-held missile weapon it was compatible with their traditional infantry tactics. In fact, the Granadans seemed to have embraced the handgun before the Ottomans, who were reluctant to supplant their very effective composite-bow infantry contingents. It is tempting to draw a parallel here with the English relationship to the longbow and the responsiveness in accepting firearms.

After launching crossbow bolts and regular arrows, the Granadan and Maghribi warriors threw javelins and released sling shots. Finally in close battle, they used their spears as short pikes, along with flails and swords. Infantry swords are generally depicted with straight blades in contemporary images. More than one of the carvings in the Cathedral of Toledo choir stalls show Muslim foot combatants brandish wide-blade, cutlass-like swords which appear to be a *falchion* (*alfanje* in Spanish).[179] Although the *falchion* was used for some time in medieval Europe, the curve suggests possible Middle Eastern origin.[180] The ultimate close-fighting weapon was the dagger, and all combatants had at least one dagger.

The Granadan warriors are shown with considerably less body protection than their Christian assailants. The Toledo carvings show a few Muslims wearing what appear to be *brigandines*, leather jackets with scales (bone or metal) sewn inside. Granadans are shown wearing very little mail, and rarely any plate metal protection. The sporadic appearance of metal body protection suggests these items were obtained from fallen enemies and does not suggest an indigenous style. This perception on the part of contemporary Christian artisans, or the conclusion one may draw from inspecting contemporary images, may be inaccurate regarding the amount of body protection worn by the Spanish Muslims. It was the custom of early Muslim warriors to wear civilian attire or a burnous over body protective garments.[181] This is another difference between the Hispano-Maghribi warriors and the mail (sometimes with pieces of plate metal) worn by the contemporary Muslim Ottomans to the East. The Spanish Muslim spearman relied primarily on leather *lamt* shields for parrying blows, and appears to have worn little body protection. Wooden *turs* shields were more familiar to the Maghribi forces. The distinctive kidney-shaped leather *daraqa* was used by some Granadan infantry as well as by light cavalry.

Contemporary images show a disparity between the Muslims and Christian warriors in wearing head protection.[182] A few Muslims are shown wearing steel or hard leather helmets of Italian design – possibly captured, but easily accessible through robust trade with Genoa. In the Toledo Cathedral carvings, there is a noticeable number of Muslim leaders wearing turbans. However, it is more difficult to discern in these images the real nature of the headgear worn by many of the Granadan town defenders. These Muslim combatants appear to be wearing soft, wide-brim hats, with the front section rolled back in such a manner as to suggest felt or straw material. Wide-brim hats were popular peasant hats in warm Mediterranean climates and are shown worn by civilians in near contemporary art renderings.[183]

There is an important distinction between the Granadan army and military trends in other Muslim societies of the late medieval era. The institution of 'slave armies' was not incorporated in the Nasrid military system. The Spanish Umayyads of Córdoba had used slaves for some military units and for some administrative posts in the caliphal government. Upon the dissolution of the Cordoban Caliphate, several of the minor kingdoms were ruled by descendants of such 'slave' ministers. The Almoravids and Almohads made only 'moderate use' of military slaves.[184] The Nasrid king Muhammad V found security in acquiring a personal guard of 'mamalik' slave-soldiers in 1359, but the example evolved into later monarchs employing foreign mercenaries.[185] Many of these mercenaries in the Granadan service were from Europe and European chroniclers felt compelled to describe them as 'renegades' or 'slaves'. Harvey explains that practices reminiscent of the Ottomans and of other Muslim domains to the east were not reflected in the incidents of senior Granadan government officials being identified as former captives or children of slaves. 'Recruitment by slave raiding was … never more than sporadic in Granada, whereas in the Ottoman East the practice became institutionalized. Nothing like a corps of janissaries could ever emerge in Spain, and the foreign militia for Granada was … North African'.[186]

Artillery

The brief review of Granadan non-gunpowder artillery here balances the attention given earlier to the dramatic impact of Castilian offensive gunpowder artillery in the War of Granada. It must be noted that there was a significant amount of non-gunpowder artillery used by both sides in the war; and that artillery was used defensively, as well as offensively in siege operations. Convention describes non-gunpowder artillery weapons as 'machines' or 'engines' of war.

Three main categories of war engines (*engeños* in Spanish, *al-majanech* in Arabic) were represented in late medieval non-gunpowder artillery. Catapults and ballistas were ancient artillery weapons, which underwent a few modifications in their medieval configurations. Trébuchets, the third hurling machine, were distinctly a medieval weapon in Europe. The catapult (*cabrita* in Spanish) was generally called a mangonel (*manganiq* in Arabic) in the medieval era. The mangonel [mangon] was a throwing engine for lobbing stones and numerous destructive objects. It had a long arm, held upright by twisted ropes at the lower end, with a fixed cup at the top. When the arm was forced down to a near horizontal position a potential torsion force was induced by the twisted ropes. When released from the horizontal, the torsion force rotated the arm rapidly upwards ejecting the contents which had been placed in the cup.

The ballista (*balista* in Spanish, *arrada* in Arabic) was a large crossbow with a cranking device to draw the bow, largely used as an anti-personnel weapon against formations or massed groups. It was a direct shooting weapon that fired large bolts and small objects. Mostly the ballista worked on the simple tension principle of the hand-held crossbow. There were some which were modified to use twisted rope and work under torsion.

The trébuchet represented a more powerful throwing engine than the mangonel and was particularly effective in throwing heavy and large projectiles in high trajectory, over fortress walls. It operated on a counter-weight [counterpoise] principle. A distinctive feature of the trébuchet was a long pivoting arm that had a sling or cup at the throwing end of the shaft. The throwing end was far from the pivot point. The other end supported a large container in which weight stones were placed. The long arm was winched down (often assisted by crews concurrently pulling on ropes) to near-horizontal and the sling loaded. When released, the force of the counter-weights on the short arm rotated the long arm upward about the pivot. A clear Arabic term for the trébuchet is not apparent. In his work on medieval sieges, Jim Bradbury suggests that many of the Muslim weapons described as 'mangonels' were probably the pivot-type machines, and may more correctly be categorized as trébuchets.[187]

Gunpowder artillery in general has already been largely covered in earlier sections, noting the unusually strong showing of the Castilian artillery. It need only be noted further that the Granadans definitely were aware of and employed cannon at its earliest stages. It is possible that the first use of cannon in warfare in the Iberian Peninsula was by Muslims at the siege of Huéscar (1324). The debate hinges largely on interpretation of the word '*naft*'. This

Arabic term was used to mean various flammable substances – Greek Fire, gunpowder, or cannon – during different phases of the medieval era.[188] Luis Seco de Lucena Paredes mentions that sometime after 14 Aug 1340, the Africans and the Granadans surrounded Tarifa, then under the power of Castile, in the Strait and used artillery (called *anfat*) in the siege.[189] The first strong confirmation of the Granadans' use of cannon was against Alfonso XI's Siege of Algeciras (1342–43).[190]

From the very beginning of the fifteenth century, Granadans were well experienced with gunpowder artillery. In the Antequera War (1406–10), artillery was employed by both Christians and Muslims. Ferdinand, Regent for the young Juan II of Castile, made artillery his principal weapon in his successful Siege of Antequera (1410). Interestingly, the Granadan defending gunners managed to strike the platform holding the Castilians' large crossbows (*ballestas de garrocha*), which were doing more damage than the siege artillery.[191] Cook refers to Granadan advisors in the use of gunpowder weapons and Granadan-crewed bombards assisting the Maghribi attempt to retake Portuguese-held Ceuta, Morocco, in 1419. Granadan gunners were sought by Maghribi leaders to repel a Portuguese expedition against Tangier in 1437.[192]

Though more advanced in knowledge of gunpowder weapons that their North African brethren, the Spanish Muslims were seriously behind the Christian Spanish in artillery at the onset of the War of Granada. The only clear records of their artillery assets suggest that they were largely acquired by capture from the Christians. There is no evidence of their importation or production of significant amounts of artillery. The Granadans were praised for their skilled *espingarderos*, who had an indispensable role in the mountain skirmishes during the war, but gunpowder artillery '... was not an innovation that the Muslim side seems to have known how to exploit in the conditions of warfare of those days'.[193]

Harvey finds Granada's lack of preparedness in gunpowder artillery to be 'comprehensible': 'Since the Granadans were on the defensive and besieged very few Christian towns of this period, clearly the Christians had an incentive to develop and perfect the new weapon, while for the Muslims the cannon was a military toy of dubious use'.[194] Prescott's narrative of the War of Granada reveals a dramatic contrast between Ferdinand's later campaigns and the opening sieges, which did not give significant weight to artillery. In fact, Abul Hacen did not give artillery priority in his initial attempt to retake Alhama in 1482. Nor did the Andalusian Christian Spanish forces emphasize artillery, preferring sudden attacks and scaling as the dominant tactical methods. Accounts of the early incidents in the War of Granada mention guns largely as anti-personnel weapons. Non-gunpowder war machines were used well into the early sixteenth century in Europe, when gunpowder artillery became fully established. Wonder at the Granadan failure to develop their gunpowder artillery should be tempered with acknowledgement that medieval non-gunpowder heavy weaponry was very effective.

IV How the War has been Appraised by Authors

Generally, modern scholars agree with J.N. Hillgarth's observation that 'Prescott's analysis of the general means by which the conquest was achieved remains valid'.[195] Prescott's analysis was interwoven with his narrative. His main observations as to the reasons for the victory of the Catholic Sovereigns could be summarized as follows:

- Adoption of a bold strategy of siege-warfare which emphasized the newly emerging technology of gunpowder weapons
- Raids of devastation upon the Granadan food crops
- Strategic sea and area land blockades
- Joint naval support of siege operations
- Change from employing irregular-sized medieval levies for limited periods, to fielding forces of unprecedented size and duration in the field
- Building, upon an already fine tradition, a hardy, disciplined, and adaptable infantry arm
- Ferdinand's leadership in strategic direction of the war, and in personal command of the major campaigns
- Isabella's dedicated and successful acquisition of military resources and supervision of delivery.

These observations are echoed, in part, by twentieth-century scholars who have re-examined the war from a military perspective. Miguel Quesada emphasized the factors for the Catholic Sovereigns' success as due to the great size of the Castilian standing force, the employment of artillery, and the dominant infantry prowess.[196] While almost all who review the war are compelled to acknowledge the unusual artillery effort undertaken by Ferdinand, there is a tendency to relegate the accomplishment as an automatic product of material technology. Weston Cook's 'The Cannon Conquest of Nasrid Spain', is a necessary argument to appreciate Ferdinand's daring adoption of a radically new strategy, based upon the advancements in artillery that had been recently developed in France. Cook's theme links the War of Granada, to the modern elements of gunpowder warfare, other than trying to cast it as a mere final episode and inevitable outcome of the *Reconquista*. Placing the siege artillery as the critical element, Cook considers that the decisive phase of the conquest of Granada was when the Spanish first acquired 'a firsthand appreciation for the value of concentrated artillery firepower' at the sieges of Illora and Tajara in 1483, not 1484 (with the taking of Alora and Setenil), nor 1487, when the strategic fortress of Málaga fell.[197]

Paul Stewart, whose study observes the transformation of the Spanish

military under the Catholic Sovereigns over a longer period than just the War of
Granada (as did Prescott's primary work), finds particular praise for Ferdinand's
performance as a 'modern military commander'. Stewart discerns evidence of
Ferdinand's strategic vision in the methodical structure of his campaigns and in
his political acumen in dealing with the Nasrid leaders. Stewart goes on to
comment on how the war against the Spanish Muslims taught some valuable
traits that served the Castilian army well in the later Italian wars. These positive
lessons led to the Spanish army's readiness to adapt to new combat requirements, acquiring extensive infantry and light cavalry combat experience, and
appreciating the value of joint naval and military actions.[198]

Numerous books and articles on the fall of the Kingdom of Granada explain
the amirate's demise as a socio-economic phenomenon. While the event did
coincide with one of the worst disruptions within the Nasrid sultanate, it was by
no means the only time such disorders had occurred as the Christians contemplated advancing the *Reconquista*. Looking at the preceding Castilian civil
war and the relative wealth of the two monarchies in 1481, there was nothing
economically that foredoomed the Nasrid Amirate. The victory of the Christian
Spanish was most predicated upon the intelligence, tenacity, and complementary aptitudes of each of the Spanish sovereigns – a remarkable and most
unusual monarchial arrangement.

This leads to one unique factor in any assessment of the military aspects of
the war – the role of the Queen, Isabella. In his *The Decisive Battles of the Western
World*, J.F.C. Fuller remarks that Isabella 'proved herself to be one of the ablest
quartermaster-generals in history'.[199] Prescott describes her critical and central
role in raising funds, organizing manufacture and distribution of the full
complement of artillery, arranging for road construction, and ensuring timely
distribution to sustained lengthy campaigns. She promoted two novel orga-
nizations, a corps of field messengers and a medical service. Isabella embodied
the dominant, individual spirit of the Castilian military conquest of Granada.

NOTES

1. Charles W.C. Oman, *A History of the Art of War in the Sixteenth Century*, (London,
   1989), p.6.
2. In both the European eastern and the western frontiers, there were cross-
   influences between the Muslim (largely of Middle Eastern and Central Asian
   origins) and European (largely of Roman, Germanic and Slavic origins) military
   systems. The various medieval dynasties and kingdoms that predominately
   practised either Muslim or European military conventions were often adversaries,
   but sometimes allies. Either way, the contact fostered an inevitable cross-
   fertilization of warfare concepts and weapons. In the late medieval era it is difficult to label the origin of some weapons or tactics as purely Muslim (more
   precisely: Arab, Persian, Egyptian, Berber, etc.) or European (or more precisely:
   Frankish, Slavic, Italian, Visigoth, etc.).

3. Frederick G. Heymann's John *Žižka and the Hussite Revolution* provides an
   enthusiastic argument for recognizing the contribution of the Hussite Wars to
   European warfare. Heymann articulates as well as anyone that the Hussite armies
   under Žižka 'really revolutionized warfare. At least as much as the famous
   mercenary infantry of the Swiss, and perhaps even more effectively, it was the
   Hussite forms of military organization, Hussite methods of fighting, and the
   development of the recently invented fire weapons by the Hussites under Žižka
   which led to the eclipse of the knightly cavalry of the Middle Ages' (p.13).
   Heymann claims (p.452) that the Hussite Wars provided an 'enormous influence
   upon the development of armies, weapons and tactics in fifteenth and early
   sixteenth centuries, especially in central and eastern Europe'. His observations
   deserve careful consideration. Heymann does not establish a tangible link from
   the events or persons of the Hussite Wars to the tactical developments in
   Western Europe. In fact, Žižka's experience as a participant at the Battle of
   Agincourt (25 October 1415) suggests that he may have learned from the West
   the ability of disciplined infantry, in a tactical defensive posture and on carefully
   selected terrain, to withstand the charge of armed knights. As will be argued later
   in this Introduction, the success of gunpowder weapons in Western Europe
   depended upon technical developments still to come – improved gunpowder
   mixture and lock firing mechanisms. It is very conceivable that the Hussite
   experience encouraged the noted robust gun manufacturing that emerged early
   in the German states, and spread quickly to adjacent Flemish and Northern
   Italian communities. There is some evidence to suggest that the Hungarians had
   matchlock handguns equal to those possessed by the Christian and Muslim
   Spanish at the time of the Granadan War. Reportedly an 'early' fifteenth-century
   matchlock is exhibited in the Brukenthal Museum, Sibiu, Romania [David
   Nicolle's *Hungary and the Fall of Eastern Europe (1000–1568)*, (London, 1988),
   p.6].

   It is conjecture whether the Hussite tactical scheme was conscientiously copied
   by the French and Spanish at the end of the fifteenth century. However, it is
   conceivable that these armies, confronting a common need to acquire massed
   missile fire and lacking a large resource of trained bowmen, solved their shared
   dilemma, separately but in parallel, by the acquisition of handgunners and the
   employment of medium to small sized cannon in the field.

   The first apparent replica of Žižka's tactical use of guns, without the wagons,
   but skilfully adapting to favourable defensive terrain is at Castillon (1453).
   However, this was against an infantry attack, not cavalry. The two tactical
   schemes differ from the more casual and earlier employment of guns reported at
   Crécy (1346), by Flemish militia outside Bruges (1381) and in Italy at Cas-
   tagnaro (1382). The Hussites' and Jean Bureau's employments both placed
   primary emphasis on the guns in face of determined professional armies, and the
   deliberate tactical positions were critical to their successes.

4. Oman, *A History of the Art of War in the Middle Ages*, (London, 1991), vol.2,
   p.435, and *Art of War in the Sixteenth Century*, p.30.

5. As mentioned in Prescott's notes, Fernández de Córdoba distinguished himself as
   an officer in the War of Granada. His title of *el Gran Capitán* was earned from his
   brilliant military performance in the Italian Wars of 1495–1504.

6. Paul J. Stewart, Jr. doctorate dissertation, *The Army of the Catholic Kings: Spanish Military Organization and Administration in the Reign of Ferdinand and Isabella, 1474–1516*, p.268.

7. Survey studies that try to encompass broad time frames of European warfare have to be carefully evaluated. For example, it is interesting to note the coverage the War of Granada receives in the well-known works of F.L. Taylor, Charles Oman, and Hans Delbrück.

In Taylor's *The Art of War in Italy, 1494–1529*, most of the references to earlier military events concern Italian, French, and German cases. Though he praises the Spanish army's performance in the Italian wars, Taylor refers to very few of the Spanish chroniclers, relying instead on writers of the other nations. Compared with the attention he gives to the past histories of other European armies in the Italian Wars, Taylor has a meagre interest in the Spanish army's earlier development. He refers only seldom to the war with the 'infidels', as if it were some minor event. He lets the Italian and German sources convince him that the creation of the Spanish war machine was the result of the Spanish army's exposure to the Swiss in the Italian Wars – apparently unaware that there had been a Swiss contingent in the War of Granada.

Oman's time frame in his *Art of War in the Middle Ages* covers the period 378–1485, not completely to the end of the fifteenth century. His view is that the last phase of the Hundred Years' War and the War of the Roses (1455–85) represented the fulfilment of warfare of the Middle Ages. He sees the Italian Wars, begun by Charles VIII of France in 1494, as beginning a new era and belonging to his study of sixteenth-century warfare. Oman's introduction to his *Art of War in the Sixteenth Century* refers to the 'last war of Granada being the only event of importance in the nine intervening years' between the points where he left off his examination of warfare in the Middle Ages and took up his study of the sixteenth century. In *Art of War in the Middle Ages*, Oman observes the significant emergence of formidable gunpowder artillery at the end of the Hundred Years' War. However, he fails to follow the theme to its conclusion in the Middle Ages with the War of Granada. Instead, he takes up the English War of the Roses, only to conclude that the war had no impact on the broader developments in warfare. By omitting an examination of the progress of European warfare in the War of Granada, Oman could not properly assess the rise of the Spanish military might which triumphed at the very end of the Middle Ages and announced a new era in European warfare. Oman's selective reference to some late fifteenth-century events in the Spanish *Reconquista* reveal his failure to understand the significance of the War of Granada. His conclusions drawn from his brief reflection on the Battle of Higueruela (1431) (*Art of War in the Middle Ages*, vol.2, pp.180–1) have little to do with the dramatic change in Spanish warfare that took place between 1481 and 1492, in the War of Granada.

Hans Delbrück's *History of the Art of War* series, translated by Walter J. Renfroe, Jr. has two volumes that could address the War of Granada: *Medieval Warfare* (volume III) and *The Dawn of Modern Warfare* (volume IV). Together, the titles appear comprehensive, but geographic coverage in explaining the development of modern infantry omits reference to the Spanish before the Italian Wars. He acknowledges his failure to study the Spanish before the Italian Wars

(*The Dawn of Modern Warfare*, p.15). Delbrück was aware of a Swiss unit deployed 'as a model' to King Ferdinand during the struggle with Granada in 1483, and asked a Dr. Karl Hadank to research the Spanish archives, but he obtained 'only meager results'. Delbrück seems to have relied mostly on *Vita Consalvi Cordubae*, the life of Gonzalo of Córdoba, by the Italian writer, Jovius (Giovio).

8. The Italian Wars which followed the War of Granada had many phases. For the purposes of this examination, the primary importance is with the initial phases of the Italian Wars that took place between 1495 and 1504. More particularly, the first expedition under Gonzalo Fernández de Córdoba, which introduced the Spanish military experience from the War of Granada into the cauldron of wars from which emerged Western European modern armies. The Spanish military took on new dimensions during the Italian Wars and, after their initial expedition, the transformation of the Spanish military must more rightfully be examined in light of their collective experiences in Italy.

9. After suffering a severe defeat in attempting to seize Almería from the Moors in 1309, Jaime II, 'the Just', (1291–1327) King of Aragón, decided to place more emphasis in expanding the Aragonese domains eastward, into the Mediterranean. Aragonese expansion to the north or west was blocked by France and Castile. The opening had been made during the War of the Sicilian Vespers (1282–1302), when Pedro III (1239–85) of Aragón assisted Sicilian rebels in overthrowing the rule of the French Charles of Anjou. This led to Sicily, Sardinia, and Corsica coming under Aragonese domination. See J.N. Hillgarth, *The Spanish Kingdoms*, (Oxford, 1978), vol. 1, p.19.

10. Michael Mallett's *Mercenaries and Their Master: Warfare in Renaissance Italy* provides a fine summary of Italian military advancements during the fifteenth century.

11. Duke Charles of Burgundy (1467–77) was the fourth in the line of Valois dukes of Burgundy. During his time he was referred to as '*le Hardi*' ('the Bold'). Many later historians have given him the sobriquet '*le Téméraure*' ('the Rash') to describe his character more aptly.

12. The tactical concept of the English longbow is discussed in a later section on infantry. It developed in English battles with the Welsh and Scots. During the Welsh Wars of 1277–95, Edward I of England formed a professional army that he could keep in the field throughout the winter, and he first emphasized the employment of massed archers at the Battle of Falkirk (1298) to defeat the Scots. At the Battle of Halidon Hill (1333), Edward III employed the archers much as Edward I, and also in conjunction with cavalry. See Oman, *Art of War in the Middle Ages*, vol.2, pp.62, 67, 80, and 111.

13. Though men-at-arms [Spanish: *hombres de armas*] were originally mounted, there were exceptions.

14. The *routes* were usually about 50 men-at-arms. *Batailles* would comprise various multiples of the *routes*, generally amounting to between 300 and 500 men-at-arms. There were usually three *batailles* in a field army prepared for combat: a Vaward, Main, and Rearward. Such contingents were formed entirely of the heavily armed cavalrymen. Infantry forces and light cavalrymen were organized separately, even if they were part of the *lance* of the principal man-at-arms. The *lance* was the smallest administrative unit of medieval cavalry. It consisted of one

mounted and equipped man-at-arms, accompanied by retinue that varied according to country and time-period. In 1360, the English lance consisted of a knight, a squire, and a mounted archer. Later, the number of archers increased. The French lance of 1450 had a man-at-arms, a squire, two mounted archers, and a light cavalryman. In Spain at the time of the late *Reconquista* the lance was usually only a single man-at-arms.

15. The technique was inherently vulnerable to almost any sound tactical response by an opponent. It is amazing that the situation lasted so long before such responses were made. One possible explanation is that the men-at-arms monopolized the profession of warfare for most of the medieval era. They had been imbued with a fighting code that stressed personal bravery and direct confrontation with an enemy. Another view (more in line with modern military examples) is that the military leaders were secure in their existing skills of warfare, and really did not want to consider alternatives. If examined closely, many changes in warfare techniques are not so much sparked by new technologies as by perceived need (in terms of conquest or defensive posture) to challenge a prevailing dominant military system.

16. 'Without cavalry, a fifteenth-century army was unlikely to achieve a decisive victory on the field of battle.' (Malcolm Vale, *War and Chivalry*, p.127). If a combat force found itself at a disadvantage but maintained cohesion, it had a chance of withdrawing from an opponent's infantry. Exceptions, of course, were when the force found their retreat geographically constrained by mountains or wide bodies of water.

17. Vale, *War and Chivalry*, p.127.

18. Charles Oman's observation that the *jinetes* were driven from the field at the First Battle of Seminara (28 June 1495) is countered by those who have examined Spanish sources. It appears that the retreat of the *jinetes* was feigned, but Gonzalo's Neapolitan allies misunderstood and fled. The apparent withdrawal to lure the enemy into a hasty and disorganized pursuit was consistent with Hispano-Maghribi warfare methods, and was repeated successfully by the Spanish during the course of the Italian campaigns. At Seminara, the ruse was not understood by Gonzalo's allied Calabrian militia. See: Oman, *Art of War in the Sixteenth Century* (1989), p.52; W.H. Prescott, *The Reign of Ferdinand and Isabella*, (Philadelphia, 1892), vol.2, p.45.; Stewart, *Army of the Catholic Kings*, p.238; and Curt Johnson, 'Lanza Gineta: Spanish Light Cavalry of the Early Italian Wars, Toward Cerignola, No.1', *Scenarios for Wargamers*, vol.1, no.1, (November 1992), p.34.

19. Johnson, 'Lanza Gineta', p.34.

20. In this last campaign, which won the Swiss their independence, the cantons were aided by the French. This led to a long association where the Swiss mercenaries, maintaining their own tactical integrity and company leaders, became the principal infantry component of the French armies in the Italian wars.

At the end of the fifteenth century, France had not developed a strong indigenous infantry component to their army. As one of many attempts to acquire a contingent along the lines of the English infantry bowman, the French attempted to create a militia of infantry bowman, the *francs-archers*. The failure of the 'free archers' was dramatically exposed by their rout at the Battle of Guinegatte

(August 1479) when the French forces of Louis XI were defeated by the Emperor Maximilian I.

21. The Swiss-style pike tactic may have been tested at the Battle of Stoke Field (16 June 1487), where the English King Henry VII destroyed rebel forces which had a contingent of German mercenary *landsknechts*. The *landsknechts*, lightly armoured pikemen, like the Swiss, proved to be vulnerable to the English longbows. (Oman, *Art of War in the Sixteenth Century*, p.76.)

22. The English were not the only West European army to make significant use of the regular (straight) bow. Burgundian archers of Philip 'the Good's' prevailed over the Flemish pole-armed infantry at the Battle of Gavere (22 July 1453), which reflected a general pattern in similar engagements as the Burgundian dukes suppressed Flemish uprisings. Apparently the Burgundians employed English longbowmen in these efforts. Certainly the Burgundian army of Charles 'the Rash's' had a small contingent of English longbowmen at Morat (1476) and Nancy (1477), but they could not save him from the disaster of his poor leadership.

23. Eventually the vulnerability of the Swiss system was unmasked during the Italian Wars when faced with Spanish firearms, deployed behind field fortification that effectively stalled the momentum of the Swiss attack. Some of the most dramatic losses of the Swiss to firearms were at the battles of Cerignola (26 April 1503) and Bicocca (27 April 1522).

24. Maximilian I (1459–1519), son of the Holy Roman Emperor Frederick III, and Archduke of Austria, married in 1477 the daughter and heiress of the last duke of Burgundy, Charles 'the Rash'. He warred with Louis XI of France to maintain the Flemish territory of Burgundy. Upon the death of his father in 1493 Maximilian became Emperor. His defeat by the Swiss in 1499 at Dornach essentially gave the Confederation its independence from Austria. Maximilian's son Philip married Juana, daughter of Ferdinand and Isabella of Castile, and Maximilian was succeeded as Emperor by his grandson from that union, Charles V.

25. Delbrück states that the term '*landsknecht*' was 'a defined concept' by 1486. See *Dawn of Modern Warfare*, pp.9–10. The *landsknechts* went on to imitate the early Spanish infantry formations of pike and handguns that developed during the Italian Wars of the early sixteenth century.

26. In his *The Agincourt War*, (London, 1956), A.H. Burne observes that during the phase of the Hundred Years' War identified as the 'Du Guesclin War' (1369–96), 'nothing worthy of the name of battle was fought' (p.20). English loss of command of the sea also contributed to their reverses during this period which preceded the dramatic English victory at Agincourt (1415).

27. Delbrück points out in *Medieval Warfare*, pp.459 & 461, that the real innovation at Crécy (26 August 1346) was neither the longbow as a new weapon nor the mere dismounting of men-at-arms. The spectacular imbalance of that outcome resulted largely from the way the forces were employed by both sides. The undisciplined attack of the French knights into a missile barrage contributed as much to the dramatic casualties as did the positioning of the English archers. The theme was repeated in the battles of Poitiers (1356), Agincourt (1415), Verneuil (1424), and several smaller engagements during the Hundred Years' War.

28. See Burne's *Agincourt War*, pp.315– 45. At the Battle of Formigny (15 April

1450) the French brought up two culverins in what appears to have been an afterthought, and managed to disrupt the English longbowmen who were drawn up in their traditional firing position. The English archers charged and temporarily seized the French culverins. In doing so, the English bowmen became vulnerable to a counter-charge of mounted French men-at-arms who arrived upon the English flank. The Battle of Castillon (17 July 1453) was not a contest between longbows and handguns. At Castillon, the English attacked gunpowder weapons fired from prepared field fortifications. In effect, the English went against the very tactical scheme that made the longbow effective, but the missiles were different – shot instead of arrows. Castillon's significance is addressed further under field artillery.

29. A factor worth noting was the 'independent' status of the Spanish frontier towns during much of the *Reconquista*. This was a rare occurrence in Western Europe at the time of the late fifteenth century. In Spain, it was most pronounced in the towns bordering al-Andalus. Northern Castile and Aragón had passed this phase. Not surprisingly, it was the towns of southern Castile that provided the most aggressive infantries in the War of Granada. The Andalusian frontier fostered a sense of self-reliance similar to that held by Swiss cantons. The condition certainly contributed to instilling a sense of responsibility and an acceptance of discipline by the military forces that were raised in these communities.

30. Mallett, *Mercenaries and Their Master*, p.156.

31. Philippe Contamine identified a category of Italian infantry in the third quarter of the fifteenth century as *rotulari*, using small round shields. See *War in the Middle Ages*, p.135.

32. One of the valuable aids to study the combatants in the War of Granada is the fifty-four bas-relief carvings, depicting scenes of the Conquest of Granada, located in the lower choir stalls of the Cathedral of Toledo. The work was completed during 1489–93 by a German sculptor Rodrigo Alemán. The carvings provide an important record of armour and military weapons of the period. Since the images were executed contemporaneously with the events, they were very probably reviewed by participants in the war and are given considerable credibility by Spanish historians. Compared with other contemporary images, the carvings appear to provide detailed renderings of west European combatants' arms. However, the depictions of the Muslim warriors suggest an unreasonable lack of sophistication in their weapons for the time. The obvious propaganda nature of the carvings must be recognized. The complete images are in J. De Mata Carriazo's *Los Relieves de la Guerra de Granada en la Silleria del Coro de la Catedral de Toledo*.

33. 'The effects of firearms were specific and dramatic: they raised problems of tactics, equipment, and supply; wars cost more, new methods of fortification had to be devised, but they had little effect in the fortunes of campaigns as a whole or on the balance of political power.' – J.R. Hale, 'Gunpowder and the Renaissance: an Essay in the History of Ideas', in *From Renaissance to the Counter Reformation*, p.114. This comment is typical in many works which ignore the specific engagements in the late fifteenth-century French and Spanish wars of reconquest. This general statement of Hale's seems to be at odds with many more specific observations made in his article. For example on page 126, Hale states: 'The

acceptance of firearms did not, of course, depend on the issue of a debate. Fundamentally, guns came to stay because they worked: they won battles, they demolished walls.'

34. See Carlo M. Cipolla's *Guns, Sails, and Empires: Technological Innovation and the Early Phases of European Expansion 1400–1700*; and John F. Guilmartin's *Gunpowder and Galleys: Changing Technology and Mediterranean Warfare at Sea in the Sixteenth Century*.

35. See Weston F. Cook's 'The Cannon Conquest of Nasrid Spain and the End of the Reconquista', *JMH*, (January 1993); and Clifford J. Rogers, 'Military Revolution of the Hundred Years' War', *JMH*, (April 1993).

36. Cook, 'The Cannon Conquest of Nasrid Spain', p.44.

37. Rogers, 'Military Revolution of the Hundred Years' War', p.172: Rogers addresses 'a series of interconnected innovations [which] synergistically improved the powder and efficiency of gunpowder artillery' between 1400 and 1430. A brief summary of the innovations are:
   - hooped-staves method (as used in making wine barrels) made possible longer barrels and led to improved accuracy, power and rate of fire (due to faster cooling)
   - new iron refining process and increasing skills made guns cheaper
   - corned powder made guns more powerful.

   Rogers states that these innovations meant that the 'number and size of guns in use increased rapidly'. He notes that technology made the 'revolution occur in the art of war around the 1420s to 1430s, as gunpowder artillery overturned the centuries-old dominance of the defensive in siege warfare' (p.266). However, his most convincing examples are from the late 1440s and 1450s (pp.265–6).

38. The differences in gunpowder artillery are not easily apparent given the vast amount of what is so obviously common to earlier siege operations. The great sieges were massive undertakings of engineering and logistical management. Roads and bridges had to be made. Enormous quantities of material had to be transported. Many of the large siege devices, even cannon in some cases, were constructed on site. Repair of the siege weapons was continuous. In all, the siege required the construction of a whole new town to provide the most sophisticated technical services of the era.

39. Burne, *Agincourt War*, pp.41–3.

40. Rogers, 'Military Revolution of the Hundred Years' War', p.264.

41. Rogers, 'Military Revolution of the Hundred Years' War', pp.266–72. Rogers provides considerable detail on gun barrel design, improvements in metallurgy, and the introduction of 'corned' gunpowder. Corned gunpowder was a granulated form of all the components of gunpowder held in an equal dispersion. Prior to this discovery, the separate components of gunpowder tended to settle out during storage and travel. The mixing of the components in the field was dangerous and also led to non uniform performance of the explosive charge before corned powder.

42. D.W. Lomax, *The Reconquest of Spain*, p.166.
   Rachel Arié believes that 'Greek Fire' was used by Ismail I at Huéscar. The debate on when gunpowder weapons were first used by Muslims seems to hinge around the contemporary meaning of the Arabic word *'naft'* (*L'Espagne musulmane au*

temps des Nasrides (1232–1492), p.261). Similar problems with discerning the initial introduction of gunpowder weapons exist with English terms 'crekys' and 'artillery', which applied to earlier non-gunpowder-propelled throwing machines as well.

43. Jorge Vigón, *Historia de la artillería Española*, vol.1, p.26.

J.R. Partington, in *A History of Greek Fire and Gunpowder*, p.193, believes that Muslims did not have cannon at Alicante. Ada Bruhn Hoffmeyer, *Arms and Armour in Spain, A Short Survey*, vol.2, (Madrid, 1982), p.217, finds the report of Muslim gunpowder weapons at Alicante in 1331 to be the first of any 'historical worth'; and she finds it fully 'trustworthy' that King Alfonso XI of Castile and the Muslims used 'gunpowder as propulsor for projectiles' at Algeciras in 1342.

44. L.P. Harvey notes that Ferdinand, co-Regent with Catherine of Lancaster for young Juan II of Castile, took Zahara in 1407 using siege artillery. See Harvey, *Islamic Spain, 1250 to 1500*, p.231. Ferdinand would later acquire the sobriquet 'of Antequera' after he seized that Granadan city in 1410 and even later would be chosen King Ferdinand I of Aragón (1412–16).

45. This is the very Zahara that was retaken by the Spanish Muslims in a surprise night attack in late December, 1481. The event is generally accepted as the first military action of the War of Granada.

46. Cook 'Cannon Conquest', p.48.

47. Rogers' 'Military Revolution of the Hundred Years' War', pp.241–78 argues well for the 'revolutionary' technological developments in artillery. The operational and logistical aspects of the impressive achievements of Charles VII's artillery under the management of the Bureau brothers are usually only hinted at in most English writings on medieval warfare. See: Oman, *Art of War in the Middle Ages*, vol.2, pp.397–404 and 425–31; and Burne, *Agincourt War*, pp.289–345. A brief explanation of the French system at the time can be found in Beaucourt's *Histoire de Charles VII*, vol.IV, pp.387–400. However, even French literature on their artillery of this period suggests more research is warranted to adequately explain the effect this artillery had on the reconquests.

48. Rogers, 'Military Revolution of the Hundred Years' War', pp.262–6. Rogers notes that not all one hundred strong points had to be besieged. On learning of the severe damage the French artillery could do to their walls, many positions surrendered. This same pattern recurred several times during the Catholic Sovereigns' cannon conquest of Granada.

49. Burne designates the event 'important as making a distinct step in the evolution of siege artillery. Cannon had recently increased in size and power in the French army, and a man had arisen who understood how to use it.' (Burne, *Agincourt War*, pp.301–2).

Burne's tribute to Jean Bureau is interesting. Like many who study the war, Burne would like to know more about Bureau's organization and methods, for it appears that he never undertook a siege that failed. In contrast, Rogers disclaims anything special about the French artillerist's methods. Rogers 'looks elsewhere for the developments which enabled the artillery of the 1450s to tumble down the walls of the strongest fortresses'. He sees the answers 'included in the design and manufacture of the guns themselves, in loading methods, and in powder formulation'. Rogers goes on to remark that probably 'the most important of these involved the lengthening of gun barrels'. ('Military Revolution of the Hundred Years' War', pp.266–7.)

Tarassuk & Blair's *Encyclopedia of Arms & Weapons* (p.50) states that Jean Bureau is 'credited with having standardized gun calibers to take projectiles of 2, 4, 8, 16 and 64 lbs'. The authors also state that the artillery was organized so that '(a) heavy ordnance was formed into an artillery park and remained apart from the troops, until it was to be brought into action for besieging operations; and (b) light artillery was divided between the various units, supporting both infantry and cavalry in their engagement on the battlefield'. Such claims very likely apply to a period after the final major gunpowder victory at Castillon in 1453, as the Bureaus continued in their senior managerial positions over the French artillery.

50. Oman's remark that this 'was probably the first event of supreme importance whose result was determined by the power of artillery' (*Art of War in the Middle Ages*, vol.2, p.357) must be based upon the size of the operation and the fact that the fortress was formidable and politically symbolic. He goes on to speculate whether Muhammad II had heard of Jean Bureau's 1450–51 campaign in France. The Ottomans appear to have lagged behind the foremost artillery in Western Europe at the time. The Sultan found it necessary to hire the Hungarian artillerist, Urban, to make the large siege guns used at Constantinople in 1453.

51. Some discount the effect of the bombardment against the formidable fortress since the defenders repaired the breaches in the walls, and the Ottomans gained entrance into the city by a minor force penetrating an unguarded gate. However, the total picture has to acknowledge the continued strain on the defenders, who were fully distracted defending against a massive assault upon a new breach in the wall. This caused what would otherwise have been a minor incursion to become fatal.

52. Stewart, *Army of the Catholic Kings*, pp.232–3.

53. A new momentum in artillery manufacture developed with the arrival, in 1484, of French masters at the manufacturing sites of Córdoba and Ecija. See: Miguel Angel Ladero Quesada, *Castilla y la Conquista del Reino de Granada*, p.123.

54. Hillgarth (*Spanish Kingdoms*, vol.2, p.376) states that the large Spanish guns (*bombardas*) had a maximum range of 2,000 metres, and fired once per hour. To be effective they had to be placed much closer than the maximum range. A large number of the Spanish cannon were of longer barrel and smaller bore diameter (*pasavolantes* and *cerbatanas*). These latter pieces allowed for a faster rate-of-fire. Rogers explains (p.268) that lengthening of the barrels allowed faster cooling of the barrels and permitted faster reloading and firing. Unlike the larger *bombardas*, the narrower cannon were breech-loaders. Each cannon had several removable breech-chambers which allowed for separate, safe packing of powder and shot. This avoided the risk of packing in a recently used (therefore hot) firing chamber.

55. Cook, 'Cannon Conquest', p.51.

56. Nothing appears more trivial to understanding warfare, the conduct of battles, or the developing impact of gunpowder artillery in particular, than the endless debates to substantiate the presence of cannon at the Battle of Crécy (1346). Charles Oman reviewed the various claims. His observations incline him to doubt the presence of English cannon on the field. More importantly, he states that had

there been cannon at Crécy, they certainly 'had no perceptible influence' on the outcome of the battle. (Oman, *Art of War in the Middle Ages*, vol.2, pp.217–20.)

57. Oman, *Art in the Middle Ages*, vol.2, pp.400–4, 431, *Agincourt War*, pp.315–45. In neither battle were the handguns and gunpowder artillery the deciding factor, but they contributed to the outcomes. The effect of the French *culverins* at the Battle of Formigny (15 Apr 1450) is discussed earlier in note 28. The Battle of Castillon (17 Jul 1453) was a set-piece battle, planned with deliberate care by the French Master Artillerist, Jean Bureau. The French prepared a field fortification out of gun range of the town they would later besiege. Their position was designed primarily to engage an expected English relief force, with carefully selected fields of fire for 300 artillery pieces and a hidden cavalry reserve. When the attack came, it was gunfire rather than bow-shots that diminished the frontal assault and set the scene for the *coup de grâce* by the cavalry. The large quantity of French gunpowder weapons reported to be at Castillon leads to the suspicion that many were handguns, rather than cannon.

There were, no doubt, many instances of early gunpowder weapons being fired in open battle that do not receive recognition in general military histories. For example, there is far more authority than supports gunpowder weapons at Crécy (26 August 1346) to show such weapons were employed during the Flemish revolts against the French-supported Count of Flanders in the late fourteenth century. In 1382, townsmen from Ghent marched against the town of Bruges (loyal to the count) and dispersed a sortie from the town with gunpowder weapons. Unlike at Crécy, there is no doubt that the discharge of the guns before Ghent influenced the outcome of the engagement. However, unlike the use of gunpowder weapons by the Hussite armies during the early part of the fifteenth century, the employment of guns in this engagement did not suggest a tactical scheme.

Through the first half of the fifteenth century, gunpowder weapons appeared with increasing numbers on the battlefields of Europe. The use of guns by the French at Formigny (1450) is similar to that of the townsmen's before Bruges in 1382, except that the former engagement is distinctive for markedly countering the formidable English longbow tactic. Castillon and the Hussite battles reflect the employment of guns in a deliberate tactical scheme – launching mass missile fire from a defensive position – which becomes a consistent pattern in the Italian Wars at the end of the fifteenth century.

58. Oman, *Art of War in the Middle Ages*, vol.2, p.216.
59. Stewart, *Army of the Catholic Kings*, p.235, referencing the *Historia de Ponce de León*, pp.275–6.
60. Vigón, *Historia de la artillería Española*, vol.1, pp.34–40.
61. O.F.G. Hogg states that there is a gap in English artillery matter between the end of the fourteenth century and the beginning of the sixteenth century (*Artillery: Its Origin, Heyday and Decline*, p.47), at a time when Rogers says that artillery improvements were most significant ('Military Revolution of the Hundred Years' War', p.172). Between the 1450s and 1470s the modern two-wheeled carriage, trunnions, and iron cannonballs were adopted. Large bombards gave way to smaller, cheaper, more easily transportable guns, particularly cast bronze mussel-loaders (Rogers, p.172).

62. Cipolla, *Guns, Sails, and Empires* and Guilmartin, *Gunpowder and Galleys*.

63. Charles VIII of France had an impressive field artillery when he invaded Italy in 1494. The performance had to do with 'excellent organization. The centralization of the administration of the Kingdom of France had enabled the organization of a "weapon system", equipped with an excellent artillery park and also a remount service....' See: Eric Egg 'From the Beginning of the Battle of Marignano – 1515', in *Guns*, ed. Joseph Jobé, p.22. Egg agrees with Oman that the 'Italian campaign conducted by Charles VIII ... heralded a new era'. (Egg, p.23; and Oman, *Art of War in the Middle Ages*, vol.2, p.425.)

64. Vigón, *Historia de la artillería Española*, vol.1, p.27.

65. Delbrück refers to some of the earliest uses of firearms (1331 and 1334) being in Germany and northern Italy. He refers to the original records using the various expressions relating to *spingardarum* and *sclopeta* to denote the weapons. (*Dawn of Modern Warfare*, p.25.)

66. Medieval Latin, *colubrina*, from Latin *colubra*, a serpent. See: Vale, *War and Chivalry*, p.134.

67. Leonid Tarassuk and Claude Blair, *The Complete Encyclopedia of Arms & Weapons*, p.46.

Writers do not agree on a precise definition for the term *arquebuse*. Like so many weapons of this early period, the original chroniclers discerned no need to describe the weapons in detail for future generations. The decision to use *arquebuse* as synonymous with the first general configuration of matchlock firearms is an arbitrary one, but it appears to be the convention followed by many writers familiar with the period. Of course, the expression was not common among the many armies of the late fourteenth century.

68. The late fifteenth-century *arquebuse* should not be confused with the heavier, musket firearm developed by the Spanish in the sixteenth century. The Spanish musket, which was heavier, longer, and needed a rest-arm, became a highly effective and powerful infantry missile weapon. Neither is the arquebus of the late fifteenth century the 'arquebuse' used by mounted troops in the mid sixteenth century. The later 'arquebuse' was a more advanced, wheel-lock system. It probably received its name because it was smaller than the contemporary musket.

69. General description is taken from Tarassuk and Blair, *The Complete Encyclopedia of Arms & Weapons*. The authors note that the *serpentine* was a device that held a match, recognized as early as 1411 in a Vienna manuscript. During the last quarter of the fifteenth century, other improvements to the matchlock appeared in the form of the spring, the sear, and the trigger (or rather, sear levels) (p.219).

70. Evidence from stock designs and contemporary images indicates that European crossbows were not supported against the shoulder earlier than the end of the fifteenth century. Even at this time, not all stocks appear to have been distinctly configured so that the butt-end fitted into the shoulder.

71. Mallett, *Mercenaries and Their Master*. See caption to illustration (4c) of a photograph of a late fifteenth-century Italian arquebus (Museo di Castel S. Angelo, Rome) on unnumbered plate page facing p.55. The weapon depicted shows crossbow-like trigger and serpentine holder for match, and shoulder stock. The weapon appears very much like the *espingarda* displayed, without its lock, in the Madrid Army Museum.

72. Vigón, *Historia de la artillería Española*, vol.1, p.40.

73. Kelly DeVries (*Medieval Military Technology*, pp.37–8, 44) gives the range for the longbow 'drawn to the ear', rather than to the chest, to be as far as '400 meters'; and the arrow could pierce chain mail at '200 meters'. He gives the rate-of-fire of the longbow in battles as ten flights per minute. Some general writings give estimates of six aimed arrows per minute to twelve unaimed shots per minute for the English longbow. DeVries gives the range for fifteenth-century crossbow, made entirely of steel, to 'vary from between 370 to 500 meters, with sufficient force to pierce even the best plate armor'. The rate-of-fire for crossbow depended upon the mechanisms employed to draw the strings, and it was well behind that of the longbow. The best estimates are that crossbowmen reloaded and shot a single bolt in just less than a minute. Mechanisms to aid in drawing the steel bows (windlass or *cranequin*) were attached to the stock, thereby adding weight and costs, as well as making the weapon more awkward to use. Though slow when compared to the longbow, the loading time for the crossbow probably outweighed the multi-tasked loading of early firearms.

74. 'No serious comparison of the range, firepower or practicability of the hand-gun and the crossbow has yet been attempted, but it is clear that the former was steadily replacing the latter as the principal infantry missile weapon from a fairly early moment in the fifteenth century. This was to some extent because the hand-gun and its ammunition were cheaper to produce and easier to use than the crossbow, rather than because of its superiority as a weapon.' (Mallett, *Mercenaries and Their Master*, p.158.)

75. Oman, *Art of War in the Middle Ages*, vol.2, p.356–7. Apparently firearms were not in the Ottoman army as late as the Second Battle of Kossovo (17 October 1448). Oman suspects Hussite origins behind the German and Bohemian mercenary handgunners employed by Hunyadi (of Hungary) in the battle. Though the Hungarian cavalry wings eventually gave way to superior numbers of Ottoman cavalry, the Hungarian centre of gunmen held until they had to withdraw to keep from being enveloped. The considerable thrashing received by the *janissaries* from the handgunners during the two-day battle, Oman further suggests, may have influenced the *janissaries*' subsequent adoption of firearms.

76. By the mid sixteenth century, Spanish writers used the term *espingarda* to denote the long-barrelled firearms used by the Moors in North Africa. It was a different weapon.

77. Oman, *Art of War in the Middle Ages*, vol.2, among plates between pp.182–3. The Battle of Higueruela (1431) is sometimes called the battle of the 'Sierra Elvira' by European writers, and 'Andaraxemel' by Muslims. Luis Seco de Lucena Paredes considers it, and the capture of Alhama (1482), among the most important military actions, in Spain, of the fifteenth century (*Book of the Alhambra*, p.64). The event was a crushing defeat of the Nasrid army of Muhammad IX by the Castilian army of Juan II, under the leadership of his constable, Alvaro de Luna. A famous painting of the battle is in the Room of Battles at the Escorial, near Madrid. The work was executed in 1587 by Italian artists under the service of Philip II, after a painting found in the Alcazar of Segovia; the latter has not survived, but is believed to have been made contemporary to the event (Arié, p.252).

78. Ladero Quesada, *Castilla y la conquista reino de granada*, p.128.

79. *Ibid.* p.128.

80. Oman and Taylor express surprise at the Spanish army's positive response to firearms. In *Art of War in the Sixteenth Century*, Oman comments, 'For causes which it is impossible to discover, the Spaniards had taken to the smaller firearms much earlier than the French or the English or the Italians', (p.52). On p.67 of the same work, Oman emphasizes that the Swiss never employed their firearms with noticeable effectiveness as the Spanish did. In *Art of War in Italy*, Taylor observes, 'Already before 1494 the Spanish army had shown an exceptional appreciation of the importance of small-arms' (p.42). Taylor recognizes both the strong proportion of arquebusiers in the Spanish forces and their aggressive, un-Swiss tactical employment with such weapons, but somehow he declares that they are only 'developing' from a Swiss pattern (p.44). It is as if he cannot explain any other reason for the Spanish battlefield competence in the early part of the Italian Wars. But, as mentioned elsewhere, the works of neither writer really cover the War of Granada.

81. Oman, *Art of War in the Middle Ages*, p.428, expresses the same view as Vale, *War and Chivalry*, p.103. Vale states that 'by mid sixteenth century, firearms and field artillery posed a far greater threat to mounted men-at-arms than had English longbows or Swiss pikes'. (*War and Chivalry*, p.128.)

82. Stewart, *Army of the Catholic Kings*, p.237.

83. Paul J. Stewart, 'Military Command and the Development of the Viceroyalty Under Ferdinand and Isabella', *The Journal of Medieval and Renaissance Studies*, vol.5, no.2, (Fall 1975), p.226.

84. Charles VII's sobriquet 'the well served' alludes to the generally exceptional abilities of his senior ministers, such as Jacques Coeur and the Bureau brothers. These few provided remarkable talents that resurrected a nearly destroyed Valois monarchy to the forefront of late medieval European governments, and were essential for successful reconquest of French lands in the Hundred Years' War.

85. Rogers, 'Military Revolution of the Hundred Years' War', p.172.

86. *Ibid.* p.273.

87. Oman, *Art of War in the Middle Ages*, vol.2, p.432.

88. Stewart, *Army of the Catholic Kings*, p.13.

89. The development of sailing naval power and the relationship to shipboard cannon is well covered in Cipolla's *Guns, Sails, and Empires*. The impact of gunpowder weapons on Mediterranean naval operations at the very end of the fifteenth century is touched upon in Guilmartin's *Gunpowder and Galleys: Changing Technology and Mediterranean Warfare at Sea in the Sixteenth Century*. Unfortunately, the War of Granada just barely falls outside the time period of Guilmartin's examination.

90. Cipolla, *Guns, Sails, and Empires*, p.70.

91. Gutierre Díez de Games, *El Victorial: Crónica de don Pero Niño, Conde de Buelna*, ed. Juan de Mata Carriazo, English translation by Joan Evans of sections published as '*The Unconquered Knight*', *the Chronicle of Don Pero Niño, Count of Buelna*.

92. Often overlooked in many accounts of the Hundred Years' War is the critical importance of the English King Edward III's naval victories at the Battle of Sluys (24 Jun 1340), over the French fleet, and Les-Espagnols-sur-Mer [Winchelsea] (19 Aug 1350), over a Castilian fleet.

93. Harvey, *Islamic Spain*, p.184, and Arié's *L'Espagne musulmane au temps des Nasrides*, pp.266–8, provide a fine summary of these events.

94. Ada Bruhn Hoffmeyer states that the Aragonese navy used a bombard in 1359, and that Castile had cannon at La Rochelle in 1371 (p.218). She relates that Aragón's navy had two to three bombards on a ship in the early fifteenth century (p.220). See: *Arms and Armour in Spain*, vol.2.

95. Henry Kamen, *Spain 1469–1714; a Society in Conflict*, p.12.

96. Angus MacKay, *Spain in the Middle Ages, From Frontier to Empire, 1000–1500*, p.128.

97. Contemporary pictures of Mediterranean ports and ships show a variety of sailing vessels which do not subscribe to a specific design. Many thirteenth-century sailing ships had one to three masts, and two stern oar-rudders, like the galleys. During the fourteenth century, sailing ships began adopting the stern rudder, and mostly had two to three masts. The *caravel* appeared in the mid thirteenth century, and appears to have achieved its full design concept by the late fifteenth century. The Spanish generally referred to *carabela* and *nao* types of sailing ships. The latter term was apparently used for ships larger than the *caravel*, such as the *carrack*. There were various ship designs that combined sail and oar, such as the Turkish *galliot* and the Venetian *galleass*. (Björn Landström, *The Ship, An Illustrated History* (NY, 1961), pp.101–6; DeVries, *Medieval Military Technology*, Part IV: 'Warships', pp.281–308.)

98. The agreement was re-confirmed in 1480 and 1481 treaties. (Weston F. Cook, *The Hundred Years War for Morocco*, p.116.)

99. Weston F. Cook, 'Warfare and Firearms in Fifteenth Century Morocco, 1400–1492', *War & Society*, vol.11, no.1, (October, 1993), p.27.

100. MacKay, *Spain in the Middle Ages*, p.150.

101. The Castilian fleet was reconstituted over several months, and consisted largely of Genoese galleys. However, 12 of the 15-galley fleet were lost in an October storm of the same year (Hillgarth, *Spanish Kingdoms*, vol.1, p.341).

102. Spanish galleys continued to harry the English coasts until the truce of 1389. (Hillgarth, *Spanish Kingdoms*, vol.1, p.398.)

103. Luis Suárez Fernández's '*El atlántico y el mediterráneo en los objetivos de la casa de Trastámara*', in *Spain in the Fifteenth Century, 1369–1516, Essays and Extracts by Historians of Spain*, ed. R. Highfield, translations by Frances M. López-Morillas, p.60–3.

104. The Treaty of Bayonne (15 Aug 1402) and the marriage of Enríque III to Catherine of Lancaster initiated a rapprochement with England, Castile and Portugal. When Catherine of Lancaster died in 1418, Anglo-Castilian relations again deteriorated.

105. MacKay, *Spain in the Middle Ages*, p.51.

106. Cook, *Hundred Years' War for Morocco*, p.74.

107. Stewart, *Army of the Catholic Kings*, p.241.

108. Ladero Quesada reviews the importance of the Spanish Christian navies in *Castilla y la Conquista del Reino de Granada*, pp.146–51. He mentions that Count de Palamós y Trevento was captain-general over the fleet at Málaga (p.150).

109. Stewart assesses the broad strategy in Gonzalo's second campaign in the Italian wars: 'The warfare of 1502–1503 was decided almost as much on sea as on land,

and only a nation-state such as Spain could have conducted this kind of warfare on the scale that was required.' (*Army of the Catholic Kings*, p.240.)

110. Ladero Quesada, *Castilla y la Conquista del Reino de Granada*, pp.146–51.

111. The Ottoman Empire recovered quickly after Tamerlane's invasion of Anatolia (1400–03) and the catastrophic defeat of Bayazid I (1389–1403) by Timur at Battle of Angora [Ankara] (20 July 1402). The Sultans were able to continue the drive for conquest and empire as if it had not been interrupted.

112. Andrew C. Hess, 'The Ottoman Seaborne Empire, 1453–1525', *American Historical Review*, no.75 (Dec 70), pp.1,904–05.

113. The Spanish–Habsburg victory at the Battle of Lepanto (7 October 1571) generally receives more attention in Western military histories than do the two Lepanto engagements mentioned here, and was important in marking the beginning of the decline of the Ottoman naval power.

114. Cook observes that Western Europe was predisposed to accelerate their ship-building, while the Muslim states discerned 'no compelling need to compete with Europe in naval endeavors'. An exception was the Ottomans who saw naval power to be essential for their designs of conquest. Most of the other Muslim states perceived that their commerce and trade were secure with Muslims' control over the land routes to Asia. Large armies were more important to these Muslim domains. (*Hundred Years War for Morocco*, p.73.)

115. Cook, 'Warfare and Firearms in Fifteenth Century Morocco', p.28.

116. Maghribi corsairs (*qarasin*) raided in the small-to-medium Maghribi galliot (the *qarib*), which used sail and oars, and were excellent for quick strikes and withdrawals to coastal coves. They became a source of harassment long after the War of Granada. The status of the Maghrib during this timeframe is summarized from: Cook, *The Hundred Years War for Morocco*, p.75.

117. Cook accuses the Wattas of remaining neutral in the War of Granada, in part to benefit from Castilian purchases of their wheat (p.126). Cook mentions that Muhammad ash-Shaykh al-Wattas agreed in 1471 to a ten-year peace – note, this goes to 1481 – with Portugal and officially surrendered Arzila, Tangier, Ceuta and Qasr-s-Saghir to the Portuguese king Affonso (p.31). (Cook, *Hundred Years' War for Morocco*.)

118. Arié provides a fine treatment of the Nasrid maritime situation. See Arié, *L'Espagne musulmane au temps des Nasrides*, pp.265–76.

119. *Ibid.* p.266.

120. *Ibid.* pp.267–68.

121. The watch towers along the Andalusian coast were used for the same purpose by the Christian Spanish for years after the conquest of Granada, and many remain to be seen in the late twentieth century.

122. Arié, *L'Espagne musulmane au temps des Nasrides*, p.267.

123. See Hess's 'The Ottoman Seaborne Empire', p.1,905.

124. Caravels and galliots were employed by the Christian navies at Málaga (Arié, *L'Espagne musulmane au temps des Nasrides*, p.269).

125. Stewart observes Ferdinand's 'all-controlling royal hand ... best seen in combined [joint] naval and military actions', which were part of his strategic awareness. (Stewart, *Army of the Catholic Kings*, p.240.)

126. Lomax, *The Reconquest of Spain*, p.166.

127. Stewart, *Army of the Catholic Kings*, p.241. Naval warfare figured prominently in the War of Granada, '... encounters between Christian and Muslim fleets in the straits were common' (Joseph F. O'Callaghan, *A History of Medieval Spain*, p.602).

128. Material in this section draws heavily upon Chapter VII, 'The Development of a National Royal Army', in Stewart's *Army of the Catholic Kings*, pp.176–223.

129. Stewart, *Army of the Catholic Kings*, p.191.

130. The Castilian ordinances promulgated in 1387 were an imitation of the Swiss regulations. The troops directly under Ferdinand's command wore the distinctive red cross on white background of the Swiss (Ladero Quesada, *Castilla y la Conquista del Reino de Granada*, p.144).

131. Ladero Quesada, *Castilla y la Conquista del Reino de Granada*, p.141.

132. Stewart, *Army of the Catholic Kings*, p.188.

133. Stewart, *Army of the Catholic Kings*, fn 17, p.179. Hillgarth, *Spanish Kingdoms*, vol.2, p.399.

134. Stewart, *Army of the Catholic Kings*, p.184.

135. *Ibid.* fn 25, p.181.

136. *Ibid.* p.181.

137. *Ibid.* p.181–2.

138. *Ibid.* p.183.

139. *Ibid.* p.184.

140. 'The title "*capitán*" had always been used and was used for the heads of royal garrisons along the Granadan frontier, and companies of footmen in royal service were called *captaincies* (in the case of the horse "lance" (*lanza*) was used).' (Stewart, *Army of the Catholic Kings*, pp.185, 202.)

141. Stewart, *Army of the Catholic Kings*, p.185.

142. In 1488, *Hermandad* companies each contained 720 *lanzas* and 80 *espingarderos* plus administration and command. It was divided into sixteen 50-man squads, whose leaders (*cuadrilleros*) were directly responsible for the men. 'The 800-man companies of the *Hermandad* seem in function and size almost like regiments, and the battles into which they were formed in tactical situations can be called *de facto* regiments.' (Stewart, *Army of the Catholic Kings*, p.206.) Further examination of the organizational structure can be found in Clonard's *Historia orgánica de les armes de infanteria y caballeria espanolas desde la creacion del ejercito permanente hasta el dia*, vol.2, pp.158–66.

143. Much of this description of the organization is based on Paul Stewart and Weston Cook's review of Jorge Vigón's *Artillería española* and Pulgar's *Crónica*.

144. Ladero Quesada, *Castilla y la Conquista del Reino de Granada*, pp.123–4.

145. Stewart, *Army of the Catholic Kings*, p.189.

146. Stewart states that for 'the development of an infantry-oriented standing army one must look to the royal bodyguard' which was established by Ferdinand in 1504 [or early 1505] 'under the captaincy of Gonzalo de Ayora; initially consisting of 50 halberdiers, drilled by veterans from Italy to function as disciplined infantry'. (*Army of the Catholic Kings*, fn 93, p.194.)

147. Ladero Quesada, *Castilla y la Conquista del Reino de Granada*, pp.227–86.

148. Stewart, *Army of the Catholic Kings*, pp.165, 202.

149. Ladero Quesada, *Castilla y la Conquista del Reino de Granada*, p.106–8.

150. *Ibid.* pp.117, 132.

151. The best sources for trying to understand traditional military institutions of the Spanish Muslims are by French scholars: E. Lévi-Provençal, *Histoire de l'Espagne musulmane*, 3 vols.; Ferdinand Lot, *L'Art Militaire et les Armées au Moyen Age en Europe et dans le Proche Orient*, vol.2, pp.248–322; Arié, *L'Espagne musulmane au temps des Nasrides*. Louis Mercier provides abridged versions of works by a late fourteenth-century Granadan, Ibn Hudhayl, in *L'Ornement des âmes et la devise des habitents de l'Andalouise* and *La Parue des cavaliers et l'insigne des preux*. For English readers desiring carefully documented presentation of the Muslim military of the period, there are the works of Cook: 'Cannon Conquest', and *Hundred Years War for Morocco*. The latter work provides a special focus on the Granadan–Maghribi military relationship.

 Useful overviews of the Granadan army, which synthesize the many disparate sources, without specific notations, are provided in the following: Ian Heath's *Armies of the Middle Ages*, vol.1, and David Nicolle's *El Cid and the Reconquista 1050–1492*, with fine illustrations by Angus McBride. Nicolle also covers the Muslim Eastern military in other works which assist in understanding both similarities and many differences among the medieval Muslim armies. See bibliography for other related works by Nicolle and Cook.

152. 'The general size of the *usul*, given that the system was designed for numerical flexibility, could range from 10 to 50 thousand troops.' Cook, *Hundred Years War for Morocco*, p.41.

153. From Lévi-Provençal, pp.77–8. This structure is also related by the late fourteenth-century Granadan chronicler, Ibn Hudhayl, in his thesis on 'holy war' (Tuhfat al-Anfus), translated by Mercier in *L'Ornement des âmes et la devise des habitents de l'Andalouise*, p.162.

154. Cook, *Hundred Years War for Morocco*, pp.40–2.

155. *Ibid.* p.41.

156. *Ibid.* pp.43, 46.

157. Cook quotes from Ibn Khaldun's *Muqaddimah*, wherein that Arabic historian praises the formal battle formation of the *tabiya*. Cook reviews other Arabic writings on medieval warfare and observes that the tactics were not mere copies of bedouin raids, but were 'complex' and 'demanded disciplined forces to execute'. *Ibid.* pp.41–5.

158. Cook refers to Mercier's translation of Ibn Hudhayl. Hudhayl did not address the recovery of lost Spanish Muslim territory, but merely the need to defend it. Cook observes that: 'The *ribat* was no longer a frontier from which to launch an offensive *jihad*, but rather a fortified position and military assembly area.' *Ibid.* p.47.

159. Where gunpowder artillery had already begun to have an impact, in France and Italy, new fortress designs were emerging to deal with the new military era.

160. Though many of the Spanish Muslim defensive structures have been drastically altered over time, there remain some impressive sights for the late-twentieth-century-visitor. The *alcazaba*, linked with its Gebalfaro, at Málaga, and the remaining walls of the mountain-ensconced town of Ronda are just a few impressive examples. Pictures are inadequate, compared with a personal inspection, to convey the awesome military challenge these features presented.

161. Cook, 'Cannon Conquest', p.54.

162. This description of the Nasrid defensive force posture has been paraphrased from Cook's 'Cannon Conquest', p.55.
163. *Ibid.* pp.54–5.
164. The Marinids occupied much of what is present day Morocco. To their east was a contending Maghribi kingdom, the Wattasids, with whom they warred during the 1460s.
165. 'The North African "Volunteers for the Faith" had by long-established custom been commanded by members of the royal family, the Banu Abd al-Haqq, but from 1372 the Volunteers were under direct Nasrid command.' (Harvey, *Islamic Spain*, p.216.)
166. Their descendants played a crucial role as units of the Free French in the Italian campaign of the Second World War. The Moroccan *'Goumiers'* led the 1944 Allied breach of the Axis' Gustav Line in the rugged mountains of Monte Cassino.
167. Cook, 'Cannon Conquest', p.54.
168. In the fourteenth century, Ibn al-Hatib reported that the use of Christian material and equipment was abandoned in his time (Arié, *L'Espagne musulmane au temps des Nasrides*, pp.250–1).
169. Harvey attributed the Muslim loss at Salado (1340) to the 'highly-developed heavy cavalry charge' of the Christians. It was fought on terrain which restricted the mobility of the Muslim (Granadan and Marinid) light cavalry. See: Harvey, *Islamic Spain*, p.193.
170. Muhammad XI's Granadan forces were defeated at the Battle fought near the village of Alporchones (1452), 15 kilometres east of Lorca. (Harvey, pp.258–9.)
171. The sword of the Spanish Muslims was a *saif* (shown on p.19, in Zaky's article in *Gladius*). In contrast to the more impressive and unusual *'espada jinéta'*, the *saif* had a simple hilt, and some had knuckle guards on the handle. While the *saif* reflects the Muslims' preference for sabre (cutting, slashing) capabilities in their swords, it could be used effectively as a thrusting weapon.

The scimitar appears to be a name derived from the Persian *shamshir* (George Stone, *A Glossary of the Construction, Decoration and Use of Arms and Armor, in All Countries and in All Times*, pp.550–3) which had an extremely curved and relatively narrow blade, and was only a cutting weapon. An early Turkish *kilij* (one of circa 1467 is shown by Stone, p.356) had a broader, shorter, and less curved blade than the Persian *shamshir* and remained mainly a slashing weapon with only modest use in thrusting.

At best, the scimitar is only distantly related to the *falchion* (*fauchon*), the broad, slightly curved, broad-bladed sword of the Middle Ages (Stone, p.224, shows a fifteenth-century German one). A Granadan infantry warrior in one of the panels in the Toledo Cathedral holds a *falchion*. Some Spanish writers refer to the weapon in the carvings as an *alfanje*, which generally translates into English as 'scimitar' or 'cutlass'. The different terms and variations of meaning over time is understandable. However, the images suggest that the Spanish Muslims in the Granadan wars did not employ the narrow, highly curved bladed Turkish/Persian type swords that the Western observer generally associates with a 'scimitar'. Many important aspects about Muslim swords are contained in David Nicolle's *Early Medieval Islamic Arms and Armour*.

The *espada jinéta* was a Hispano-Moresque straight sword with a distinctive hilt and was carried in a scabbard hung from a baldric. Boabodil's *espada jinéta* and scabbard displayed at the Muséo del Ejercito, Madrid, provides an example of a highly decorative one. The museum also holds a sword of the same design, but simpler hilt, that is attributed to the Granadan war-leader Ali Atar. Some poorly preserved illustrations in the Alhambra suggest that such swords were used by the Hispano-Maghrib light cavalry.

172. Cook, 'Cannon Conquest', p.54.

173. The Maghrib and al-Andalus of the late fifteenth century may not have had a distinct Arabic word for a handgun. G.S. Colin mentions some early Arabic Maghrib terms, which may not have been as early as the War of Granada, but appear soon after: *midfa* (firearm), *kabus* (arcabus), *shkubbita* (escopeta), *bundukiyya* (arquebus at the beginning of the sixteenth century); see G.S. Colin, 'Barud: Maghrib', in *the Encyclopedia of Islam*, 2nd Edition, p.1057. It is very possible that the Granadans used *'espingarda'* like the Christian Spanish.

174. Arié, *L'Espagne musulmane au temps des Nasrides*, p.251. DeVries, *Medieval Military Technology*, p.39 mentions that the crossbow was even described by Byzantine as 'a barbarian weapon', suggesting their lack of familiarity with it.

175. Cook, *Hundred Years War for Morocco*, p.57.

176. Vernard Floey, George Palmer and Werner Soedel, 'The Crossbow', *Scientific American*, vol.252, no.1, (January 1985), p.107.

177. Cook mentions that the al-Andalus late fourteenth-century chronicler Ibn Hudhayl named the crank-wound crossbow *az-zanburak* or *gaws ifranji* in Arabic. (*Hundred Years War* for Morocco, p.49.)

178. A wall painting (probably fourteenth-century) in the Torre de las Damas of the Alhambra of Granada depicts two mounted bowmen, one with a regular bow and the other with a crossbow. The composition suggests that the archers may be an accompaniment to a Nasrid knight who rides ahead with his lance. It is doubtful that mounted troops used steel crossbows as the various mechanical spanning devices would be awkward and heavy for horse- or mule-mounted crossbowmen, who very likely used lighter crossbows which could be spanned by hand or the simple belt-claw. There was also a 'goat's foot' lever device, which could be used by mounted troops.

179. Fifty-four bas-relief carvings in the choir stalls of the Cathedral of Toledo show an interesting array of weapons used by Muslims, such as the sling and *falchion*. Photographs of the carvings are in Mata Carriazo's *Los Relieves de la Guerra de Granada*.

180. R. Ewart Oakeshott, in his *The Archaeology of Weapons*, (pp.135–8), discusses more than one type of *falchion*. One type based upon the Viking 'sax' went out of style by the fourteenth century. *Falchions* used in the late fifteenth century appear to be of Eastern origin.

181. Nicolle, *Early Medieval Islamic Arms and Armour*, p.8.

182. Besides the casual references made in the chronicles, the comparative battle dress between the Christian and Muslim warriors on the Iberian Peninsula can be examined from the few works of art of the general period. Two good examples are Schongauer's engraving of the *Battle of St. James at Calavijo*, executed circa 1470–75 (in Alan Shestack's *Fifteenth Century Engravings of Northern Europe*, (National

Gallery of Art, Washington, DC, 1967), p.33) and the already mentioned carvings in the choir stalls of the Cathedral of Toledo.

183. Seco de Lucena Paredes, *Book of the Alhambra*, pp.72–4.

184. Daniel Pipes, *Slave Soldiers and Islam, the Genesis of a Military System*, p.48.

185. Arié, *L'Espagne musulmane au temps des Nasrides*, p.244.

186. '... an essential difference between the Turkish practice and that of the Gran- adans was that no impediment seems to have been placed in Granada in the way of the neo-Muslim offspring following him [his father] into government, whereas Turks and Mamluks sought to avoid corruption by banning the transmission of offices from father to son.' (Harvey, *Islamic Spain*, p.247.)

187. Jim Bradbury states that the Muslim machine used a cup rather than a sling. He mentions that the Arabic expressions for 'long-haired' (probably to do with all the ropes stringing from the machine) seemed to apply to trébuchet-like machines. He mentions an Arabic expression: *umm farwa* (mother of the hair) for such a machine. (Bradbury's *The Medieval Siege*, pp.259–70.)

188. 'What may help to decide against Greek fire is that both Ibn al-Khatib and another eyewitness stress the thunderous noise made by the device as it projected its iron ball (*kurra hadidin*). If this interpretation is correct, Granada must have been in the forefront of technical innovation in the world at this time. The new weapon was a success, for Huéscar hastened to surrender, but there is nothing to indicate that it had any more general impact on the fighting.' (Harvey, *Islamic Spain*, p.184.) Also see Arié, p.261 on earliest Granadan use of gunpowder artillery.

189. Seco de Lucena Paredes, *Book of the Alhambra*, p.38.

190. The reader is reminded of an earlier part of this introduction discussing gun- powder artillery in the Iberian Peninsula. Also it should be recalled that medieval writers were not consistent in their description of these artillery weapons. As has been mentioned, this obscured distinguishing when some engines were merely launching fiery projectiles rather than representing the earliest true gunpowder weapons.

191. Harvey, *Islamic Spain*, pp.240–1: his source: *Crónica de Juan II*. On p.241, Harvey mentions that the fortress was taken by a surprise scaling on 16 Sep. This incident pre-dates when gunpowder artillery would dominate the siege.

192. Cook, 'Warfare and Firearms in Fifteenth Century Morocco', pp.28–9.

193. Harvey, *Islamic Spain*, p.230. Cook's assessment: 'Wed to static urban defense and horse-borne war, Granada lacked the technological depth and martial cohesion to carry the war far into Castile.' (Cannon Conquest', pp.56–7.)

194. Harvey, *Islamic Spain*, p.230.

195. Hillgarth, *Spanish Kingdoms*, vol.2, p.374.

196. Ladero Quesada, *Granada: Historia de un país Islámico (1232–1571)*, p.12.

197. Cook, 'Cannon Conquest', p.62.

198. Stewart, *Army of the Catholic Kings*, pp.239–40.

199. J.F.C. Fuller, *The Decisive Battles of the Western World, 480 BC–1757*, vol.1, p.538.

INTRODUCTION, PART II

LA RECONQUISTA AND CHRISTIAN SPAIN ON THE EVE OF THE WAR

I THE EPIC OF THE *RECONQUISTA*

In historical context, the conquest of Granada must be viewed as the last act of *La Reconquista*, the eight-hundred-year epic of reconquest of Spain by the Christian peoples of the Iberian Peninsula. The strategic geography was a dynamic cross-roads even before the Muslim conquest. Coastal parts of the Iberian Peninsula had been colonized by Phoenicians and Greeks during the first millennium B.C. The original inhabitants were given the name 'Iberians' by the Greek geographers. Carthaginians moved in upon the coastal areas in the fourth century B.C., as barbarian migrants, largely Celts from northern Europe, moved into the central and western regions of the Peninsula. Rome conquered the Carthaginian-controlled and Celtic areas as the Punic Wars began, around 218 B.C. The Romans named the peninsula 'Hispania', incorporated it into their empire, and made Córdoba the centre of administration in 151 B.C. In the fifth century A.D., the Roman Empire disintegrated under waves of various Germanic invaders. By 415 A.D., one of these groups, the Visigoths, dominated and consolidated their conquest of Hispania. Already partially Romanized, the Visigoths were able to establish an effective administration, centred at Toledo. Christianity became prevalent in conjunction with the Visigothic conquest. The Christian clergy acquired considerable influence and forced conversions of non-Christians began as early as 600 A.D.

Just as the Visigoths had swept over the old Roman Hispania, in the fifth century, so did the Islamic Arabs storm over the old Roman region of Mauritania, in North Africa, during the eighth century. The Arabs quickly converted the indigenous Berber inhabitants to the Muslim faith. Flush with proselytizing zeal, the Arab warrior leaders looked north across the narrow waters to the Iberian Peninsula, much as the Carthaginians had done centuries earlier. The fall of the Visigoth, Christian, kingdom was dramatic, swift, and so complete that to most observers it suggested no reversal was possible for centuries thereafter.

Conquest of Spain by the Muslims began in July 710 when the Arab governor of all the Maghrib (today's Morocco, Algeria, and Tunisia), Musa ibn Nusayr, sent the governor of Tangier, Tariq ibn Ziyad, across the Strait to the Iberian Peninsula, which was under the dominion of a Christianized Visigoth kingdom.[1] Tariq defeated the forces of the Visigoth king, Rodrigo [Roderic], at the Battle of Barbate [*Wadi Lago*] (19 July 711).[2] The loosely administered Visigoth kingdom was helpless against the aggressive conquest of the Arab-led North African Berber armies. The invaders were known as 'Moors' by the Christians.[3] By the end of 711, Tariq had conquered almost half of the peninsula, the Visigoth capital of Toledo falling in October. Musa followed, crossing over with a larger army in 712, and conquered the entire Iberian Peninsula except for remote enclaves in the north. In this mountainous region, called Asturias, a Visigothic leader known as Pelayo led a successful uprising during the years (approximately) 716 to 726.[4] Some accounts mark this resistance as the beginning of the *Reconquista*. It is not clear why this resistance was successful given the overwhelming military power available to the Muslims at the time. One possible explanation is that the Muslim conquerors were not concentrating on subduing this difficult region. Rather they continued the momentum of their triumph further north into the domains of the Franks.

Distrustful of regional governors who gained too much power, the supreme caliph in Damascus recalled Musa, and appointed a series of short-term governors to pursue the conquest further north. Crossing the Pyrenees Mountains, the Muslims seized Narbonne (719) and later Carcassone and Nîmes. Duke Eudes of Aquitaine defeated the first Muslim attack on Toulouse (721) but then suffered a reverse, and sought help from Charles Martel, the 'Mayor of the Palace' of the Frankish king. Charles deployed with a force of Frankish warriors toward Tours, where the Muslims, led by the governor, Abd al-Rahman, were raiding, and defeated them in the celebrated Battle of Tours [Poitiers] (October 732).[5] This engagement was the 'high water mark' of the Muslim advance into Western Europe. The Frankish kingdom grew in strength, and the Muslims were expelled from Provence in 738. Charles Martel's son, Pepin III, retook Narbonne in 751, ending the last Muslim conquest north of the Pyrenees, and his grandson, Charlemagne, conducted several expeditions south. By 785 the Franks pushed past the eastern Pyrenees and began seizing a northeastern section of the Iberian Peninsula, which became known as Catalonia. Barcelona was taken in 801.[6]

Frustrated in their attempts to expand the conquest north, the Muslims fought a strategic defence against the Franks in the northeast, and turned to subdue the troublesome region of Asturias in the northwest. Muslim military operations were further hampered by internal upheavals in the Muslim Empire.

In Syria, the Abbasids overthrew the Umayyads and attempted to exterminate members of the former ruling dynasty. The new Abbasid caliphate established itself in Baghdad (750). One of the Umayyads, Abd al-Rahman, escaped to North Africa, then proceeded to Spain in 755, and seized Córdoba in 756. He reigned, independent of Baghdad, as leader of the Muslim amirate in al-Andalus until 788. Continual uprisings kept the Cordoban amir from conducting aggressive expeditions against the Frankish frontier or the region of Asturias.

Abd al-Rahman I managed to recapture the strategic Pyrenees town of Pamplona in 781, an outpost which the Muslims had acquired in 718 but later lost. Eventually the town was seized around 799 by a Navarrese chieftain, Iñigo. The town maintained a precarious existence as an objective of Spanish Muslims, Franks, and the various small Christian kingdoms emerging in Northern Spain.

At the end of the eighth century, the Cordoban amirate's greatest threat was Frankish imperialism. Amir Abd al-Rahman I established three military regions under governors with wide powers: a northern frontier ruled from Zaragoza, a middle frontier ruled from Toledo, and a southern frontier ruled from Mérida. The governors of these military defensive regions were either Arab nobles or aristocratic Hispano-Visigoths with strong propensities for independent action and, at times, scheming against either one another or the amir.

INITIAL RECONQUEST TO THE DUERO AND EBRO (878–981)

The Spanish Christians, with Frankish assistance, slowly commenced the *Reconquista*.[7] The 780 years of the *Reconquista* developed in uneven pulses, and incurred several reverses.[8] Taking advantage of the distractions and intrigues plaguing the Cordoban amirate, the dynamic king of Asturias, Alfonso I (739–57), expanded his borders into Galicia in northwest Spain. New Christian provinces, León, Navarra, and Aragón, appeared along side Asturias and the French *marche* of Barcelona. Alfonso I continued to expand the domains of Asturia south to the Duero River, as far as Salamanca, Ávila and Segovia. Alfonso II (791–842), grandson of Alfonso I, also continued the expansion and annexed León. Eventually his kingdom extended eastward to include headwaters of the Ebro River. In this latter region, there emerged a new frontier province moulded by the nature of the continuous conflict. More than any of the other Iberian Peninsula's Christian kingdoms, Castile would grow and thrive with the progress of the *Reconquista*.

Towards the end of the tenth century, a wide frontier zone was created between the Muslim and Christian controlled regions. In this frontier both sides conducted raids to obtain booty and slaves, and to force towns to pay tribute. The impulse of the Christian counter-offensive increased, and at the battles of Polvoraria and Valdemora (878), Alfonso III's victories compelled the amirate

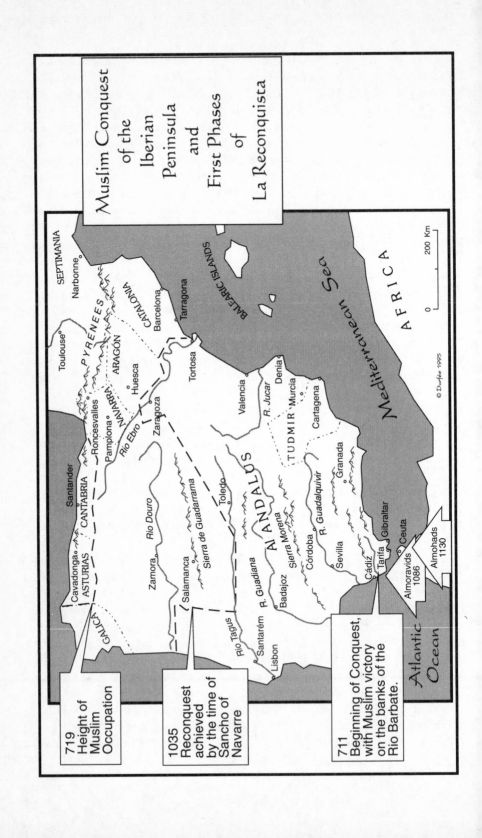

Muslim Conquest of the Iberian Peninsula and First Phases of La Reconquista

© Durfee 1995

200 Km

0

SEPTIMANIA

Narbonne

Toulouse

PYRENEES

Roncesvalles

Pamplona

NAVARRA

CATALONIA

Barcelona

Tarragona

Tortosa

BALEARIC ISLANDS

Mediterranean Sea

AFRICA

Santander

CANTABRIA

ARAGÓN

Huesca

Zaragoza

Rio Ebro

Valencia

R. Jucar

Denia

TUDMIR Murcia

Cartagena

Cavadonga

ASTURIAS

GALICA

Rio Douro

Zamora

Salamanca

Sierra de Guadarrama

Toledo

AL ANDALUS

R. Guadiana

Sierra Morena

Córdoba

R. Guadalquivir

Granada

Sevilla

Rio Tagus

Santarém

Lisbon

Badajoz

Cádiz

Tarifa

Gibraltar

Ceuta

Almoravids 1086

Almohads 1130

Atlantic Ocean

719
Height of Muslim Occupation

1035
Reconquest achieved by the time of Sancho of Navarre

711
Beginning of Conquest, with Muslim victory on the banks of the Rio Barbate.

to seek peace, revealing a shift of power. At the Battle of Simancas (934), Ramiro II of León's heavy cavalry defeated a Spanish Muslim army in an open battle, and with such a clear margin of victory that some mark this the true beginning of the Spanish Christian *Reconquista*. Another distinct victory was won when a Christian host defeated a Muslim army besieging Zamora (939), north of Madrid. The Duero River delineated the general southern boundary of the *Reconquista* by the year 1000.

Spanish Christian settlements arising in the reconquered areas were, of necessity, responsible for much of their own security. This responsibility imparted to the Spanish townships an 'egalitarian peasant society, organized for war and governed by relatively democratic assemblies'.[9] This created a social substructure in Christian Spain that significantly differed from the feudal systems of the Christian domains to the north. As the frontier moved south, the secured regions took on more of the feudal aspects of the rest of Europe. However, the frontier ensured the presence of a sizable, urban warrior class.[10]

The Spanish Muslim kingdom's failure to defend its northern boundaries can be partly attributed to the disruptions precipitated by the existence of disparate ethnic, tribal, and religious groups in their society. Abd al-Rahman II was distracted by rebellions (especially in Toledo 829–37, and later at Mérida). The reverses on its periphery did not fully alarm the Cordoban amirate, which prospered richly within its own borders, in spite of civil disturbances.

Abd al-Rahman III established a caliphate in 929 and placed Córdoba on the political level of Baghdad. Andalus (al-Andalus) benefited as a commercial centre due to Muslim sea-power in the Mediterranean, providing access to eastern trade routes denied to most of northern Europe. Many other aspects of this high-point are covered in Chapter I. The apogee of the Cordoban caliphate was during the reigns of Abd al-Rahman III (913–61) and al-Hakam II (961–76). The descent of the Umayyad dynasty in Spain began with al-Hisham II (976–1009), but the inner decay of its government was temporarily hidden by a brilliant display of military prowess.[11]

It was during this last period that the weak caliph's skilful warrior–Prime Minister (*hajib*), al-Mansur (Almanzor), 'The Victorious', reorganized the Muslim army. He led it in numerous successful expeditions against the adjoining Muslim challengers and Christian kingdoms. During al-Mansur's time, the Spanish Christian *Reconquista*, barely started, was abruptly halted. Particularly crushing was his defeat of the combined forces of Castile, León, and Navarre at the Battle of Rueda (981). Al-Mansur sacked Barcelona (987), León (988), and Christian towns at will. Sometimes he temporarily occupied them, as with Zamora in 988. His prowess forced the Christians to abandon some towns on the frontier. Al-Mansur was not interested in conquering new territory. He preferred to treat the Christian kingdoms as a garden, to prune for loot and captives with which to enrich the Moorish realm.[12]

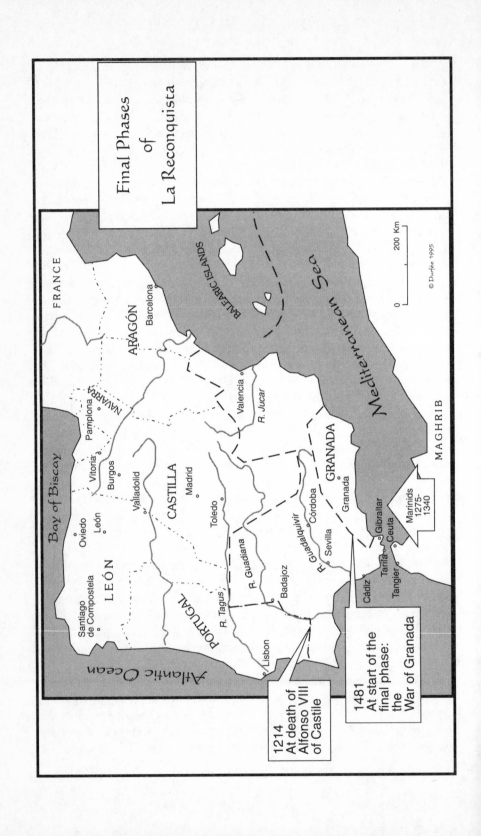

Final Phases
of
La Reconquista

FRANCE

Bay of Biscay

Atlantic Ocean

Santiago
de Compostela

Oviedo

León

LEÓN

PORTUGAL

Valladolid

Burgos

Vitoria

Pamplona

NAVARRA

ARAGÓN

Barcelona

BALEARIC ISLANDS

Mediterranean Sea

© Durfee 1995

0   200 Km

MAGHRIB

Madrid

CASTILLA

Toledo

Valencia

R. Jucar

GRANADA

Granada

Córdoba

Sevilla

R. Guadalquivir

Marinids
1275-
1340

Gibraltar

Ceuta

Tarifa

Tangier

Cádiz

Badajoz

R. Guadiana

Lisbon

R. Tagus

1214
At death of
Alfonso VIII
of Castile

1481
At start of the
final phase:
the
War of Granada

FURTHER RECONQUEST TO THE TAJO (1031–85)

With the death of the great Muslim military commander the Spanish Christian advance pushed on to the Tajo (Tagus) River. The effort was facilitated by the collapse of the Cordoban Umayyad caliphate (1031), which left separate *taifa* (small party) kingdoms.

At the beginning of the eleventh century, the Iberian Peninsula was separated generally north and south by religion. The Christian kingdoms were Navarra, Aragón, León, and Castile, which along with the French *marche* of Barcelona (Catalonia) represented the various independent Christian domains in northern Spain. In the south were the independent Muslim cities and regions (remnants of the former caliphate defence zones) of Zaragoza, Toledo, Sevilla, Badajoz, and Granada. The Muslim *taifas*, while sharing a common faith, continued to be fragmented by ethnic (Berber versus Arab) and tribal differences. They were not motivated to unite in a common cause for either conquest or defence. It was difficult for the Spanish Muslim communities to perceive a serious threat from the separate, small Christian kingdoms, and easy for the southernmost Spanish Muslim *taifas* to bask in the shelter of those Muslim communities contending with intermittent warfare on the frontier to the north.[13]

In contrast, although they often quarrelled among themselves and occasionally allied with separate Spanish Muslim states against a local Christian ruler, the Christian dynasties had considerable ethnic cohesion and a growing sense of a common goal to regain the lost land of the old Visigoth kingdom. Alfonso II (791–842), of Asturias, had constructed a monument to St. James at Santiago de Compostela as an inspiration to the *Reconquista*. The vision of a great crusade was promoted by a growing number of monasteries being established and an increased employment of monks in court administrative positions in the fledgling Spanish Christian kingdoms. These clerics provided popular, psychological and religious motivations that coincided with the aspirations of the monarchs, and the Christian communities began to identify their actions as part of a larger quest.[14]

Various dynamic leaders of the Spanish Christian kingdoms took advantage of the weakened Muslim domain. Castile was the most active. Ferdinand I, 'the Brave' (1037–65), of Castile began by making Zaragoza, Badajoz, and Sevilla pay tribute to him.[15] Eventually Ferdinand undertook conquests of small towns such as Lamego (1057), Viseu (1058), and Coimbra (1064).[16]

The most aggressive Christian offensives were led by Alfonso VI, 'the Brave' (1072–1109), of Castile [includes León from 1072–1157]. He captured Toledo (May 1085), which effectively thrust the centre of the frontier border to the Tajo River. This gave the Christians a threatening strategic salient into the Spanish Muslim domains. The triumph had an important psychological significance for the Christians, as Toledo had been the former capital of the Visigoth kingdom in Spain.

This was the time of the near-legendary El Cid. Rodrigo Díaz de Bivar, 'El Cid' (1040?–99), was a soldier of fortune who, when he fell out of favour with his Christian sovereign, Alfonso VI, served the Muslim amir of Zaragoza (1081). El Cid's propensity to fight for and against either Christian or Muslim was not unusual. Rigid distinctions between loyalties based upon religious belief grew slowly. The confused loyalties that prevailed during the *Reconquista*, especially prior to the final war for Granada, are hidden by the mantle of a 'holy crusade' that Christian chroniclers drew over the fundamental impetus of greed and power behind the struggle.

WARS AGAINST THE ALMORAVIDS AND THE ALMOHADS

Toledo's fall removed the comfortable buffer for the remaining Spanish Muslim rulers and forced them to recognize their weakness. They reluctantly invited help from the Muslim rulers of North Africa in 1086. In doing so, they knew that they risked being conquered by their saviours, in turn. The Almoravids had conquered Morocco and Algiers in 1082, and were known to be strong warriors. As such, they were not well disposed to fight as equal allies for a society, Muslim or not, which they perceived as dissipated and unworthy. When the Almoravids came, they came to rule Andalus.

Led by Yusuf ibn Tashfin (1061–1161), the Almoravids invaded, and, with Moorish allies, defeated a Castilian–Aragonese force under Alfonso VI at the Battle of Zallaqa [Sagrajas] (1086). The Almoravids beat Alfonso again at the Siege of Badajoz (1088). El Cid was invited back to serve under Alfonso VI and to fight against the invading Almoravids. He conquered Valencia (1091) and held it as his own fiefdom. He warded off the Almoravids at the battles of Cuarte (1094) and Balren (1097) and defended Valencia until his death 1099. Unfortunately, there were not enough El Cids, and even he was bested in his last, small engagment outside Valencia. The Almoravids captured Valencia (1102), conquered all Muslim Spain (1091), and won over the Christians at the Battle of Uclés [Ecles] (1108). In 1097, Almoravids defeated Castile at Consuegra and Cuenca. The Almoravids took Zaragoza in 1110, their northernmost posession.

The Almoravids proved to be poor rulers. In time, they were unable to keep control of their conquered domains. While they were preoccupied with threats in North Africa, they were overthrown by revolutions in Spain. Another era of small *taifa* kingdoms formed in the remaining Spanish Muslim regions (1131). Aragón moved quickly in to retake Zaragoza (1118). However, the risks remained high. At the Battle of Lerida [Fraga] (1134), Alfonso I of Aragón was killed in an ambush following an otherwise successful raid on the town.

Portugal gained a degree of autonomy with their defeat of Almoravids at Ourique (1139). Alfonso VII (1126–57) of Castile took up the *Reconquista*, only to be confronted by a new invasion from North Africa.

In 1130, the new fundamentalist Berber sect, the Almohads, overthrew the Almoravids in Morocco. They looked upon Andalus much as did the Almoravids, and they invaded Spain with new warrior vigour. The Almohads captured Sevilla (1147) and ruled the entire Muslim domain by 1150. Alfonso VII of Castile was killed fighting the Almohads at Muradel (1157). However, intermittent warfare between León and Castile (1170–80) made the Christians vulnerable to the invasion. The Almohads defeated Castile at Alarcos (1195). An exception to the Almohad success was in the far west of the peninsula where the newly emerging Portugal, under Affonso I (1112–85), aggressively stemmed the Muslim tide.[17] Finally, a united Castilian–Aragonese force defeated the Almohads at the Battle of Las Navas de Tolosa (16 July 1212), one of the most decisive events in the *Reconquista*.

EARLY WARS AGAINST THE NASRIDS AND THE MARINIDS

In 1179, Castile and Aragón agreed to partition Andalus. A final reunion of León and Castile took place in 1230, under Ferdinand III (1217–52), who became known as 'Saint Ferdinand'. Ferdinand III led the greater Castilian forces in an offensive that captured Baeza (1225), Jerez (1233), Córdoba (1236), Jaén (1246), and Sevilla (1248), the capital of the Almohad Andalus. During the first part of the thirteenth century, the *Reconquista* paused at the vast Morena mountain range. South of this massive range lay the last remaining Muslim domain of Granada under its new Nasrid dynasty, which came to power in 1248. However, the Nasrid kingdom had been reduced to vassal status under Castile. Their amir submitted to Ferdinand III and even assisted him in fighting other Muslims, such as at the seizure of Sevilla.[18]

While Castile was advancing along the western areas, Aragón captured Valencia (1246) and then had to contend with a Muslim revolt in that city (1247–56). Nevertheless, under Jaime [James] I (1213–76), 'the Conqueror', the *Reconquista* was continued down the eastern part of the Iberian Peninsula and pushed out into the Mediterranean. Aragón captured the Balearic Islands in 1229–35.

Midway into the thirteenth century, periodic civil wars broke out in Castile (1252 and after). Taking advantage of the situation, the Nasrid sultan of Granada, Ibn al-Ahmar [Muhammad I Alahmar, 1231–72] refused support to Alfonso X (1252–84) of Castile. Alfonso X's punitive expedition was defeated by the Granadan army at Alcalá de Ben Zaide (1252).[19] A general Muslim revolt broke out in 1264–67 in Castile's Andalusian towns. In 1269, Ibn al-Ahmar sought help from the Marinids, another Berber dynasty. The Marinids had overthrown the Almohads (1227) and established their new dynasty at Fez, Morocco by 1250.

The first of four Marinid expeditions to Spain (1275) led to the Battle of Ecija (1275). This was a great victory for the coalition of Muslim forces, who obtained large quantities of captured Spanish materiel, especially artillery.[20] The Spanish Muslims regained momentum while the Spanish Christians were disunited and preoccupied with other ventures. Muslims revolted in Valencia (1276–80) while Aragón was focused upon a kingdom in Naples. The Aragonese kings Pedro III, 'el Grande', (1276–85) and Alfonso III, 'el Liberal' (1285–91), became distracted in fighting with the French House of Anjou over succession to the throne of Naples and over Catalonia. With Aragón's conquest of Sicily (1282–83) and repluse of a French invasion (1284), the Spanish Christian kingdoms renewed their interests in Andalus.

In 1291 Castile and Aragón effected another coalition and undertook expeditions of conquest. Jaime II, 'el Justiciero' (1291–1327), of Aragón besieged Almería (1309).[21] Ferdinand IV, 'el Emplazado' (1295–1312), of Castile, captured Tarifa (1292) from Marinids.[22] Unfortunately, civil wars plagued Castile again between 1295 and 1302.

The distractions from a concerted Castilian–Aragonese effort in the Reconquista opened a window of opportunity for the Muslims. Ismail I (1313–25), the fifth Nasrid amir, proved to be their most sucessful military leader. He led a coalition force of Granadan and North African troops that completely defeated an allied Christian host in the mountains of Elvira (1319). The amir then led the Granadan army in an expedition to Baza, Huéscar, and other towns in 1324. However, he was assassinated and the defence of Granada then relied upon an uneasy alliance with the Marinids in Africa.

The strategically important port cities around the Strait of Gibraltar were bitterly contested once the Spanish Christians' frontier was close enough to support strong expeditions into the area. Castile captured Gibraltar in 1320; Granada retook it in 1462 with the aid of North African expeditionary forces. Alfonso XI, 'el Noble' (1312–50), of Castile employed gunpowder artillery in an attempt to take Algeciras (1333).[23] The important seaport was finally seized by Aragonese and Castilian forces under Alfonso XI in 1344. The Marinids of Africa tried to gain a foothold in Spain at the expense of the weakened Nasrid dynasty of Granada. However, a force of Marinids, with some Granadan allies, was soundly defeated at the Battle of Salado (1340) by Alfonso XI, who was assisted by forces of Alfonso IV of Portugal. This ended further major invasions by the Marinids, or any other large contingent from North Africa to the Iberian Peninsula.

Despite the weakness of Nasrid Granada by the middle of the fourteenth century, dynastic wars within and among the Christian kingdoms, and the Hundred Years' War (1337–1453) between England and France impeded the onslaught of potential strength possessed by allied Spanish Christian kingdoms. The *Reconquista* had progressed to the point at which Portugal occupied territory much as it has today. Castile possessed western and central Spain, with Navarra contained in a small section in northern Spain, and Aragón extended down the eastern quarter of the peninsula to Murcia and eastward to include the Balearic Islands and Sardinia.

Lulls in the Hundred Years' War attracted unemployed companies of armed adventurers to take sides in the Castilian Civil Wars 1295–1302 and various Portuguese–Castilian dynastic struggles. The most important military events were the Battle of Nájera [Navarrette] (1367), the Battle of Montiel (1369), the English Duke of Lancaster's invasion in 1386–87, and the Battle of Aljubarrota (1385).[24] There were many other confrontations between the Spanish Christian kingdoms in which their northern neighbours took sides. In general, France assisted Castile, while England would ally itself with any of the Iberian Peninsula kingdoms (at various times: Navarra, Aragón, or Portugal) that might have France as an opponent.

At the beginning of the fifteenth century, Castile continued to struggle with frequent internal problems, but managed some renewed effort toward the *Reconquista*. Enríque III, 'el Enfermo' (1390–1406), and Juan II (1406–54) conducted what is sometimes called the 'Antequera War' between Granada and Castile (1404–10). Two notable conquests by the Christians were Zahara (1407) and Antequera (1410), along with a few raids into the Vega of Granada. Early in his reign Juan II, with the Constable Álvaro de Luna, won the Battle of Higueruela (1431).[25] However, progress of the *Reconquista* was lacklustre compared with earlier achievements. Although a strong rebel nobility of Castile was defeated by royalists at the Battle of Olmedo (1445), the authority of the king remained threatened. The situation remained depressing during the reign of the successor to Juan II, Enríque IV of Castile, 'el Impotente' (1454–74).[26]

Two main factors kept the Spanish Muslims from taking advantage of the weak state of Castile during the early part of the fifteenth century: the aggressive strength of Portugal as a maritime power and the even worse intra-dynastic problems in Granada. The Portuguese captured the North African port of Ceuta in 1415, occupied Madeira (1420), and the Azores (1431–45). Recovering from a brief civil war, Portugal went on to capture a number of ports along the Moroccan Atlantic coast in 1458–91. The confusion of Castile's leadership was mild when compared with that in Nasrid Granada. From 1391 to 1492, twelve sultans occupied the throne of Granada in twenty separate reigns.[27] The disunity of the Granadan kingdom made it especially vulnerable in the incessant warfare taking place on the frontier in northern Andalus. Although truces existed between the rulers of Granada and Castile, the regional nobles felt free to undertake sporadic raids as opportunities presented themselves. One of several, but certainly one of the most important of these adventurous expeditions, was the Duke of Medina Sidonia's capture of Gibraltar in 1462.

In contrast to the turmoil that festered in the Nasrid dynasty of Granada during the late fifteenth century, the monarchy of Castile made a remarkable recovery.

II CHRISTIAN SPAIN AT THE END OF THE FIFTEENTH CENTURY

Castile's emergence from its power hiatus of the first part of the fifteenth century is almost a fairytale. The central event was the union of Castile and Aragón through the marriage, in 1469, of Ferdinand, son of Juan II (1458–79) of Aragón, and Isabella, daughter of Juan II (1406–54) of Castile, and half-sister of Enríque IV (1454–74) of Castile.[28] However, this was not the product of a fully mutual arrangement by both ruling houses. The marriage came about largely due to the diplomatic initiatives of Juan II of Aragón and the choice of the strong-willed Isabella, who wished to avoid less desirable matches being planned for her by Enríque IV and his advisors. Complicating the issue was the young daughter, Juana ['*La Beltraneja*'], born to Enríque IV and his second queen, Juana of Avís, who was sister to the King of Portugal, Affonso V (1438–81). Isabella married Ferdinand without the consent of Enríque IV, who thereupon affirmed that Juana would inherit the crown.[29]

Upon Enríque IV's death, Isabella immediately had herself declared queen of Castile. Part of Isabella's claim was the assertion that Enríque was impotent and could not be the father of Juana.[30] Isabella's proclamation was supported by most of the leading nobles and cities in Castile. She was challenged by a faction of nobles who sought help from Juana's uncle, Affonso V, King of Portugal. Affonso invaded Castile in 1475 to assist the Castilian factions supporting Juana. Civil war ensued, consisting of isolated actions. The major action involved Isabella's husband taking the field with an army to confront Affonso V's forces at Toro (June–July 1475). Initially, Affonso avoided battle and was deserted by some of his Castilian allies. The Portuguese king received reinforcements and fought Ferdinand in the Battle of Toro (1 March 1476). Although not a clearly won victory, the outcome persuaded the rebellious cites and nobles to submit to Isabella's rule.

The new sovereigns of Castile had survived a precarious start. The challenge from Portugal was not as threatening as the possible ambitions of the more powerful kingdom of France under Louis XI. Already France held Cerdaña and Rosellon [Roussillon], which were claimed by Castile–Aragón. Various city-fortresses in Andalusia and Galicia, taking advantage of the contested Castilian succession, sought independence from their previous vassal status and had to be subdued with sieges and military threats. Isabella and Ferdinand demonstrated

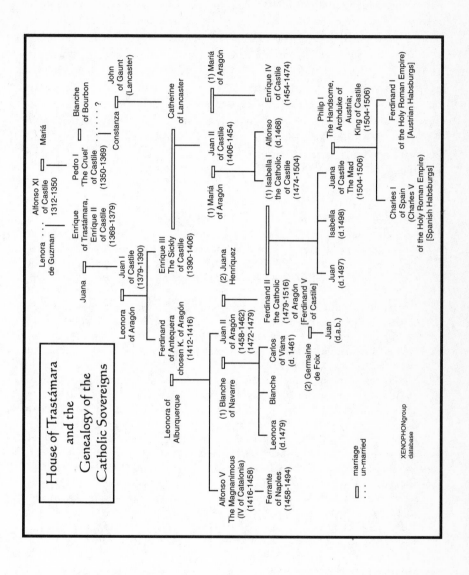

House of Trastámara
and the
Genealogy of the
Catholic Sovereigns

XENOPHONgroup
database

marriage ▯
un-married · · ·

diplomatic and administrative skill and wise command of military force in dealing with all these factors.

As far as the *Reconquista* was concerned, the war of succession for the Castilian throne produced a more unified and a more militarily competent Christian Spain. On the eve of the War of Granada, the most powerful Spanish Christian domain was poised to undertake the task so close to the heart of the highly devout, intelligent, and strong-willed queen, who had fortunately married a very capable military leader. Castile–Aragón, in their many earlier coalition pacts, had made the major advances of the *Reconquista*. Now the young sovereigns of these two kingdoms were to proceed against a Spanish Muslim kingdom with considerable capability, even though it critically lacked stable leadership. In this undertaking Ferdinand and Isabella were to win their claim and famous joint title in history as *Los Reyes Católicos* ('The Catholic Sovereigns').[31]

NOTES

1. The strait was known as the 'Pillars of Hercules' to the ancients, due to the two large rock formations on either side. On the coast of North Africa there was 'Abyla' (modern Ceuta), and on the southern coast of the Iberian Peninsula there was 'Calpe', now known as Gibraltar. The name Gibraltar is derived from the Arabic words *Gebel Tariq* (rock of Tariq) to commemorate Tariq ibn Ziyad's landing there.

2. The battle is sometimes erroneously identified as having been fought by the Guadalete River near Jerez de la Frontera, rather than by the Barbate River, in Wadi Bekka near Medina Sidonia. King Rodrigo [Roderic] apparently died while fleeing from the battle. He was never heard from again (Joseph O'Callaghan, *A History of Medieval Spain*, p.92).

3. The expression 'Moors' was derived from the Latin *'mauri'*, for the people who lived in the ancient Roman province of Mauritania in North Africa. In general, written histories use the term 'Moors' to include all peoples of the Islamic faith in southern Europe. Although often led by families of Persian or Arab descent from Syria and Arabia, the vast majority of Moors were people native to North Africa. They referred to themselves by their tribal names. One of the more appropriate European appellations for them is 'Berbers'. The expressions 'Berber' or 'Barbary' originate from Greek and Latin terms (*barbaroi, barbari*) for foreign people who speak an 'uncivilized' (unknown to the Greeks and Romans) language. Arabic terms (*barabir*, sing *barbari*) apparently derive from the Roman expressions. The Arabs also referred to them as *'Maghribis'* (westerners, or men of the west).

4. This resistance is sometimes described as a single battle, led by Pelayo (718–37) and fought at Covadonga (approximately 722). D.W. Lomax's *The Reconquest of Spain* is a comprehensive study of the subject and admits that dates and the leader are uncertain. Lomax allows between 716 to 719 for the uprising and 721–26 for the decisive engagement. See also O'Callaghan, *History of Medieval Spain*, p.99.

5. Ferdinand Lot is one of several authorities who identify this famous victory of Charles Martel, 'The Hammer', as being near Poitiers and not Tours (Lot, *L'Art*

Militaire et les Armées au Moyen Age en Europe et dans le Proche Orient, volume 2, p.252).

The Franks fought on foot, in a solid phalanax, and repulsed a series of Muslim cavalry attacks until nightfall. The Moorish leader, Abd al-Rahman, was killed during the battle, and the Muslim forces withdrew during the night. The name 'Abd al-Rahman' is a common name among Muslims. The governor by that name, who was at the Battle of Tours, should not be confused with the renowned amirs and caliphs who ruled later in Córdoba. See Charles Oman, *A History of the Art of War in the Middle Ages*, vol.I, p.58.

6. There were many Frankish incursions. Oddly the most famous incident, the defeat of a small Frankish force at Roncesvalles (778), near Pamplona in the Pyrenees, was not typical. The rearguard's destruction was a minor engagement, in the course of Charlemagne's expedition withdrawing north after an otherwise successful campaign. Charlemagne's son Louis I ('The Pious'), who governed the southern Franks from his centre of power at Toulouse, took Barcelona in 801. The northeast region of Spain became the French frontier outpost (a *marche*) for the next three centuries.

7. The Spanish Christians were further aided in their fledgling reconquest by years of bad harvests and resultant famine experienced by Berber settlers. The Berber settlers' abandonment of the plains around the Duero River (741–50) depleted the northern *thughur* (frontier zone) of resident warriors. See Lomax, *Reconquest of Spain*, p.26.

8. The outline for the summary of the Reconquest sketched here borrows heavily from the outline in Lomax's *Reconquest of Spain*. He identifies the main phases as:

Struggle for the Duero (842–1008): The Leonese empire forms and Castile emerges.

Advance to the Tajo [Tagus] (1008–85): Collapse of Cordoban Caliphate, leaving weak *taifa* kingdoms.

War against the Almoravids (1086–94): The Almoravids from North Africa arrive.

War against the Almohads (1147–1212): Another North African Berber sect follows and overthrows the Almoravids.

War against the surviving Nasrid kingdom of Granada (1481–92).

9. Lomax, *Reconquest of Spain*, p.38.

10. The way in which this special environment contributed to the performance of the Spanish infantry in the late fifteenth century is addressed in the Editor's Introduction, Part I.

11. Lot, *L'Art Militaire et les Armées au Moyen Age*, vol.2, pp.254–5.

12. Not many works exist in English describing the military operations of al-Mansur (976–1002). His name was Muhammad ibn Abi Amir, but following his brilliant victory over a coalition Christian host at the Battle of Rueda and devastating expedition into León, he took the name of al-Mansur. Arabic works translated by the famous Dutch orientalist, Dozy, provide probably the best primary source. See Reinhart Dozy, *Spanish Islam, A History of the Moslems in Spain*, translated by Francis G. Stokes, pp.457–533. A fine analysis of al-Mansur's military exploits is in E. Lévi-Provençal's *Histoire de l'espagne musulmane*, vol.2, pp.222–72.

13. It should not be difficult to appreciate the reluctance of the educated and elite Spanish Muslims to perceive the northern, former barbarian, 'Goth' communities

as just what they had been only a few generations before. The Spanish Muslims reasoned that the military prowess shown by the Christians was mere chance, and would not be sustained against a superior culture supported by 'the true faith'.

14. Benedictine monks from the great Cluny abbey in France were particularly influential and came as part of a broad French involvement. Nobles of Catalonia and Navarra had links, through marriage, with their northern neighbours of Aquitaine and Burgundy. The French undertook military expeditions into the Spanish Muslim territories, such as the Norman and Burgundian Siege of Barbastro (1064). (O'Callaghan, *History of Medieval Spain*, pp.310–11; Lomax, *Reconquest of Spain*, pp.39–41, 55–6.)

15. In compensation for such tribute, Ferdinand I protected his Muslim clients against other Christian attacks. For example, Ferdinand sent El Cid to assist the vassal of Zaragoza, when Ramiro I (1035–63) of Aragón tried to seize the Muslim town of Graus (1063). Ramiro was killed in the attempt.

16. 'Coimbra was the first example of capitulation terms which became standard.' If a Muslim town surrendered immediately, the residents' lives, religious practice, and property would be spared. If they surrendered during a siege, the residents could depart with all they could carry. Should the town have to be stormed, the population would be killed or enslaved. (Lomax, *Reconquest of Spain*, pp.53–5.)

17. With the aid of English crusaders, the Portuguese captured Lisbon (1147). The success of Portugal's Affonso (I) Henriques in repelling the Almohads effectively established Portugal's independence, which had been recognized by Castile in the Treaty of Zamora (1143). Affonso was captured at Battle of Badajoz (1169).

18. Oddly, the Sultan of Sevilla had earlier assisted Ferdinand III in the capture of Muslim Córdoba.

19. Luis Seco de Lucena Paredes, *The Book of the Alhambra*, p.23.

20. L.P. Harvey, *Islamic Spain 1250 to 1500*, pp.156–7.

21. The disastrous failure of the siege of Almería (1309) induced Aragón to seek expansion further into the Mediterranean, and effectively left the *Reconquista* to be run by Castile. (J.N. Hillgarth, *The Spanish Kingdoms*, vol.1, p.17.)

22. Muhammad II of Granada, who feared the Banu Marin of Morocco more than the Christians, aided Castile in the seizure of Tarifa (1292). (Hillgarth, *Spanish Kingdoms*, vol.1, p.20.)

23. Muslims demolished a Castilian fleet near the Strait, off Algeciras (1 April 1340). This was part of many land and naval operations in that region during 1340. Seco de Lucena Paredes mentions that some time after 14 Aug 1340, the Africans and the Granadans surrounded Tarifa, then under the power of Castile, and used artillery (called *anfat*) in the siege. (Seco de Lucena Paredes, *Book of the Alhambra*, p.38.)

24. The Battle of Nájera (1367) was fought between two coalition forces supporting the contenders for the Castilian throne, Pedro I, 'the Cruel', and Enríque of Trastámara, Pedro's half-brother. Pedro's allies consisted of the English Black Prince, Edward, and some Muslim vassals. Enríque was supported by the French Constable, Bertrand Du Guesclin. Although the force supporting Pedro decisively won the battle, the English prince later withdrew his vital support of the Castilian king. Enríque of Trastámara finally triumphed, at the Battle of Montiel (1369). French men-at-arms remained with Enríque II of Castile [formerly 'of Trastá-

mara'] (1368–79) and were present to assist his successor, Juan I (1379–90) of Castile in defeating the English Duke of Lancaster's invasion in 1386–87. In turn, Castilian naval forces aided the French in their Hundred Years' War struggle. Castilian ships defeated English naval forces at La Rochelle (1372) and raided English towns along the Channel.

The Battle of Aljubarrota (1385) was fought when Juan I of Spain claimed the crown of Portugal. England allied with the Portuguese claimant, Juan of Avís [a Burgundian who became João I of Portugal (1385–1433)]. French forces joined with Juan I of Castile. The decisive English–Portuguese victory in this battle assured Portugal's independence.

25. The Battle of Higueruela [Andaraxemel] (1 Jul 1431) is ignored in many of the military summaries of this period – Oman's work being an exception. Military historians who address the developments of the era in detail find the battle interesting even though no great conquest resulted. The battle is 'documented' in unique detail in a 1587 fresco in the Battle Gallery of the famous Escorial, near Madrid.

26. The situation is covered in the aptly titled 'The Confusions of Castile, 1416–1474', in Hillgarth's *Spanish Kingdoms*, vol.2, pp.300–47.

27. 'The last years of Muhammad VII's reign coincided with the early fifteenth century of the Christian era. A century-long civil war began with the overthrow of Muhammad VIII. Twelve sultans were to occupy the [Nasrid] throne in less than 100 years; this amounted to the proclamation of twenty different [reigns] in the following order of Succession:'

Muhammad VII	
Yusuf III	
Muhammad VIII 'the Little'	1st time
Muhammad IX 'the Left-handed'	1st time
Muhammad VIII 'the Little'	2nd and last time
Muhammad IX 'the Left-handed'	2nd time
Yusuf IV *'ben al-Mawl'*	
Muhammad IX 'the Left-handed'	3rd time
Muhammad X 'the Lame'	1st time
Yusuf V (Aben Ismail)	1st time
Muhammad IX 'the Left-handed'	4th and last time; reign shared by
Muhammad XI 'the Tiny'	
Sa'd (or 'Ciriza')	1st time
Yusuf V (Aben Ismail)	2nd and last time
Sa'd (or 'Ciriza')	2nd and last time
Abul Hacén Ali	1st time
Muhammad XII (Boabdil)	1st time
Abul Hacén Ali	2nd and last time
Muhammad XIII 'the Lad' (al-Zagal)	
Muhammad XII (Boabdil)	2nd and last time; last Granadan monarch

Seco de Lucena Paredes, *Book of the Alhambra*, p.58.

28. The marriage of Ferdinand and Isabella did not, in itself, ensure a political union of Aragón and Castile. Upon Isabella's death in 1504, her will gave the crown of Castile to the couple's eldest surviving child, Juana. Ferdinand remained King of Aragón, but was relegated to be Regent of Castile until Juana and her husband, Philip of Austria, came from The Netherlands to assume the throne of Castile. In March 1506, the situation became uncertain when Ferdinand married the niece of the King of France, Germaine de Foix. This act suggested that Ferdinand was seeking to have an heir to Aragón who would be independent from Castile. Juana and Philip arrived and assumed their sovereign positions in Castile in May 1506, but Philip died in September of the same year. Mental illness prevented Juana from assuming her sovereign duties. Cardinal Cisneros became Regent until 1507, when Ferdinand took over as an administrative governor and became effectively the sole ruler of Castile until his death in 1516. Ferdinand and Germaine de Foix's only son died as an infant in 1509. After Ferdinand's death, Cisneros assumed the Regency again until Charles of Ghent, son of Juana and Philip (grandson of Ferdinand and Isabella) was old enough to assume the crown as Carlos I of Spain (1516–56), a truly united Castile and Aragón. When his other grandfather, Emperor Maximilian I died, Carlos I of Spain also became Charles V (1519–58) of the Holy Roman Empire. See: Henry Kamen, *Spain 1469–1714; a Society in Conflict*, p.4.

29. Isabella claimed that Enríque IV recognized her as heir in 1468. Enríque did not openly deny this, even though he had earlier proclaimed Juana as heiress in 1462. Enríque appeared to have acquiesced to his strong willed stepsister until she married without his permission. After Isabella's marriage to Ferdinand, Enríque began to treat Juana as his heiress. However, no clear will existed, and both claimants were supported by opposing factions of nobles whom Enríque seemed unable to control. (Hillgarth, *Spanish Kingdoms*, vol.2, p.355; R.G. Merriman, *The Rise of the Spanish Empire*, pp.46–9.)

30. Some historians see the charge of Juana's illegitimacy to be a product of propaganda perpetuated by the court of Isabella. The Spanish chroniclers' frequent references to Enríque IV as 'the impotent' were to reinforce Isabella's claim. (Hillgarth, *Spanish Kingdoms*, vol.2, pp.352–64.)

31. Though not unique, the arrangement of shared power between Ferdinand and Isabella was certainly unusual. The terms were due to Isabella's kingdom of Castile being the more powerful of the two domains. Her personality was also instrumental in the negotiated arrangement. There are many assessments of this cooperative rule in the histories of Spain. In the course of his relating the War of Granada, Prescott gives several evaluations. J.N. Hillgarth presents a view which does not put Isabella as high on a pedestal as Prescott and other writers who have relied on her historian as a dominant source. See Hillgarth, *Spanish Kingdoms*, vol.2, pp.352–4.

On the other hand, one may find the fullest picture in reviewing the War of Granada itself. This great challenge revealed the characters of the two, as individuals and as a royal team. The formal arrangements of their shared power may not have been so important as the complementary aspects of their separate talents and personalities.

CHAPTER 1

THE SPANISH MUSLIMS PREVIOUS TO THE WAR OF GRANADA

Conquest of Spain by the Muslims. – Cordoban Empire. – High Civilization and Prosperity. – Its Dismemberment. – Kingdom of Granada. – Luxurious and Chivalrous Character. – Literature of the Spanish Muslims. – Progress in Science. – Historical Merits. – Useful Discoveries. – Poetry and Romance. – Influence on the Christian Spanish.

We have now arrived at the commencement of the famous war of Granada, which terminated in the subversion of the Islamic empire in Spain, after it had subsisted for nearly eight centuries, and with the consequent restoration to the Castilian crown of the fairest portion of its ancient domain. In order to [reach] a better understanding of the character of the Spanish Muslims, or Moors, who exercised an important influence on that of their Christian neighbours, the present chapter will be devoted to a consideration of their previous history in the Peninsula, where they probably reached a higher degree of civilization than in any other part of the world.[1]

It is not necessary to dwell upon the causes of the brilliant successes of Islam at its outset: the dexterity with which, unlike all other religions, it was raised upon, not against the principles and prejudices of preceding sects; the military spirit and discipline, which it established among all classes, so that the multifarious nations who embraced it, assumed the appearance of one vast, well-ordered camp;[2] the union of ecclesiastical with civil authority intrusted to the caliphs, which enabled them to control opinions, as absolutely as the Roman pontiffs in their most despotic hour;[3] or lastly, the peculiar adaptation of the doctrines of Muhammad to the character of the wild tribes among whom they were preached.[4] It is sufficient to say, that these latter, within a century after the coming of their apostle, having succeeded in establishing their religion over vast regions in Asia, and on the northern shores of Africa, arrived before the Strait of Gibraltar, which, though a temporary, were destined to prove an ineffectual bulwark for Christendom.

The causes which have been currently assigned for the invasion and conquest of Spain, even by the most credible modern historians, have scarcely any foundation in contemporary records. The true causes are to be found in the rich spoils offered by the Gothic monarchy, and in the thirst of enterprise in the Muslims, which their long uninterrupted career of victory seems to have sharpened, rather than satisfied.[5] The fatal battle, which terminated with the slaughter of King Rodrigo [Roderic] and the flower of his nobility, was fought in the summer of 711, on a plain washed by the Guadalete near Jerez, about two leagues distant from Cádiz.[6] The Goths appear never to have afterward rallied under one head, but their broken detachments made many a gallant stand in such strong positions as were afforded throughout the kingdom; so that nearly three years elapsed before the final achievement of the conquest. The policy of the conquerors, after making the requisite allowance for the evils necessarily attending such an invasion,[7] may be considered liberal. Such of the Christians, as chose, were permitted to remain in the conquered territory in undisturbed possession of their property. They were allowed to worship in their own way; to be governed, within prescribed limits, by their own laws; to fill certain civil offices, and serve in the army; their women were invited to intermarry with the conquerors;[8] and, in short, they were condemned to no other legal badge of servitude than the payment of somewhat heavier imposts than those exacted from their Muslim brethren. It is true the Christians were occasionally exposed to suffering from the caprices of despotism, and, it may be added, of popular fanaticism.[9] But, on the whole, their condition may sustain an advantageous comparison with that of any Christian people under the Muslim dominion of later times, and affords a striking contrast with that of our Saxon ancestors after the Norman conquest, which suggests an obvious parallel in many of its circumstances to the Saracen.[10]

After the further progress of the Muslims in Europe had been checked by the memorable defeat at Tours [or Poitiers (732) – ED], their energies, no longer allowed to expand in the career of conquest, recoiled on themselves, and speedily produced the dismemberment of their overgrown empire. Spain was the first of the provinces, which fell off. The Umayyad family, under whom this revolution was effected, continued to occupy the throne as independent princes, from the middle of the eighth to the close of the eleventh century, a period which forms the most honourable portion of the Islamic annals.

The new government was modelled on the eastern caliphate. Freedom shows itself under a variety of forms; while despotism, at least in the institutions founded on the Koran, seems to wear but one. The sovereign was the depositary of all power, the fountain of honour, the sole arbiter of life and fortune. He styled himself 'Commander of the Faithful', and, like the caliphs of the east, assumed an entire spiritual as well as temporal supremacy. The country was distributed into six *capitnías* or provinces, each under the administration of a

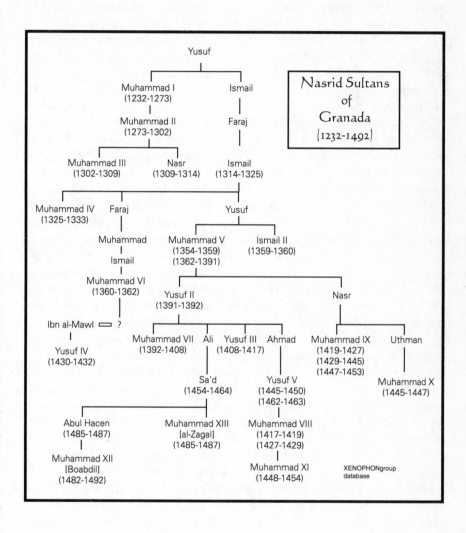

Yusuf

Muhammad I
(1232-1273)

Ismail

Nasrid Sultans of Granada (1232-1492)

Muhammad II
(1273-1302)

Faraj

Muhammad III
(1302-1309)

Nasr
(1309-1314)

Ismail
(1314-1325)

Muhammad IV
(1325-1333)

Faraj

Yusuf

Muhammad

Muhammad V
(1354-1359)
(1362-1391)

Ismail II
(1359-1360)

Ismail

Muhammad VI
(1360-1362)

Yusuf II
(1391-1392)

Nasr

Ibn al-Mawl ▭ ?

Yusuf IV
(1430-1432)

Muhammad VII
(1392-1408)

Ali

Yusuf III
(1408-1417)

Ahmad

Muhammad IX
(1419-1427)
(1429-1445)
(1447-1453)

Uthman

Muhammad X
(1445-1447)

Sa'd
(1454-1464)

Yusuf V
(1445-1450)
(1462-1463)

Abul Hacen
(1485-1487)

Muhammad XIII
[al-Zagal]
(1485-1487)

Muhammad VIII
(1417-1419)
(1427-1429)

Muhammad XII
[Boabdil]
(1482-1492)

Muhammad XI
(1448-1454)

XENOPHONgroup
database

wali, or governor, with subordinate officers, to whom was intrusted a more immediate jurisdiction over the principal cities. The immense authority and pretensions of these petty satraps became a fruitful source of rebellion in later times. The caliph administered the government with the advice of his *mexuar*, or council of state, composed of his principal *cadis* and *hajibs*, or secretaries. The office of prime minister, or chief hajib, corresponded, in the nature and variety of its functions, with that of a Turkish grand vizier. The caliph reserved to himself the right of selecting his successor from among his numerous progeny; and this adoption was immediately ratified by an oath of allegiance to the heir apparent from the principal officers of state.[11]

The princes of the blood, instead of being condemned, as in Turkey, to waste their youth in the seclusion of the harem, were intrusted to the care of learned men, to be instructed in the duties befitting their station. They were encouraged to visit the academies, which were particularly celebrated in Córdoba, where they mingled in disputation, and frequently carried away the prizes of poetry and eloquence. Their riper years exhibited such fruits as were to be expected from their early education. The Umayyads need not shrink from a comparison with any other dynasty of equal length in modern Europe. Many of them amused their leisure with poetical composition, of which numerous examples are preserved in Condé's History, and some left elaborate works of learning, which have maintained a permanent reputation with Arabian scholars. Their long reigns, the first ten of which embrace a period of two centuries and a half, their peaceful deaths, and unbroken line of succession in the same family for so many years, show that their authority must have been founded in the affections of their subjects. Indeed, they seem, with one or two exceptions, to have ruled over them with a truly patriarchal sway; and, on the event of their deaths the people, bathed in tears, are described as accompanying their relics to the tomb, where the ceremony was concluded with a public eulogy on the virtues of the deceased, by his son and successor. This pleasing moral picture affords a strong contrast to the sanguinary scenes which so often attend the transmission of the sceptre from one generation to another, among the nations of the east.[12]

The Spanish caliphs supported a large military force, frequently keeping two or three large armies in the field at the same time. The flower of these forces was a body guard, gradually raised to twelve thousand men, one third of them Christians, superbly equipped, and officered by members of the royal family. Their feuds with the eastern caliphs and the Barbary pirates required them also to maintain a respectable navy, which was fitted out from the numerous dockyards, that lined the coast from Cádiz to Tarragona.

The munificence of the Umayyads was most ostentatiously displayed in their public edifices, palaces, mosques, hospitals, and in the construction of commodious quays, fountains, bridges, and aqueducts, which, penetrating the sides of the mountains, or sweeping on lofty arches across the valleys, rivalled in their proportions the monuments of ancient Rome. These works, which were scattered more or less over all the provinces, contributed especially to the embellishment of Córdoba, the capital of the empire. The delightful situation of this city in the midst of a cultivated plain washed by the waters of the Guadalquivir, made it very early the favourite residence of the Spanish Muslims, who loved to surround their houses, even in the cities, with groves and refreshing fountains, so delightful to the imagination of a wanderer of the desert.[13] The public squares and private court-yards sparkled with *jets d'eau*, fed by copious streams from the Sierra Morena, which, besides supplying nine hundred public baths, were conducted into the interior of the edifices, where they diffused a grateful coolness over the sleeping-apartments of their luxurious inhabitants.[14]

Without adverting to that magnificent freak of the caliphs, the construction of the palace of Azahra, of which not a vestige now remains, we may form a sufficient notion of the taste and magnificence of this era from the remains of the far-famed mosque, now the cathedral of Córdoba. This building, which still covers more ground than any other church in Christendom, was esteemed the third in sanctity by the Muslim world, being inferior only to the Alaksa of Jerusalem and the temple of Mecca. Most of its ancient glories have indeed long since departed. The rich bronze which embossed its gates, the myriads of lamps which illuminated its aisles, have disappeared; and its interior roof of odoriferous and curiously carved wood has been cut up into guitars and snuff-boxes. But its thousand columns of variegated marble still remain; and its general dimensions, notwithstanding some loose assertions to the contrary, seem to be much the same as they were in the time of the Muslims. European critics, however, condemn its most elaborate beauties as 'heavy and barbarous'. Its celebrated portals are pronounced 'diminutive, and in very bad taste'. Its throng of pillars gives it the air of 'a park rather than a temple', and the whole is made still more incongruous by the unequal length of their shafts, being grotesquely compensated by a proportionate variation of size in their bases and capitals, rudely fashioned after the Corinthian order.[15]

But if all this gives us a contemptible idea of the taste of the Muslims at this period, which indeed, in architecture seems to have been far inferior to that of the later princes of Granada, we cannot but be astonished at the adequacy of their resources to carry such magnificent designs into execution. Their revenue, we are told in explanation, amounted to eight millions of *mitcales* of gold or nearly six millions sterling; a sum fifteen-fold greater than that which William the Conqueror, in the subsequent century, was able to extort from his subjects, with all the ingenuity of feudal exaction. The tone of exaggeration, which distinguishes the Asiatic writers, entitles them perhaps to little confidence in their numerical estimates. This immense wealth, however, is predicated of other Muslim princes of that age; and their vast superiority over the Christian states of the north, in arts and effective industry, may well account for a corresponding superiority in their resources.

The revenue of the Cordoban sovereigns was derived from the fifth of the spoil taken in battle, an important item in an age of unintermitting war and rapine; from the enormous exaction of one tenth of the produce of commerce, husbandry flocks, and mines; from a capitation tax on Jews and Christians; and from certain tolls on the transportation of goods. They engaged in commerce on their own account, and drew from mines, which belonged to the crown, a conspicuous part of their income.[16]

Before the discovery of America, Spain was to the rest of Europe, what her colonies have since become, the great source of mineral wealth. The Carthaginians, and the Romans afterward, regularly drew from her large masses of the precious metals. Pliny, who resided some time in the country, relates that three of her provinces were said to have annually yielded the incredible quantity of sixty thousand pounds of gold.[17] The Muslims with their usual activity penetrated into these arcana of wealth. Abundant traces of their labours are still to be met with along the barren ridge of mountains that covers the north of Andalusia; and the diligent Bowles has enumerated no less than five thousand of their excavations in the kingdom or district of Jaén.[18]

But the best mine of the caliphs was in the industry and sobriety of their subjects. The Muslim colonies have been properly classed among the agricultural. Their acquaintance with the science of husbandry is shown in their voluminous treatises on the subject, and in the monuments which they have everywhere left of their peculiar culture. The system of irrigation, which has so long fertilized the south of Spain, was derived from them. They introduced into the Peninsula various tropical plants and vegetables, whose cultivation has departed with them. Sugar, which the modern Spaniards have been obliged to import from foreign nations in large quantities annually for their domestic consumption, until within the last half [of the nineteenth] century when they have been supplied by their island of Cuba, constituted one of the principal exports of the Spanish Muslim. The silk manufacture was carried on by them extensively. The Nubian geographer [see author's comments at end of chapter], in the beginning of the twelfth century, enumerates six hundred villages in Jaén as engaged in it, at a time when it was known to the Europeans only from their circuitous traffic with the Greek empire. This together with fine fabrics of cotton and wool, formed the staple of an active commerce with the Levant, and especially with Constantinople, whence they were again diffused, by means of the caravans of the north, over the comparatively barbarous countries of Christendom.

The population kept pace with this general prosperity of the country. It would appear from a census instituted at Córdoba, at the close of the tenth century, that there were at that time in it six hundred temples and two hundred thousand dwelling-houses; many of these latter being, probably, mere huts or cabins, and occupied by separate families. Without placing too much reliance on any numerical statements, however, we may give due weight to the inference of an intelligent writer, who remarks that their minute cultivation of the soil, the cheapness of their labour, their particular attention to the most nutritious esculents, many of them such as would be rejected by Europeans at this day, are indicative of a crowded population, like that, perhaps, which swarms over Japan or China, where the same economy is necessarily resorted to for the mere sustenance of life.[19]

Whatever consequence a nation may derive, in its own age, from physical resources, its intellectual development will form the subject of deepest interest to posterity. The most flourishing periods of both not infrequently coincide. Thus the reigns of Abd al-Rahman III (913–61), al-Hakam II (961–76), and the regency of al-Mansur (976–1002), embracing the latter half of the tenth century, during which the Spanish Muslims reached their highest political importance, may be regarded as the period of their highest civilization under the Umayyads; although the impulse then given carried them forward to still further advances, in the turbulent times which followed. This beneficent impulse is, above all, imputable to al-Hakam. He was one of those rare beings, who have employed the awful engine of despotism in promoting the happiness and intelligence of his species. In his elegant tastes, appetite for knowledge, and munificent patronage, he may be compared with the best of the Medici. He assembled the eminent scholars of his time, both natives and foreigners, at his court where he employed them in the most confidential offices. He converted his palace into an academy, making it the familiar resort of men of letters, at whose conferences he personally assisted in his intervals of leisure from public duty. He selected the most suitable persons for the composition of works on civil and natural history, requiring the prefects of his provinces and cities to furnish, as far as possible, the necessary intelligence. He was a diligent student, and left many of the volumes which he read, enriched with his commentaries. Above all, he was intent upon the acquisition of an extensive library. He invited illustrious foreigners to send him their works, and munificently recompensed them. No donative was so grateful to him as a book. He employed agents in Egypt, Syria, Iraq, and Persia, for collecting and transcribing the rarest manuscripts; and his vessels returned freighted with cargoes more precious than the spices of the east. In this way he amassed a magnificent collection, which was distributed, according to the subjects, in various apartments of his palace; and which, if we may credit the Muslim historians, amounted to six hundred thousand volumes.[20]

If all this be thought to savour too much of eastern hyperbole, still it cannot be doubted that an amazing number of writers swarmed over the Peninsula at this period. Casiri's multifarious catalogue bears ample testimony to the emulation, with which not only men, but even women of the highest rank devoted themselves to letters; the latter contending publicly for the prizes, not merely in eloquence and poetry, but in those recondite studies which have usually been reserved for the other sex. The prefects of the provinces, emulating their master, converted their courts into academies, and dispensed premiums to poets and philosophers. The stream of royal bounty awakened life in the remotest districts. But its effects were especially visible in the capital. Eighty free schools were opened in Córdoba. The circle of letters and science was publicly expounded by professors, whose reputation for wisdom attracted not only the scholars of Christian Spain, but of France, Italy, Germany, and the British Isles. For this period of brilliant illumination with the Muslims corresponds precisely with that of the deepest barbarism of Europe; when a library of three or four hundred volumes was a magnificent endowment for the richest monastery; when scarcely 'a priest south of the Thames', in the words of Alfred, 'could translate Latin into his mother tongue', when not a single philosopher, according to Tiraboschi, was to be met with in Italy, save only the French Pope Sylvester II, who drew his knowledge from the schools of the Spanish Muslims, and was esteemed a necromancer for his pains.[21]

Such is the glowing picture presented to us of Arabian scholarship, in the tenth and succeeding centuries, under a despotic government and a sensual religion; and, whatever judgment may be passed on the real value of their boasted literature, it cannot be denied that the nation exhibited a wonderful activity of intellect, and an apparatus for learning (if we are to admit their own statements) unrivalled in the best ages of antiquity.

The Muslim governments of that period rested on so unsound a basis, that the season of their greatest prosperity was often followed by precipitate decay. This had been the case with the eastern caliphate, and was now so with the western. During the life of al-Hakam II's successor, the empire of the Umayyads was broken up into a hundred petty principalities; and their magnificent capital of Córdoba, dwindling into a second-rate city, retained no other distinction than that of being the Mecca of Spain. These little states soon became a prey to all the evils arising out of a vicious constitution of government and religion. Almost every accession to the throne was contested by numerous competitors of the same family; and a succession of sovereigns, wearing on their brows but the semblance of a crown, came and departed, like the shadows of Macbeth. The motley tribes of Asiatics, of whom the Spanish Muslim population was composed, regarded each other with ill-disguised jealousy. The lawless, predatory habits, which no discipline could effectually control in an Arab, made them ever ready for revolt. The Muslim states, thus reduced in size and crippled by faction were unable to resist the Christian forces, which were pressing on them from the north. By the middle of the ninth century, the Christian Spanish had reached the Douro and the Ebro. By the close of the eleventh, they had advanced their line of conquest, under the victorious banner of the Cid, to the Tajo. The swarms of Africans who invaded the Peninsula, during the two following centuries, gave substantial support to their Muslim brethren; and the cause of Christian Spain trembled in the balance for a moment on the memorable day of Navas de Tolosa [1212]. But the fortunate issue of that battle, in which, according to the lying letter of Alfonso IX [1188–1230], 'one hundred and eighty-five thousand infidels perished, and only five and twenty Spaniards', gave a permanent ascendancy to the Christian arms. The vigorous campaigns of Jaime I ['the Conqueror' (1213–76)], of Aragón, and of Ferdinand III ['the Saint' (c.1200–52)], of Castile, gradually stripped away the remaining territories of Valencia, Murcia, and Andalusia; so that, by the middle of the thirteenth century, the constantly contracting circle of the Moorish dominion had shrunk into the narrow limits of the province of Granada. Yet on this comparatively small point of their ancient domain, the Muslims erected a new kingdom of sufficient strength to resist, for more than two centuries, the united forces of the Spanish monarchies.

The Muslim territory of Granada contained, within a circuit of about one hundred and eighty leagues, all the physical resources of a great empire. Its broad valleys were intersected by mountains rich in mineral wealth, whose hardy population supplied the state with husbandmen and soldiers. Its pastures were fed by abundant fountains, and its coasts studded with commodious ports, the principal marts in the Mediterranean. In the midst, and crowning the whole, as with a diadem, rose the beautiful city of Granada. In the days of the Spanish Muslims it was encompassed by a wall, flanked by a thousand and thirty towers, with seven portals.[22] Its population, according to a contemporary, at the beginning of the fourteenth century, amounted to two hundred thousand souls;[23] and various authors agree in attesting, that, at a later period, it could send forth fifty thousand warriors from its gates. This statement will not appear exaggerated, if we consider that the native population of the city was greatly swelled by the influx of the ancient inhabitants of the districts lately conquered by the Christian Spanish.

On the summit of one of the hills of the city was erected the royal fortress or palace of the Alhambra, which was capable of containing within its circuit forty thousand men.[24] The light and elegant architecture of this edifice, whose magnificent ruins still form the most interesting monument in Spain for the contemplation of the traveller, shows the great advancement of the art since the construction of the celebrated mosque of Córdoba. Its graceful porticoes and colonnades, its domes and ceilings, glowing with tints, which, in that transparent atmosphere, have lost nothing of their original brilliancy, its airy halls, so constructed as to admit the perfume of surrounding gardens and agreeable ventilation of the air, and its fountains, which still shed their coolness over its deserted courts, manifest at once the taste, opulence, and Sybarite luxury of its proprietors. The streets are represented to have been narrow, many of the houses lofty, with turrets of curiously wrought larch or marble, and with cornices of shining metal, 'that glittered like stars through the dark foliage of the orange groves'; and the whole is compared to 'an enamelled vase, sparkling with hyacinths and emeralds'.[25] Such are the florid strains in which the Arabic writers fondly descant on the glories of Granada.

At the foot of this fabric of the genii [specially endowed region] lay the cultivated *vega*, or plain, so celebrated as the arena, for more than two centuries, of Muslim and Christian chivalry, every inch of whose soil may be said to have been fertilized with human blood. The Spanish Muslims exhausted on it all their powers of elaborate cultivation. They distributed the waters of the Genil [Xenil], which flowed through it, into a thousand channels for its more perfect irrigation. A constant succession of fruits and crops was obtained throughout the year. The products of the most opposite latitudes were transplanted there with success; and the hemp of the north grew luxuriant under the shadow of the vine and the olive. Silk furnished the principal staple of a traffic that was carried on through the ports of Almería and Málaga. The Italian cities, then rising into opulence, derived their principal skill in this elegant manufacture from the Spanish Muslims. Florence, in particular, imported large quantities of the raw material from them as late as the fifteenth century. The Genoese are mentioned as having mercantile establishments in Granada; and treaties of commerce were entered into with this nation, as well as with the crown of Aragón. Their ports swarmed with a motley contribution from 'Europe, Africa, and the Levant', so that 'Granada', in the words of the historian, 'became the common city of all nations'. 'The reputation of its citizens for trust-worthiness', says a Spanish writer, 'was such, that their bare word was more relied on, than a contract is now among us'; and he quotes the saying of a Catholic bishop, that 'Moorish works and Spanish faith were all that were necessary to make a good Christian'.[26]

The revenue, which was computed at twelve hundred thousand ducats, was derived from similar, but, in some respects, heavier impositions than those of the caliphs of Córdoba. The crown, besides being possessed of valuable plantations in the vega, imposed the onerous tax of one seventh on all the agricultural produce of the kingdom. The precious metals were also obtained in considerable quantities, and the royal mint was noted for the purity and elegance of its coin.[27]

The sovereigns of Granada were for the most part distinguished by liberal tastes. They freely dispensed revenues in the protection of letters, the construction of sumptuous public works, and, above all, in the display of courtly pomp, unrivalled by any of the princes of that period. Each day presented a succession of *fêtes* and tourneys, in which the knight seemed less ambitious of the hardy prowess of Christian chivalry, than of displaying his inimitable horsemanship, and his dexterity in the elegant pastimes peculiar to his nation.

The people of Granada, like those of ancient Rome, seem to have demanded a perpetual spectacle. Life was with them one long carnival, and the season of revelry was prolonged until the enemy was at the gate.

During the interval, which had elapsed since the decay of the Umayyads, the Christian Spanish had been gradually rising in civilization to the level of their Muslim enemies; and, while their increased consequence secured them from contempt, with which they had formerly been regarded by the Muslims, the latter, in their turn, had not so far sunk in the scale, as to have become the objects of the bigoted aversion, which was, in after days, so heartily visited on them by the Christian Spaniards. At this period, therefore, the two nations viewed each other with more liberality probably, than at any previous or succeeding time. Their respective monarchs conducted their mutual negotiations on a footing of perfect equality. We find several examples of Muslim sovereigns visiting in person the court of Castile. These civilities were reciprocated by the Christian princes. As late as 1463, Enríque IV [1425–74] had a personal interview with the king of Granada, in the dominions of the latter. The two monarchs held their conference under a splendid pavilion erected in the vega, before the gates of the city; and, after an exchange of presents, the Spanish sovereign was escorted to the frontiers by a body of Muslim cavaliers. These acts of courtesy relieve in some measure the ruder features of an almost uninterrupted warfare, that was necessarily kept up between the rival nations.[28]

The Spanish Muslim and Christian knights were also in the habit of exchanging visits at the courts of their respective masters. The latter were wont to repair to Granada to settle their affairs of honour, by personal rencounter, in the presence of its sovereign. The disaffected nobles of Castile, among whom Mariana especially notices the Velas and the Castros, often sought an asylum there, and served under the Muslim banner. With this interchange of social courtesy between the two nations, it could not but happen that each should contract somewhat of the peculiarities natural to the other. The Spaniard acquired something of the gravity and magnificence of demeanour proper to the Muslim; and the latter relaxed his habitual reserve, and above all, the jealousy and gross sensuality which characterize the nations of the east.[29]

Indeed, if we were to rely on the pictures presented to us in the Spanish ballads or *romances*, we should admit as unreserved an intercourse between the sexes to have existed among the Spanish Muslims, as with any other people of Europe. The Moorish lady is represented there as an undistinguished spectator of the public festivals; while her knight, bearing an embroidered mantle or scarf, or some other token of her favour, contends openly in her presence for the prize of valour, mingles with her in the graceful dance of the Zambra, or sighs away his soul in moonlight serenades under her balcony.[30]

Other circumstances, especially the frescoes still extant on the walls of the Alhambra, may be cited as corroborative of the conclusions afforded by the *romances*, implying a latitude in the privileges accorded to the sex, similar to that in Christian countries, and altogether alien from the genius of Islam.[31] The chivalrous character ascribed to the Spanish Muslims appears, moreover, in perfect conformity to this. Thus some of their sovereigns, we are told, after the fatigues of the tournament, were wont to recreate their spirits with 'elegant poetry, and florid discourses of amorous and knightly history'. The ten qualities, enumerated as essential to a true knight, were 'piety, valour, courtesy, prowess, the gifts of poetry and eloquence, and dexterity in the management of the horse, the sword, lance, and bow'.[32] The history of the Spanish Muslims, especially in the latter wars of Granada, furnishes repeated examples, not merely of the heroism, which distinguished the European chivalry of the thirteenth and fourteenth centuries, but occasionally of a polished courtesy, that might have graced a Bayard or a Sidney. This combination of oriental magnificence and knightly prowess shed a ray of glory over the closing days of the Islamic empire in Spain, and served to conceal, though it could not correct, the vices which it possessed in common with all Muslim institutions.

The government of Granada was not administered with the same tranquillity as that of Córdoba. Revolutions were perpetually occurring, which may be traced sometimes to the tyranny of the prince, but more frequently to the factions of the seraglio, the soldiery, or the licentious populace of the capital. The latter, indeed, more volatile than the sands of the deserts from which they originally sprung, were driven by every gust of passion into the most frightful excesses, deposing and even assassinating their monarchs, violating their palaces, and scattering abroad their beautiful collections and libraries; while the kingdom, unlike that of Córdoba, was so contracted in its extent, that every convulsion of the capital was felt to its farthest extremities. Still, however, it held out, almost miraculously, against the Christian arms, and the storms that beat upon it incessantly, for more than two centuries, scarcely wore away any thing from its original limits.

Several circumstances may be pointed out as enabling Granada to maintain this protracted resistance. Its concentrated population furnished such abundant supplies of soldiers, that its sovereigns could bring into the field an army of a hundred thousand men.[33] Many of these were drawn from the regions of the Alpujarras [Alpuxarras], whose rugged inhabitants had not been corrupted by the soft effeminacy of the plains. The ranks were occasionally recruited, moreover, from the warlike tribes of Africa. The Muslims of Granada are praised by their enemies for their skill with the cross-bow, to the use of which they were trained from childhood.[34] But their strength lay chiefly in their cavalry. Their spacious vegas afforded an ample field for the display of their matchless horsemanship; while the face of the country, intersected by mountains and intricate defiles, gave a manifest advantage to the Arabian light-horse over the steel-clad cavalry of the Christians, and was particularly suited to the wild *guerrilla* warfare, in which the Granadans so much excelled. During the long hostilities of the country, almost every city had been converted into a fortress. The number of these fortified places in the territory of Granada was ten times as great as is now to be found throughout the whole Peninsula.[35] Lastly, in addition to these means of defence, may be mentioned their early acquaintance with gunpowder, which, like the Greek fire of Constantinople, contributed perhaps in some degree to prolong their precarious existence beyond its natural term.

But after all, the strength of Granada, like that of Constantinople, lay less in its own resources than in the weakness of its enemies, who, distracted by the feuds of a turbulent aristocracy, especially during the long minorities with which Castile was afflicted, perhaps more than any other nation in Europe, seemed to be more remote from the conquest of Granada at the death of Enríque IV, than at that of St. Ferdinand in the thirteenth century. Before entering on the achievement of this conquest by Ferdinand and Isabella, it may not be amiss to notice the probable influence exerted by the Spanish Muslims on European civilization.

Notwithstanding the high advances made by the Muslims in almost every branch of learning, and the liberal import of certain sayings ascribed to Muhammad, the spirit of his religion was eminently unfavourable to letters. The Koran, whatever be the merit of its literary execution, does not, we believe, contain a single precept in favour of general science.[36] Indeed during the first century after its promulgation, almost as little attention was bestowed upon this by the Muslims, as in their 'days of ignorance', as the period is stigmatized which preceded the advent of their apostle.[37] But, after the nation had reposed from its tumultuous military career, the taste for elegant pleasures, which naturally results from opulence and leisure, began to flow in upon it. It entered upon this new field with all its characteristic enthusiasm, and seemed ambitious of attaining the same preeminence in science, that it had already reached in arms.

It was at the commencement of this period of intellectual fermentation, that the last of the Umayyads, escaping into Spain, established there the kingdom of Córdoba, and imported along with him the fondness for luxury and letters, that had begun to display itself in the capitals of the east. His munificent spirit descended upon his successors; and on the breaking up of the empire, the various capitals, Sevilla, Murcia, Málaga, Granada, and others, which rose upon its ruins, became the centres of so many intellectual systems, that continued to emit a steady lustre through the clouds and darkness of succeeding centuries. The period of this literary civilization, reached far into the fourteenth century, and thus, embracing an interval of six hundred years, may be said to have exceeded in duration that of any other literature ancient or modern.

There were several auspicious circumstances in the condition of the Spanish

Muslims, which distinguished them from their Muslim brethren. The temperate climate of Spain was far more propitious to robustness and elasticity of intellect than the sultry regions of Arabia and Africa. Its long line of coast and convenient havens opened to an enlarged commerce. Its numbers of rival states encouraged a generous emulation, like that which glowed in ancient Greece and modern Italy; and was infinitely more favourable to the development of the mental powers than the far-extended and sluggish empires of Asia. Lastly, a familiar intercourse with the Europeans served to mitigate in the Spanish Muslims some of the more degrading superstitions incident to their religion, and to impart to them nobler ideas of the independence and moral dignity of man, than are to be found in the slaves of eastern despotism.

Under these favourable circumstances, provisions for education were liberally multiplied, colleges, academies, and gymnasiums springing up spontaneously, as it were, not merely in the principal cities, but in the most obscure villages of the country. No less than fifty of these colleges or schools could be discerned scattered over the suburbs and populous plains of Granada. Seventy public libraries are enumerated in Spain by a contemporary, at the beginning of the fourteenth century. Every place of note seems to have furnished materials for a literary history. The copious catalogues of writers, still extant in the Escorial, show how extensively the cultivation of science was pursued, even through its minutest subdivisions; while a biographical notice of blind men, eminent for their scholarship in Spain, proves how far the general avidity for knowledge triumphed over the most discouraging obstacles of nature.[38]

The Spanish Muslims emulated their countrymen of the east in their devotion to natural and mathematical science. They penetrated into the remotest regions of Africa and Asia, transmitting an exact account of their proceedings to the national academies. They contributed to astronomical knowledge by the number and accuracy of their observations, and by the improvement of instruments and the erection of observatories, of which the noble tower of Sevilla is one of the earliest examples. They furnished their full proportion in the department of history, which, according to an Arabic author cited by D'Herbelot, could boast of thirteen hundred writers. The treatises on logic and metaphysics amount to one ninth of the surviving treasures of the Escorial; and, to conclude this summary of naked details, some of their scholars appear to have entered upon as various a field of philosophical inquiry, as would be crowded into a modern encyclopedia.[39]

The results, it must be confessed, do not appear to have corresponded with this magnificent apparatus and unrivalled activity of research. The mind of the Muslims was distinguished by the most opposite characteristics, which sometimes, indeed, served to neutralize each other. An acute and subtle perception was often clouded by mysticism and abstraction. They combined a habit of classification and generalization, with a marvellous fondness for detail; a vivacious fancy with a patience of application, that a German of our day might envy; and, while in fiction they launched boldly into originality, indeed extravagance, they were content in philosophy to tread servilely in the track of their ancient masters. They derived their science from versions of the Greek philosophers; but, as their previous discipline had not prepared them for its reception, they were oppressed rather than stimulated by the weight of the inheritance. They possessed an indefinite power of accumulation, but they rarely ascended to general principles, or struck out new and important truths; at least, this is certain in regard to their metaphysical labours.

Hence Aristotle, who taught them to arrange what they had already acquired, rather than to advance to new discoveries, became the god of their idolatry. They piled commentary on commentary, and, in their blind admiration of his system, may be almost said to have been more of Peripatetics than the Stagirite himself. The Cordoban Averroes was the most eminent of his Muslim commentators, and undoubtedly contributed more than any other individual to establish the authority of Aristotle over the reason of mankind for so many ages. Yet his various illustrations have served, in the opinion of European critics, to darken rather than dissipate the ambiguities of his original, and have even led to the confident assertion that he was wholly unacquainted with the Greek language.[40]

The Muslims gave an entirely new face to pharmacy and chemistry. They introduced a great variety of salutary medicaments into Europe. The Spanish Muslims, in particular, are commended by Sprengel above their brethren for their observations on the practice of medicine.[41] But whatever real knowledge they possessed was corrupted by their inveterate propensity for mystical and occult science. They too often exhausted both health and fortune in fruitless researches after the elixir of life and the philosopher's stone. Their medical prescriptions were regulated by the aspect of the stars. Their physics were debased by magic, their chemistry degenerated into alchemy, their astronomy into astrology.

In the fruitful field of history, their success was even more equivocal. They seem to have been wholly destitute of the philosophical spirit, which gives life to this kind of composition. They were the disciples of fatalism and the subjects of a despotic government. Man appeared to them only in the contrasted aspects of slave and master. What could they know of the finer moral relations, or of the higher energies of the soul, which are developed only under free and beneficent institutions? Even could they have formed conceptions of these, how would they have dared to express them? Hence their histories are too often mere barren chronological details, or fulsome panegyrics on their princes, unenlivened by a single spark of philosophy or criticism.

Although the Spanish Muslims are not entitled to the credit of having wrought any important revolution in intellectual or moral science, they are commended by a severe critic, as exhibiting in their writings 'the germs of many theories, which have been reproduced as discoveries in later ages',[42] and they silently perfected several of those useful arts, which have had a sensible influence on the happiness and improvement of mankind. Algebra, and the higher mathematics, were taught in their schools, and thence diffused over Europe. The manufacture of paper, which, since the invention of printing, has contributed so essentially to the rapid circulation of knowledge, was derived through them. Casiri has discovered several manuscripts on cotton paper in the Escorial as early as 1009, and of linen paper of the date of 1106;[43] the origin of which latter fabric Tiraboschi has ascribed to a Italian of Trevigi, in the middle of the fourteenth century.[44] Lastly, the application of gunpowder to military science, which has wrought an equally important revolution, though of a more doubtful complexion, in the condition of society, was derived through the same channel.[45]

The influence of the Spanish Muslims, however, is discernible not so much in the amount of knowledge, as in the impulse, which they communicated to the long dormant energies of Europe. Their invasion was coeval with the commencement of that night of darkness, which divides the modern from the ancient world. The soil had been impoverished by long, assiduous cultivation. The Muslims came like a torrent, sweeping down and obliterating even the landmarks of former civilization, but bringing with it a fertilizing principle, which, as the waters receded, gave new life and loveliness to the landscape. The writings of the Saracen were translated and diffused throughout Europe. Their schools were visited by disciples, who, roused from their lethargy, caught somewhat of the generous enthusiasm of their masters; and a healthful action was given to the European intellect, which, however ill directed at first, was thus prepared for the more judicious and successful efforts of later times.

It is comparatively easy to determine the value of the scientific labours of a people, for truth is the same in all languages; but the laws of taste differ so widely in different nations, that it requires a nicer discrimination to pronounce fairly upon such works as are regulated by them. Nothing is more common than to see the poetry of the east condemned as timid, over-refined, infected with meretricious ornament and conceits, and, in short, as every way contravening the principles of good taste. Few of the critics, who thus peremptorily condemn, are capable of reading a line of the original. The merit of poetry, however, consists so much in its literary execution, that a person, to pronounce upon it, should be intimately acquainted with the whole import of the idiom in which it is written. The style of poetry, indeed of all ornamental writing, whether prose or verse, in order to produce a proper effect, must be raised or relieved, as it were, upon the prevailing style of social intercourse. Even where this is highly figurative and impassioned, as with the Muslims, whose Arabic language is made up of metaphor, that of the poet must be still more so. Hence the tone of elegant literature varies so widely in different countries, even in those of Europe, which approach the nearest to each other in their principles of taste, that it would be found extremely difficult to effect a close translation of the most admired specimens of eloquence from the language of one nation into that of any other. A page of Boccaccio or Bembo, for instance, done into literal English, would have an air of intolerable artifice and verbiage. The choicest morsels of Massillon, Bossuet, or the rhetorical Thomas, would savour marvellously of bombast; and how could we in any degree keep pace with the magnificent march of the Castilian! Yet surely we are not to impugn the taste of all these nations, who attach much more importance, and have paid (at least this is true of the French and Italian) much greater attention to the mere beauties of literary finish, than English writers.

Whatever may be the sins of the Muslims on this head, they are certainly not those of negligence. The Spanish Muslims, in particular, were noted for the purity and elegance of their idiom; insomuch that Casiri affects to determine the locality of an author by the superior refinement of his style. Their copious philological and rhetorical treatises, their arts of poetry, grammars, and rhyming dictionaries, show to what an excessive refinement they elaborated the art of composition. Academies, far more numerous than those of Italy, to which they subsequently served for a model, invited by their premiums frequent competitions in poetry and eloquence. To poetry, indeed, especially of the tender kind, the Spanish Muslims seem to have been as indiscriminately addicted as the Italians in the time of Petrarch; and there was scarcely a doctor in church or state, but at some time or other offered up his amorous incense on the altar of the muse.[46]

With all this poetic feeling, however, the Muslims never availed themselves of the treasures of Grecian eloquence, which lay open before them. Not a poet or orator of any eminence in that language seems to have been translated by them.[47] The temperate tone of Attic composition appeared tame to the fervid conceptions of the east. Neither did they venture upon what in Europe are considered the higher walks of the art, the drama and the epic.[48] None of their writers in prose or verse shows much attention to the development or dissection of character. Their inspiration exhaled in lyrical effusions, in elegies, epigrams, and idylls. They sometimes, moreover, like the Italians, employed verse as the vehicle of instruction in the grave and recondite sciences. The general character of their poetry is bold, florid, impassioned, richly coloured with imagery, sparkling with conceits and metaphors, and occasionally breathing a deep tone of moral sensibility, as in some of the plaintive effusions ascribed by Condé to the royal poets of Córdoba. The compositions of the golden age of the Abbasids, and of the preceding period, do not seem to have been infected with the taint of exaggeration, so offensive to a European, which distinguishes the later productions in the decay of the empire.

Whatever be thought of the influence of the Arabic on European literature in general, there can be no reasonable doubt that it has been considerable on the Provençale and the Castilian. In the latter especially, so far from being confined to the vocabulary, or to external forms of composition, it seems to have penetrated deep into its spirit, and is plainly discernible in that affectation of stateliness and oriental hyperbole, which characterizes Spanish writers even at the present day; in the subtitles and conceits with which the ancient Castilian verse is so liberally bespangled; and in the relish for proverbs and prudential maxims, which is so general that it may be considered national.[49]

A decided effect has been produced on the romantic literature of Europe by those tales of fairy enchantment, so characteristic of oriental genius, and in which it seems to have revelled with uncontrolled delight. These tales, which furnished the principal diversion of the East, were imported by the Muslims into Spain; and we find the monarchs of Córdoba solacing their leisure hours with listening to their *rawis*, or novelists, who sang to them

'Of ladye-love and war, romance, and knightly worth.'[50]

The same spirit, penetrating into France, stimulated the more sluggish inventions of the *trouvère*, and, at a later and more polished period, called forth the imperishable creations of the Italian muse.[51]

It is unfortunate for the Arabians, that their literature should be locked up in a character and idiom so difficult of access to European scholars. Their wild, imaginative poetry, scarcely capable of transfusion into a foreign tongue, is made known to us only through the medium of bald prose translation; while their scientific treatises have been done into Latin with an inaccuracy, which, to make use of a pun of Casiri's, merits the name of perversions rather than versions of the originals.[52] How obviously inadequate, then, are our means of forming any just estimate of their merits!

*   *   *   *   *

AUTHOR'S CHAPTER COMMENTS

Notwithstanding the history of the Muslims is so intimately connected with that of the Spaniards, that it may be justly said to form the reverse side of it, and notwithstanding the amplitude of authentic documents in the Arabic tongue to be found in the public libraries, the Castilian writers, even the most eminent, until the latter half of the last century, with an insensibility which can be imputed to nothing else but a spirit of religious bigotry, have been content to derive their narratives exclusively from national authorities. A fire occurred in the Escorial in 1671 and consumed more than three quarters of the magnificent collection of eastern manuscripts contained in its library. The Spanish government, taking some shame to itself, as it would appear, for its past supineness, caused a copious catalogue of the surviving volumes, to the number of 1,850, to be compiled by the learned Casiri. The result was his celebrated work, *Bibliotheca Arabico-Hispana Escurialensis*, which appeared in the years 1760–70, and which would reflect credit from the splendour of its typographical execution on any press of the present day. This work, although censured by some later orientalists as hasty and superficial, must ever be highly valued as affording the only complete index to the rich repertory of Arabian manuscripts in the Escorial, and for the ample evidence which it exhibits of the science and mental culture of the Spanish Muslims. Several other native scholars, among whom Andres and Masdeu may be particularly noticed, have made extensive researches into the literary history of this people. Still their political history, so essential to a correct knowledge of the Spanish, was comparatively neglected, until Señor Cond, the late learned librarian of the Academy, who had given ample evidence of his oriental learning in his version and illustrations of the *Nubian Geographer*, and a Dissertation on Arabic Coins published in the fifth volume of the *Memoires of the Royal Academy of History*, compiled his works entitled *Historia de la Dominacion de los Arabes en España*. The first volume appeared in 1820. But unhappily the death of its author, occurring in the autumn of the same year, prevented the completion of his design. The two remaining volumes, however, were printed in the course of that and the following year from his own manuscripts; and although their comparative meagreness and confused chronology betray the want of the same paternal hand, they contain much interesting information. The relation of the conquest of Granada, especially, with which the work concludes, exhibits some important particulars in a totally different point of view from that in which they had been presented by the principal Spanish historians.

The first volume, which may be considered as having received the last touches of its author, embraces a circumstantial narrative of the great Saracen invasion, of subsequent condition of Spain under the viceroys, and of the empire of the Umayyads; undoubtedly the most splendid portion of Arabic annals, but the one, unluckily, which had been most copiously illustrated in the popular work compiled by Cardonne from the oriental manuscripts in the Royal Library at Paris. But as this author has followed the Spanish and the oriental authorities, indiscriminately, no part of his book can be cited as a genuine Arabic version, except indeed the last sixty pages, comprising the conquest of Granada, which Cardonne professes in his Preface to have drawn exclusively from an Arabian manuscript. Condé, on the other hand, professes to have adhered to his originals with such scrupulous fidelity, that 'the European reader may feel that he is perusing an Arabian author', and certainly very strong internal evidence is afforded of the truth of this assertion, in the peculiar national and religious spirit which pervades the work, and in a certain florid gasconade of style, common with the oriental writers. It is this fidelity that constitutes the peculiar value of Condé's narrative. It is the first time that the Arabians, at least those of Spain, the part of the nation which reached the highest degree of refinement, have been allowed to speak for themselves. The history, or rather tissue of histories, embodied in the translation, is certainly conceived in no very philosophical spirit, and contains, as might be expected from an Asiatic pen, little for the edification of a European reader on subjects of policy and government. The narrative is, moreover, encumbered with frivolous details and a barren muster-roll of names and titles, which would better become a genealogical table than a history. But with every deduction, it must be allowed to exhibit a sufficiently clear view of the intricate conflicting relations of the petty principalities, which swarmed over the Peninsula; and to furnish abundant evidence of a widespread intellectual improvement amid all the horrors of anarchy and a ferocious despotism. The work had already been translated or rather paraphrased into French. The necessity of an English version will doubtless be in great degree superseded by the *History of the Spanish Arabs*, preparing for the Cabinet Cyclopædia, by Mr. Southey, – a writer with whom few Castilian scholars will be willing to compare, even on their own ground; and who is, happily, not exposed to the national or religious prejudices, which can interfere with his rendering perfect justice to his subject. [Southey's English translation of Condé's *Dominion of the Arabs in Spain* appears not to have been published, but one by Mrs. J. Foster (London, 1854) is cited in the bibliography to this book. Prescott refers to Condé's *Nubian Geographer*, evidently the Arabic text of al-Idrisi. The famous Dutch Orientalist, Dozy, also worked on this text and published it in 1866 as part of his *Description de l'Afrique et l'Espagne*. See Dozy, *Histoire des Musulmans d'Espagne*, translated by Francis Griffin Stokes, Frank Cass, London, 1972, p.xxiv. – ED]

NOTES

1. [Prescott's original note at this point merely referred to an earlier note in his large work of the *History of Ferdinand and Isabella*. The earlier note identified this chapter as the one where he would discuss in detail the Spanish Muslims. Prescott used the expression 'Spanish Arabs'. References to 'Arab' have been changed to 'Muslim' when the subject actually is the broader Islamic community, and not people of Arab ancestry. Of course, their language and literature was Arabic. – ED]

2. The Koran, in addition to the repeated assurances of Paradise to the martyr who falls in battle, contains the regulations of a precise military code. Military service in some shape or other is exacted from all. The terms to be prescribed to the enemy and the vanquished, the division of the spoil, the seasons of lawful truce, the conditions on which the comparatively small number of exempts are permitted to remain at home, are accurately defined. (Sale's Koran, chap. 2, 8, 9 *et alibi*.) When the *jihad*, or Muslim crusade, which, in its general design and immunities, bore a close resemblance to the Christian, was preached in the mosque, every true believer was bound to repair to the standard of his chief. 'The holy war', says one of the early Saracen generals, 'is the ladder of Paradise. The Apostle of God styled himself the son of the sword. He loved to repose in the shadow of banners and on the fields of battle.'

3. The successors, caliphs or vicars, as they were styled, of Muhammad, represented both his spiritual and temporal authority. Their offices involved almost equally ecclesiastical and military functions. It was their duty to lead the army in battle, and on the pilgrimage to Mecca. They were to preach a sermon, and offer up public prayers in the mosques every Friday. Many of their prerogatives resemble those assumed anciently by the popes. They conferred investitures on the Muslim princes by the symbol of a ring, a sword, or a standard. They complimented them with titles of 'defender of the faith', 'column of religion', and the like. The proudest potentate held the bridle of their mules, and paid his homage by touching their threshold with his forehead. The authority of the caliphs was in this manner founded on opinion no less than on power; and their ordinances, however frivolous or iniquitous in themselves, being enforced, as it were, by a divine sanction, became

laws which it was sacrilege to disobey. See D'Herbelot, *Bibliothèque Orientale*, (La Haye, 1777–79), voce *Khalifah*.

4. The character of the Arabs, before the introduction of Islam, like that of most rude nations, is to be gathered from their national songs and romances: the poems suspended at Mecca, familiar to us in the elegant version of Sir William Jones, and still more, the recent translation of 'Antar', a composition indeed of the age of al-Raschid, but wholly devoted to the primitive Bedouins, present us with a lively picture of their peculiar habits, which, notwithstanding the influence of a temporary civilization, may be thought to bear resemblance to those of their descendants at the present day.

5. Startling as it may be, there is scarcely a vestige of any of the particulars, circumstantially narrated by the national historians (Mariana, Zurita, Abarca, Moret, etc.) as the immediate causes of the supervision of Spain, to be found in the chronicles of the period. No intimation of the persecution, or of the treason of the two sons of Witiza is to be met with in any Spanish writer, as far as I know, until nearly two centuries after the conquest; none earlier than this, of the defection of Archbishop Oppas, during the fatal conflict near Jerez; and none, of the tragical amours of Rodrigo [Roderic] and the revenge of Count Julian, before the writers of the thirteenth century. Nothing indeed can be more than the original narratives of the invasion. The continuation of the *Chronicon del Biclarense*, and the *Chronicon del Isidoro Pacense* or *de Beja*, which are contained in the voluminous collection of Florez, (*España Sagrade*, tom.vi and viii) afford the only histories contemporary with the event. Condé is mistaken in his assertion (*Dominacion de los Arabes*, Pról. p.vii), that the work of Isidore de Beja was the only narrative written during that period. Spain had not the pen of a Bede or an Eginhart to describe the memorable catastrophe. But the few and meagre touches of the contemporary chroniclers have left ample scope for conjectural history, which had been most industriously improved.

The reports, according to Condé, (*Dominacion de los Arabs*, tom. i. p.36) greedily circulated among the Saracens, of the magnificence and general prosperity of the Gothic monarchy, may sufficiently account for its invasion by an enemy flushed with uninterrupted conquests, and whose fanatical ambition was well illustrated by one of their own generals, who on reaching the western extremity of Africa, plunged his horse into the Atlantic, and sighed for other shores on which to plant the banners of Islam. See Cardonne, *Histoire de l'Afrique et de l'Espagne sous la Domination des Arabes*, (Paris, 1765) tom. i. p.37.

6. The laborious diligence of Masdeu may be thought to have settled the epoch, about which so much learned dust has been raised. The fourteenth volume of his *Historia Crítica de España y de la Cultura Española* (Madrid, 1783–1805) contains an accurate table, by which the minutest details of the Muslim lunar year are adjusted by those of the Christian era. The fall of Rodrigo on the field of battle is attested by both the domestic chroniclers of that period, as well as by the Saracens. (Incerti Auctoris Additio ad Joannem Biclarensein, apud Florez, *España Sagrada*, tom.vi. p.430 – Isidori Pacensis Episcopi Chronicon, apud Florez, *España Sagrada*, tom.viii. p.290.) The tales of the ivory and marble chariot, of the gallant steed Orelia and magnificent vestments of Rodrigo, discovered after the fight on the banks of the Guadalete [sic, now believed to have taken place on the banks of the Barbate –

ED.}, of his probable escape and subsequent seclusion among the mountains of Portugal, which have been thought worthy of Spanish history, have found a much more appropriate place in their romantic national ballads, as well as in the more elaborate productions of Scott and Southey.

7. 'Whatever curses,' says an eyewitness, whose meagre diction is quickened on this occasion into something like sublimity, 'whatever curses were denounced by the prophets of old against Jerusalem, whatever fell upon ancient Babylon, whatever miseries Rome inflicted upon the glorious company of the martyrs, all these were visited upon the once happy and prosperous, but now desolated Spain.' Pacensis Chronicon apud Florez, *España Sagrada*, tom.viii. p.292.

8. The frequency of this alliance may be inferred from the extraordinary, though, doubtless, extravagant statement cited by Zurita. The ambassadors of Jaime II, of Aragón, in 1311, represented to the sovereign pontiff, Clement V, that, of the 200,000 souls, which then composed the population of Granada, there were not more than 500 of pure Moorish descent. *Anales*, tom.iv. fol.314.

9. The famous persecutions of Córdoba under the reigns of Abd al-Rahman II, and his son, which, to judge from the tone of Castilian writers, might vie with those of Nero and Diocletian, are admitted by Morales (*Obras*, tom. X, p.74) to have occasioned the destruction of only forty individuals. Most of these unhappy fanatics solicited the crown of martyrdom, by an open violation of the Muslim laws and usages. The details are given by Florez, in the tenth volume of his collection.

10. Bleda, *Corónica de los Moros de España*, (Valencia, 1618), lib. 2, cap. 16, 17. – Cardonne, *Hist. d'Afrique et d'Espagne*, tom.i, pp.83 *et seq.* 179. – Condé, *Dominacion de los Arabes*, Pról., p.vii and tom.i, pp.29–54, 75, 87. – Morales, *Orbas*, tom.vi. pp.407–417; tom.vii, pp.262– 264. – Florez, *España Sagrada*, tom.X, pp.237– 270. – Fuero Juzgo, Int. p.40.

11. Condé, *Dominacion de los Arabes*, part 2, cap. 1–46.

12. *Ibid. ubi supra.* – Masdeu, *Historia Crítica*, tom.xiii, pp.178, 187.

13. 'Aussi dès que vous approchez, en Europe ou en Asie, d'une terre possédée par les Musulmans, vous la reconnaissez de loin au riche et sombre voile de verdure qui totte gracieusement sur elle: – des arabes pour s'asseoir à leur ombre, des fontaines utillissantes pour rêver à leur bruit, du silence et des mosquées aux légers minarets, s'élevant à chaque pas du sein d'une terre pieuse.' Lamartine, *Voyage en Orient*, tome i, p.172.

14. Condé, *Dominacion de los Arabes*, tom.i, pp.199, 265, 284, 285, 417, 446, 447, *et alibi*. –Cardonne, *Hist. d'Afrique et d'Espagne*, tom.i, pp.227–30 *et seq*.

15. Condé, *Dominacion de los Arabes*, tom.i, pp.211, 212, 226. – Swinburne, *Travels through Spain*, (London, 1787) let. 35. – Xerif Aledris, conocido por El Nubiense, *Descripcion de España*, con Traduccion y Notas de Condé, (Madrid, 1799) pp.161, 162 – Morales, *Obras*, tom.x, p.61 – Chenier, *Recherches Historiques sur les Maures, et Histoire de l'Empire de Maroc*, (Paris, 1787) tom.ii, p.312.

16. Condé, *Dominacion de los Arabes*, tom.i, pp.214, 228, 270, 611. – Masdeu, *Historia Crítica*, tom.xiii, p.118. – Cardonne, *Hist d'Afrique et d'Espagne*, tom.i, pp.338– 343. – Casiri quotes from an Arabic historian the conditions on which Abd al-Rahman I proffered his alliance to the Christian princes of Spain, viz the annual tribute of 10,000 ounces of gold, 10,000 pounds of silver, 10,000 horses, etc. The absurdity of this story, inconsiderately repeated by historians, if any argument

were necessary to prove it, becomes sufficiently manifest from the fact, that the instrument is dated in the 142d year of the *Hegira*, being a little more than fifty years after the conquest. See *Bibliotheca Arabico-Hispana Escurialensis*, (Matriti, 1760) tom.ii, p.104.

17. *Hist. Naturalis*, lib.33, cap.4.

18. Introduction à l'*Histoire Naturelle de l'Espagne*, traduite par Flavigny, (Paris, 1776), p.411.

19. See a sensible essay by Abbé Correa de Serra on the husbandry of the Spanish Muslims, contained in tom.i, of *Archives Littéraires de l'Europe*, (Paris, 1804). – Masdeu, *Historia Crítica*, tom.xiii, pp.115, 117, 127, 131. – Condé, *Dominacion de los Arabes*, tom.i, cap.44. – Casiri, *Bibliotheca Escurialensis*, tom.i, p.338.

An absurd story has been transcribed from Cardonne, with little hesitation, by almost every succeeding writer upon this subject. According to him (*Hist. d'Afrique et d'Espagne*, tom.i p.338), 'the banks of the Guadalquivir were lined with no less than twelve thousand villages and hamlets'. The length of the river, not exceeding three hundred miles, would scarcely afford room for the same number of farmhouses. Condé's version of the Arabic passage represents twelve thousand hamlets, farms, and castles, to have 'been scattered over the regions watered by the Guadalquivir'; indicating by this indefinite statement nothing more than the extreme populousness of the province of Andalusia.

20. Casiri, *Bibliotheca Escurialensis*, tom.ii, pp.38, 202. – Condé, *Dominacion de los Arabes*, part.2, cap.88.

21. *Storia della Letteratura Italiana*, (Roma, 1782–97) tom.iii, p.231. – Turner, *History of the Anglo-Saxons*, (London, 1820), vol.iii. p.137. – Andres, *Dell' Origine, de Progressi e dello Stato Attuale d'Ogni Letteratura*, (Venezia, 1783) part.1, cap.8, 9. – Casiri, *Bibliotheca Escurialensis*, tom.ii, p.149. – Masdeu, *Historia Crítica*, tom.xiii, pp.165, 171. – Condé, *Dominacion de los Arabes*, part 2, cap.93. – Among the accomplished females of this period, Valadata, the daughter of the Caliph Muhammad, is celebrated as having frequently carried away the palm of eloquence in her discussions with the most learned academicians. Others again, with an intrepidity that might shame the degeneracy of a modern *blue*, plunged boldly into the studies of philosophy, history, and jurisprudence.

22. Garibay, *Compendio*, lib.39, cap.3.

23. Zurita, *Anales*, lib.20, cap.42.

24. L. Marineo, *Cosas Memorables*, fol.169.

25. Condé, *Dominaciion de los Arabes*, tom.ii, p.147. – Casiri, *Bibliotheca Escurialensis*, tom.ii, pp.248 et seq. – Pedraza, Antiguedad y Excelencias de Granada (Madrid, 1608) lib.1. – Pedraza has collected the various etymologies of the term *Granada*, which some writers have traced to the fact of the city having been the spot where the *pomegranate* was first introduced from Africa; others to the large quantity of *grain* in which its vega abounded; others again to the resemblance which the city, divided into two hills thickly sprinkled with houses, bore to a half-opened pomegranate. (Lib.2, cap.17.) The arms of the city which were in part composed of pomegranate, would seem to favour the derivation of its name from that of the fruit.

26. Pedraza, *Antiguedad de Granada*, fol.101. – Denina, *Delle Rivoluzioni d'Italia* (Venezia, 1816). *Capmany y Montpalau, Memorias Históricas sobre la Marina,*

Comerico, y Artes de Barcelona, (Madrid, 1779–92) tom.iii, p.218; tom.iv, pp.67 et seq. – Condé, *Dominacion de los Arabes*, tom.iii, cap.26. – The ambassador of the Emperor Frederic III, on his passage to the court of Lisbon in the middle of the fifteenth century, contrasts the superior cultivation, as well as general civilization, of Granada at this period with that of the other countries of Europe through which he had travelled. Sismondi, *Histoire des Républiques Italiennes du Moyen-Age* (Paris, 1818) tom.ix, p.405.

27. Casiri, *Bibliotheca Escurialensis*, tom.ii, pp.250–8. – The fifth volume of the royal Spanish Academy of History contains an erudite essay by Condé on Arabic money, principally with reference to that coined in Spain; pp.225–315.

28. A specification of a royal donative in that day may serve to show the martial spirit of the age. In one of these, made by the King of Granada to the Castilian sovereign, we find twenty noble steeds of the royal stud, reared on the banks of the Genil, with superb caparisons, and the same number of scimitars richly garnished with gold and jewels; and in another, mixed up with perfumes and cloth of gold, we meet with a litter of tame lions. (Condé, *Dominacion de los Arabes*, tom.iii, pp.163, 183.) This latter symbol of royalty appears to have been deemed peculiarly appropriate to the kings of León. Ferreras informs us that the ambassadors from France at the Castilian court, in 1434, were received by Juan II, with a full grown domesticated lion crouching at his feet. (*Hist. d'Espagne*, tom.vi, p.401.) The same taste appears still to exist in Turkey. Dr. Clarke, in his visit to Constantinople, met with one of these terrific pets, who used to follow his master, Hassan Pacha, about like a dog.

29. Condé, *Dominacion de los Arabes*, tom.iii, cap.28. – Henriquez del Castillo (*Crónica*, cap.138) gives an account of an intended duel between two Castilian nobles, in the presence of the king of Granada, as late as 1470. One of the parties, Don Alfonso de Aguilar, failing to keep his engagement, the other rode round the lists in triumph, with his adversary's portrait contemptuously fastened to the tail of his horse.

30. It must be admitted, that these ballads, as far as facts are concerned, are too inexact to furnish other than a very slippery foundation for history. The most beautiful portion perhaps of the Moorish ballads, for example, is taken up with the feuds of the Abencerrages in the later days of Granada. Yet this family, whose romantic story is still repeated to the traveller amid the ruins of the Alhambra, is scarcely noticed, as far as I am aware, by contemporary writers, foreign or domestic, and would seem to owe its chief celebrity to the apocryphal version of Ginés Perez de Hyta, whose 'Milesian tales', according to the severe sentence of Nic. Antonio, 'are fit only to amuse the lazy and the listless'. (*Bibliotheca Nova*, tom.i, p.536.)

But although the Spanish ballads are not entitled to the credit of strict historical documents, they may yet perhaps be received in evidence of the prevailing character of the social relations of the age; a remark indeed predictable of most works of fiction, written by authors contemporary with the events they describe, and more especially so of that popular minstrelsy, which emanating from a simple, uncorrupted class, is less likely to swerve from the truth, than more ostentatious works of art. The long cohabitation of the Saracens with the Christians, (full evidence of which is afforded by Capmany, (Mem. de Barcelona, tom.iv., Apend. no.11) who quotes a document from the public archives of Catalonia, showing the great number of Saracens residing in Aragón even in the thirteenth and fourteenth centuries, the most flourishing period of the Granadan empire) had enabled many of them confessedly to speak and write the Spanish language with purity and elegance. Some of the graceful little songs which are still chanted by the peasantry of Spain in their dances, to the accomplishment of the castanet, are referred by a competent critic (Condé, *De la Poesía Oriental*, MS) to an Arabian origin. There can be little hazard, therefore, in imputing much of this peculiar minstrelsy to the Arabians themselves, the contemporaries, and perhaps the eyewitnesses of the events they celebrate.

31. Casiri (*Bibliotheca Escurialensis*, tom.ii, p.250) has transcribed a passage from an Arabian author of the fourteenth century, inveighing bitterly against the luxury of the Moorish ladies, their gorgeous apparel and habits of expense, 'amounting almost to insanity', in a tone which may remind one of the similar phillippic by his contemporary Dante, against his fair countrywomen of Florence. – Two ordinances of a king of Granada, cited by Condé in his History, prescribe the separation of the women from the men in the mosques; and prohibit their attendance on certain festivals, without the protection of their husbands or some near relative. – Their *femmes savantes*, as we have seen, were in the habit of conferring freely with men of letters, and of assisting in person at the academical *séances*. – And lastly, the frescoes alluded to in the text represent the presence of females at the tournaments, and the fortunate knight receiving the palm of victory from their hands.

32. Condé, *Dominacion de los Arabes*, tom.i, p.340; tom.iii, p.119.

33. Casiri, on Arabian authority, computes it at 200,000 men. *Bibliotheca Escurialensis*, tom.i, p.338.

34. Pulgar, *Reyes Católicos*, p.250.

35. *Mem. de la Acad. de Hist*, tom.vi, p.169. – These ruined fortifications still thickly stud the border territories of Granada; and many an Andalusian mill, along the banks of the Guadayra and the Guadalquivir, retains its battlemented tower, which served for the defence of its inmates against the forays of the enemy.

36. D'Herbelot, (*Bib. Orientale*, tom.i, p.630) among other authentic traditions of Muhammad, quotes one as indicating his encouragement of letters, viz. 'That the ink of the doctors and the blood of the martyrs are of equal price.' M. Œlsner (*Des Effets de la Religion de Mohammed*, Paris, 1810) has cited several others of the same liberal import. But such traditions cannot be received in evidence of the original of the prophet. They are rejected as apocryphal by the Persians and the whole sect of the Shiites and are entitled to little weight with a European.

37. When the Caliph al-Mamun [c.827] encouraged, by his example as well as patronage, a more enlightened policy, he was accused by the more orthodox Muslims of attempting to subvert the principles of their religion. See Pococke, *Spec. Hist. Arabum*. (Oxon, 1650) p.166.

38. Andres, *Letteratura*, part.1, cap.8, 10. – Casiri, *Bibliotheca Escurialensis*, tom.ii, pp.71, 251, *et passim*.

39. Casiri mentions one of these universal geniuses, who published no less than a thousand and fifty treatises on the various topics of Ethics, History, Law, Medicine, etc. *Bibliotheca Escurialensis*, tom.ii, p.107. – See also tom.i, p.370; tom.ii, p.71 *et alibi*. – Zuñiga, *Annales de Sevilla*, p.22. – D'Herbelot, *Bib. Orientale, voce Tarikh*. – Masdeu, *Historia Crítica*, tom.xiii, pp.203, 205. – Andres, Letteratura, part 1, cap.8.

40. Consult the sensible, though perhaps severe, remarks of Degerando on Arabian science. (*Hist. de la Philosophie*, tom.iv, cap.24.) – The reader may also peruse with advantage a disquisition on Arabian metaphysics in Turner's *History of England* (vol.vi, pp.405–449. – Brucker, Hist. Philosophiae, tom.iii, p.105). – Ludovicus Vives seems to have been the author of the imputation in the text. (Nic. Antonio, *Bibliotheca Vetus*, tom.ii, p.394). Averroes translated some of the philosophical works of Aristotle from the Greek into Arabic; a Latin version of which translation was afterwards made. Though D'Herbelot is mistaken (*Bib. Orientale*, art. *Roschd*) in saying that Averroes was the first to translate Aristotle into Arabic; as this has been done two centuries before, at least, by Honain and others in the ninth century, (see Casiri, *Bibliotheca Escurialensis*, tom.i, p.304) and Bayle had shown that a Latin version of the Stagirite was used by the Europeans before the alleged period. See art. *Averroes*.

41. Sprengel, *Histoire de la Médecine*, traduite par Jourdan (Paris, 1815) tom.ii, pp.263 et seq.

42. Degerando, *Hist. de la Philosophie*, tom.iv, *ubi supra*.

43. *Bibliotheca Escurialensis*, tom.ii, p.9. – Andres, *Letteratura*, part. 1, cap. 10.

44. *Letteratura Italiana*, tom.v, p.87.

45. The Battle of Crécy [1346] furnishes [one of] the earliest in instance[s] on record of the use of artillery by the European Christians; although Du Cange, among several examples which he enumerates, has traced a distinct notice of its existence as far back as 1338. (*Glossarium ad Scriptores Mediæ et Infinæ Latinitatis*, (Paris, 1739) and Supplement (Paris, 1766) *voce Bombarda*.) The history of the Spanish Muslims carries it to a much earlier period. It was employed by the Nasrid king of Granada at the siege of Baza in 1312 and 1325. (Condé, *Dominacion de los Arabes*, tom.iii, cap.18. – Casiri, *Bibliotheca Escurialensis*, tom.ii, p.7.) It is distinctly noticed in an Arabian treatise as ancient as 1249; and, finally, Castri quotes a passage from a Spanish author at the close of the eleventh century, (whose MS., according to Nic. Antonio, though familiar to scholars, lies still entombed in the dust of libraries), which describes the use of artillery in a naval engagement of that period between the Muslims of Tunis and Sevilla. Casiri, *Bibliotheca Escurialensis*, tom.ii, p.8. – Nic. Antonio, *Bibliotheca Vetus*, tom.ii, p.12. [Some of the reported earliest uses of gunpowder artillery by the Spanish Muslims have been questioned. This is reviewed, with other military aspects, in Part 1 of the Introduction. – ED.]

46. Petrarch complains in one of his letters from the country, that 'jurisconsults and divines, nay his own valet, had taken to rhyming; and he was afraid the very cattle might begin to low in verse'; *apud* De Sade, *Mémoires pour La Vie de Pétrarque*, tom.iii, p.243.

47. Andres, *Letteratura*, part. 1, cap.11. – Yet this popular assertion is contradicted by Reinesius, who states that both Homer and Pindar were translated into Arabic by the middle of the eighth century. See Fabricius, *Bibliotheca Græca* (Hamb, 1712–38) tom.xii, p.753.

48. Sir William Jones, *Traité sur la Poésie Orientale*, Sec. 2. – Sismondi says that Sir W. Jones is mistaken in citing the history of Timour by Ebn Arabschah, as an Arabic epic. (*Littérature du Midi*, tom.i, p.57.) It is Sismondi who is mistaken, since the English critic states that the Muslims have no heroic poem, and that this poetical prose history is not accounted such even by the Muslims themselves.

49. It would require much more learning that I am fortified with, to enter into the merits of the question, which has been raised respecting the probable influence of the Arabian on the literature of Europe. A.W. Schlegel, in a work of little bulk, but much value in refuting with his usual vivacity, the extravagant theory of Andres, has been led to conclusions of an opposite nature, which may be thought perhaps scarcely less extravagant. (*Observations sur la Langue et la Littérature Provençales*, p.64.) It must indeed seem highly improbable that the Muslims, who, during the middle ages were so far superior in science and literary culture to the Europeans, could have resided so long in immediate contact with them, and in those very countries indeed which gave birth to the most cultivated poetry of that period, without exerting some perceptible influence upon it. Be this as it may, its influence on the Castilian cannot reasonably be disputed. This has been briefly traced by Condé in an 'Essay on Oriental Poetry', *Poesia Oriental*, whose publication he anticipates in the Preface to his *History of the Spanish Arabs*, but which still remains in manuscript. (The copy I have used is in the Library of Mr. George Ticknor.) He professes in this work to discern in the earlier Castilian poetry, in the Cid, the Alexander, in Berceo's, the arch priest of Hita's, and others of similar antiquity, most of the peculiarities and varieties of Arabic verse; the same cadences and number of syllables, the same intermixture of assonances and consonances, the double hemistich and prolonged repetition of the final rhyme. From the same source he derives much of the earlier rural minstrelsy of Spain, as well as the measure of its romances and seguidillas; and in the Preface to his History, he has ventured on the bold assertion, that the Castilian owes so much of its vocabulary to the Arabic, that it may be almost accounted a dialect of the latter. Condé criticisms, however, must be quoted with reserve. His habitual studies had given him such a keen relish for oriental literature, that he was in a manner, *denaturalized* from his own.

50. Byron's beautiful line may seem almost a version of Condé's Spanish text, 'sucesos de armas y de amores con muy estraños lances y en elegante estilo.' – *Dominacion de los Arabes*, tom.i, p.457.

51. Sismondi, in his *Littérature du Midi* (tom.i, pp.267 *et seq*), and more fully in his *Républiques Italiennes* (tom.xvi, p.448 et seq), derives the jealousy of the sex, the ideas of honour, and the spirit of revenge, which distinguished the southern nations of Europe in the fifteenth and sixteenth centuries, from the Arabians. Whatever he thought of the jealousy of the sex, it might have been supposed, that the principles of honour and the spirit of revenge might, without seeking further, find abundant precedent in the feudal habits and institutions of our European ancestors.

52. '*Quas perversiones potius, quam scrsiones meritò dixeris*' *Bibliotheca Escurialensis*, tom.i, p.266.

CHAPTER 2

THE WAR OF GRANADA
OPENING PHASE (1481–82)

Zahara surprised by the Spanish Muslims. – Marquis of Cádiz. – His Expedition against Alhama. – Valour of the Citizens. – Desperate Struggle. – Fall of Alhama. – Consternation of the Spanish Muslims. – Vigorous Measures of the Queen.

No sooner had Ferdinand and Isabella restored internal tranquillity to their dominions, and made the strength effective, which had been acquired by their union under one government, than they turned their eyes to those fair regions of the peninsula, over which the Muslim crescent had reigned triumphant for nearly eight centuries. Fortunately an act of aggression on the part of the Spanish Muslims furnished a pretext for entering on their plan of conquest, at the moment when it was ripe for execution. Aben Ismail [Yusuf V (1408–17 and 1462)], who had ruled in Granada during the latter part of Juan II's reign [of Castile (1406–54)], and [for a short time at] the commencement of Enríque IV's [of Castile (1454–74)], had been partly indebted for his throne to the former monarch. Sentiments of gratitude, combined with a naturally amiable disposition, had led him to foster as amicable relations with the Christian princes as the jealousy between the natural enemies would permit. Not withstanding an occasional border foray, or the capture of a frontier fortress, such a correspondence was maintained between the two kingdoms, that the nobles of Castile frequently resorted to the court of Granada. There, forgetting their ancient feuds, they mingled with the Granadan cavaliers in the generous pastimes of chivalry. Abul Hacen [Hasan] Ali, who succeeded his father [Sa'd (1454–62 and 1462–64)] in 1464, was of a very different temperament. His fiery character prompted him, when very young, to violate the truce by an unprovoked inroad into Andalusia and, although after his accession domestic troubles occupied him too closely to allow leisure for foreign war, he still cherished in secret the same feelings of animosity against the Christians. When, in 1476 the Spanish sovereigns required as the condition of a renewal of the truce, which he solicited, the payment of the annual tribute imposed on his

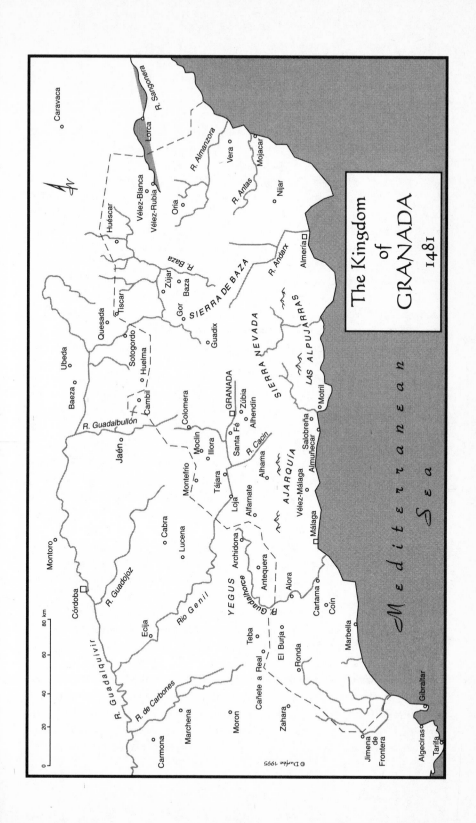

The Kingdom of GRANADA 1481

© Dunlee 1995

predecessors, he proudly replied that 'the mints of Granada coined no longer gold, but steel'. His subsequent conduct did not belie the spirit of this Spartan answer.[1]

At length, toward the close of the year 1481, the storm which had been so long gathering burst upon Zahara, a small fortified town on the frontier of Andalusia, crowning a lofty eminence, washed at its base by the River Guadalete, which from its position seemed almost inaccessible. The garrison, trusting to these natural defences, suffered itself to be surprised on the night of the 26th of December by the Nasrid monarch; who, scaling the walls under favour of a furious tempest, which prevented his approach from being readily heard, put to the sword such of the guard as offered resistance, and swept away the whole population of the place, men, women, and children, in slavery to Granada.

The intelligence of this disaster caused deep mortification to the Spanish sovereigns, especially to Ferdinand, by whose grandfather Zahara had been recovered from the Spanish Muslims. Measures were accordingly taken for strengthening the whole line of frontier, and the utmost vigilance was exerted to detect some vulnerable point of the enemy, on which retaliation might be successfully inflicted. Neither were the tidings of their own successes welcomed, with the joy that might have been expected, by the people of Granada. The prognostics, it was said, afforded by the appearance of the heavens, boded no good. More sure prognostics were afforded in the judgments of thinking men, who deprecated the temerity of awakening the wrath of a vindictive and powerful enemy. 'Woe is me!' exclaimed an ancient Alfaki, on quitting the hall of audience, 'The ruins of Zahara will fall on our own heads; the days of the Muslim empire in Spain are now numbered!'[2]

It was not long before the desired opportunity for retaliation presented itself to the Spaniards. One Juan de Ortega, a captain of *escaladores*, or scalers, so denominated from the peculiar service in which they were employed in besieging cities, who had acquired some reputation under Juan II, in the wars of Rosellon, reported to Diego de Merlo, assistant of Sevilla, that the fortress of Alhama, situated in the heart of the Muslim territories, was so negligently guarded, that it might be easily carried by an enemy, who had skill enough to approach it. The fortress, as well as the city of the same name, which it commanded, was built, like many others in that turbulent period, along the crest of a rocky eminence, encompassed by a river at its base, and, from its natural advantages, might be deemed impregnable. This strength of position, by rendering all other precautions apparently superfluous, lulled its defenders into a security like that which had proved so fatal to Zahara. Alhama, as this Arabic name implies, was famous for its baths, whose annual rents are said to have amounted to five hundred thousand ducats. The monarchs of Granada, indulging the taste common to the people of the east, used to frequent this

place, with their court, to refresh themselves with its delicious waters, so that
Alhama became embellished with all the magnificence of a royal residence. The
place was still further enriched by its being the *dépôt* of the public taxes on land,
which constituted a principal branch of the revenue, and by its various manufactures of cloth, for which its inhabitants were celebrated throughout the
kingdom of Granada.[3]

Diego de Merlo, although struck with the advantages of this conquest, was
not insensible to the difficulties with which it would be attended; since Alhama
was sheltered under the very wings of Granada, from which it lay scarcely eight
leagues distant, and could be reached only by traversing the most populous
portion of the Muslim territory, or by surmounting a precipitous *sierra*, or chain
of mountains, which screened it on the north. Without delay, however, he
communicated the information which he had received to Don Rodrigo Ponce de
León, Marquis of Cádiz, as the person best fitted by his capacity and courage for
such an enterprise. This nobleman, who had succeeded his father, the Count of
Arcos, in 1469, as head of the great house of Ponce de León, was at this period
about thirty-nine years of age. Although a younger and illegitimate son, he had
been preferred to the succession in consequence of the extraordinary promise
which his early youth exhibited. When scarcely seventeen years old, he achieved
a victory over the Muslims, accompanied with a signal display of personal
prowess.[4] Later in life, he formed a connection with the daughter of the Marquis
of Villeama, the factious minister of Enríque IV, through whose influence he
was raised to the dignity of Marquis of Cádiz. This alliance attached him to the
fortunes of Enríque, in his disputes with his brother Alfonso, and subsequently
with Isabella, on whose accession, of course, Don Rodrigo looked with no
friendly eye. He did not, however, engage in any overt act of resistance, but
occupied himself with prosecuting an hereditary feud, which he had revived
with the Duke of Medina Sidonia, the head of the Guzmáns; a family, which
from ancient times had divided with his own the great interests of Andalusia.
The pertinacity with which this feud was conducted, and the desolation which it
carried not only into Sevilla, but into every quarter of the province, have been
noticed in the preceding pages. The vigorous administration of Isabella
repressed these disorders, and, after abridging the overgrown power of the two
nobles, effected an apparent (it was only apparent) reconciliation between them.
The fiery spirit of the Marquis of Cádiz, no longer allowed to escape in domestic
broil, urged him to seek distinction in more honourable warfare; and at this
moment he lay in his castle at Arcos, looking with a watchful eye over the
borders and waiting, like a lion in ambush, [for] the moment when he could
spring upon his victim.

Without hesitation, therefore, he assumed the enterprise proposed by Diego
de Merlo, imparting his purpose to Don Pedro Enríquez, *adelantado* of Andalusia, a relative of Ferdinand, and to the alcaides of two or three neighbouring

fortresses. With the assistance of these friends he assembled a force, which, including those who marched under the banner of Sevilla, amounted to two thousand five hundred horse and three thousand foot. His own town of Marchena was appointed as the place of rendezvous. The proposed route lay by the way of Antequera, across the wild sierras of Alzerifa. The mountain passes, sufficiently difficult at a season when their numerous ravines were choked up by the winter torrents, were rendered still more formidable by being traversed in the darkness of night; for the party, in order to conceal their movements, lay by during the day. Leaving their baggage on the banks of the Yeguas, that they might move forward with greater celerity, the whole body at length arrived, after a rapid and most painful march, on the third night from their departure, in a deep valley about half a league from Alhama. Here the Marquis first revealed the real object of the expedition to his soldiers, who, little dreaming of any thing beyond a mere border inroad, were transported with joy at the prospect of the rich booty so nearly within their grasp.[5]

The next morning, being the 28th of February [1482], a small party was detached, about two hours before dawn, under the command of Juan de Ortega for the purpose of scaling the citadel, while the main body moved forward more leisurely under the Marquis of Cádiz, in order to support them. The night was dark and tempestuous, circumstances which favoured their approach in the same manner as with the Granadans at Zahara. After ascending the rocky heights which were crowned by the citadel, the ladders were very silently placed against the walls, and Ortega, followed by about thirty others, succeeded in gaining the battlements unobserved. A sentinel, who was found sleeping on his post, they at once despatched, and, proceeding cautiously forward to the guard-room, put the whole of the little garrison to the sword, after the short and ineffectual resistance that could be opposed by men suddenly roused from slumber. The city in the mean time was alarmed, but it was too late; the citadel was taken; and the outer gates, which opened into the country, being thrown open, the Marquis of Cádiz entered with trumpet sounding and banner flying, at the head of his army, and took possession of the fortress.[6]

After allowing the refreshment necessary to the exhausted spirits of his soldiers, the Marquis resolved to sally forth at once upon the town, before its inhabitants could muster in sufficient force to oppose him. But the citizens of Alhama, showing a resolution rather to have been expected from men trained in a camp, than from peaceful burghers of a manufacturing town, had sprung to arms at the first alarm, and, gathering in the narrow street on which the portal of the castle opened, so completely enfiladed it with their arquebuses and crossbows, that the Spaniards, after an ineffectual attempt to force a passage, were compelled to recoil upon their defences, amid showers of bolts and balls which occasioned the loss, among others, of two of their principal alcaides.

A council of war was then called, in which it was even advised by some, that the fortress, after having been dismantled, should be abandoned as incapable of defence against the citizens on the one hand, and the succours which might be expected speedily to arrive from Granada, on the other. But this counsel was rejected with indignation by the Marquis of Cádiz, whose fiery spirit rose with the occasion; indeed, it was not very palatable to most of his followers, whose cupidity was more than ever inflamed by the sight of the rich spoil, which, after so many fatigues, now lay at their feet. It was accordingly resolved to demolish part of the fortifications, which looked toward the town, and at all hazards to force a passage into it. This resolution was at once put into execution; and the marquis, throwing himself into the breach thus made, at the head of his men-at-arms, and shouting his war-cry of 'St. James and the Virgin', precipitated himself into the thickest of the enemy. Others of the Spaniards, running along the out-works contiguous to the buildings of the city, leaped into the street, and joined their companions there, while others again sallied from the gates, now opened for the second time.[7]

The Granadans, unshaken by the fury of this assault, received the assailants with brisk and well-directed volleys of shot and arrows; while the women and children, thronging the roofs and balconies of the houses, discharged on their heads boiling oil, pitch, and missiles of every description. But the weapons of the Granadans glanced comparatively harmless from the mailed armour of the Castilians, while their own bodies, loosely arrayed in such habiliments as they could throw over them in the confusion of the night, presented a fatal mark to their enemies. Still they continued to maintain a stout resistance, checking the progress of the Castilians by barricades of timber hastily thrown across the streets; and, as their entrenchments were forced one after another, they disputed every inch of ground with the desperation of men who fought for life, fortune, liberty, all that was most dear to them. The contest hardly slackened till the close of day, while the kennels literally ran with blood, and every avenue was choked up with the bodies of the slain.

At length, however, Castilian valour proved triumphant in every quarter, except where a small and desperate remnant of the Granadans, having gathered their wives and children around then, retreated as a last resort into a large mosque near the walls of the city, from which they kept up a galling fire on the closed ranks of the Christians. The latter after enduring some loss, succeeded in sheltering themselves so effectually under a roof or canopy constructed of their own shields, in the manner practised in war previous to the exclusive use of firearms, that they were enabled to approach so near the mosque, as to set fire to its doors; when its tenants, menaced with suffocation, made a desperate sally, in which many perished, and the remainder surrendered at discretion. The prisoners thus made were all massacred on the spot without distinction of sex or age, according to the Saracen accounts. But the Castilian writers make no mention of this: and, as the appetites of the Spaniards were not yet stimulated

Siege of Alhama (1482).
Relief carving from Toledo Cathedral. (Rodrigo Alemán, c.1492)

by that love of carnage, which they afterward displayed in their American wars, and which was repugnant to the chivalrous spirit with which their contests with the Muslims were usually conducted, we may be justified in regarding it as an invention of the enemy.[8]

Alhama was now delivered up to the sack of the soldiery, and rich indeed was the booty which fell into their hands, – gold and silver plate, pearls, jewels, fine silks and cloths, curious and costly furniture, and all the various appurtenances of a thriving, luxurious city. In addition to which, the magazines were found well stored with the more substantial, and at the present juncture, more serviceable supplies of grain, oil, and other provisions. Nearly a quarter of the population is said to have perished in the various conflicts of the day, and the remainder, according to the usage of the time, became the prize of the victors. A considerable number of Christian captives, who were found immured in the public prisons, were restored to freedom, and swelled the general jubilee with their grateful acclamations. The contemporary Castilian chroniclers record also, with no less satisfaction, the detection of a Christian renegade, notorious for his depredations on his countrymen, whose misdeeds the Marquis of Cádiz requited by causing him to be hung up over the battlements of the castle, in the face of the whole city. Thus fell the ancient city of Alhama, the first conquest, and achieved with a gallantry and daring unsurpassed by any other during this memorable war.[9]

The report of this disaster fell like the knell of their own doom on the ears of the inhabitants of Granada. It seemed as if the hand of Providence itself must have been stretched forth to smite the stately city, which, reposing as it were under the shadow of their own walls, and in the bosom of a peaceful and populous country, was thus suddenly laid low in blood and ashes. Men now read the fulfilment of the disastrous omens and predictions which ushered in the capture of Zahara. The melancholy *romance* or ballad, with the burden of *Ay de mi Alhama* 'Woe is me, Alhama', composed probably by some one of the nation not long after this event, shows how deep was the dejection which settled on the spirits of the people. The old king, Abul Hacen, however, far from resigning himself to useless lamentation, sought to retrieve his loss by the most vigorous measures. A body of a thousand horse was sent forward to reconnoitre the city, while he prepared to follow with as powerful levies, as he could enforce, of the militia of Granada.[10]

The intelligence of the conquest of Alhama diffused general satisfaction throughout Castile, and was especially grateful to the sovereigns who welcomed it as an auspicious omen of the ultimate success of their designs upon the Spanish Muslims. They were attending mass in their royal palace of Medina del Campo, when they received despatches from the Marquis of Cádiz, informing them of the issue of his enterprise. 'During all the while he sat at dinner,' says a precise chronicler of the period, 'the prudent Ferdinand was revolving in his mind the course best to be adopted.' He reflected that the Castilians would soon be beleaguered by an overwhelming force from Granada, and he determined at all hazards to support them. He accordingly gave orders to make instant preparation for departure; but, first, accompanied the Queen, attended by a solemn procession of the court and clergy, to the cathedral church of St. James; where *Te Deum* was chanted, and a humble thanksgiving offered up to the Lord of Hosts for the success with which he had crowned their arms. Toward evening, the King set forward on his journey to the south, escorted by such nobles and cavaliers as were in attendance on his person, leaving the queen to follow more leisurely, after having provided reinforcements and supplies requisite for the prosecution of the war.[11]

On the 5th of March [1482], the King of Granada appeared before the walls of Alhama, with an army which amounted to three thousand horse and fifty thousand foot. The first object which encountered his eyes was the mangled remains of his unfortunate subjects, which the Christians, who would have been scandalized by an attempt to give them the rites of sepulture, had from dread of infection thrown over the walls, where they now lay half-devoured by birds of prey and the ravenous dogs of the city. The Muslim troops, transported with horror and indignation at this hideous spectacle, called loudly to be led to the attack. They had marched from Granada with so much precipitation, that they were wholly unprovided with artillery, in the use of which they were expert for that period; and which was now the more necessary, as the Spaniards had diligently employed the few days which intervened since their occupation of the place, in repairing the breaches in the fortifications, and in putting them in a posture of defence. But the Spanish Muslim ranks were filled with the flower of their chivalry, and their immense superiority of numbers enabled them to make their attacks simultaneously on the most distant quarters of the town, with such un-intermitted vivacity, that the little garrison, scarcely allowed a moment for repose, was wellnigh exhausted with fatigue.[12]

At length, however, Abul Hacen, after the loss of more than two thousand of his bravest troops in these precipitated assaults, became convinced of the impracticability of forcing a position, whose natural strength was so ably seconded by the valour of its defenders, and he determined to reduce the pace by the more tardy but certain method of blockade. In this he was favoured by one or two circumstances. The town, having but a single well within its walls, was almost wholly indebted for its supplies of water to the river which flowed at its base. The Granadans, by dint of great labour, succeeded in diverting the stream so effectually, that the only communication with it, which remained open to the besieged, was by a subterraneous gallery or mine, that had probably been contrived with reference to some such emergency by the original inhabitants. The mouth of this passage was commanded in such a manner by the Granadan archers, that no egress could be obtained without a regular skirmish, so that every drop of water might be said to be purchased with the blood of Christians; who, 'if they had not possessed the courage of Spaniards,' says a Castilian writer, 'would have been reduced to the last extremity'. In addition to this calamity, the garrison began to be menaced with scarcity of provisions, owing to the improvident waste of the soldiers, who supposed that the city, after being plundered, was to be razed to the ground and abandoned.[13]

At this crisis they received the unwelcome tidings of the failure of an expedition destined for their relief by Alonso de Aguilar. This cavalier, the chief of an illustrious house since rendered immortal by the renown of his younger brother, Gonzalo de Córdoba, had assembled a considerable body of troops, on learning the capture of Alhama, for the purpose of supporting his friend and companion in arms, the Marquis of Cádiz. On reaching the shores of the Yeguas, he received, for the first time, advice of the formidable host which lay between him and the city, rendering hopeless any attempt to penetrate into the latter with his inadequate force. Contenting himself, therefore, with recovering the baggage, which the Marquis's army in its rapid march, as has been already noticed, had left on the banks of the river, he returned to Antequera.[14]

Under these depressing circumstances, the indomitable spirit of the Marquis of Cádiz seemed to infuse itself into the hearts of his soldiers. He was ever in the front of danger, and shared the privations of the meanest of his followers; encouraging them to rely with undoubting confidence on the sympathies which their cause must awaken in the breasts of their countrymen. The event proved that he did not miscalculate. Soon after the occupation of Alhama, the Marquis, foreseeing the difficulties of his situation, had despatched missives, requesting the support of the principal lords and cities of Andalusia. In this summons he had omitted the Duke of Medina Sidonia, as one who had good reason to take umbrage at being excluded from a share in the original enterprise. Enríque de Guzmán, Duke of Medina Sidonia, possessed a degree of power more considerable than any other chieftain in the south. His yearly rents amounted to nearly sixty thousand ducats, and he could bring into the field, it was said, from his own resources an army little inferior to what might be raised by a sovereign prince. He had succeeded to his inheritance in 1468, and had very early given his support to the pretensions of Isabella. Notwithstanding his deadly feud with the Marquis of Cádiz, he had the generosity, on the breaking out of the present war, to march to the relief of the Marchioness when beleaguered, during her husband's absence, by a party of Muslims from Ronda, in her own castle of Arcos. He now showed a similar alacrity in sacrificing all personal jealousy at the call of patriotism.[15]

No sooner did he learn the perilous condition of his countrymen in Alhama, than he mustered the whole array of his household troops and retainers, which, when combined with those of the Marquis de Villena, of the Count de Cabra, and those from Sevilla, in which city the family of the Guzmáns had long exercised a sort of hereditary influence, swelled to the number of five thousand horse and forty thousand foot. The Duke of Medina Sidonia, putting himself at the head of this powerful body, set forward without delay on his expedition.

When King Ferdinand in his progress to the south had reached the little town of Adamuz, about five leagues from Córdoba, he was informed of the advance of the Andalusian chivalry, and instantly sent instructions to the Duke to delay his march, as he intended to come in person and assume the command. But the latter, returning a respectful apology for his disobedience, represented to his master the extremities to which the besieged were already reduced, and without waiting for a reply pushed on with the utmost vigour for Alhama. The Nasrid monarch, alarmed at the approach of so powerful a reinforcement, saw himself in danger of being hemmed in between the garrison on the one side, and these new enemies on the other. Without waiting [for] their appearance on the crest of the eminence which separated him from them, he hastily broke up his encampment, on the 29th of March, after a siege of more than three weeks, and retreated on his capital.[16]

The garrison of Alhama viewed with astonishment the sudden departure of their enemies; but their wonder was converted into joy, when they beheld the bright arms and banners of their countrymen, gleaming along the declivities of the mountains. They rushed out with tumultuous transport to receive them, and pour forth their grateful acknowledgements, while the two commanders, embracing each other in the presence of their united armies, pledged themselves to a mutual oblivion of all past grievances; thus affording to the nation the best possible earnest of future successes, in the voluntary extinction of a feud, which had desolated it for so many generations.

Notwithstanding the kindly feelings excited between the two armies, a dispute had wellnigh arisen respecting the division of the spoil, in which the duke's army claimed a share, as having contributed to secure the conquest which their more fortunate countrymen had effected. But these discontents were appeased, though with some difficulty, by their noble leader, who besought his men not to tarnish the laurels already won, by mingling a sordid avarice with the generous motives which had prompted them to the expedition. After the necessary time devoted to repose and refreshment, the combined armies proceeded to evacuate Alhama, and having left in garrison Don Diego Merlo, with a corps of troops of the *hermandad*, returned into their own territories.[17]

King Ferdinand, after receiving the reply of the Duke of Medina Sidonia, had pressed forward his march by the way of Córdoba, as far as Lucena, with the intention of throwing himself at all hazards into Alhama. He was not without much difficulty dissuaded from this by his nobles, who represented the temerity of the enterprise, and its incompetency to any good result, even should he succeed, with the small force of which he was master. On receiving intelligence that the siege was raised, he returned to Córdoba, where he was joined by the Queen toward the latter part of April. Isabella had been employed in making vigorous preparation for carrying on the war, by enforcing the requisite supplies, and summoning the crown vassals, and the principal nobility of the north, to hold themselves in readiness to join the royal standard in Andalusia. After this, she proceeded by rapid stages to Córdoba, notwithstanding the state of pregnancy, in which she was then far advanced. Here the sovereigns received the unwelcome information, that the King of Granada, on the retreat of the Castilians, had again sat down before Alhama having brought with him artillery, from the want of which he had suffered so much in the preceding siege. This news struck a damp into the hearts of the Castilians, many of whom recommended the total evacuation of a place, 'which' they said, 'was so near the capital that it must be perpetually exposed to sudden and dangerous assaults, while, from the difficulty of reaching it, it would cost the Castilians an incalculable waste of blood and treasure in its defence. It was experience of these evils, which had led to its abandonment in former days, when it had been recovered by the Spanish arms from the Saracens'.

Isabella was far from being shaken by these arguments. 'Glory,' she said, 'was not to be won without danger. The present war was one of peculiar difficulties and danger, and these had been well calculated before entering upon it. The strong and central position of Alhama made it of the most importance, since it might be regarded as the key of the enemy's country. This was the first blow struck during the year, and honour and policy alike forbade them to adopt a measure, which could not fail to damp the ardour of the nation.' This opinion of the Queen, thus decisively expressed, determined the question, and kindled a spark of her own enthusiasm in the breasts of the most desponding.[18]

It was settled that the King should march to the relief of the besieged, taking with him the most ample supplies of forage and provisions, at the head of a force strong enough to compel the retreat of the Nasrid monarch. This was effected without delay; and, Abul Hacen once more breaking up his camp on the rumour of Ferdinand's approach, the latter took possession of the city without opposition, on the 14th of May. The King was attended by a splendid train of his prelates and principal nobility; and he prepared with their aid to dedicate his new conquest to the service of the cross, with all the formalities of the Romish church. After the ceremony of purification, the three principal mosques of the city were consecrated by the cardinal of Spain, as temples of Christian worship. Bells, crosses, a sumptuous service of plate, and other sacred utensils, were liberally furnished by the Queen; and the principal church of Santa Maria de la Encarnación long exhibited a covering of the altar, richly embroidered by her own hands. Isabella lost no opportunity of manifesting that she had entered into the war, less from motives of ambition than of zeal for the exaltation of the true faith. After the completion of these ceremonies,

Ferdinand, having strengthened the garrison with new recruits under the command of Portocarrero, Lord of Palma, and victualled it with three months' provisions, prepared for a foray into the vega of Granada. This he executed in the true spirit of that merciless warfare, so repugnant to the more civilized usage of later times, not only by sweeping away the green, unripened crops, but by cutting down the trees, and eradicating the vines; and then, without so much as having broken a lance in the expedition, returned in triumph to Córdoba.[19]

Isabella in the mean while was engaged in active measures for prosecuting the war. She issued orders to the various cities of Castile and León, as far as the borders of Biscay and Guipuscoa, prescribing the *repartimiento*, or subsidy of provisions, and the quota of troops, to be furnished by each district respectively, together with an adequate supply of ammunition and artillery. The whole were to be in readiness before Loja, by the 1st of July [1482]; when Ferdinand was to take the field in person at the head of his chivalry, and besiege that strong post. As advices were received, that the Spanish Muslims of Granada were making efforts to obtain the cooperation of their African brethren in support of the Islamic empire in Spain, the Queen caused a fleet to be manned under the command of her two best admirals, with instructions to sweep the Mediterranean as far as the Strait of Gibraltar, and thus effectually cut off all communication with the Barbary coast.[20]

NOTES

1. Cardonne, *Hist. d'Afrique et d'Espagne*, tom.iii, pp.467–9. – Condé, *Dominacion de los Arabes*, cap.32, 34.

   [As explained in the Preface to this work, Prescott repeats some of Condé's errors in addressing the succession of Nasrid rulers of Granada. Prescott's original text implied that Abul Hacen was the son of, and directly followed Yusuf V to the throne of Granada. Abul Hacen did succeed his father, the Sultan Sa'd, who murdered Yusuf V in 1462. Yusuf and Sa'd were among others who had interlocking and disrupted reigns during this period of the Nasrid kingdom. See note 27 to Part II of the Introduction; Arié, *L'Espagne Musulmane au Temps des Nasrides*, p.147; and Paredes, *The Book of the Alhambra*, p.58; Harvey, *Islamic Spain, 1250 to 1500*, pp.243–74. – ED]

2. Bernaldez, *Reyes Católicos*, MS. cap.31. – Condé, *Dominacion de los Arabes*, tom.iii, cap.34. – Pulgar, *Reyes Católicos*, p.180. – L. Marineo, *Cosas Memorables*, fol.171. – Marmol, *Historia del Rebelion y Castigo de los Moriscos*, (Madrid, 1797), lib.1, cap.12.

   Lebrija states, that the revenues of Granada, at the commencement of this war, amounted to a million of gold ducats, and that it kept in pay 7,000 horsemen on its peace establishment, and could send forth 21,000 warriors from its gates. The last of these estimates would not seem to be exaggerated. Rerum, *Gestarum Decades*, ii, lib.1, cap.1.

   [Arié (*L'Espagne Musulmane au Temps des Nasrides*, pp.152–3) records that the Granadan force that took Zahara on 27 December, 1481, consisted of 300 cavalry and 4,000 infantry, and was led by Ibrahim al-Hakim (Abrahen Alhaquine). – ED]

3. Estrada, *Poblacion de España*, tom. ii, pp. 247, 248. – El Nubiense, *Description de España*, p.222, nota. – Pulgar, *Reyes Católicos*, p.181. – Marmol, *Historia del Rebelion y Castigo de los Moriscos*, (Madrid, 1797), lib.1, cap.12.

4. Zuñiga, *Annales de Sevilla*, pp.349, 392. This occurred in the fight of Madroño, when Don Rodrigo stopping to adjust his buckler, which had been unlaced, was suddenly surrounded by a party of Muslims. He snatched a sling from one of them, and made such brisk use of it, that after disabling several, he succeeded in putting them to flight; for which feat, says Zuñiga, the King complimented him with the title of 'the youthful David'.

   Don Juan, Count of Arcos, had no children born in wedlock, but a numerous progeny by his concubines. Among these latter, was Doña Leonora Nuñez de Prado, the mother of Don Rodrigo. The brilliant and attractive qualities of this youth so far won the affection of his father, that the latter obtained the royal sanction (a circumstance not infrequent in an age, when the laws of descent were very unsettled) to bequeath him his titles and estates, to the prejudice of more legitimate heirs.

5. Bernaldez, *Reyes Católicos*, MS. cap.52. – L. Marineo, *Cosas Memorables*, fol.171. – Pulgar computes the marquis's army at 3,000 horse and 4,000 foot. *Reyes Católicos*, p.181. – Condé, *Dominacion de los Arabes*, tom.iii, cap.34. [Arié, *L'Espagne Musulmane au Temps des Nasrides*, p.154, records that the Marquis assembled his troops at the town of Marchena, and departed with 2,500 cavalry and 3,000 infantry to arrive in two days at Alhama the morning of 28 February 1482. – ED]

   [Prescott's reference to the 'sierras of Alzerifa' appears to apply to a mountainous region around today's towns of Zafarraya and Ventas de Zafarraya. These are just southwest of Alhama. A few maps show an unnamed river, originating in the mountains near Zafarraya, that feeds into a large lake (*La Laguna*) near the town of Sierra de Yeguas. The lake is about 50 kilometres west of Alhama. This river appears to be the Yeguas River in Prescott's description of the routes taken by the Marquis of Cádiz and his men. – ED]

6. Lebrija, *Rerum Gestarum Decades*, ii, lib.1, cap.2. – Carbajal, *Anales*, MS., año 1482. – Bernaldez, *Reyes Católicos*, MS, cap.52. – Zurita, *Anales*, tom.iv, fol.315. – Cardonne, *Hist. d'Afrique et d'Espagne*, tom.iii, pp.252, 253.

7. Bernaldez, *Reyes Católicos*, MS. *ubi supra*. – Condé, *Dominacion de los Arabes*, tom.iii, p.34. – L. Marineo, *Cosas Memorables*, fol.172.

8. Condé, *Dominacion de los Arabes, ubi supra*. – Pulgar, *Reyes Católicos*, pp.182, 183. – Mariana, *Hist. de España*, tom.ii, pp.545, 546.

9. Bernaldez, *Reyes Católicos*, MS. cap.52. – Pulgar, *Reyes Católicos, ubi sup.* – Cardonne, *Hist. d'Afrique et d'Espagne*, tom.iii, p.254.

10. *Passeavase el Rey Moro*
    Por la ciudad de Granada,
    Desde las puertas de Elvira
    Hasta las de Bivarambia.
           Ay de mi Alhama!

    Cartas le fueron venides
    Que Alhama era ganada
    Las cartas echó en el fuego,
    Y al mensagero matava.
           Ay de mi Alhama!

Hombres, niños y mugeres,
Lloran tan grande perdida.
Lloravan todas las damas
Quantas en Granada avia.
          Ay de mi Alhama!

Per las calles y ventanas
Mucho luto parecia;
Llora el Rey como fembra.
Qu'es mucho lo que perdia.
          Ay de mi Alhama!

The *romance*, according to Hyta (not the best voucher for a fact) caused such general lamentation, that it was not allowed to be sung by the Moors after the conquest. (*Guerras Civiles de Granada*, tom.i, p.350.) Lord Byron, as the reader recollects, has done this ballad into English. The version has the merit of fidelity. It is not his fault if his Muse appears to little advantage in the plebeian dress of the Moorish minstrel.

11. L. Marineo, *Cosas Memorables*, fol.172. – Condé, *Dominacion de los Arabes*, tom.iii, p.34. – Carbajal, *Annales*, MS., año 1482. – Mariana, *Hist. de España*, tom.ii, pp.545, 546.

12. Bernaldez, *Reyes Católicos*, MS. cap.52. – Bernaldez swells the Muslim army to 5,500 horse, and 80,000 foot, but I have preferred the more moderate and probable estimate of the Arabic authors. Condé, *Dominacion de los Arabes*, tom.iii, cap.34. – Pulgar, *Reyes Católicos, loc cit*. [Condé (Foster's English translation) *History of the Dominion of the Arabs in Spain*, p.346 says Abul Hacen had 3,000 cavalry and 50,000 infantry. – ED]

13. Garibay, *Compendio*, tom.ii, lib.18, cap.23. – Pulgar, *Reyes Católicos*, pp.183, 184. [Arié, *L'Espagne Musulmane au Temps des Nasrides*: p.145, reports that Abul Hacen arrived at Alhama four days after it fell, conducted his unsuccessful siege for 25 days, and departed 29 March 1482; p.155, states that the Muslims made three more unsuccessful attempts to regain Alhama during the spring and summer of 1482. – ED]

14. Bernaldez, *Reyes Católicos*, MS. cap.52.
[Part II of Prescott's *History of the Reign of Ferdinand and Isabella* (from Part I of which the text of this work is extracted) describes the later great military exploits of 'The Great Captain' Gonzalo de Córdoba in the Italian wars against Charles VIII of France. Prescott remarks about Gonzalo (p.41, Part II): 'The long war of Granada ... was the great school in which his military discipline was perfected. He did not ... occupy so eminent a position in these campaigns as some chiefs of riper years and more enlarged experience; but on various occasions he displayed uncommon proofs both of address and valour. He particularly distinguished himself at the capture of Tajara, Illora, and Monte Frio. At the last place, he headed the scaling party, and was first to mount the walls in the face of the enemy. He wellnigh closed his career in a midnight skirmish before Granada, which occurred a short time before the end of the war. In the heat of the struggle, his horse was slain; and Gonzalo, unable to extricate himself from the morass in which he was entangled, would have perished, but for a faithful servant of the family,

who mounted him on his own horse, ... Gonzalo escaped, but his brave follower
paid for his loyalty with his life.' Prescott goes on to report that Gonzalo, due to his
familiarity with Arabic, played a key role in early secret negotiations for the
capitulation of Granada. – ED]

15. Zuñiga, *Annales de Sevilla*, p.360. – L. Marineo, *Cosas Memorables*, fol.24, 172. –
    Lebrija, *Rerum Gestarum Decades*, ii, lib.1, cap.3.
16. Pulgar, *Reyes Católicos*, pp.183, 184. – Bernaldez, *Reyes Católicos*, MS. cap.53. –
    Ferreras, *Hist. d'Espagne*, tom.vii, p.572. – Zuñiga, *Annales de Sevilla*, pp.392, 393.
    – Cardonne, *Hist. d'Afrique et d'Espagne*, tom.iii, p.257.
17. Pulgar, *Reyes Católicos*, pp.183–6. – Oviedo, *Quincuagenas*, MS., bat.1, quinc.1 dial.
    28.
18. Bernaldez, *Reyes Católicos*, MS. cap.43, 54. – Pulgar states that Ferdinand took the
    more southern route of Antequera, where he received the tidings of the Moorish
    king's retreat. The discrepancy is of no great consequence; but as Bernaldez, whom
    I have followed, lived in Andalusia, the theatre of action, he may be supposed to
    have more accurate means of information. Pulgar, *Reyes Católicos*, pp.187, 188.
19. Oviedo, *Quincuagenas*, MS., bat.1, quinc 1, dial.28. – Bernaldez, *Reyes Católicos*, MS.
    cap.54, 55. – Lebrija, *Rerum Gestarum Decades*, ii, lib.1, cap.6. – Condé, *Dominacion
    de los Arabes*, cap.34. – Salazar de Mendoza, *Crón. del Gran Cardenal*, pp.180. –
    Marmol, *Historia del Rebelion y Castigo de los Moriscos*, (Madrid, 1797), lib.1, cap.12.

    During this second siege, a body of Muslim knights to the number of forty,
    succeeded in scaling the walls of the city in the night, and had nearly reached the
    gates with the intention of throwing them open to their countrymen, when they
    were overpowered after a desperate resistance, by the Christians, who acquired a
    rich booty, as many of them were persons of rank. There is considerable variation
    in the authorities, in regard to the date of Ferdinand's occupation of Alhama. I
    have been guided, as before, by Bernaldez.
20. Pulgar, *Reyes Católicos*, pp.188, 189.

CHAPTER 3

UNSUCCESSFUL ATTEMPT ON LOJA AND
DEFEAT IN THE AJARQUÍA (1482–83)

Siege of Loja. – Revolution in Granada. – Expedition to the Ajarquía. – Military Array. – Muslim Preparations. – Bloody Conflict among the Mountains. – The Castilians Force a Passage. – The Marquis of Cádiz Escapes.

Loja stands not many leagues from Alhama, on the banks of the Genil [Xenil], which rolls its clear current through a valley luxuriant with vineyards and olive-gardens; but the city is deeply entrenched among hills of so rugged an aspect, that it has been led not inappropriately to assume as the motto on its arms, 'A flower among thorns.' Under the Spanish Muslims, it was defended by a strong fortress, while the Genil, circumscribing it like a deep moat upon the south, formed an excellent rampart against the approaches of a besieging army; since the river was fordable only in one place, and traversed by a single bridge, which might be easily commanded by the city. In addition to these advantages, the king of Granada, taking warning from the fate of Alhama, had strengthened its garrison with three thousand of his choicest troops, under the command of a skilful and experienced warrior, named Ali Atar.[1]

In the mean while, the efforts of the Spanish sovereigns to procure supplies adequate to the undertaking against Loja, had not been crowned with success. The cities and districts of which the requisitions had been made, had discovered the tardiness usual in such unwieldy bodies, and their interest, moreover, was considerably impaired by their distance from the theatre of action. Ferdinand on mustering his army, toward the latter part of June [1482], found that it did not exceed four thousand horse and twelve thousand, or indeed, according to some accounts, eight thousand foot; most of them raw militia, who, poorly provided with military stores and artillery, formed a force obviously inadequate to the magnitude of his enterprise. Some of his counsellors would have persuaded him, from these considerations, to turn his arms against some weaker and more assailable point than Loja. But Ferdinand burned with a desire for distinction in

the new war, and suffered his ardour for once to get the better of his prudence.
The distrust felt by the leaders seems to have infected the lower ranks, who
drew the most unfavourable prognostics from the dejected mien of those who
bore the royal standard to the cathedral of Córdoba, in order to receive the
benediction of the church before entering on the expedition.[2]

Ferdinand, crossing the Genil at Ecija, arrived again on its banks before Loja,
on the 1st of July [1482]. The army encamped among the hills, whose deep
ravines obstructed communication between its different quarters; while the
level plains below were intersected by numerous canals, equally unfavourable to
the manoeuvres of the men-at-arms. The Duke of Villa Hermosa, the King's
brother, and Captain-General of the Hermandad, an officer of large experience,
would have persuaded Ferdinand to attempt, by throwing bridges across the
river lower down the stream, to approach the city on the other side. But his
counsel was overruled by the Castilian officers, to whom the location of the
camp had been intrusted, and who neglected, according to Zurita, to advise
with the Andalusian chiefs, although far better instructed than themselves in
Moorish warfare.[3]

A large detachment of the army was ordered to occupy a lofty eminence, at
some distance, called the Heights of Albohacen, and to fortify it with such few
pieces of ordnance as they had, with the view of annoying the city. This
commission was intrusted to the Marquises of Cádiz and Villena, and the Grand
Master of Calatrava; which last nobleman had brought to the field about four
hundred horse and a large body of infantry from the places belonging to his
order in Andalusia. Before the entrenchment could be fully completed, Ali
Atar, discerning the importance of this commanding station, made a sortie from
the town, for the purpose of dislodging his enemies. The latter poured out from
their works to encounter him; but the Muslim general, scarcely waiting to
receive the shock, wheeled his squadrons round, and began a precipitate retreat.
The Castilians eagerly pursued; but, when they had been drawn to a sufficient
distance from the redoubt, a party of Granadan *jinetes*, or light cavalry, who had
crossed the river unobserved during the night and laid in ambush, after the wily
fashion of Arabian tactics, darted from their place of concealment, and galloping into the deserted camp, plundered it of its contents, including the
lombards, or small pieces of artillery, with which it was garnished. The Castilians, too late perceiving their error, halted from the pursuit, and returned
with as much speed as possible to the defence of their camp. Ali Atar, turning
also, hung close on their rear, so that, when the Christians arrived at the summit
of the hill, they found themselves hemmed in between the two divisions of the
Muslim army. A brisk action now ensued, and lasted nearly an hour; when the
advance of reinforcements from the main body of the Castilian army, which had
been delayed by distance and impediments on the road, compelled the
Granadans to a prompt but orderly retreat into their own city. The Christians

sustained a heavy loss, particularly in the death of Rodrigo Tellez Girón, Grand Master of Calatrava. He was hit by two arrows, the last of which, penetrating the joints of his harness beneath his sword-arm, as he was in the act of raising it, inflicted on him a mortal wound, of which he expired in a few hours, says an old chronicler, after having confessed, and performed the last duties of a good and faithful Christian. Although scarcely twenty-four years of age, this cavalier had given proofs of such signal prowess, that he was esteemed one of the best knights of Castile; and his death threw a general gloom over the army.[4]

Ferdinand now became convinced of the unsuitableness of a position, which neither admitted of easy communication between the different quarters of his own camp, nor enabled him to intercept the supplies daily passing into that of his enemy. Other inconveniences also pressed on him. His men were so badly provided with the necessary utensils for dressing their food, that they were obliged either to devour it raw, or only half cooked. Most of them being new recruits, unaccustomed to the privations of war, and many exhausted by a wearisome length of march before joining the army, they began openly to murmur, and even to desert in great numbers. Ferdinand therefore resolved to fall back as far as Rio Frio, and await there patiently the arrival of such fresh reinforcements as might put him in condition to enforce a more rigorous blockade.

Orders were accordingly issued to the cavaliers occupying the Heights of Albohacen to break up their camp, and join themselves to the main body of the army. This was executed on the following morning before dawn, being the 4th of July. No sooner did the Granadans of Loja perceive their enemy abandoning his strong position, than they sallied forth in considerable force to take possession of it. Ferdinand's men, who had not been advised of the proposed manoeuvre, no sooner beheld the Muslim array brightening the crest of the mountain, and their own countrymen rapidly descending, than they imagined that these latter had been surprised in their entrenchments during the night, and were now flying before the enemy. An alarm instantly spread through the whole camp. Instead of standing to their defence, each one thought only of saving himself by as speedy a flight as possible. In vain did Ferdinand, riding along their broken files, endeavour to reanimate their spirits and restore order. He might as easily have calmed the winds, as the disorder of a panic-struck mob, unschooled by discipline or experience. Ali Atar's practised eye speedily discerned the confusion which prevailed through the Christian camp. Without delay, he rushed forth impetuously at the head of his whole array from the gates of Loja, and converted into a real danger, what had before been only an imaginary one.[5]

At this perilous moment, nothing but Ferdinand's coolness could have saved the army from total destruction. Putting himself at the head of the royal guard, and accompanied by a gallant band of cavaliers, who held honour dearer than life, he made such a determined stand against the Nasrid advance, that Ali Atar was compelled to pause in his career. A furious struggle ensued betwixt this devoted little band and the whole strength of the Muslim army. Ferdinand was repeatedly exposed to imminent peril. On one occasion he was indebted for his safety to the Marquis of Cádiz, who, charging at the head of about sixty lances, broke the deep ranks of the Nasrid column, and compelling it to recoil, succeeded in rescuing his sovereign. In this adventure, he narrowly escaped with his own life, his horse being shot under him, at the very moment when he had lost his lance in the body of a Muslim. Never did the Christian Spanish chivalry shed its blood more freely. The Constable, Count of Haro, received three wounds in the face. The Duke of Medina Celi was unhorsed and brought to the ground, and saved with difficulty by his own men; and the Count of Tendilla, whose encampment lay nearest the city, received several severe blows, and would have fallen into the hands of the enemy, had it not been for the timely aid of his friend, the young Count of Zuñiga.

The Spanish Muslims, finding it so difficult to make a impression on this iron band of warriors, began at length to slacken their effort, and finally allowed Ferdinand to draw off the remnant of his forces without further opposition. The king continued his retreat without halting, as far as the romantic site of the Peña de los Enamorados, about seven leagues distant from Loja; and, abandoning all thoughts of offensive operations for the present, soon after returned to Córdoba. Abul Hacen arrived the following day with a powerful reinforcement from Granada, and swept the country as far as Rio Frio. Had he come but a few hours sooner, there would have been few Christian Spanish cavaliers left to tell the tale of the rout of Loja.[6]

The loss of the Christians must have been very considerable, including the greater part of the baggage and the artillery. It occasioned deep mortification to the Queen; but, though a severe, it proved a salutary lesson. It showed the importance of more extensive preparations for a war, which must of necessity be a war of posts; and it taught the nation to entertain greater respect for an enemy, who, whatever might be his natural strength, must become formidable when armed with the energy of despair.

At this juncture, a division among the Spanish Muslims themselves did more for the Christians, than any successes of their own. This division grew out of the vicious system of polygamy, which sows the seeds of disorder among those, whom nature and our own happier institutions unite most closely. The old king of Granada had become so deeply enamoured of a Greek slave, that the Sultana Aysha, jealous lest the offspring of her rival [Zoraya] should supplant her own in the succession, secretly contrived to stir up a spirit of discontent with her husband's government. The King, becoming acquainted with her intrigues, caused her to be imprisoned in the fortress of the Alhambra. But the Sultana, binding together the scarfs and veils belonging to herself and attendants, succeeded, by means of this perilous conveyance, in making her escape, together with her children, from the upper apartments of the tower in which she was lodged. She was received with joy by her own faction. The insurrection soon spread among the populace, who, yielding to the impulses of nature, are readily roused by a tale of oppression; and the number was still further swelled by many of higher rank, who had various causes of disgust with the oppressive government of Abul Hacen.[7] The strong fortress of the Alhambra, however, remained faithful to him. A war now burst forth in the capital which deluged its streets with the blood of its citizens. At length the Sultana triumphed; Abul Hacen was expelled from Granada, and sought a refuge in Málaga, which, with Baza, Guadix, and some other places of importance, still adhered to him; while Granada, and by far the larger portion of the kingdom proclaimed the authority of his elder son, Abu Abdallah, or Boabdil, as he is usually called by the Castilian writers. The Spanish sovereigns viewed with no small interest these proceedings of the Muslims, who were thus wantonly fighting the battles of their enemies. All proffers of assistance on their part, however, being warily rejected by both factions, notwithstanding the mutual hatred of each other, they could only await with patience the termination of a struggle, which, whatever might be its results in other respects, could not fail to open the way for the success of their own arms.[8]

No military operations worthy of notice occurred during the remainder of the campaign, except occasional *cavalgadas* or inroads, on both sides, which, after the usual unsparing devastation, swept away whole herds of cattle, and human beings, the wretched cultivators of the soil. The quantity of booty frequently carried off on such occasions, amounting, according to the testimony of both Christians and Muslim writers, to twenty, thirty, and even fifty thousand head of cattle, shows the fruitfulness and abundant pasturage in the southern regions of the Peninsula. The loss inflicted by these terrible forays fell, eventually, most heavily on Granada, in consequence of her scant territory and insulated position, which cut her off from all foreign resources.

Toward the latter end of October [1482], the [Castilian] court passed from Córdoba to Madrid, with the intention of remaining there the ensuing winter. Madrid, it may be observed, however, was so far from being recognized as the capital of the monarchy at this time, that it was inferior to several other cities, in wealth and population, and was even less frequented than some others, as Valladolid for example, as a royal residence. On the 1st of July [1482], while the court was at Córdoba, Alfonso de Carillo died. He was the factious archbishop of Toledo who contributed more than any other to raise Isabella to the throne, and who, with the same arm, had wellnigh hurled her from it. He passed the close of his life in retirement and disgrace at his town of Alcalá de Henares, where he devoted himself to science, especially to alchemy; in which illusory pursuit he is said to have squandered his princely revenues with such prodigality, as to leave them encumbered with a heavy debt. He was succeeded in the primacy by his ancient rival, Don Pedro González de Mendoza, Cardinal of Spain; a prelate whose enlarged and sagacious views gained him deserved ascendancy in the councils of his sovereigns.[9]

The importance of their domestic concerns did not prevent Ferdinand and Isabella from giving a vigilant attention to what was passing abroad. The conflicting relations growing out of the feudal system occupied most princes, till the close of the fifteenth century, too closely at home to allow them often to turn their eyes beyond the borders of their own territories. This system was, indeed, now rapidly melting away. But Louis XI [of France (1461–83)] may perhaps be regarded as the first monarch, who showed anything like an extended interest in European politics. He informed himself of the interior proceedings of most of the neighbouring courts, by means of secret agents whom he pensioned there. Ferdinand obtained a similar result by the more honourable expedient of resident embassies, a practice, which he is said to have introduced,[10] and which, while it has greatly facilitated commercial intercourse, has served to perpetuate friendly relations between different countries, by accustoming them to settle their differences by negotiation rather than the sword.

The position of the Italian states, at this period, whose petty feuds seemed to blind them to the invasion which menaced them from the Ottoman Empire, was such as to excite a lively interest through out Christendom, and especially in Ferdinand, as Sovereign of Sicily. He succeeded, by means of his ambassadors at the papal court, in opening a negotiation between the belligerent, and in finally adjusting the terms of a general pacification, signed December 12th, 1842. The Castilian court, in consequence of its friendly mediation on this occasion, received three embassies with suitable acknowledgments, on the part of the Pope Sixtus IV, the College of Cardinals, and the city of Rome; and certain marks of distinction were conferred by his Holiness on the Castilian envoys, not enjoyed by those of any other potentate. This event is worthy of notice as the first instance of Ferdinand's interference in the politics of Italy, in which at a later period he was destined to act so prominent a part.[11]

The affairs of Navarra [Navarre] at this time, were such as to engage still more deeply the attention of the Spanish sovereigns. The crown of that kingdom had devolved, on the death of Leonora, the guilty sister of Ferdinand, on her grandchild, Francis Phœbus, whose mother, Magdeleine of France, held the reins of government during her son's minority.[12] The relationship of this princess to Louis XI, gave that monarch an absolute influence in the councils of Navarra. Louis made use of this to bring about a marriage between the young king, Francis Phœbus, and Juana 'the Beltraneja', Isabella's former competitor for the crown of Castile, notwithstanding this princess had long since taken the veil in the convent of Santa Clara at Coimbra. It is not easy to unravel the tortuous politics of King Louis. The Spanish writers impute to him the design of enabling Juana by this alliance to establish her pretensions to the Castilian throne, or at least to give such employment to its present proprietors, as should effectually prevent them from disturbing him in the possession of Rosellon [Roussillon]. However this may be, his intrigues with Portugal were disclosed to Ferdinand by certain nobles of that court, with whom he was in secret correspondence. The Spanish sovereigns, in order to counteract this scheme, offered the hand of their own daughter Juana, afterwards mother of Charles V [of the Holy Roman Empire, Carlos I of Spain], to the King of Navarra. But all negotiations relative to this matter were eventually defeated by the sudden death of this young prince, not without strong suspicions of poison. He was succeeded on the throne by his sister Catharine. Propositions were then made by Ferdinand and Isabella, for the marriage of this princess, then thirteen years of age, with their infant son Juan, heir apparent of their united monarchies.[13] Such an alliance, which would bring under one government nations corresponding in origin, language, general habits, and local interests, presented great and obvious advantages. It was however evaded by the Queen Dowager [Magdeleine], who still acted as regent, on the pretext of disparity of age in the parties. Information being soon after received that Louis XI was taking measures to make himself master of the strong places in Navarra, Isabella transferred her residence to the frontier town of Logroño, prepared to resist by arms, if necessary, the occupation of that country by her insidious and powerful neighbour. The death of the King of France, which occurred not long after, fortunately relieved the sovereigns from apprehensions of any immediate annoyance on that quarter.[14]

Amid their manifold concerns, Ferdinand and Isabella kept their thoughts anxiously bent on their great enterprise, the conquest of Granada. At a congress general of the deputies of the *hermandad*, held at Pinto, at the commencement of the present year, 1483, with the view of reforming certain abuses in that institution, a liberal grant was made of eight thousand men and sixteen thousand beasts of burden, for the purpose of conveying supplies to the garrison in Alhama. But the sovereigns experienced great embarrassment from the want of funds. There is probably no period in which the princes of Europe felt so sensibly their own penury, as at the close of the fifteenth century; when, the demesnes of the crown having been very generally wasted by the lavishness or imbecility of its proprietors, no substitute had as yet been found in that searching and well-arranged system of taxation, which prevails at the present day. The Spanish sovereigns, notwithstanding the economy which they had introduced into the finances, felt the pressure of these embarrassments, peculiarly, at the present juncture. The maintenance of the royal guard and of the vast national police of the *hermandad*, the incessant military operations of the late campaign, together with the equipment of a navy not merely for war, but for maritime discovery, were so many copious drains of the exchequer.[15] Under these circumstances, they obtained from the pope a grant of one hundred thousand ducats, to be raised out of the ecclesiastical revenues in Castile and Aragón. A bull of crusade was also published by his Holiness, containing numerous indulgences for such as should bear arms against the infidel, as well as those who should prefer to commute their military service for the payment of a sum of money. In addition to these resources, the government was enabled on its own credit, justified by the punctuality with which it had redeemed its past engagements, to negotiate considerable loans with wealthy individuals.[16]

With these funds the sovereigns entered into extensive arrangements for the ensuing campaign; causing cannon, after the rude construction of that age, to be fabricated at Huesca, and a large quantity of stone balls, then principally used, to be manufactured in the Sierra de Constantina; while the magazines were carefully provided with ammunition and military stores.

An event not unworthy of notice is recorded by Pulgar, as happening about this time. A common soldier, named Juan de Corral, contrived under false pretences, to obtain from the King of Granada a number of Christian captives, together with a large sum of money, with which he escaped into Andalusia. The man was apprehended by the warden of the frontier of Jaén; and, the transaction being reported to the sovereigns, they compelled an entire restitution of the money, and consented to such a ransom for the liberated Christians as the king of Granada should demand. This act of justice, it should be remembered, occurred in an age when the church itself stood ready to sanction any breach of faith, however glaring, toward heretics and infidels.[17]

While the court was detained in the north, tidings were received of a reverse sustained by the Spanish arms, which plunged the nation in sorrow far deeper than that occasioned by the rout at Loja. Don Alonso de Cárdenas, Grand Master of Santiago [St. James], an old and confidential servant of the crown, had been intrusted with the defence of the frontier of Ecija. While on this station, he was strongly urged to make a descent on the environs of Málaga, by his *adalides* or scouts, men who, being for the most part Moorish deserters, *renegadoes*, were employed by the border chiefs to reconnoitre the enemy's country, or to guide them in their marauding expeditions.[18] The district around Málaga was famous under the Muslims for its silk manufactures, of which it annually made large exports to other parts of Europe. It was to be approached by traversing a savage sierra, or chain of mountains, called the Ajarquía [Axarquía], whose margin occasionally afforded good pasturage, and was sprinkled over with Moorish villages. After threading its defiles, it was proposed to return by an open road that turned the southern extremity of the sierra along the sea-shore. There was little to be apprehended, it was stated, from pursuit, since Málaga was almost wholly unprovided with cavalry.[19]

The Grand Master, falling in with the proposition communicated it to the principal chiefs on the borders; among others, to Don Pedro Enríquez [de Ribera], *adelantado* of Andalusia, Don Juan de Silva, Count of Cifuentes, Don Alonso de Aguilar, and the Marquis of Cádiz. These noblemen, collecting their retainers, repaired to Antequera, where the ranks were quickly swelled by recruits from Córdoba, Sevilla, Jerez, and other cities of Andalusia, whose chivalry always readily answered the summons to an expedition over the border.[20]

In the mean while, however, the Marquis of Cádiz had received such intelligence from his own *adalides*, as led him to doubt the expediency of a march through intricate defiles, inhabited by a poor and hardy peasantry; and he strongly advised to direct the expedition against the neighbouring town of Almojia. But in this he was overruled by the Grand Master and the other partners of his enterprise; many of whom, with the rash confidence of youth, were excited rather than intimidated by the prospect of danger.

On Wednesday, the 19th of March, this gallant little army marched forth from the gates of Antequera. The van was intrusted to the *adelantado* Enríquez and Don Alonso de Aguilar. The centre divisions were led by the Marquis of Cádiz, and the Count of Cifuentes, and the rear-guard, by the Grand Master of Santiago. The number of foot, which is uncertain, appears to have been considerably less than that of the horse, which amounted to about three thousand, containing the flower of Andalusian knighthood, together with the array of Santiago, the most opulent and powerful of the Christian Spanish military orders. Never, says an Aragonese historian, had there been seen in these times a more splendid body of chivalry; and such was their confidence, he adds, that they deemed themselves invincible by any force which the Muslims could bring against them. The leaders took care not to encumber the movements of the army with artillery, camp equipage, or even much forage and provisions, for which they trusted to the invaded territory. A number of persons, however, followed in the train, who, influenced by desire rather of gain than of glory, had come provided with money, as well as commissions from their friends, for the purchase of rich spoil, whether of slaves, stuffs, or jewels, which they expected would be won by the good swords of their comrades, as in Alhama.[21]

After travelling with little intermission through the night, the army entered the winding defiles of the Ajarquía; where their progress was necessarily so much impeded by the character of the ground, that most of the inhabitants of the villages, through which they passed, had opportunity to escape with the greater part of their effects to the inaccessible fastnesses of the mountains. The Christian Spaniards, after plundering the deserted hamlets of whatever remained, as well as of the few stragglers, whether men or cattle, found still lingering about them, set them on fire. In this way they advanced, marking their line of march with the usual devastation that accompanied these ferocious forays, until the columns of smoke and fire, which rose above the hill-tops, announced to the people of Málaga the near approach of an enemy.

The old king Abul Hacen, who lay at this time in the city, with a numerous and well-appointed body of horse, contrary to the reports of the *adalides*, would have rushed forth at once at their head, had he not been dissuaded from it by his younger brother Abdallah [Muhammad XIII], who is better known in history by the name of al-Zagal, or 'the Valiant', an Arabic epithet, given to him by his countrymen to distinguish him from his nephew, the ruling King of Granada [al-Zagal is also known as 'the Lad']. To this prince Abul Hacen intrusted the command of the corps of picked cavalry, with instructions to penetrate at once into the lower level of the sierra, and encounter the Christians entangled in its passes; while another division, consisting chiefly of arquebusiers and archers, should turn the enemy's flank by gaining the heights under which he was defiling. This last corps was placed under the direction of Reduan Benegas, a chief of Christian lineage, according to Bernaldez, and who may perhaps be identified with the Reduan, that, in the later Moorish ballads, seems to be shadowed forth as the personification of love and heroism.[22]

The Castilian army in the mean time went forward with a buoyant and reckless confidence, and with very little subordination. The divisions occupying the advance and centre, disappointed in their expectations of booty, had quitted the line of march, and dispersed in small parties in search of plunder over the adjacent country; and some of the high-mettled young cavaliers had the audacity to ride up in defiance to the very walls of Málaga. The Grand Master of Santiago was the only leader who kept his columns unbroken, and marched forward in order of battle. Things were in this state, when the Spanish Muslim cavalry under al-Zagal, suddenly emerging from one of the mountain passes, appeared before the astonished rear-guard of the Christians. The Muslims spurred on to the assault, but the well disciplined chivalry of Santiago remained unshaken. In the fierce struggle which ensued, the Andalusians became embarrassed by the narrowness of the ground on which they were engaged, which afforded no scope for the manoeuvres of cavalry; while the Muslims, trained to the wild tactics of mountain warfare, went through their usual evolutions, retreating and returning to the charge, with a celerity, that sorely distressed their opponents and at length threw them into some disorder. The Grand Master in consequence despatched a message to the marquis of Cádiz, requesting his support. The latter, putting himself at the head of such of his scattered forces as he could hastily muster, readily obeyed the summons. Discerning on his approach the real source of the Grand Master's embarrassment, he succeeded in changing the field of action by drawing off the Granadans to an open reach of the valley, which allowed free play to the movements of the Andalusian horse, when the combined squadrons pressed so hard on the Muslims, that they were soon compelled to take refuge within the depths of their own mountains.[23]

In the mean while, the scattered troops of the advance, alarmed by the report of the action, gradually assembled under their respective banners, and fell back upon the rear. A council of war was then called. All further progress seemed to be effectually intercepted. The country was everywhere in arms. The most that could now be hoped, was that they might be suffered to retire unmolested with such plunder as they had already acquired. Two routes lay open for this purpose. The one winding along the sea-shore, wide and level but circuitous, and swept through the whole range of its narrow entrance by the fortress of Málaga. This determined them unhappily to prefer the other route, being that by which they had penetrated the Ajarquía, or rather a shorter cut, by which the *adalides* undertook to conduct them through its mazes.[24]

The little army commenced its retrograde movement with undiminished spirit. But it was now embarrassed with the transportation of its plunder, and by the increasing difficulties of the sierra, which, as they ascended its sides, was matted over with impenetrable thickets, and broken up by formidable ravines or channels, cut deep into the soil by the mountain torrents. The Spanish Muslims were now seen mustering in considerable numbers along the heights, and, as they were expert marksmen, being trained by early and assiduous practice, the shots from their arquebuses and cross-bows frequently found some assailable point in the harness of the Spanish Christian men-at-arms. At length, the army, through the treachery or ignorance of the guides, was suddenly brought to a halt by arriving in a deep glen or enclosure, whose rocky sides rose with such boldness as to be scarcely practicable for infantry, much less for horse. To add to their distresses, daylight, without which they could scarcely hope to extricate themselves, was fast fading away.[25]

In this extremity no other alternative seemed to remain, than to attempt to regain the route from which they had departed. As all other considerations were now subordinate to those of personal safety, it was agreed to abandon the spoil acquired at so much hazard, which greatly retarded their movements. As they painfully retraced their steps, the darkness of the night was partially dispelled by numerous fires, which blazed along the hill-tops, and which showed the figures of their enemies flitting to and fro like so many spectres. It seemed, says Bernaldez, as if ten thousand torches were glancing along the mountains. At length, the whole body, faint with fatigue and hunger, reached the borders of a little stream, which flowed through a valley, whose avenues, as well as the rugged heights by which it was commanded, were already occupied by the enemy, who poured down mingled volleys of shot, stones, and arrows on the heads of the Christians. The compact mass presented by the latter afforded a sure mark to the artillery of the Nasrids; while they, from their scattered position, as well as from the defences afforded by the nature of the ground, were exposed to little annoyance in return. In addition to lighter missiles, the Spanish Muslims occasionally dislodged large fragments of rock, which, rolling with tremendous violence down the declivities of the hills, spread frightful desolation through the Christian ranks.[26]

The dismay occasioned by these scenes, occurring amidst the darkness of night, and heightened by the shrill war-cries of the Muslims, which rose around them on every quarter, seems to have completely bewildered the Christian Spanish, even their leaders. It was the misfortune of the expedition, that there was but little concert between the several commanders, or, at least, that there was no one so preeminent above the rest as to assume authority at this awful moment. So far, it would seem, from attempting escape, they continued in their perilous position, uncertain what course to take, until midnight; when at length, after having seen their best and bravest followers fall thick around them, they determined at all hazards to force a passage across the sierra in the face of the enemy. 'Better lose our lives,' said the Grand Master of Santiago, addressing his men, 'in cutting a way through the foe, than be butchered without resistance, like cattle in the shambles.'[27]

The Marquis of Cádiz, guided by a trusty *adalid*, and accompanied by sixty or seventy lances, was fortunate enough to gain a circuitous route less vigilantly guarded by the enemy, whose attention was drawn to the movements of the main body of the Castilian army. By means of this path, the marquis with his little band succeeded, after a painful march, in which his good steed sunk under him oppressed with wounds and fatigue, in reaching a valley at some distance from the scene of action, where he determined to wait the coming up of his friends, who he confidently expected would follow on his track.[28]

But the Grand Master and his associates, missing this track in the darkness of the night, or perhaps preferring another, breasted the sierra in a part where it proved difficult of ascent. At every step the loosened earth gave way under the pressure of the foot, and, the infantry endeavouring to support themselves by clinging to the tails and manes of the horses, the jaded animals borne down with the weight, rolled headlong with their riders on the ranks below, or were precipitated down the sides of the numerous ravines. The Spanish Muslims, all the while, avoiding a close encounter, contented themselves with discharging on the heads of their opponents an un-intermitted shower of missiles of every description.[29]

It was not until the following morning, that the Castilians having sur-mounted the crest of the eminence, began the descent into the opposite valley, which they had the mortification to observe was commanded on every point by their vigilant adversary, who seemed now in their eyes to possess the powers of ubiquity. As the light broke upon the troops, it revealed the whole extent of their melancholy condition. How different from the magnificent array which, but two days previous, marched forth with such high and confident hopes from the gates of Antequera! Their ranks {were now] thinned, their bright arms defaced and broken, their banners rent in pieces, or lost – as had been that of St.

James, together with its gallant *alferez*, Diego Becerra, in the terrible passage of
the preceding night – their countenances aghast with terror, fatigue, and
famine. Despair now was in every eye, all subordination was at an end. No one,
says Pulgar, heeded any longer the call of the trumpet, or the wave of the
banner. Each sought only his own safety, without regard to his comrade. Some
threw away their arms; hoping by this means to facilitate their escape, while in
fact it only left them more defenceless against the shafts of their enemies. Some,
oppressed with fatigue and terror, fell down and died without so much as
receiving a wound. The panic was such, that, in more than one instance, two or
three Muslim soldiers were known to capture thrice their own number of
Christians. Some, losing their way, strayed back to Málaga and were made
prisoners by females of the City, who overtook them in the fields. Others
escaped to Alhama or other distant places, after wandering seven or eight days
among the mountains, sustaining life on such wild herbs and berries as they
could find, and lying close during the day. A greater number succeeded in
reaching Antequera, and, among these, most of the leaders of the expedition.
The Grand Master of Santiago, the *adelantado* Enríquez, and Don Alonso de
Aguilar effected their escape by scaling so perilous a part of the sierra that their
pursuers cared not to follow. The Count de Cifuentes was less fortunate.[30] That
nobleman's division was said to have suffered more severely than any other. On
the morning after the bloody passage of the mountain, he found himself
suddenly cut off from his followers, and surrounded by six Muslim cavaliers,
against whom he was defending himself with desperate courage, when their
leader, Reduan Benegas, struck with the inequality of the combat, broke in,
exclaiming, 'Hold, this is unworthy of good knights.' The assailants sunk back
abashed by the rebuke, and left the count to their commander. A close
encounter then took place between the two chiefs; but the strength of the
Castilian was no longer equal to his spirit, and, after a brief resistance, he was
forced to surrender to his generous enemy.[31]

The Marquis of Cádiz had better fortune. After waiting till dawn for the
coming up of his friends, he concluded that they had extricated themselves by a
different route. He resolved to provide for his own safety and that of his followers, and, being supplied with a fresh horse, accomplished his escape, after
traversing the wildest passages of the Ajarquía for the distance of four leagues,
and got into Antequera with but little interruption from the enemy. But,
although he secured his personal safety, the misfortunes of the day fell heavily
on his house; for two of his brothers were cut down by his side, and a third
brother, with a nephew, fell into the hands of the enemy.[32]

The amount of slain in the two days' actions, is admitted by the Spanish
Christian writers to have exceeded eight hundred, with double that number of
prisoners. The Spanish Muslim force is said to have been small, and its loss
comparatively trifling. The numerical estimates of the Spanish historians, as

usual, appear extremely loose; and the narrative of their enemies is too meagre in this portion of their annals, to allow any opportunity of verification. There is no reason, however, to believe them in any degree exaggerated.

The best blood of Andalusia was shed on this occasion. Among the slain, Bernaldez reckons two hundred and fifty, and Pulgar four hundred persons of quality, with thirty commanders of the military fraternity of Santiago. There was scarcely a family in the south, but had to mourn the loss of some one of its members by death or captivity; and the distress was not a little aggravated by the uncertainty which hung over the fate of the absent, as to whether they had fallen in the field, or were still wandering in the wilderness, or were pining away existence in the dungeons of Málaga Granada.[33]

Some imputed the failure of the expedition to treachery in the *adalides*, some to want of concert among the commanders. The worthy Curate of Los Palacios concludes his narrative of the disaster in the following manner: 'The number of the Moors was small, who inflicted this grievous defeat on the Christians. It was, indeed, clearly miraculous, and we may discern in it the special inter-position of Providence, justly offended with the greater part of those that engaged in the expedition; who, instead of confessing, partaking the sacrament, and making their testaments, as becomes good Christians, and men that are to bear arms in defence of the Holy Catholic Faith, acknowledged that they did not bring with them suitable dispositions, but, with little regard to God's service, were influenced by covetousness and love of ungodly gain.'[34]

NOTES

1. Estrada, *Poblacion de España*, tom.ii, pp.242, 243. – Zurita, *Anales*, tom.iv, fol.317. – Cardonne, *Hist. d'Afrique et d'Espagne*, tom.iii, p.261.

2. Bernaldez, *Reyes Católicos*, MS. cap. 58. – Mariana, *Hist. de España*, tom.ii, pp.249, 250. – Cardonne, *Hist. d'Afrique et d'Espagne*, tom.iii, pp.259, 260.

3. L. Marineo, *Cosas Memorables*, fol.173. – Pulgar, *Reyes Católicos*, p.187. – Zurita, *Anales*, tom.iv, fol.316, 317.

4. Rades y Andrada, *Las Tres Ordenes*, fol.80, 81. – L. Marineo, *Cosas Memorables*, fol.173. – Lebrija, *Rerum Gestarum Decades*, ii, lib.1, cap.7. – Condé, *Dominacion de los Arabes*, tom.iii, p.214. – Carbajal, *Annales*, MS., año 1482.

5. Pulgar, *Reyes Católicos*, pp.189–91. – Bernaldez, *Reyes Católicos*, MS. cap.58. – Condé, *Dominacion de los Arabes*, tom.iii, pp.214–17. – Cardonne, *Hist. d'Afrique et d'Espagne*, tom.iii, pp.260, 261.

6. Bernaldez, *Reyes Católicos*, MS. cap.58. – Condé, *Dominacion de los Arabes*, tom.iii, pp.214– 17. – Pulgar, *Reyes Católicos, ubi supra.* – Lebrija, *Rerum Gestarum Decades*, ii, lib.1, cap.7. – The *Peña de los Enamorados* received its name from a tragic incident in Moorish history. A Christian slave succeeded in inspiring the daughter of his master, a wealthy Muslim of Granada, with a passion for himself. The two lovers, after some time, fearful of the detection of their intrigue, resolved to make their escape into the Spanish territory. Before they could effect their purpose, however, they were hotly pursued by the damsel's father at the head of a party of Moorish

horsemen, and overtaken near a precipice which rises between Archidona and Antequera. The unfortunate fugitives, who had scrambled to the summit of the rocks, finding all further escape impracticable, after tenderly embracing each other, threw themselves headlong from the dizzy heights, preferring this dreadful death to falling into the hands of their vindictive pursuers. The spot consecrated as the scene of this tragic incident has received the name of *Rock of the Lovers*. The legend is prettily told by Mariana (*Hist. de España*, tom.ii, pp.253, 254), who concludes with the pithy reflection that 'such constancy would have been truly admirable had it been shown in defence of the truth faith, rather than in the gratification of lawless appetite'.

7. Condé, *Dominacion de los Arabes*, tom.iii, pp.214–17. – Cardonne, *Hist. d'Afrique et d'Espagne*, tom.iii, pp.262–3. – Marmol, *Historia del Rebelion y Castigo de los Moriscos*, (Madrid, 1797), lib.1, cap.12. – Bernaldez states that great umbrage was taken at the influence which the king of Granada allowed a person of Christian lineage, named Vanegas, to exercise over him. Pulgar hints at the bloody massacre of the Abencerrajes, which, without any better authority that I know of, forms the burden of many an ancient ballad, and had lost nothing of its romantic colouring under the hand of Ginés Perez de Hyta.

[The name of the favourite wife (or concubine) was Zoraya. It was not Aisha (Ayesha, Ayxa), as some state, like Prescott, who relied on Condé's translations. Prescott's original text switched the names of these women in Abul Hacen's harem. The names have been corrected in this work: Aisha was Boabdil's mother and adversary of Zoraya.

The inner-harem and political intrigues of this event appear to be supported mainly by romantic accounts. Washington Irving's narrative of the conquest of Granada explains the participants more clearly than Prescott introduces them. To paraphrase Washington Irving: During a foray into Christian territories, the younger daughter of a noble, Sancho Jimenes [Ximenes] de Solis, was captured by the Muslims. Brought to Granada, the young girl was raised and educated in the Muslim faith and given the name of Fatima. As she grew to be an attractive woman, she was given the surname of Zoraya, or 'Morning Star'. Sultan Abul Hacen took her as a wife. Zoraya's favour with the Sultan was resented by his noble-born wife, Aisha (also: Ayesha or Ayxa) la Horra. Some writers refer to Aisha as Fatima, a common name, and one which was initially even given to the young girl Zoraya. Aisha was the daughter of an earlier Nasrid sultan, Muhammad IX, and widow of Sultan Muhammad XI before becoming Abul Hacen's wife. Her family's Arab lineage provided her considerable prestige. Aisha was the mother of the principal heir to the Granadan throne, Abu Abdallah (commonly referred to as Boabdil). Boabdil became Muhammad XII, the last Nasrid sultan.

Legend states that astrologers predicted, at the time of his birth, that Boabdil would one day assume the throne, and that he would also bring the downfall of the kingdom. He was not well favoured by his father and became a target of the ambitious Zoraya, who conspired with the chief advisor to Abul Hacen (Abul Cacem Vanegas) to have one of her two sons be designated heir to the sultanate. Vanegas, like Zoraya, was a captured Christian infant who rose to become a most influential Muslim in Granada. A powerful, traditional faction in Granada, the Abencerrajes, resented Hacen's reliance on both Vanegas and Zoraya. The

Abencerrajes conspired to have Boabdil replace his father on the throne of Granada. Abul Hacen, alerted of the plot, had Aisha and her sons confined to a tower. However, Aisha arranged for them to escape and flee to the town of Guadix. See Irving's *The Chronicle of the Conquest of Granada*, vol.I, pp.18–21, 29–30. – ED]

8. Cardonne, *Hist. d'Afrique et d'Espagne, ubi supra.* – Condé, *Dominacion de los Arabes, ubi supra.*

  Boabdil was surnamed '*el Chico*', '*the Little*', by the Spanish writers, to distinguish him from an uncle of the same name; and '*el Zogoybi*', '*the Unfortunate*', by the Moors, indicating that he was the last of his race to wear the diadem of Granada. The Muslims, with great felicity, frequently select names significant of some quality in the objects they represent. Examples of this may be readily found in the southern regions of the Peninsula, where the Spanish Muslims lingered the longest. The etymology of *Gibraltar Tarik*, is well known. Thus, Algeciras comes from an Arabic word which signifies an island; Alpujarras comes from a term signifying *herbage* or *pasturage*; Arrecife from another, signifying *causeway* or *high road*, etc. The Arabic word *wad* stands for *river*. This without much violence has been changed into *quad*, and enters into the names of many of the southern streams; for example, Guadalquivir, *great river*, Guadiana, *narrow* or *little river*, Guadalete, etc. In the same manner the term Medina, Arabic, 'city', has been retained as a prefix to the names of many of the Spanish towns as Medina Celi, Medina del Campo, etc. See Condé's notes to El Nubiense, *Descripcion de España*, passim.

9. Salazar de Mendoza, *Crón. del Gran Cardenal*, p.181. – Pulgar, *Claros Varonnes*, tit.20. – Carbajal. *Annales*, MS., *año* 1483. – Aleson, *Annales de Navarra*, tom.v, p.11, ed.1766. – Peter Martyr, *Opus Epist*, epist. 158.

10. Fred. Marslaar, *De Leg.*2, 11. – M. de Wicquefort derives the word *ambassadeur* (anciently in English *embassador*) from the Spanish word *embiar*, 'to send'. See Rights of Embassadors, translated by Digby, (London, 1740) book 1, chap 1.

11. Sismondi, *Républiques Italiennes*, tom.xi, cap.88. – Pulgar, *Reyes Católicos*, pp.195–8. – Zurita, *Anales*, tom.iv, fol.218.

12. Aleson, *Annales de Navarra*, lib.34, cap.1. – *Histoire du Royaume de Navarre*, p.558.

  Leonora's son, Gaston de Foix, Prince of Viana, was slain by an accidental wound from a lance, at a tourney at Lisbon, in 1469. By the Princess Magdeleine, his wife, sister of Louis XI, he left two children, a son and daughter, each of whom in turn succeeded to the crown of Navarra. Francis Phœbus ascended the throne on the demise of his grandmother Leonora [de Foix], in 1479. He was distinguished by his personal graces and beauty, and especially by the golden lustre of his hair from which, according to Aleson, he derived his cognomen of Phœbus. As it was an ancestral name, however, such an etymology may be thought somewhat fanciful.

13. Ferdinand and Isabella had at this time four children; the infant Don Juan, four years and a half old, but who did not live to come to the succession, and the Infantas Isabella, Juana, and Maria; the last born at Córdoba during the summer of 1482. [Catherine, future Queen of Henry VIII of England, was born in 1485. – ED]

14. Aleson, *Annales de Navarra*, lib.34, cap.2; lib.35, cap.1. – *Histoire du Royaume de Navarre*, pp.578, 579. – La Clède, *Hist. de Portugal*. tom.iii, pp.438–41. – Pulgar, *Reyes Católicos*, p.199. – Mariana, *Hist. de España*, tom.ii, p.551.

15. Lebrija, *Rerum Gestarum Decades*, ii, lib.2, cap.1.

Besides the armada in the Mediterranean, a fleet under Pedro de Vera was prosecuting a voyage of discovery and conquest to the Canaries at this time.

16. Pulgar, *Reyes Católicos*, p.199. – Mariana, *Hist. de España*, tom.ii, p.551. – Coleccion de Cédulas y Otros Documentos, (Madrid, 1829) tom.iii, no.25.

For this important collection, a few copies of which, only, were printed for distribution, at the expense of the Spanish government, I am indebted to the politeness of Don A. Calderon de la Barca.

17. Bernaldez, *Reyes Católicos*, MS. cap.58. – Pulgar, *Reyes Católicos*, p.202.

Juan de Corral imposed on the king of Granada by means of certain credentials, which he had obtained from the Spanish Sovereigns without any privity on their part to his fraudulent intentions. The story is told in a very blind manner by Pulgar.

It may not be amiss to mention here a doughty feat performed by another Castilian envoy, of much higher rank, Don Juan de Vera. This knight, while conversing with certain Moorish cavaliers in the Alhambra, was so much scandalized by the freedom with which one of them treated the immaculate conception, that he gave the circumcised dog the lie, and smote him a sharp blow on the head with his sword. Ferdinand, says Bernaldez, who tells the story, was much gratified with the exploit, and recompensed the good knight with many honours.

18. The *adalid* was a guide, or scout whose business it was to make himself acquainted with the enemy's country, and to guide invaders into it. Much dispute has arisen respecting the authority and functions of this officer. Some writers regard him as an independent leader, or commander; and the Dictionary of the Academy defines the term *adalid* by these very words. The State Partidas, however, explain at length the peculiar duties of this officer, conformably to the account I have given. [Ed. de la Real Acad (Madrid, 1807) part 2, tit 2, leyes 1–4.] Bernaldez, Pulgar, and the other chroniclers of the Granadan war, repeatedly notice him in this connection. When he is spoken of as a captain, or leader, as he sometimes is in these and other ancient records, his authority, I suspect, is intended to be limited to the persons, who aided him in the execution of his peculiar office. – It was common for the great chiefs, who lived on the borders, to maintain in their pay a number of these *adalides*, to inform them of the fitting time and place for making a foray. The post, as may well be believed, was one of great trust and personal hazard.

19. Pulgar, *Reyes Católicos*, p.206. – L. Marineo, *Cosas Memorables*, fol.173. – Zurita, *Anales*, tom.iv, fol.320.

20. Oviedo, *Quincuagenas*, MS, bat. 1, quinc. 1, dial. 36. – Lebrija, *Rerum Gestarum Decades*, ii, lib.1, cap.2.

The title of *adelantado* implies in its etymology one preferred or placed before others. The office is of great antiquity; some have derived it from the reign of St. Ferdinand in the thirteenth century, but Mendoza proves its existence at a far earlier period. The *adelantado* was possessed of very extensive judicial authority in the province or district in which he presided, and in war was invested with supreme military command. His functions, however, as well as the territories over which he ruled, have varied at different periods. An *adelantado* seems to have been generally established over a border province, as Andalusia for example. Marina discusses the civil authority of this officer, in his *Teoria*, tom.ii, cap.23. See also Salazar de Mendoza, *Dignidades*, lib.2, cap.15.

21. Bernaldez, *Reyes Católicos*, MS. cap.60. – Rades y Andrada, *Las Tres Ordenes*, fol.71. – Zurita, *Anales*, tom.iv, fol.320. – Zuñiga, *Annales de Sevilla*, pp.395. – Lebrija, *Rerum Gestarum Decades*, ii, lib.1, cap.2. – Oviedo, *Quincuagenas*, MS., bat.1, quinc.1 dial.36.

22. Condé, *Dominacion de los Arabes*, tom.iii, p.217. – Cardonne, *Hist. d'Afrique et d'Espagne*, tom.iii, pp.265–7. – Bernaldez, *Reyes Católicos*, MS, cap.60.

23. Condé, *Dominacion de los Arabes*, tom.iii, p.217. – Pulgar, *Reyes Católicos*, p.204. – Rades y Andrada, *Las Tres Ordenes*, fol.71, 72.

24. Mariana, *Hist. de España*, tom.ii, pp.552, 553. – Pulgar, *Reyes Católicos*, p.205. – Zurita, *Anales*, tom.iv, fol.321.

25. Pulgar, *Reyes Católicos*, p.205. – Garibay, *Compendio*, tom.ii, p.636.

26. Bernaldez, *Reyes Católicos*, MS. cap. 60. – Pulgar, *Reyes Católicos, ubi supra.* – Cardonne, *Hist. d'Afrique et d'Espagne*, tom.iii, pp.264–7.

27. Pulgar, *Reyes Católicos*, p.206. – Rades y Andrada, *Las Tres Ordenes*, fol.71, 72.

28. Pulgar, *Reyes Católicos, loc. cit.* – Bernaldez, *Reyes Católicos*, MS. cap.60.

29. Pulgar, *Reyes Católicos*, p.206.
    Mr. Irving, in his *Conquest of Granada*, states that the scene of greatest slaughter in this rout is still known to the inhabitants of the Ajarquia by the name of *La Cuesta de la Matanza*, or 'the hill of the Massacre'.

30. Oviedo, who devotes one of his dialogues to this nobleman, says of him, '*Fue una de las buenas lanzas de nuestra España en su tiempo; y muy sabio y prudente caballero. Hallose en grandes cargos y negicios de paz y de guerra.*' *Quincuagenas*, MS, bat.1, quinc.1, dial.36.

31. Condé, *Dominacion de los Arabes*, tom.iii, p.218. – Zurita, *Anales*, tom.iv, fol.321. – Carbajal, *Annales*, MS, año 1483. – Pulgar, *Reyes Católicos, ubi supra.* – Bernaldez, *Reyes Católicos*, MS. cap.60. – Cardonne, *Hist. d'Afrique et d'Espagne*, tom.iii, pp.266, 267. – The count, according to Oviedo, remained a long while a prisoner in Granada, until he was ransomed by payment of several thousand doblas of gold. *Quincuagenas*, MS, bat.1, quinc.1, dial.36.

32. Bernaldez, *Reyes Católicos*, MS, cap. 60. – Marmol says that three brothers and two nephews of the marquis, whose names he gives, were all slain, *Rebelion de Moriscos*, lib.1, cap.12

33. Zuñiga, *Annales de Sevilla*, fol.395. – Bernaldez, *Reyes Católicos*, MS., *ubi supra.* – Pulgar, *Reyes Católicos*, p.206. – Oviedo, *Quincuagenas*, MS., bat.1, quinc.1, dial.36. – Marmol, *Rebelion de Moriscos*, lib.1, cap.12.

34. *Reyes Católicos*, MS., cap.60.
    Pulgar had devoted a large space to the unfortunate expedition to the Ajarquía. His intimacy with the principal persons of the court, enable him, no doubt, to verify most of the particulars which he records. The Curate of Los Palacios, from the proximity of his residence to the theatre of action, may be supposed also to have had ample means for obtaining the requisite information. Yet their several accounts, although not strictly contradictory, are not always easy to reconcile with one another. The narratives of complex military operations are not likely to be simplified under the hands of monkish bookmen. I have endeavoured to make out a connected tissue from comparison of the Muslim with the Castilian authorities. But here the meagreness of the Muslim annals compels us to lament the premature death of Condé. It can hardly be expected, indeed, that the Moors should have

dwelt with much amplification on this humiliating period. But there can be little doubt that far more copious memorials of theirs, than any now published, exist in the Spanish libraries; and it were much to be wished that some oriental scholar would supply Condé's deficiency, by exploring these authentic records of what may be deemed, as far as Christian Spain is concerned, the most glorious portion of her history.

CHAPTER 4

GENERAL VIEW OF THE POLICY PURSUED IN THE CONDUCT OF THIS WAR (1483–87)

Defeat and Capture of Boabdil. – Policy of the Sovereigns. – Large Trains of Artillery. – Description of the Pieces. – Stupendous Roads. – Isabella's Care of the Troops. – Her Perseverance. – Discipline of the Army. – Swiss Mercenaries. – The English 'Lord Scales'. – Magnificence of the Nobles. – Isabella visits the Camp. – Ceremonies on the Occupation of a City.

The young monarch, Boabdil [Abu Abdallah, Muhammad XII], was probably the only person in Granada, who did not receive with unmingled satisfaction the tidings of the rout in the Ajarquía. He beheld with secret uneasiness the laurels thus acquired by the old king his father, or rather by his ambitious uncle al-Zagal [Muhammad XIII], whose name now resounded from every quarter as the successful champion of the Muslims. He saw the necessity of some dazzling enterprise, if he were to maintain an ascendancy even over the faction which had seated him on the throne. He accordingly projected an excursion, which instead of terminating in a mere border foray should lead to the achievement of some permanent conquest.

He found no difficulty, while the spirits of his people were roused, in raising a force of nine thousand foot, and seven hundred horse, the flower of Granada's chivalry. He strengthened his army still further by the presence of Ali Atar, the defender of Loja, the veteran of a hundred battles, whose military prowess had raised him from the common file up to the highest post in the army; and whose plebeian blood had been permitted to mingle with that of royalty, by the marriage of his daughter with the young King Boabdil.

With this gallant array, the Nasrid monarch sallied forth from Granada. As he led the way through the avenue which still bears the name of the Gate of Elvira,[1] the point of his lance came in contact with the arch, and was broken. This sinister omen was followed by another more alarming. A fox, which crossed the path of the army, was seen to run through the ranks, and, notwithstanding the showers of missiles discharged at him, to make his escape unhurt. Boabdil's counsellors would have persuaded him to abandon, or at least postpone, an enterprise of such ill augury. But the king, less superstitious, or from the obstinacy with which feeble minds, when once resolved, frequently persist in their projects, rejected their advice, and pressed forward on his march.[2]

The advance of the party was not conducted so cautiously, but that it reached the ear of Don Diego Fernandez de Córdoba, *alcaide de los donzeles*, or captain of the royal pages, who commanded in the town of Lucena, which he rightly judged was to be the principal object of attack. He transmitted the intelligence to his uncle, the Count of Cabra, a nobleman of the same name with himself, who was posted at his own town of Baena, requesting his support. He used all diligence in repairing the fortifications of the City, which, although extensive and originally strong, had fallen somewhat into decay; and, having caused such of the population as were rendered helpless by age or infirmity to withdraw into the interior defences of the place, he coolly waited the approach of the enemy.[3]

The Muslim army, after crossing the borders, began to mark its career through the Christian territory with the usual traces of devastation, and, sweeping across the environs of Lucena, poured a marauding foray into the rich *campina* of Córdoba, as far as the walls of Aguilar; whence it returned, glutted with spoil, to lay siege to Lucena about the 21st of April [1483].

The Count of Cabra, in the meanwhile, who had lost no time in mustering his levies, set forward at the head of a small but well-appointed force, consisting of both horse and foot, to the relief of his nephew. He advanced with such celerity that he had well nigh surprised the beleaguering army. As he traversed the sierra, which covered the Muslims' flank, his numbers were partially concealed by the inequalities of the ground; while the clash of arms and the shrill music, reverberating among the hills, exaggerated their real magnitude in the apprehension of the enemy. At the same time the *alcaide de los donzeles* supported his uncle's advance by a vigorous sally from the city. The Granadan infantry, anxious only for the preservation of their valuable booty, scarcely waited for the encounter, before they began a dastardly retreat, and left the battle to the cavalry. The latter, composed, as has been said, of the strength of the Muslim chivalry, men accustomed in many a border foray to cross lances with the best knights of Andalusia, kept their ground with their wonted gallantry. The conflict, so well disputed, remained doubtful for some time, until it was determined by the death of the veteran chieftain Ali Atar 'the best lance', as a Castilian writer has styled him, 'of all Morisma', who was brought to the ground after receiving two wounds, and thus escaped by an honourable death the melancholy spectacle of his country's humiliation.[4]

The enemy, disheartened by this loss, soon began to give ground. But, though hard pressed by the Spaniards, they retreated in some order, until they reached the borders of the Genil, which were thronged with the infantry, vainly attempting a passage across the stream, swollen by excessive rains to a height much above its ordinary level. The confusion now became universal, horse and foot mingling together; each one, heedful only of life, no longer thought of his booty. Many, attempting to swim the stream, were borne down, steed and rider, promiscuously in its waters. Many more, scarcely making show of resistance, were cut down on the banks by the pitiless Spaniards.

The young King Boabdil, who had been conspicuous during that day in the hottest of the fight, mounted on a milk-white charger richly caparisoned, saw fifty of his loyal guard fall around him. Finding his steed too much jaded to stem the current of the river, he quietly dismounted and sought a shelter among the reedy thickets that fringed its margin, until the storm of battle should have passed over. In this lurking place, however, he was discovered by a common soldier named Martin Hurtado, who, without recognizing his person, instantly attacked him. The prince defended himself with his scimitar [More likely not, but rather a straight bladed *jenete espada*. – ED], until Hurtado, being joined by two of his countrymen, succeeded in making him prisoner. The men, overjoyed at their prize (for Boabdil had revealed his rank, in order to secure his person from violence), conducted him to their general, the Count of Cabra. The latter received the royal captive with a generous courtesy, the best sign of noble breeding, and which, recognized as a feature of chivalry, affords a pleasing contrast to the ferocious spirit of ancient warfare. The good count administered to the unfortunate prince all the consolations which his state would admit; and subsequently lodged him in his castle of Baena, where he was entertained with the most delicate and courtly hospitality.[5]

Nearly the whole of the Muslim cavalry were cut up, or captured, in this fatal action. Many of them were persons of rank, commanding high ransoms. The loss inflicted on the infantry was also severe, including the whole of their dear-bought plunder. Nine, or indeed, according to some accounts, two and twenty banners fell into the hands of the Christians in this action; in commemoration of which the Spanish sovereigns granted to the Count of Cabra, and his nephew, the *alcaide de los donzeles*, the privilege of bearing the same number of banners on their escutcheon, together with the head of a Nasrid king, encircled by a golden coronet, with a chain of the same metal around the neck.[6]

Great was the consternation occasioned by the return of the Muslim fugitives to Granada, and loud was the lament through its most populous streets; for the pride of many a noble house was laid low on that day, and their king (a thing unprecedented in the annals of the monarchy) was a prisoner in the land of the Christians. 'The hostile star of Islam,' exclaims an Arabic writer, 'now scattered its malignant influences over Spain, and the downfall of the Muslim empire was decreed.'[7]

The Sultana Aisha, however, was not of a temper to waste time in useless lamentation. She was aware that a captive king, who held his title by so precarious a tenure as did her son Boabdil, must soon cease to be a king even in name. She accordingly despatched a numerous embassy to Córdoba, with proffers of such a ransom for the prince's liberation, as a despot only could offer, and few despots could have the authority to enforce.

King Ferdinand, who was at Vitoria with the Queen, when he received tidings of the victory of Lucena, hastened to the south to determine on the destination of his royal captive. With some show of magnanimity, he declined an interview with Boabdil, until he should have consented to his liberation. A debate of some warmth occurred in the royal council at Córdoba, respecting the policy to be pursued, some contending that the Nasrid monarch was too valuable a prize to be so readily relinquished, and that the enemy, broken by the loss of their natural leader, would find it difficult to rally under one common head, or to concert any effective movement. Others, and especially the Marquis of Cádiz, urged his release, and even the support of his pretensions against his competitor, the old King of Granada [Abul Hacen]; insisting that the Spanish Muslim empire would be more effectually shaken by internal divisions, than by any pressure of its enemies from without. The various arguments were submitted to the Queen, who still held her court in the north, and who decided for the release of Boabdil, as a measure best reconciling sound policy with generosity to the vanquished.[8]

The terms of the. treaty, although sufficiently humiliating to the Muslim prince, were not materially different from those proposed by the Sultana Aisha. It was agreed that a truce of two years should be extended to Boabdil, and to such places in Granada as acknowledged his authority. In consideration of which, he stipulated to surrender four hundred Christian captives without ransom, to pay twelve thousand doblas of gold annually to the Spanish sovereigns, and to permit a free passage, as well as furnish supplies, to their troops passing through his territories, for the purpose of carrying on the war against that portion of the kingdom which still adhered to his father. Boabdil moreover bound himself to appear when summoned by Ferdinand, and to surrender his own son, with the children of his principal nobility, as sureties for his fulfilment of the treaty. Thus did the unhappy prince barter away his honour and his country's freedom for the possession of immediate, but most precarious sovereignty; a sovereignty, which could scarcely be expected to survive the period when he could be useful to the master whose breath had made him.[9]

The terms of the treaty being thus definitively settled, an interview was arranged to take place between the two monarchs at Córdoba. The Castilian courtiers would have persuaded their master to offer his hand for Boabdil to salute, in token of his feudal supremacy; but Ferdinand replied, 'Were the king of Granada in his own dominions, I might do this; but not while he is a prisoner in mine.' The Nasrid prince entered Córdoba with an escort of his own knights, and a splendid throng of Christian Spanish chivalry, who had marched out of the city to receive him. When Boabdil entered the royal presence, he would have prostrated himself on his knees; but Ferdinand, hastening to prevent him, embraced him with every demonstration of respect. An Arabic interpreter, who acted as orator, then expatiated, in florid hyperbole, on the magnanimity and princely qualities of the Christian Spanish King, and the loyalty and good faith of his own master. But Ferdinand interrupted his eloquence, with the assurance that 'his panegyric was superfluous, and that he had perfect confidence that the sovereign of Granada would keep his faith as became a true knight and a king'. After ceremonies so humiliating to the Nasrid prince, notwithstanding the veil of decorum studiously thrown over them, he set out with his attendants for his capital, escorted by a body of Andalusian horse to the frontier, and loaded with costly presents by the Castilian King, and the general contempt of his court.[10]

Notwithstanding the importance of the results in the war of Granada, a detail of the successive steps by which they were achieved would be most tedious and trifling. No siege or single military achievement of great moment occurred until nearly four years from this period, in 1487; although, in the intervening time, a large number of fortresses and petty towns, together with a very extensive tract of territory, were recovered from the enemy. Without pursuing the chronological order of events, it is probable that the end of history will be best attained by presenting a concise view of the general policy pursued by the sovereigns in the conduct of the war.

The Moorish wars under preceding monarchs had consisted of little else than *cavalgadas*, or inroads into the enemy's territory,[11] which, pouring like a torrent over the land, swept away whatever was upon the surface, but left it in its essential resources wholly unimpaired. The bounty of nature soon repaired the ravages of man, and the ensuing harvest seemed to shoot up more abundantly from the soil, enriched by the blood of the husbandmen. A more vigorous system of spoliation was now introduced. Instead of one campaign, the army took the field in spring and autumn, intermitting its efforts only during the intolerable heats of summer, so that the green crop had no time to ripen, ere it was trodden down under the iron heel of war.

The apparatus for devastation was also on a much greater scale than had ever before been witnessed. From the second year of the war, thirty thousand foragers were reserved for this service, which they effected by demolishing farmhouses, granaries, and mills (which last were exceedingly numerous in a land watered by many small streams), by eradicating the vines, and laying waste the olive gardens and plantations of oranges, almonds, mulberries, and all the rich varieties that grew luxuriant in this highly favoured region. This merciless devastation extended for more than two leagues on either side of the line of march. At the same time, the Mediterranean fleet cut off all supplies from the Barbary coast, so that the whole kingdom might be said to be in a state of

perpetual blockade. Such and so general was the scarcity occasioned by this
system, that the Spanish Muslims were glad to exchange their Christian captives for provisions, until such ransom was interdicted by the sovereigns, as
tending to defeat their own measures.[12]

Still there was many a green and sheltered valley in Granada, which yielded
its returns unmolested to the Granadan husbandman; while his granaries were
occasionally enriched with the produce of border foray. The Spanish Muslims
too, although naturally a luxurious people, were patient of suffering, and
capable of enduring great privation. Other measures, therefore, of a still more
formidable character, became necessary in conjunction with this rigorous
system of blockade.

The Granadan towns were for the most part strongly defended, presenting
within the limits of Granada, as has been said, more than ten times the number
of fortified places that are now scattered over the whole extent of the Peninsula.
They stood along the crest of some precipice, or bold sierra, whose natural
strength was augmented by the solid masonry with which they were surrounded, and which, however insufficient to hold out against modern artillery,
bade defiance to all the enginery of battering warfare known previously to the
fifteenth century. It was this strength of fortification, combined with that of
their local position, which frequently enabled a slender garrison in these places
to laugh and to scorn all the efforts of the proudest Castilian armies.

The Spanish sovereigns were convinced, that they must look to their artillery
as the only effectual means for the reduction of these strong-holds. In this, they
as well as the Spanish Muslims were extremely deficient, although Spain
appears to have furnished earlier examples of its use than any other country in
Europe. Isabella, who seems to have had the particular control of this
department, caused the most skilful engineers and artisans to be invited into the
kingdom from France, Germany, and Italy. Forges were constructed in the
camp, and all the requisite materials prepared for the manufacture of cannon,
balls, and powder. Large quantities of the last were also imported from Sicily,
Flanders, and Portugal. Commissaries were established over the various
departments, with instructions to provide whatever might be necessary for the
operatives; and the whole was intrusted to the supervision of Don Francisco
Ramírez, an *hidalgo* of Madrid, a person of much experience, and extensive
military science, for that day. By these efforts, unremittingly pursued during
the whole of the war, Isabella assembled a train of artillery, such as was
probably not possessed at that time by any other European potentate.[13]

Still the clumsy construction of the ordnance betrayed the infancy of the art.
More than twenty pieces of artillery used at the siege of Baza, during this war,
are still to be seen in that City, where they long served as columns in the public
marketplace. [Most, if not all, are now part of the fine collection in the *Museo del
Ejército* (Army Museum), Madrid – ED.] The largest of the lombards, as the

heavy ordnance was called, are about twelve feet in length, consisting of iron bars two inches in breadth, held together by bolts and rings of the same metal. These were firmly attached to their carriages, incapable either of horizontal or vertical movement. It was this clumsiness of construction, which led Machiavelli, some thirty years after, to doubt the expediency of bringing cannon into field engagements; and he particularly recommends in his treatise on the *Art of War* that the enemy's fire should be evaded, by intervals in the ranks being left open opposite to his cannon.[14]

The balls thrown from these engines were sometimes of iron, but more usually of marble. Several hundred of the latter have been picked up in the fields around Baza, many of which are fourteen inches in diameter, and weigh a hundred and seventy-five pounds. Yet this bulk, enormous as it appears, shows a considerable advance in the art since the beginning of the century, when the stone-balls discharged, according to Zurita, at the siege of Balaguer, weighed not less than five hundred and fifty pounds. It was very long before the exact proportions requisite for obtaining the greatest effective force could be ascertained.[15]

The awkwardness with which their artillery was served, corresponded with the rudeness of its manufacture. It is noticed as a remarkable circumstance by the chronicler, that two batteries, at the siege of Albahar, discharged one hundred and forty balls in the course of a day.[16] Besides this more usual kind of ammunition the Castilians threw from their engines large globular masses, composed of certain inflammable ingredients mixed with gunpowder, 'which, scattering long trains of light,' says an eyewitness, 'in their passage through the air, filled the beholders with dismay, and, descending on the roofs of the edifices, frequently occasioned extensive conflagration.'[17]

The transportation of their bulky engines was not the least of the difficulties which the Spaniards had to encounter in this war. The Granadan fortresses were frequently entrenched in the depths of some mountain labyrinth, whose rugged passes were scarcely accessible to cavalry. An immense body of pioneers, therefore, was constantly employed in constructing roads for the artillery across these sierras, by levelling the mountains, filling up the intervening valleys with rocks, or with cork trees and other timber that grew prolific in the wilderness and throwing bridges across the torrents and precipitous *barrancos*. Pulgar had the curiosity to examine one of the causeways thus constructed, preparatory to the siege of Cambil, which, although six thousand pioneers were constantly employed in the work, was attended with such difficulty, that it advanced only three leagues in twelve days. It required, says the historian, the entire demolition of one of the most rugged parts of the sierra, which no one could have believed practicable by human industry.[18]

The Granadan garrisons, perched on their mountain fastnesses, which, like the eyry of some bird of prey, seemed almost inaccessible to man, beheld with astonishment the heavy trains of artillery, emerging from the passes, where the foot of the hunter had scarcely been known to venture. The walls which encompassed their cities, although lofty, were not of sufficient thickness to withstand long the assaults of these formidable engines. The Spanish Muslims were deficient in heavy ordnance. The weapons on which they chiefly relied for annoying the enemy at a distance were the arquebus and crossbow, with the last of which they were unerring marksmen, being trained to it from infancy. They adopted a custom, rarely met with in civilized nations of any age, of poisoning their arrows; distilling for this purpose the juice of aconite, or wolfsbane, which grew rife in the *Sierra Nevada*, or Snowy Mountains, near Granada. A piece of linen or cotton cloth steeped in this decoction was wrapped round the point of the weapon, and the wound inflicted by it, however trivial in appearance, was sure to be mortal. Indeed a Spanish Christian writer, not content with this, imputes such malignity to the virus, that a drop of it, as he asserts, mingling with the blood oozing from a wound, would ascend the stream into the vein, and diffuse its fatal influence over the whole system![19]

Ferdinand, who appeared at the head of his armies throughout the whole of this war, pursued a sagacious policy in reference to the beleaguered cities. He was ever ready to meet the first overtures to surrender, in the most liberal spirit; granting protection of person, and such property as the besieged could transport with them, and assigning them a residence, if they preferred it, in his own dominions. Many, in consequence of this, migrated to Sevilla and other cities of Andalusia, where they were settled on estates which had been confiscated by the inquisitors; who looked forward, no doubt, with satisfaction to the time, when they should be permitted to thrust their sickle into the new crop of heresy, whose seeds were thus sown amid the ashes of the old one. Those who preferred to remain in the conquered Muslim territory, as Castilian subjects, were permitted the free enjoyment of personal rights and property, as well as of their religion; and, such was the fidelity with which Ferdinand redeemed his engagements during the war, by the punishment of the least infraction of them by his own people, that many, particularly of the Granadan peasantry, preferred abiding in their early homes to removing to Granada, or other places of the Muslim dominion. It was, perhaps, a counterpart of the same policy, which led Ferdinand to chastise any attempt at revolt, on the part of his new Muslim subjects, the Mudejares, as they were called, with an unsparing rigour, which merits the reproach of cruelty. Such was the military execution inflicted on the rebellious town of Benemaquez, where he commanded one hundred and ten of the principal inhabitants to be hung above the walls, and, after consigning the rest of the population, men, women, and children, to slavery, caused the place to be razed to the ground. The humane policy, usually pursued by Ferdinand, seems to have had a more favourable effect on his enemies, who were exasperated, rather than intimidated, by this ferocious act of vengeance.[20]

The magnitude of the other preparations corresponded with those for the ordnance department. The amount of forces assembled at Córdoba, we find variously stated at ten or twelve thousand horse, and twenty, and even forty thousand foot, exclusive of foragers. On one occasion, the whole number, including men for the artillery service and the followers of the camp, is reckoned at eighty thousand. The same number of beasts of burden were employed in transporting the supplies required for this immense host, as well as for provisioning the conquered cities standing in the midst of a desolated country. The Queen, who took this department under her special cognizance, moved along the frontier, stationing herself at points most contiguous to the scene of operations. There, by means of posts regularly established, she received hourly intelligence of the war. At the same time she transmitted the requisite munitions for the troops, by means of convoys sufficiently strong to secure them against the irruptions of the wily enemy.[21]

Isabella, solicitous for everything that concerned the welfare of her people, sometimes visited the camp in person, encouraging the soldiers to endure the hardships of war, and relieving their necessities by liberal donations of clothes and money. She caused also a number of large tents, known as 'the queen's hospitals', to be always reserved for the sick and wounded, and furnished them with the requisite attendants and medicines, at her own charge. This is considered the earliest attempt at the formation of a regular camp hospital, on record.[22]

Isabella may be regarded as the soul of this war. She engaged in it with the most exalted views, less to acquire territory, than to reestablish the empire of the Cross over the ancient domain of Christendom. On this point, she concentrated all the energies of her powerful mind, never suffering herself to be diverted by any subordinate interest from this one great and glorious object. When the King, in 1484, would have paused awhile from the Granadan war, in order to prosecute his claims to Rossellon against the French, on the demise of Louis XI, Isabella strongly objected to it; but, finding her remonstrance ineffectual, she left her husband in Aragón, and repaired to Córdoba, where she placed the Cardinal of Spain at the head of the army, and prepared to open the campaign in the usual vigorous manner. Here, however, she was soon joined by Ferdinand, who, on a cooler revision of the subject, deemed it prudent to postpone his projected enterprise.

On another occasion, in the same year, when the nobles, fatigued with the service, had persuaded the king to retire earlier than usual, the Queen, dissatisfied with the proceeding, addressed a letter to her husband, in which, after representing the disproportion of the results to the preparations, she besought him to keep the field as long as the season should serve. The grandees, says Lebrija, mortified at being surpassed in zeal for the holy war by a woman, eagerly collected their forces, which had been partly disbanded, and returned across the borders to renew hostilities.[23]

A circumstance, which had frequently frustrated the most magnificent military enterprises under former reigns, was the factions of these potent vassals, who, independent of each other, and almost of the crown, could rarely be brought to act in efficient concert for a length of time, and broke up the camp on the slightest personal jealousy. Ferdinand experienced something of this temper in the Duke of Medina Celi, who, when he had received orders to detach a corps of his troops to the support of the Count of Benavente, refused, replying to the messenger, 'Tell your master, that I came here to serve him at the head of my household troops, and they go nowhere without me as their leader.' The sovereigns managed this fiery spirit with the greatest address, and, instead of curbing it, endeavoured to direct it in the path of honourable emulation. The Queen, who as their hereditary sovereign received a more deferential homage from her Castilian subjects than Ferdinand, frequently wrote to her nobles in the camp, complimenting some on their achievements, and others less fortunate on their intentions, thus cheering the hearts of all, says the chronicler, and stimulating them to deeds of heroism. On the most deserving she freely lavished those honours which cost little to the sovereign, but are most grateful to the subject. The Marquis of Cádiz, who was preeminent above every other captain in this war for sagacity and conduct, was rewarded after his brilliant surprise of Zahara, with the gift of that city, and the titles of Marquis of Zahara and Duke of Cádiz. The warrior, however, was unwilling to resign the ancient title under which he had won his laurels, and ever after subscribed himself, Marquis Duke of Cádiz.[24] Still more emphatic honours were conferred on the Count de Cabra, after the capture of the king of Granada. When he presented himself before the sovereigns, who were at Vitoria, the clergy and cavaliers of the city marched out to receive him, and he entered in solemn procession on the right hand of the Grand Cardinal of Spain. As he advanced up the hall of audience in the royal palace, the King and Queen came forward to welcome him, and then seated him by themselves at table, declaring that 'the conqueror of kings should sit with kings'. These honours were followed by the more substantial gratuity of a hundred thousand maravedies annual rent; 'a fat donative,' says an old chronicler, 'for so lean a treasury'. The young *alcaide de los donzeles* experienced a similar reception on the ensuing day. Such acts of royal condescension were especially grateful to the nobility of a court, circumscribed beyond every other in Europe by stately and ceremonious etiquette.[25]

The duration of the war of Granada was such as to raise the militia throughout the kingdom nearly to a level with regular troops. Many of these levies, indeed, at the breaking out of the war, might pretend to this character. Such were those furnished by the Andalusian cities, which had been long accustomed to skirmishes with their Muslim neighbours. Such too was the well-appointed chivalry of the military orders, and the organized militia of the

Hermandad, which we find sometimes supplying a body of ten thousand men for the service. To these may be added the splendid throng of cavaliers and *hidalgos,* who swelled the retinues of the sovereigns and the great nobility. The King was attended in battle by a bodyguard of a thousand knights, one half light, and the other half heavy armed, all superbly equipped and mounted, and trained to arms from childhood, under the royal eye.

Although the burden of the war bore most heavily on Andalusia, from its contiguity to the scene of action, yet recruits were drawn in abundance from the most remote provinces, as Galicia, Biscay, and the Asturias, from Aragón, and even the Trastamarine dominions of Sicily. The sovereigns did not disdain to swell their ranks with levies of a humbler description, by promising an entire amnesty to those malefactors, who had left the country in great numbers of late years to escape justice, on condition of their serving in the Granadan war. Throughout this motley host the strictest discipline and decorum were maintained. The Spaniards have never been disposed to intemperance; but the passion for gaming, especially with dice, to which they seem to have been immoderately addicted at that day, was restrained by the severest penalties.[26]

The brilliant successes of the Spanish sovereigns diffused general satisfaction throughout Christendom, and volunteers flocked to the camp from France, England, and other parts of Europe, eager to participate in the glorious triumphs of the Cross. Among these was a corps of Swiss mercenaries, who are thus simply described by Pulgar: 'There joined the royal standard a body of men from Switzerland, a country in upper Germany. These men were bold of heart, and fought on foot. As they were resolved never to turn their backs upon the enemy, they wore no defensive armour, except in front; by which means they were less encumbered in fight. They made a trade of war, letting themselves out as mercenaries; but they espoused only a just quarrel, for they were devout and loyal Christians, and above all abhorred rapine as a great sin.'[27] The Swiss had recently established their military renown by the discomfiture of Charles the Bold [the Rash], when they first proved the superiority of infantry over the best appointed chivalry of Europe. Their example no doubt contributed to the formation of that invincible Spanish infantry, which, under the Great Captain and his successors, may be said to have decided the fate of Europe for more than half a Century.

Among the foreigners was one from the distant isle of Britain, the Earl of Rivers [Edward Woodville; see note 28 – ED], or *conde de Escalas,* as he is called from his patronymic, Scales, by the Spanish writers. 'There came from Britain,' says Peter Martyr, 'a cavalier, young, wealthy, and high-born. He was allied to the blood royal of England. He was attended by a beautiful train of household troops three hundred in number, armed after the fashion of their land with longbow and battle-axe.' This nobleman particularly distinguished himself by his gallantry in the second [actually the third, see note 42 – ED] siege of Loja, in

1486. Having asked leave to fight after the manner of his country, says the Andalusian chronicler, he dismounted from his good steed, and putting himself at the head of his followers, armed like himself *en blanco*, with their swords at their thighs, and battle-axes in their hands, he dealt such terrible blows around him as fills even the hardy mountaineers of the north with astonishment. Unfortunately, just as the suburbs were carried, the good knight, as he was mounting a scaling-ladder, received a blow from a stone, which dashed out two of his teeth, and stretched him senseless on the ground. He was removed to his tent, where he lay some time under medical treatment. When he had sufficiently recovered, he received a visit from the King and Queen, who complimented him on his prowess, and testified their sympathy for his misfortune. 'It is little,' replied he, 'to lose a few teeth in the service of him, who has given me all. Our Lord,' he added, 'who reared this fabric, has only opened a window, in order to discern the more readily what passes within.' A facetious response, says Peter Martyr, which gave uncommon satisfaction to the sovereigns.[28]

The Queen, not long after, testified her sense of the Earl's services, by a magnificent largess, consisting among other things, of twelve Andalusian horses, two couches with richly wrought hangings and coverings of cloth of gold, with a quantity of fine linen, and sumptuous pavilions for himself and suite. The brave knight seems to have been satisfied with this taste of the Moorish wars; for he soon after returned to England, and in 1488 passed over to France, where his hot spirit prompted him to take part in the feudal factions of that country, in which he lost his life fighting for the Duke of Brittany.[29]

The pomp with which the military movements were conducted in these campaigns, gave the scene rather the air of a court pageant, than that of the stern array of war. The war was one, which, appealing both to principles of religion and patriotism, was well calculated to inflame the imaginations of the young Christian Spanish cavaliers; and they poured into the field, eager to display themselves under the eye of their illustrious Queen, who, as she rode through the ranks mounted on her war-horse, and clad in complete mail, afforded no bad personification of the genius of chivalry. The potent and wealthy barons exhibited in the camp all the magnificence of princes. The pavilions decorated with various-coloured pennons, and emblazoned with the armorial bearings of their ancient houses, shone with a splendour, which a Castilian writer likens to that of the City of Sevilla.[30] They always appeared surrounded by a throng of pages in gorgeous liveries and at night were preceded by a multitude of torches, which shed a radiance like that of day. They vied with each other in the costliness of their apparel, equipage, and plate, and in the variety and delicacy of the dainties with which their tables were covered.[31]

Ferdinand and Isabella saw with regret this lavish ostentation, and privately remonstrated with some of the principal grandees on its evil tendency, especially in seducing the inferior and poorer nobility into expenditures beyond

GENERAL VIEW OF POLICY   185

their means. This Sybarite indulgence, however, does not seem to have impaired the martial spirit of the nobles. On all occasions, they contended with each other for the post of danger. The Duke del Infantado, the head of the powerful house of Mendoza, was conspicuous above all for the magnificence of his train. At the siege of Illora, 1486, he obtained permission to lead the storming party. As his followers pressed onward to the breach, they were received with such a shower of missiles as made them falter for a moment. 'What, my men,' cried he, 'do you fail me at this hour? Shall we be taunted with bearing more finery on our backs than courage in our hearts? Let us not, in God's name, be laughed at as mere holiday soldiers!' His vassals, stung by this rebuke, rallied, and, penetrating the breach, carried the place by the fury of their assault.[32]

Notwithstanding the remonstrances of the sovereigns against this ostentation of luxury, they were not wanting in the display of royal state and magnificence on all suitable occasions. The Curate of Los Palacios has expatiated with elaborate minuteness on the circumstances of an interview between Ferdinand and Isabella in the camp before Moclín, in 1486, where the Queen's presence was solicited for the purpose of devising a plan of future operations. A few of the particulars may be transcribed, though at the hazard of appearing trivial to readers, who take little interest in such details.

On the borders of the Yeguas, the Queen was met by an advanced corps, under the command of the Marquis Duke of Cádiz, and, at the distance of a league and a half from Moclín, by the Duke del Infantado, with the principal nobility and their vassals, splendidly accoutred. On the left was drawn up in battle array the militia of Sevilla, and the Queen, making her obeisance to the banner of that illustrious city, ordered it to pass to her right. The successive battalions saluted the queen as she advanced, by lowering their standards, and the joyous multitude announced with tumultuous acclamations her approach to the conquered city.

The Queen was accompanied by her daughter, the Infanta Isabella, and a courtly train of damsels, mounted on mules richly caparisoned. The Queen herself rode a chestnut mule, seated on a saddle-chair embossed with gold and silver. The housings were of a crimson colour, and the bridle was of satin, curiously wrought with letters of gold. The infanta wore a skirt of fine velvet, over others of brocade; a scarlet mantilla of the Moorish fashion; and a black hat trimmed with gold embroidery. The King rode forward at the head of his nobles to receive her. He was dressed in a crimson doublet, with *chausses*, or breeches, of yellow satin. Over his shoulders was thrown a cassock or mantle of rich brocade, and a sopravest of the same materials concealed his cuirass. By his side, close girt, he wore a Moorish scimitar [More likely an *espada jinéta*. – ED], and beneath his bonnet his hair was confined by a cap or headdress of the finest stuff.

Ferdinand was mounted on a noble war-horse of a bright chestnut colour. In the splendid train of chivalry which attended him, Bernaldez dwells with much satisfaction on the English 'Lord Scales'. He was followed by a retinue of five pages arrayed in costly liveries. He was sheathed in complete mail, over which was thrown a French surcoat of dark silk brocade. A buckler was attached by golden clasps to his arm, and on his head he wore a white French hat with plumes. The caparisons of his steed were azure silk, lined with violet and sprinkled over with stars of gold, and swept the ground, as he managed his fiery courser with an easy horsemanship that excited general admiration.

The King and Queen as they drew near, bowed thrice with formal reverence to each other. The Queen at the same time raising her hat, remained in her coif or headdress, with her face uncovered; Ferdinand, riding up, kissed her affectionately on the cheek, and then, according to the precise chronicler, bestowed a similar mark of tenderness on his daughter Isabella, after giving her his paternal benediction. The royal party were then escorted to the camp, where suitable accommodations had been provided for the Queen and her fair retinue.[33]

It may readily be believed that the sovereigns did not neglect in a war like the present, an appeal to the religious principle so deeply seated in the Christian Spanish character. All their public acts ostentatiously proclaimed the pious nature of the work in which they were engaged. They were attended in their expeditions by churchmen of the highest rank, who not only mingled in the councils of the camp, but, like the bold Bishop of Jaén, or the Grand Cardinal Mendoza, buckled on harness over rochet and hood, and led their squadrons to the field.[34] The Queen at Córdoba celebrated the tidings of every new success over the infidel, by solemn procession and thanksgiving, with her whole household, as well as the nobility, foreign ambassadors, and municipal functionaries. In like manner, Ferdinand, on the return from his campaigns, was received at the gates of the city, and escorted in solemn pomp beneath a rich canopy of state to the cathedral church, where he prostrated himself in grateful adoration of the Lord of Hosts. Intelligence of their triumphant progress in the war was constantly transmitted to the pope, who returned his benediction, accompanied by more substantial marks of favour, in bulls of crusade, and taxes on ecclesiastical rents.[35]

The ceremonials observed on the occupation of a new conquest were such as to affect the heart no less than the imagination. 'The royal *alferez*', says Marineo, 'raised the standard of the Cross, the sign of our salvation, on the summit of the principal fortress; and all who beheld it prostrated themselves on their knees in silent worship of the Almighty, while the priests chanted the glorious anthem, *Te Deum laudamus*. The ensign or pennon of Santiago (St. James), the chivalric patron of Spain, was then unfolded, and all invoked his blessed name. Lastly, was displayed the banner of the sovereigns, emblazoned with the royal arms; at which the whole army shouted forth, as if with one voice, "Castile, Castile!" After these solemnities, a bishop led the way to the principal mosque, which, after the rites of purification, he consecrated to the service of the true faith.'

The standard of the Cross above referred to, was of massive silver, and was a present from Pope Sixtus IV to Ferdinand, in whose tent it was always carried throughout these campaigns. An ample supply of bells, vases, missals, plate, and other sacred furniture, was also borne along the camp, being provided by the queen for the purified mosques.[36]

The most touching part of the incidents usually occurring at the surrender of a Granadan city, was the liberation of Christian captives immured in its dungeons. On the capture of Ronda, in 1485, more than four hundred of these unfortunate persons, several of them cavaliers of rank, some of whom had been taken in the fatal expedition of the Ajarquía, were restored to the light of heaven. On being brought before Ferdinand, they prostrated themselves on the ground bathing his feet with tears, while their wan and wasted figures, their dishevelled locks, their beards reaching down to their girdles, and their limbs loaded with heavy manacles, brought tears into the eye of every spectator. They were then commanded to present themselves before the Queen at Córdoba, who liberally relieved their necessities, and, after the celebration of public thanksgiving, caused them to be conveyed to their own homes. The fetters of the liberated captives were suspended in the churches, where they continued to be revered by succeeding generations as the trophies of Christian warfare.[37]

Ever since the victory of Lucena, the sovereigns had made it a capital point of their policy to foment the dissensions of their enemies. The young King Boabdil, after his humiliating treaty with Ferdinand, lost whatever consideration he had previously possessed. Although the sultana Aisha, by her personal address, and the lavish distribution of the royal treasures, contrived to maintain a faction for her son, the better classes of his countrymen despised him as a renegade, and a vassal of the Christian king. As their old monarch [Abul Hacen Ali] had become incompetent, from increasing age and blindness, to the duties of his station in these perilous times, they turned their eyes on his brother Abdullah [Muhammad XIII], surnamed al-Zagal, or 'The Valiant', who had borne so conspicuous a part in the rout of the Ajarquía. The Castilians depict this chief in the darkest colours of ambition and cruelty; but the Muslim writers afford no such intimation, and his advancement to the throne at that crisis seems to be in some measure justified by his eminent talents as a military leader.

On his way to Granada, al-Zagal encountered and cut to pieces a body of Calatrava knights from Alhama, and signalized his entrance into his new capital by bearing along the bloody trophies of heads dangling from his saddlebow, after the barbarous fashion long practised in these wars.[38] It was observed that the old King Abul Hacen did not long survive his brother's accession.[39] The young King Boabdil sought the protection of the Castilian sovereigns in Sevilla, who, true to their policy, sent him back into his own dominions with the means of making headway against his rival. The *alfakies* and other considerate persons of Granada, scandalized at these fatal feuds, effected a reconciliation, on the basis of a division of the kingdom between the parties. But wounds so deep could not be permanently healed. The site of the Nasrid capital was most propitious to the purposes of faction. It covered two swelling eminences, divided from each other by the deep waters of the Darro. The two factions possessed themselves respectively of these opposite quarters. Boabdil was not ashamed to strengthen himself by the aid of Christian mercenaries; and a dreadful conflict was carried on for fifty days and nights, within the city, which swam with the blood, that should have been shed only in its defence.[40]

Notwithstanding these auxiliary circumstances, the progress of the Christians was comparatively slow. Every cliff seemed to be crowned with a fortress; and every fortress was defended with the desperation of men willing to bury themselves under its ruins. The old men, women, and children, on occasion of a siege, were frequently despatched to Granada. Such was the resolution, or rather ferocity of the Muslims, that Málaga closed its gates against the fugitives from Alora, after its surrender, and even massacred some of them in cold blood. The eagle eye of al-Zagal seemed to take in at a glance the whole extent of his little territory, and to detect every vulnerable point in his antagonist, whom he encountered where he least expected it; cutting off his convoys, surprising his foraging parties, and retaliating by a devastating inroad on the borders.[41]

No effectual and permanent resistance, however, could be opposed to the tremendous enginery of the Christians. Tower and town fell before it. Besides the principal towns of Cártama, Coín, Setenil, Ronda, Marbella, Illora, termed by the Granadans 'the right eye', Moclín, 'the shield' of Granada, and Loja, after a third desperate siege in the spring of 1486, Bernaldez enumerates more than seventy subordinate places in the Val de Cartama, and thirteen others after the fall of Marbella. Thus the Castilians advanced their line of conquest more than twenty leagues beyond the western frontier of Granada. This extensive tract they strongly fortified and peopled, partly with Christian subjects, and partly with Muslims, the original occupants of the soil who were secured in the possession of their ancient lands under their own law.[42]

Thus the strong posts, which may be regarded as exterior defences of the city of Granada, were successively carried. A few positions alone remained of sufficient strength to keep the enemy at bay. The most considerable of these was Málaga, which from its maritime situation afforded facilities for a communication with the Barbary Muslims, that the vigilance of the Castilian cruisers could not entirely intercept. On this point, therefore, it was determined to concentrate all the strength of the monarchy, by sea and land, in the ensuing campaign of 1487.

* * * * *

AUTHOR'S CHAPTER COMMENTS

Two of the most important authorities for the war of Granada are Fernando del Pulgar, and Antonio de Lebrija, or Nebrissensis, as he is called from the Latin *Nebrissa*.

Few particulars have been preserved respecting the biography of the former. He was probably a native of Pulgar, near Toledo. The Castilian writers recognize certain provincialisms in his style belonging to that district. He was secretary to Enríque IV [of Castile], and was charged with various confidential functions by him. He seems to have retained his place on the accession of Isabella, by whom he was appointed national historiographer in 1482, when, from certain remarks in his letters, it would appear be was already advanced in years. This office, in the fifteenth century, comprehended, in addition to the more obvious duties of an historian, the intimate and confidential relations of a private secretary. 'It was the business of the chronicler,' says Bernaldez, 'to carry on foreign correspondence in the service of his master, acquainting himself with whatever was passing in other courts and countries, and, by the discreet and conciliatory tenor of his epistles, to allay such feuds as might arise between the king and his nobility, and establish harmony between them.' From this period Pulgar remained near the royal person, accompanying the queen in her various progresses though the kingdom, as well as in her military expeditions into the Muslim territory. He was consequently an eyewitness of many of the warlike scenes which he describes, and, from his situation at the court, had access to the most ample and accredited sources of information. It is probable he did not survive the capture of Granada, as his history falls somewhat short of that event. Pulgar's *Chronicle*, in the portion containing a retrospective survey of events previous to 1482, may be charged with gross inaccuracy. But, in all the subsequent period, it may be received as perfectly authentic, and has all the air of impartiality. Every circumstance relating to the conduct of the war, is developed with equal fullness and precision. His manner of narration, though prolix, is perspicuous, and may compare favourably with that of contemporary writers. His sentiments may compare still more advantageously in point of liberality, with those of the Castilian historians of a later age.

Pulgar left some other works, of which his commentary on the ancient satire of *Mingo Revulgo*, his *Letters*, and his *Claros Varones*, or sketches of illustrious men, have alone been published. The last contains notices of the most distinguished individuals of the court of Enríque IV, which, although too indiscriminately encomiastic, are valuable subsidiaries to an accurate acquaintance with the prominent actors of the period. The last and most elegant edition of Pulgar's *Chronicle* was published at Valencia, in 1780, from the press of Benito Montfort, in large folio.

Antonio de Lebrija was one of the most active and erudite scholars of this period. He was born in the province of Andalusia, in 1444. After the usual discipline at Salamanca, he went at the age of nineteen to Italy, where he completed his education in the university of Bologna. He returned to Spain ten years after, richly stored with classical learning and the liberal arts that were then taught in the flourishing schools of Italy. He lost no time in dispensing to his countrymen his various acquisitions. He was appointed to the two chairs of grammar and poetry (a thing unprecedented) in the university of Salamanca, and lectured at the same time in these distinct departments. He was subsequently preferred by Cardinal Jimenes [Ximenes] to a professorship in his university of Alcalá de Henares, where his services were liberally requited, and where he enjoyed the entire confidence of his distinguished patron, who consulted him on all matters affecting the interests of the institution. Here he continued, delivering his lectures and expounding the ancient classics to crowded audiences, to the advanced age of seventy-eight, when he was carried off by an attack of apoplexy.

Lebrija, besides his oral tuition, composed works on a great variety of subjects, philological, historical, theological, etc. His emendation of the sacred text was visited with the censure of the Inquisition, a circumstance which will not operate to his prejudice with posterity. Lebrija was far from being circumscribed by the narrow sentiments of his age. He was warmed with a generous enthusiasm for letters, which kindled a corresponding flame in the bosoms of his disciples, among whom may be reckoned some of the brightest names in the literary annals of the period. His instruction effected for classical literature in Spain, what the labours of the great Italian scholars of the fifteenth century did for it in their country; and he was rewarded with the substantial gratitude of his own age, and such empty honours as could be rendered by posterity. For very many years, the anniversary of his death was commemorated by public services, and a funeral panegyric, in the university of Alcalá.

The circumstances attending the composition of his Latin *Chronicle*, so often quoted in this history, are very curious. Carbajal says, that he delivered Pulgar's *Chronicle*, after that writer's death, into Lebrija's hands for the purpose of being translated into Latin. The latter proceeded in his task, as far as the year 1486. His history, however, can scarcely be termed a translation, since, although it takes up the same thread of incident, it is diversified by many new ideas and particular facts. This unfinished performance was found among Lebrija's papers, after his decease, with a preface containing not a word of acknowledgment to Pulgar. It was accordingly published for the first time, in 1545 (the edition referred to in this history), by his son Sancho, as an original production of his father. Twenty years after, the first edition of Pulgar's original *Chronicle* was published at Valladolid, from the copy which belonged to Lebrija, by his grandson Antonio. This work appeared also as Lebrija's. Copies however of Pulgar's *Chronicle* were preserved in several private libraries; and two years later, 1567, his just claims were vindicated by an edition at Saragossa, inscribed with his name as its author. [A 1943, Madrid, publication of Pulgar's *Crónica de los Reyes Católicos* is available in some American libraries. – ED]

Lebrija's reputation has sustained some injury from this transaction, though most undeservedly. It seems probable, that he adopted Pulgar's text as the basis of his own, intending to continue the narrative to a later period. His unfinished manuscript being found among his papers after his death, without reference to any authority, was naturally enough given to the world as entirely his production. It is more strange, that Pulgar's own *Chronicle*, subsequently printed as Lebrija's, should have contained no allusion to its real author. The History, although composed as far as it goes with sufficient elaboration and pomp of style, is one that adds, on the whole, but little to the fame of Lebrija. It was at best but adding a leaf to the laurel on his brow, and was certainly not worth a plagiarism.

[Prescott also used Jerónimo Zurita's *Anales* as an important source. Zurita (d.1580) was secretary to Philip II and official chronicler of Aragón. – ED]

NOTES

1. *Por esa puerto de Elvira*
   sale muy gran cabalgada:
   cuánto del hidalgo moro,
   cuánto de la yetua baya.

   * * *

   Cuánta pluma y gentileza,
   cuánto capellar de grana,
   cuánto bayo borceguf,
   cuánto raso que se esmalta,

   Cuánto de espuela de oro,
   cuánta estribera de plata!
   Toda es gente valerosa,
   y esperta para batalla.

   En medio de todos ellos
   va el rey Chico de Granada,
   mirando las damas moras
   de las torres del Alhambra.

   La reina mora su madre
   de esta manera le habla:
   'Alá te guarde, mi hijo,
   Mahoma vaya en tu guarda.'

   – Hyta, *Guerras de Granada,*
   tom.i, p.232.

2. Condé, *Dominacion de los Arabes*, tom.iii, cap.36. – Cardonne, *Hist. d'Afrique et d'Espagne*, tom.iii, pp.267–71. – Bernaldez, *Reyes Católicos*, MS. cap.60. – Pedraza, *Antiguedad de Granada*, fol.10. – Marmol, *Rebelion de Moriscos*, lib.1, cap.12.

3. Pulgar, *Reyes Católicos*, part.3, cap.20.

   The *donzeles*, of which Diego de Córdoba was *alcaide*, or captain, were a body of young cavaliers, originally brought up as pages in the royal household, and organized as a separate corps of militia. Salazar de Mendoza, *Dignidades*, p.259. – See also Morales, *Obras*, tom.xiv, p.80.

4. Condé, *Dominacion de los Arabes*, tom.iii, cap.36. – Abarca, *Reyes de Aragón*, tom.ii, fol.302. – Carbajal, *Anales*, MS., año 1483. – Bernaldez, *Reyes Católicos*, MS., cap.61. – Pulgar, *Reyes Católicos*, cap.20. – Marmol, *Rebelion de Moriscos*, lib.1, cap.12.

5. Garibay, *Compendio*, tom.ii, p.637. – Pulgar, *Reyes Católicos, ubi supra*. – Bernaldez, *Reyes Católicos*, MS., cap.61. – Condé, *Dominacion de los Arabes*, tom.iii, cap.36. – Cardonne, *Hist. d'Afrique et d'Espagne*, tom.iii, pp.271–4.

   The various details, even to the site of the battle, are told in the usual confused and contradictory manner by the garrulous chroniclers of the period. All authorities, however, both Christian and Muslim, agree as to its general results. [Prescott's reference to the use of scimitars is questionable. See discussion of Nasrid

cavalry in Introduction, Part I. A straight bladed *jenete espada* was most likely used
by Granadan nobles and possibly by some Christians. – ED]

6. Mendoza, *Dignidades*, p.382. – Oviedo, *Quincuagenas*, MS, bat.1, quinc.4, dial.9.
7. Condé, *Dominacion de los Arabes*, tom.iii, cap.36. – Cardonne, *Hist. d'Afrique et d'Espagne*, pp.271–4.
8. Pulgar, *Reyes Católicos*, cap. 23. – Marmol, *Rebelion de Moriscos*, lib.1, cap.12.

    Charles V does not seem to have partaken of his grandfather's delicacy in regard
to an interview with his royal captive, or indeed to any part of his deportment
towards him.

9. Pulgar, *Reyes Católicos, ubi supra*. – Condé, *Dominacion de los Arabes*, cap.36.
10. Pulgar, *Reyes Católicos, loc. cit.* – Condé, *Dominacion de los Arabes*, cap.36.
11. The term *cavalgada* seems to be used indifferently by the ancient Spanish writers to
represent a marauding party, the foray itself, or the booty taken in it.
12. Pulgar, *Reyes Católicos*, cap.22. – *Mem. de la Acad. de Hist*, tom.vi, illust.6.
13. Pulgar, *Reyes Católicos*, cap.32, 41. – Zurita, *Anales*, tom.iv, lib.20, cap.59. –
Lebrija, *Rerum Gestarum Decades*, ii, lib.3, cap.5.
14. Machiavelli, *Arte della Guerra*, lib.3.

    [Unfortunately the sources, such as Machiavelli, used by Prescott for military
historical analysis were not well equipped to do justice to the importance of
artillery in the War of Granada. This important topic is covered in the Introduction, Part I, on military aspects of the war. – ED]

15. *Mem. de la Acad. de Hist*, tom.vi. illust.6.

    According to Gibbon, the cannon used by Muhammed [II] in the siege of
Constantinople [1453], about thirty years before this time, threw stone balls,
which weighed above 600 pounds. The measure of the bore was twelve palms.
Decline and Fall of the Roman Empire, chap.68.

16. *Mem. de la Acad. de Hist*, tom.vi, illust.6.

    We get a more precise notion of the awkwardness with which the artillery was
served in the infancy of the science, from a fact recorded in the Chronicle of Juan II,
that, at the siege of Setenil, in 1407, five lombards were able to discharge only
forty shot in the course of a day. We have witnessed an invention, in our time, that
of our ingenious countryman, Jacob Perkins, by which a gun, with the aid of that
miracle-worker, steam, is enabled to throw a thousand bullets in a single minute.

17. L. Marineo, *Cosas Memorables*, fol.174. – Pulgar, *Reyes Católicos*, cap.44.

    Some writers, as the Abbé Mignot, (*Histoire des Rois Catholiques Ferdinand et
Isabelle* Paris, 1766, tom.i, p.273.), have referred the invention of bombs to the
siege of Ronda. I find no authority for this. Pulgar's words are, 'They made many
iron balls, large and small, some of which they cast in a mould, having reduced the
iron to a state of fusion, so that it would run like any other metal.'

18. Pulgar, *Reyes Católicos*, cap.51. – Bernaldez, *Reyes Católicos*, MS, cap.82.
19. Mendoza, *Guerra de Granada*, (Valencia, 1776) pp.73, 74. – Zurita, *Anales*, tom.iv,
lib.20, cap.59. – *Mem. de la Acad. de Hist.*, tom.vi. p.168. According to Mendoza, a
decoction of the quince furnished the most effectual antidote known against this
poison.
20. Abarca, *Reyes de Aragón*, tom.ii, fol.304. – Lebrija, *Rerum Gestarum Decades*, ii, lib.4,
cap.2. – Bernaldez, *Reyes Católicos*, MS., cap. 76. – Marmol, *Rebelion de Moriscos*,
lib.1, cap.12.

Pulgar, who is by no means bigoted for the age, seems to think the liberal terms granted by Ferdinand to the enemies of the faith stand in need of perpetual apology. See *Reyes Católicos*, cap.44 *et passim*.

21. Bernaldez, *Reyes Católicos*, MS. cap.75. – Pulgar, *Reyes Católicos*, cap.21, 33, 42. – Lebrija, *Rerum Gestarum Decades*, ii, lib.8, cap.6. – Marmol, *Rebelion de Moriscos*, lib.1, cap.13.

22. *Mem de la Acad. de Hist.*, tom.vi, illust.6.

23. Lebrija, *Rerum Gestarum Decades*, ii, lib.3, cap.6. – Pulgar, *Reyes Católicos*, cap.31.

24. After another daring achievement, the sovereigns granted him and his heirs the royal suit worn by the monarchs of Castile on Ladyday; a present, says Abarca, not to be estimated by its cost. *Reyes de Aragón*, tom.ii, fol.303.

25. Abarca, *Reyes de Aragón, ubi supra*. – Peter Martyr, *Opus Epist.* lib.1, epist.41. – Bernaldez, *Reyes Católicos*, MS. cap. 68. – Zurita, *Anales*, tom.iv, cap.36.

26. Pulgar, *Reyes Católicos*, cap.31, 67, 69. – Lebrija, *Rerum Gestarum Decades*, ii, lib.2, cap.10.

27. *Reyes Católicos*, cap.21.

   [The French historian Arié identifies the first time a detachment of Swiss mercenaries were known to be present with the royal Spanish force at Ferdinand's conquest of the fortress of Tájara (14 June 1483). A note on the same page also cites the presence of Gónzalo de Córdoba at the same battle. See *L'Espagne musulmane au temps des Nasrides (1232–1492)*, Paris, 1973, p.161. – ED]

28. Peter Martyr, *Opus Epist.*, lib.1, epist.62. – Bernaldez, *Reyes Católicos*, MS. cap.78. [This valiant Englishman may have been perceived by the Spanish Sovereigns as possessor of a title held by his father (First Earl of Rivers), and later by an older brother (Anthony, the Second Earl) and a younger brother (Richard, the Third and last Earl). However, according to the *Dictionary of National Biography* (Oxford University Press, Oxford, 1964–65, vol.xxi, p.887), Edward Woodville did not hold an English title. He was one of five sons of Richard Woodville, the First Lord Scales and First Earl of Rivers who with two of his other sons experienced misfortune in the English War of the Roses (1455–85). – ED]

29. Guillaume de Ialigny, *Histoire de Charles VIII*, (Paris, 1617), pp.90–4.

30. Bernaldez, *Reyes Católicos*, MS. cap. 75. – This city, even before the New World had poured its treasures into its lap, was conspicuous for its magnificence, as the ancient proverb testifies. Zuñiga, *Annales de Sevilla*, p.183.

31. Pulgar, *Reyes Católicos*, cap.41.

32. Pulgar, *Reyes Católicos*, cap.59. – This nobleman, whose name was Iñigo Lopez de Mendoza, was son of the first duke, Diego Hurtado, who supported Isabella's claims to the crown. Oviedo was present at the siege of Illora, and gives a minute description of this appearance there. 'He came,' says that writer, 'attended by a numerous body of cavaliers and gentlemen, as befitted so great a lord. He displayed all the luxuries which belong to a time of peace; and his tables, which were carefully served, were loaded with rich and curiously wrought plate, of which he had a greater profusion than any other grandee in the kingdom.' In another place he says, 'The duke Iñigo was a perfect Alexander for his liberality, in all his actions princely, maintaining unbounded hospitality among his numerous vassals and dependents, and beloved throughout Spain. His palaces were garnished with the most costly tapestries, jewels, and rich stuffs of gold and silver. His chapel was

filled with accomplished singers and musicians; his falcons, hounds, and his whole hunting establishment, including a magnificent stud of horses, not to be matched by any other nobleman in the kingdom. Of the truth of all which,' concludes Oviedo, 'I myself have been an eyewitness, and enough others can testify.' See Oviedo (*Quincuagenas*, MS., bat.1, quinc.1, dial.8) who has given the genealogy of the Mendozas and Mendozinos, in all its endless ramifications.

33. Bernaldez, *Reyes Católicos*, MS. cap.80. – The lively author of *A Year in Spain* describes among other suits of armour still to be seen in the museum of the armory at Madrid, those worn by Ferdinand and his illustrious consort, 'In one of the most conspicuous stations is the suit of armour usually worn by Ferdinand the Catholic. He seems snugly seated upon his war-horse, with a pair of red velvet breeches, after the manner of the Moors, with lifted lance and closed visor. There are several suits of Ferdinand and his Queen Isabella who was no stranger to the dangers of a battle. By the comparative heights of the armour, Isabella would seem to be the bigger of the two, as she certainly was the better.' *A Year in Spain*, by a young American [Alexander Mackenzie – ED] (Boston, 1829), p.116. [Since 1829, considerably more military artifacts have crowded into the national military collection at Spain's Army Museum (*Museo del Ejército*) in Madrid, where the suits and the Royal Standard of the Catholic Sovereigns are now exhibited. – ED]

34. Cardinal Mendoza, in the campaign of 1485, offered the Queen to raise a body of 3,000 horse, and march at its head to the relief of Alhama, and at the same time to supply her with such sums of money as might be necessary in the present exigency. Pulgar, *Reyes Católicos*, cap.50.

35. In 1486, we find Ferdinand and Isabella performing a pilgrimage to the shrine of Santiago [St. James] of Compostella. Carbajal, *Anales*, MS., año 86.

36. L. Marineo, *Cosas Memorables*, fol.173. – Bernaldez, *Reyes Católicos*, MS. cap.82, 87.

37. Pulgar, *Reyes Católicos*, cap.47. [The outer walls of the Church of San Juan de los Reyes, in Toledo, exhibit a spectacular display of the chains of freed Christian captives. Prior to the conquest of Granada, this church was intended to be the burial place of the Catholic Sovereigns and a monument to their reign. However, Granada became the shrine of their greatest achievement and they are buried there in the Capilla Real. – ED]

38. Condé, *Dominacion de los Arabes*, tom.iii, cap.37. – Cardonne, *Hist. d'Afrique et d'Espagne*, tom.iii, pp.276, 281, 282. – Abarca, *Reyes de Aragón*, tom.ii, fol.304.

> 'El enjaeza el caballo
> De las cabezas de fama,'

says one of the old Moorish ballads. A garland of Christian heads seems to have been deemed no unsuitable present from a Muslim knight to his lady love. Thus one of the Zegries triumphantly asks:

> '¿Que Cristianos habeis muerto,
> O escalado que murallas?
> ¿O que cabezas famisas
> Aveis presentado a damas?

This sort of trophy was also borne by the Christian cavaliers. Examples of this may

be found even as late as the siege of Granada. See, among others the ballad
beginning

'*A vista de los dos Reyes.*'

39. The Arabic historian alludes to the vulgar report of the old king's assassination by
his brother, but leaves us in the dark in regard to his own opinion of its credibility.
'*Algunos dicen que le procuro la muerte su hermano el Rey Zagal; pero Dios lo sabe, que es el
unico etemo e immutable.*' – Condé, *Dominacion de los Arabes*, tom.iii, cap.38. [Later
historians such as Arié and Paredes do not support the reputed assassination. – ED]

40. Condé, *Dominacion de los Arabes*, tom.iii. cap.38. – Cardonne, *Hist. d'Afrique et
d'Espagne*, pp.291, 292. – Mariana, *Hist. de España*, lib.25, cap.9. – Marmol,
Rebelion de Moriscos, lib.1, cap.12.

> '*Muy revuelta anda Granada
> en amas y fuego ardiendo,
> y los ciudadanos de ella
> duras muertes padeciendo;
>   Por tres reves que hay esquivos,
> cada uno pretendiendo
> el mando, cetro y corona
> de Granada y su gobierno,*' etc.

See this old romance, mixing up fact and fiction, with more of the former than
usual, in Hyta, *Guerras de Granada*, tom.i. p.292.

41. Among other achievements, al-Zagal surprised and beat the count of Cabra in a
night attack upon Moclín, and wellnigh retaliated on that nobleman his capture of
the Nasrid King Boabdil. Pulgar, *Reyes Católicos*, cap.48. [Arié assigns the dates 31
August–3 September 1485 to this battle. See *L'Espagne musulmane au temps des
Nasrides (1232–1492)*, Paris, 1973, p.165. – ED]

42. Bernaldez, *Reyes Católicos*, MS. cap. 75 – Pulgar, *Reyes Católicos*, cap.48. – Lebrija,
Rerum Gestarum Decades, ii, lib.3, cap.5, 7; lib.4, cap.2, 3. – Marmol, *Rebelion de
Moriscos*, lib.1, cap.12.
[The seizure of Loja holds some interest not noted in Prescott's text. Prescott's
original text refers to three sieges of Loja, but does not mention Boabdil's presence
at the third. Ferdinand besieged Loja twice following his disastrous attempt in
1482. He was repulsed again in January of 1485, before finally taking possession of
Loja, 29 May 1486. Boabdil (released soon after his capture at the Battle of Lucena
in 1483) was captured a second time with the fall of Loja in 1486. Although there
was significant ransom and exchange of Christian prisoners, Ferdinand's real
scheme in releasing Boabdil was to promote the political dissension with Granada.
Upon his release, Boabdil had to share the kingdom with his uncle, al-Zagal. A
violent civil conflict erupted between the two factions in the City of Granada
where Boabdil was situated in the Albaicin section and al-Zagal occupied the
Alhambra. In May 1486, Boabdil was forced to accept the dominant position of his
uncle, and to relocate to the town of Loja where he assumed a subordinate kingship
over the eastern part of the amirate of Granada. The Spanish sovereigns must have
been pleased with their original subversive use of Boabdil, for he was released the
second time. It was on this second capture that Boabdil had to agree to surrender

the city of Granada eight months following the surrender of Loja. References to the
sequence of sieges of Loja have been corrected in Prescott's text in this work. See
Arié, L'Espagne musulmane au temps des Nasrides (1232–1492), Paris, 1973, pp.166–
168. – ED}

CHAPTER 5

SIEGE AND CONQUEST OF MÁLAGA (1487)

*Narrow Escape of Ferdinand before Velez. – Málaga invested by Sea and Land. –
Brilliant Spectacle. – The Queen visits the Camp. – Attempt to assassinate the
Sovereigns. – Distress and Resolution of the Besieged. – Enthusiasm of the Christians. –
Outworks carried by them. – Proposals for Surrender. – Haughty Demeanour of
Ferdinand. – Málaga surrenders at Discretion. – Cruel Policy of the Victors.*

Before commencing operations against Málaga, it was thought expedient by
the Spanish council of war to obtain possession of Velez Málaga, situated
about five leagues distant from the former. This strong town stood along the
southern extremity of a range of mountains that extend to Granada. Its position
afforded an easy communication with that capital, and obvious means of
annoyance to an enemy interposed between itself and the adjacent city of
Málaga. The reduction of this place, therefore, became the first object of the
campaign.

The forces assembled at Córdoba, consisting of the levies of the Andalusian
cities principally, of the retainers of the great nobility, and of the well-appointed
chivalry which thronged from all quarters of the kingdom, amounted on this
occasion, to twelve thousand horse and forty thousand foot; a number, which
sufficiently attests the unslackened ardour of the nation in the prosecution of
the war. On the 7th of April, King Ferdinand, putting himself at the head of
this formidable host, quitted the fair city of Córdoba amid the cheering
acclamations of its inhabitants, although these were somewhat damped by the
ominous occurrence of an earthquake, which demolished a part of the royal
residence, among other edifices, during the preceding night. The route, after
traversing the Yeguas and the old town of Antequera, struck into a wild, hilly
country, that stretches toward Velez. The rivers were so much swollen by
excessive rains, and the passes so rough and difficult, that the army in part of its
march advanced only a league a day; and on one occasion, when no suitable
place occurred for encampment for the space of five leagues, the men fainted
with exhaustion, and the beasts dropped down dead in the harness. At length,
on the 17th of April, the Spanish army sat down before Velez Málaga, where in

a few days they were joined by the lighter pieces of their battering ordnance; the roads, notwithstanding the immense labour expended on them, being found impracticable for the heavier.[1]

The Granadans were aware of the importance of Velez to the security of Málaga. The sensation excited in Granada by the tidings of its danger was so strong, that the old chief, al-Zagal, found it necessary to make an effort to relieve the beleaguered city, notwithstanding the critical posture in which his absence would leave his affairs in the capital. Dark clouds of the enemy were seen throughout the day mustering along the heights, which by night were illumined with a hundred fires. Ferdinand's utmost vigilance was required for the protection of his camp against the ambuscades and nocturnal sallies of his wily foe. At length, however, al-Zagal having been foiled in a well-concerted attempt to surprise the Christian quarters by night, was driven across the mountains by the Marquis of Cádiz, and compelled to retreat on his capital, completely baffled in his enterprise. There the tidings of his disaster had preceded him. The fickle populace, with whom misfortune passes for misconduct, unmindful of his former successes, now hastened to transfer their allegiance to his rival, Boabdil, and closed the gates against him; and the unfortunate chief withdrew to Guadix, which, with Almería, Baza, and some less considerable places, still remained faithful.[2]

Ferdinand conducted the siege all the while with his usual vigour, and spared no exposure of his person to peril or fatigue. On one occasion, seeing a party of Christians retreating in disorder before a squadron of the enemy, who had surprised them while fortifying an eminence near the city, the king, who was at dinner in his tent, rushed out with no other defensive armour than his cuirass, and, leaping on his horse, charged briskly into the midst of the enemy, and succeeded in rallying his own men. In the midst of the encounter, however, when he had discharged his lance, he found himself unable to extricate his sword from the scabbard which hung from the saddlebow. At this moment he was assaulted by several Granadans, and must have been either slain or taken, but for the timely rescue of the Marquis of Cádiz, and a brave cavalier, Garcilasso de la Vega, who galloping up to the spot with their attendants, succeeded after a sharp skirmish in beating off the enemy. Ferdinand's nobles remonstrated with him on this wanton exposure of his person, representing that he could serve them more effectually with his head than his hand. But he answered, that 'he could not stop to calculate chances, when his subjects were periling their lives for his sake'; a reply, says Pulgar, which endeared him to the whole army.[3]

At length, the inhabitants of Velez, seeing the ruin impending from the bombardment of the Christians, whose rigorous blockade both by sea and land excluded all hopes of relief from without, consented to capitulate on the usual conditions of security to persons, property, and religion. The capitulation of this

Siege of an unknown Granadan stronghold.
Relief carving from Toledo Cathedral. (Rodrigo Alemán, c.1492)

place, April 27th, 1487, was followed by that of more than twenty places of inferior note lying between it and Málaga, so that the approaches to this latter city were now left open to the victorious Castilians.[4]

This ancient city, which, under the Spanish Muslims in the twelfth and thirteenth centuries, formed the capital of an independent principality, was second only to the metropolis itself, in the kingdom of Granada. Its fruitful environs furnished abundant articles of export, while its commodious port on the Mediterranean opened a traffic with the various countries washed by that inland sea, and with the remoter regions of India. Owing to these advantages, the inhabitants acquired unbounded opulence, which showed itself in the embellishments of their city, whose light forms of architecture, mingling after the eastern fashion with odoriferous gardens and fountains of sparkling water, presented an appearance most refreshing to the senses in this sultry climate.[5]

The city was encompassed by fortifications of great strength, and in perfect repair. It was commanded by a citadel, connected by a covered way with a second fortress impregnable from its position, denominated Gebalfaro, which stood along the declivities of the bold sierra of the Ajarquía, whose defiles had proved so disastrous to the Christians. The city lay between two spacious suburbs, the one on the land side being also encircled by a formidable wall; and the other declining toward the sea, showing an expanse of olive, orange, and pomegranate gardens, intermingled with the rich vineyards that furnished the celebrated staple for its export.

Málaga was well prepared for a siege by supplies of artillery and ammunition. Its ordinary garrison was reinforced by volunteers from the neighbouring towns, and by a corps of African mercenaries, Gomeres, as they were called, men of ferocious temper, but of tried valour and military discipline. The command of this important post had been intrusted by al-Zagal to a noble Muslim, named Hamet Zeli, whose renown in the present war had been established by his resolute defence of Ronda.[6]

Ferdinand, while lying before Velez, received intelligence that many of the wealthy burghers of Málaga were inclined to capitulate at once, rather than hazard the demolition of their city by an obstinate resistance. He instructed the Marquis of Cádiz, therefore, to open a negotiation with Hamet Zeli, authorizing him to make the most liberal offers to the alcayde himself, as well as his garrison, and the principal citizens of the place, on condition of immediate surrender. The sturdy chief, however, rejected the proposal with disdain, replying, that he had been commissioned by his master to defend the place to the last extremity, and that the Christian king could not offer a bribe large enough to make him betray his trust. Ferdinand, finding little prospect of operating on this Spartan temper, broke up his camp before Velez, on the 7th of May, and advanced with his whole army as far as Bezmillana, a place on the sea-board about two leagues distant from Málaga.[7]

The line of march now lay through a valley commanded at the extremity nearest the city by two eminences; the one on the seacoast, the other facing the fortress of the Gebalfaro, and forming part of the wild sierra which over-shadowed Málaga on the north. The enemy occupied both these important positions. A corps of Galicians were sent forward to dislodge them from the eminence toward the sea. But it failed in the assault, and, notwithstanding it was led up a second time by the Commander of León [Gutierre de Cárdenas] and the brave Garcilasso de La Vega,[8] was again repulsed by the intrepid foe.

A similar fate attended the assault on the sierra, which was conducted by the troops of the royal household. They were driven back on the vanguard, which had halted in the valley under command of the Grand Master of Santiago, prepared to support the attack on either side. Being reinforced, the Castilians returned to the charge with the most determined resolution. They were encountered by the enemy with equal spirit. The latter, throwing away their lances, precipitated themselves on the ranks of the assailants, making use only of their daggers, grappling closely man to man, till both rolled promiscuously together down the steep sides of the ravine. No mercy was asked, or shown. None thought of sparing or of spoiling, for hatred, says the chronicler, was stronger than avarice. The main body of the army, in the mean while, pent up in the valley, were compelled to witness the mortal conflict, and listen to the exulting cries of the enemy, which, after the Moorish custom, rose high and shrill above the din of battle, without being able to advance a step in support of their companions, who were again forced to give way before their impetuous adversaries, and fall back on the vanguard under the Grand Master of Santiago. Here, however, they speedily rallied; and, being reinforced, advanced to the charge a third time, with such inflexible courage as bore down all opposition, and compelled the enemy, exhausted, or rather overpowered by superior numbers, to abandon his position. At the same time the rising ground on the seaside was carried by the Castilians under the commander of León and Garcilasso de la Vega, who, dividing their forces, charged the Granadans so briskly in front and rear, that they were compelled to retreat on the neigh-bouring fortress of Gebalfaro.[9]

As it was evening before these advantages were obtained, the army did not defile into the plains around Málaga, before the following morning, when dispositions were made for its encampment. The eminence on the sierra, so bravely contested, was assigned as the post of greatest danger to the Marquis Duke of Cádiz. It was protected by strong works surmounted by artillery, and a corps of two thousand five hundred horse and fourteen thousand foot, was placed under the immediate command of that nobleman. A line of defence was constructed along the declivity from this redoubt to the seashore. Similar works, consisting of a deep trench and palisades, or, where the soil was too rocky to admit of them, of an embankment or mound of earth, were formed in front of the encampment, which embraced the whole circuit of the city; and the blockade was completed by a fleet of armed vessels, galleys and caravels, which rode in the harbour under the command of the Catalan admiral, Requesens, and effectually cut off all communication by water.[10]

The old chronicler Bernaldez warms at the aspect of the fair city of Málaga, thus encompassed by Christian legions, whose deep lines, stretching far over hill and valley, reached quite round from one arm of the sea to the other. In the midst of this brilliant encampment was seen the royal pavilion, proudly displaying the united banners of Castile and Aragón, and forming so conspicuous a mark for the enemy's artillery, that Ferdinand, after imminent hazard, was at length compelled to shift his quarters. The Christians were not slow in erecting counter batteries; but the work was obliged to be carried on at night, in order to screen them from the fire of the besieged.[11]

The first operations of the Castilians were directed against the suburb, on the land side of the city. The attack was intrusted to the Count of Cifuentes, the nobleman who had been made prisoner in the affair of the Ajarquía, and subsequently ransomed. The Castilian ordnance was served with such effect, that a practicable breach was soon made in the wall. The combatants now poured their murderous volleys on each other through the opening, and at length met on the ruins of the breach. After a desperate struggle the Granadans gave way. The Christians rushed into the enclosure, at the same time effecting a lodgment on the rampart; and, although a part of it, undermined by the enemy, gave way with a terrible crash, they still kept possession of the remainder, and at length drove their antagonists, who sullenly retreated step by step within the fortifications of the city. The lines were then drawn close around the place. Every avenue of communication was strictly guarded, and every preparation was made for reducing the town by regular blockade.[12]

In addition to the cannon brought round by water from Velez, the heavier lombards, which from the difficulty of transportation had been left during the late siege at Antequera, were now conducted across roads, levelled for the purpose, to the camp. Supplies of marble bullets were also brought from the ancient and depopulated city of Algeciras, where they had lain ever since its capture in the preceding century by Alfonso XI. The camp was filled with operatives, employed in the manufacture of balls and powder, which were stored in subterranean magazines, and in the fabrication of those various kinds of battering enginery, which continued in use long after the introduction of gunpowder.[13]

During the early part of the siege, the camp experienced some temporary inconvenience from the occasional interruption of the supplies transported by water. Rumours of the appearance of the plague in some of the adjacent villages caused additional uneasiness; and deserters, who passed into Málaga, reported these particulars with the usual exaggeration, and encouraged the besieged to persevere, by the assurance that Ferdinand could not much longer keep the field, and that the Queen had actually written to advise his breaking up the camp. Under these circumstances, Ferdinand saw at once the importance of the Queen's presence in order to dispel the delusion of the enemy, and to give new heart to his soldiers. He accordingly sent a message to Córdoba, where she was holding her court, requesting her appearance in the camp.

Isabella had proposed to join her husband before Velez, on receiving tidings of al-Zagal's march from Granada, and had actually enforced levies of all persons capable of bearing arms, between twenty and seventy years of age, throughout Andalusia, but subsequently disbanded them, on learning the discomfiture of the Granadan army. Without hesitation, she now set forward, accompanied by the cardinal of Spain and other dignitaries of the church, together with the Infanta Isabella, and a courtly train of ladies and cavaliers in attendance on her person. She was received at a short distance from the camp by the Marquis of Cádiz and the Grand Master of Santiago, and escorted to her quarters amidst the enthusiastic greetings of the soldiery. Hope now brightened every countenance. A grace seemed to be shed over the rugged features of war; and the young gallants thronged from all quarters to the camp, eager to win the guerdon of valour from the hands of those from whom it is most grateful to receive it.[14]

Ferdinand, who had hitherto brought into action only the lighter pieces of ordnance, from a willingness to spare the noble edifices of the city, now pointed his heaviest guns against its walls. Before opening his fire, however, he again summoned the place, offering the usual liberal terms in case of immediate compliance, and engaging otherwise, 'With the blessing of God, to make them all slaves!' But the heart of the *alcaide* was hardened like that of Pharaoh, says the Andalusian chronicler, and the people were swelled with vain hopes, so that their ears were closed against the proposal; orders were even issued to punish with death any attempt at a parley. On the contrary, they made answer by a more lively cannonade than before, along the whole line of ramparts and fortresses which overhung the city. Sallies were also made at almost every hour of the day and night on every assailable point of the Christian lines, so that the camp was kept in perpetual alarm. In one of the nocturnal sallies, a body of two thousand men from the castle of Gebalfaro succeeded in surprising the quarters of the Marquis of Cádiz, who, with his followers, was exhausted by fatigue and watching, during the two preceding nights. The Christians, bewildered with the sudden tumult which broke their slumber were thrown into the greatest confusion; and the Marquis, who rushed half armed from his tent, found no little difficulty in bringing them to order, and beating off the assailants, after receiving a wound in the arm from an arrow; while he had a still narrower escape from the ball of an arquebus, that penetrated his buckler and hit him below the cuirass, but fortunately so much spent as to do him no injury.[15]

The Granadans were not unmindful of the importance of Málaga, or the gallantry with which it was defended. They made several attempts to relieve it, whose failure was less owing to the Christians than to treachery and their own miserable feuds. A body of cavalry, which al-Zagal despatched from Guadix to throw succours into the beleaguered city, was encountered and cut to pieces by a superior force of the young King Boabdil, who consummated his baseness by sending an embassy to the Christian camp, charged with a present of Arabian horses sumptuously caparisoned to Ferdinand, and of costly silks and oriental perfumes to the Queen; at the same time complimenting them on their successes, and soliciting the continuance of their friendly dispositions toward himself. Ferdinand and Isabella requited this act of humiliation by securing to Boabdil's subjects the right of cultivating their fields in quiet, and of trafficking with the Christian Spanish in every commodity, save military stores. At this paltry price did the dastard prince consent to stay his arm, at the only moment when it could be used effectually for his country.[16]

More serious consequences had like to have resulted from an attempt made by another party of Granadans from Guadix to penetrate the Christian lines. Part of them succeeded, and threw themselves into the besieged city. The remainder were cut in pieces. There was one, however, who making no show of resistance, was made prisoner without harm to his person. Being brought before the Marquis of Cádiz, he informed that nobleman, that he could make some important disclosures to the sovereigns. He was accordingly conducted to the royal tent; but, as Ferdinand was taking his siesta in the sultry hour of the day, the Queen, moved by divine inspiration, according to the Castilian historian, deferred the audience till her husband should awake, and commanded the prisoner to be detained in the adjoining tent. This was occupied by Doña Beatriz de Bobadilla, Marchioness of Moya, Isabella's early friend, who happened to be at that time engaged in discourse with a Portuguese nobleman, Don Alvaro, son of the Duke of Braganza.[17]

The Muslim did not understand the Castilian language, and deceived by the rich attire and courtly bearing of these personages, he mistook them for the King and Queen. While in the act of refreshing himself with a glass of water, he suddenly drew a dagger from beneath the broad folds of *albornoz*, or Moorish mantle, which he had been incautiously suffered to retain, and, darting on the Portuguese prince, gave him a deep wound on the head; and then, turning like lightening on the marchioness, aimed a stroke at her, which fortunately glanced without injury, the point of the weapon being turned by the heavy embroidery of her robes. Before he could repeat his blow, the Moorish Scævola, with a fate very different from that of his Roman prototype, was pierced with a hundred wounds by the attendants, who rushed to the spot, alarmed by the cries of the marchioness, and his mangled remains were soon after discharged from a catapult into the city; a foolish bravado, which the besieged requited by slaying a Galician gentleman, and sending his corpse astride upon a mule through the gates of the town into the Christian camp.[18]

This daring attempt on the lives of the king and queen spread general consternation throughout the army. Precautions were taken for the future, by ordinances prohibiting the introduction of any unknown person armed, or any Muslim whatever, into the royal quarters; and the bodyguard was augmented by the addition of two hundred *hidalgos* of Castile and Aragón, who, with their retainers, were to keep constant watch over the persons of the sovereigns.

Meanwhile, the city of Málaga, whose natural population was greatly swelled by the influx of its foreign auxiliaries, began to be straitened for supplies, while its distress was aggravated by the spectacle of abundance which reigned throughout the Spanish camp. Still, however, the people, overawed by the soldiery, did not break out into murmurs, nor did they relax in any degree the pertinacity of their resistance. Their drooping spirits were cheered by the predictions of a fanatic, who promised that they should eat the grain which they saw in the Christian camp; a prediction, which came to be verified, like most others that are verified at all, in a very different sense from that intended or understood.

The incessant cannonade kept up by the besieging army, in the meantime, so far exhausted their ammunition, that they were constrained to seek supplies from the most distant parts of the kingdom, and from foreign countries. The arrival of two Flemish transports at this juncture, from the Emperor of Germany, whose interest had been roused in the crusade, afforded a seasonable reinforcement of military stores and munitions.

The obstinate defence of Málaga had given the siege such celebrity, that volunteers, eager to share in it, flocked from all parts of the Peninsula to the royal standard. Among others, the Duke of Medina Sidonia, who had furnished his quota of troops at the opening of the campaign, now arrived in person with a reinforcement, together with a hundred galleys freighted with supplies, and a loan of twenty thousand doblas of gold to the sovereigns for the expenses of the war. Such was the deep interest in it excited throughout the nation, and the alacrity which every order of men exhibited in supporting its enormous burdens.[19]

The Castilian army, swelled by these daily augmentations, varied in its amount, according to different estimates, from sixty to ninety thousand men. Throughout this immense host, the most perfect discipline was maintained. Gaming was restrained by ordinances interdicting the use of dice and cards, of which the lower orders were passionately fond. Blasphemy was severely punished. Prostitutes, the common pest of a camp, were excluded; and so entire was the subordination, that not a knife was drawn, and scarcely a brawl occurred, says the historian, among the motley multitude. Besides the higher ecclesiastics who attended the court, the camp was well supplied with holy men, priests, friars, and the chaplains of the great nobility, who performed the exercises of religion in their respective quarters with all the pomp and splendour of the Roman Catholic worship; exalting the imaginations of the soldiers into the high devotional feeling, which became those who were fighting the battles of the Cross.[20]

Hitherto, Ferdinand, relying on the blockade, and yielding to the Queen's desire to spare the lives of her soldiers, had formed no regular plan of assault upon the town. But, as the season rolled on without the least demonstration of submission on the part of the besieged, he resolved to storm the works, which, if attended by no other consequences, might at least serve to distress the enemy, and hasten the hour of surrender. Large wooden towers on rollers were accordingly constructed, and provided with an apparatus of drawbridges and ladders, which, when brought near to the ramparts, would open a descent into the city. Galleries were also wrought, some for the purpose of penetrating into the place, and others to sap the foundations of the walls. The whole of these operations was placed under the direction of Francisco Ramírez, the celebrated engineer of Madrid.

But the Granadans anticipated the completion of these formidable preparations by a brisk, well concerted attack on all points of the Castilian lines. They countermined the assailants, and, encountering them in the subterranean passages, drove them back, and demolished the framework of the galleries. At the same time, a little squadron of armed vessels, which had been riding in safety under the guns of the city, pushed out and engaged the Christian fleet. Thus the battle raged with fire and sword, above and under ground, along the ramparts, the ocean, and the land, at the same time. Even Pulgar cannot withhold his tribute of admiration to this unconquerable spirit in an enemy, wasted by all the extremities of famine and fatigue. 'Who does not marvel,' he says, 'at the bold heart of these infidels in battle, their prompt obedience to their chiefs, their dexterity in the wiles of war, their patience under privation, and undaunted perseverance in their purposes?'[21]

A circumstance occurred in a sortie from the city, indicating a trait of character worth recording. A noble Muslim named Abrahen Zenete fell in with a number of Christian Spanish children who had wandered from their quarters. Without injuring them, he touched them gently with the handle of his lance, saying, 'Get ye gone, varlets, to your mothers.' On being rebuked by his comrades, who inquired why he had let them escape so easily, he replied, 'Because I saw no beard upon their chins.' 'An example of magnanimity,' says the Curate of Los Palacios, 'truly wonderful in a heathen, and which might have reflected credit on a Christian *hidalgo*.'[22]

But no virtue nor valour could avail the unfortunate Málagans against the overwhelming force of their enemies, who, driving them back from every point, compelled them, after a desperate struggle of six hours, to shelter themselves within the defences of the town. The Christians followed up their success. A mine was sprung near a tower, connected by a bridge of four arches with the main works of the place. The Muslims, scattered and intimidated by the explosion, retreated across the bridge, and the Christians, carrying the tower, whose guns completely enfiladed it, obtained possession of this important pass into the beleaguered city. For these and other signal services during the siege, Francisco Ramírez, the master of the ordnance, received the honours of knighthood from the hand of King Ferdinand.[23]

The citizens of Málaga, dismayed at beholding the enemy established in their defences, and fainting under exhaustion from a siege which had already lasted more than three months, now began to murmur at the obstinacy of the garrison, and to demand a capitulation. Their magazines of grain were emptied, and for some weeks they had been compelled to devour the flesh of horses, dogs, cats, and even the boiled hides of these animals, or, in default of other nutriment, vine leaves dressed with oil, and leaves of the palm tree, pounded fine, and baked into a sort of cake. In consequence of this loathsome and unwholesome diet, diseases were engendered. Multitudes were seen dying about the streets. Many deserted to the Spanish camp, eager to barter their liberty for bread; and the city exhibited all the extremes of squalid and disgusting wretchedness, bred by pestilence and famine among an overcrowded population. The sufferings of the citizens softened the stern heart of the *alcaide*, Hamet Zeli, who at length yielded to their importunities, and, withdrawing his forces into the Gebalfaro, consented that the Málagans should make the best terms they could with their conqueror.

A deputation of the principal inhabitants, with an eminent merchant named Ali Dordux at their head, was then despatched to the Christian quarters, with the offer of the city to capitulate, on the same liberal conditions which had been uniformly granted by the Castilians. The King refused to admit the embassy into his presence, and haughtily answered through the Commander of León, 'that these terms had been twice offered to the people of Málaga, and rejected; that it was too late for them to stipulate conditions, and nothing now remained but to abide by those, which he, as their conqueror, should vouchsafe to them'.[24]

Ferdinand's answer spread general consternation throughout Málaga. The inhabitants saw too plainly that nothing was to be hoped from an appeal to sentiments of humanity. After a tumultuous debate, the deputies were despatched a second time to the Christian camp, charged with propositions in which concession was mingled with menace. They represented that the severe response of King Ferdinand to the citizens had rendered them desperate. That, however, they were willing to resign to him their fortifications, their city, in short their property of every description, on his assurance of their personal security and freedom. If he refused this, they would take their Christian captives, amounting to five or six hundred, from the dungeons in which they lay, and hang them like dogs over the battlements; and then, placing their old men, women, and children in the fortress, they would set fire to the town, and cut a way for themselves through their enemies, or fall in the attempt. 'So,' they continued, 'if you gain a victory, it shall be such a one as shall make the name of Málaga ring throughout the world, and to ages yet unborn!' Ferdinand, unmoved by these menaces, coolly replied, that he saw no occasion to change his former determination; but they might rest assured, if they harmed a single hair of a Christian, he would put every soul in the place, man, woman, and child, to the sword.

The anxious people who thronged forth to meet the embassy on its return to the city, were overwhelmed with the deepest gloom at its ominous tidings. Their fate was now sealed. Every avenue to hope seemed closed by the stern response of the victor. Yet hope will still linger; and, although there were some frantic enough to urge the execution of their desperate menaces, the greater number of the inhabitants, and among them those most considerable for wealth and influence, preferred the chance of Ferdinand's clemency to certain, irretrievable ruin.

For the last time, therefore, the deputies issued from the gates of the city, charged with an epistle to the sovereigns from their unfortunate countrymen, in which, after deprecating their anger, and lamenting their own blind obstinacy, they reminded their highnesses of the liberal terms which their ancestors had granted to Córdoba, Antequera, and other cities, after a defence as pertinacious as their own. They expatiated on the fame which the sovereigns had established by the generous policy of their past conquests, and, appealing to their magnanimity, concluded with submitting themselves, their families, and their fortunes to their disposal. Twenty of the principal citizens were then delivered up as hostages for the peaceable demeanour of the city until its occupation by the Castilians. 'Thus,' says the Curate of Los Palacios, 'did the Almighty harden the hearts of these heathen, like to those of the Egyptians, in order that they might receive the full wages of the manifold oppressions which they had wrought on his people, from the days of King Rodrigo [Roderic] to the present time!'[25]

On the appointed day, the Commander of León rode through the gates of Málaga, at the head of his well-appointed chivalry, and took possession of the *alcazaba*, or lower citadel. The troops were then posted on their respective stations along the fortifications, and the banners of Christian Spain triumphantly unfurled from the towers of the city, where the crescent had been displayed for an uninterrupted period of nearly eight centuries.

The first act was to purify the town from the numerous dead bodies, and other offensive matter, which had accumulated during this long siege, and lay festering in the streets, poisoning the atmosphere. The principal mosque was next consecrated with due solemnity to the service of Santa Maria de la Incarnacion. Crosses and bells, the symbols of Christian worship, were distributed in profusion among the sacred edifices; where, says the Catholic chronicler last quoted, 'the celestial music of their chimes, sounding at every hour of the day and night, caused perpetual torment to the ears of the infidel.'[26]

On the eighteenth day of August, being somewhat more than three months from the date of opening trenches, Ferdinand and Isabella made their entrance into the conquered city, attended by the court, the clergy, and the whole of their military array. The procession moved in solemn state up the principal streets, now deserted, and hushed in ominous silence, to the new cathedral of Santa Maria, where mass was performed, and, as the glorious anthem of the *Te Deum* rose for the first time within its ancient walls, the sovereigns, together with the whole army, prostrated themselves in grateful adoration of the Lord of Hosts, who had thus reinstated them in the domains of their ancestors.

The most affecting incident was afforded by the multitude of Christian captives, who were rescued from the Moorish dungeons. They were brought before the sovereigns, with their limbs heavily manacled, their beards descending to their waists, and their sallow visages emaciated by captivity and famine. Every eye was suffused with tears at the spectacle. Many recognized their ancient friends, of whose fate they had long been ignorant. Some had lingered in captivity ten or fifteen years; and among them were several belonging to the best families in Christian Spain. On entering the presence, they would have testified their gratitude by throwing themselves at the feet of the sovereigns; but the latter, raising them up and mingling their tears with those of the liberated captives, caused their fetters to be removed, and, after administering to their necessities, dismissed them with liberal presents.[27]

The fortress of Gebalfaro surrendered on the day after the occupation of Málaga by the Castilians. The gallant Zegri chieftain, Hamet Zeli, was loaded with chains; and, being asked why he had persisted so obstinately in his rebellion, boldly answered, 'Because I was commissioned to defend the place to the last extremity; and, if I had been properly supported, I would have died sooner than surrender now!'

The doom of the vanquished was now to be pronounced. On entering the city, orders had been issued to the Castilian soldiery, prohibiting them under the severest penalties from molesting either the persons or property of the inhabitants. These latter were directed to remain in their respective mansions with a guard set over them, while the cravings of appetite were supplied by a liberal distribution of food. At length, the whole population of the city, comprehending every age and sex, was commanded to repair to the great courtyard of the *alcazaba*, which was overlooked on all sides by lofty ramparts garrisoned by the Castilian soldiery. To this place, the scene of many a Spanish Muslim triumph, where the spoil of the border foray had been often displayed, and which still might be emblazoned with the trophy of many a Christian banner, the people of Málaga now directed their steps. As the multitude swarmed through the streets, filled with boding apprehensions of their fate, they wrung their hands, and, raising their eyes to Heaven, uttered the most piteous lamentations. 'Oh Málaga,' they cried, 'renowned and beautiful city, how are thy sons about to forsake thee! Could not thy soil on which they first drew breath, be suffered to cover them in death? Where is now the strength of thy towers, where the beauty of thy edifices? The strength of thy walls, alas, could not avail thy children, for they had sorely displeased their Creator. What shall become of thy old men and thy matrons, or of thy young maidens delicately nurtured within thy halls, when they shall feel the iron yoke of bondage? Can thy barbarous conquerors without remorse thus tear asunder the dearest ties of life?' Such are the melancholy strains, in which the Castilian chronicler has given utterance to the sorrows of the captive city.[28]

The dreadful doom of slavery was denounced on the assembled multitude. One third was to be transported into Africa in exchange for an equal number of Christian captives detained there; and all, who had relatives or friends in this predicament, were required to furnish a specification of them. Another third was appropriated to reimburse the state for the expenses of the war. The remainder were to be distributed as presents at home and abroad. Thus, one hundred of the flower of the African warriors were sent to the pope, who incorporated them into his guard, and converted them all in the course of the year, says the Curate of Los Palacios, into very good Christians. Fifty of the most beautiful Moorish girls were presented by Isabella to the Queen of Naples, thirty to the Queen of Portugal, others to the ladies of her court; and the residue of both sexes were apportioned among the nobles, cavaliers, and inferior members of the army, according to their respective rank and services.[29]

As it was apprehended that the Málagans, rendered desperate by the prospect of a hopeless, interminable captivity, might destroy or secrete their jewels, plate, and other precious effects, in which this wealthy city abounded, rather than suffer them to fall into the hands of their enemies, Ferdinand devised a politic expedient for preventing it. He proclaimed, that he would receive a certain sum, if paid within nine months, as the ransom of the whole population, and that their personal effects should be admitted in part payment. This sum averaged about thirty doblas a head, including in the estimate all those who might die before the determination of the period assigned. The ransom, thus stipulated, proved more than the unhappy people could raise, either by themselves, or agents employed to solicit contributions among their brethren of Granada and Africa; at the same time, it so far deluded their hopes, that they gave in a full inventory of their effects to the treasury. By this shrewd device, Ferdinand obtained complete possession both of the persons and property of his victims.[30]

Málaga was computed to contain from eleven to fifteen thousand inhabitants, exclusive of several thousand foreign auxiliaries, within its gates at the
time of surrender. One cannot, at this day, read the melancholy details of its
story, without feelings of horror and indignation. It is impossible to vindicate
the dreadful sentence passed on this unfortunate people for a display of heroism,
which should have excited admiration in every generous bosom. It was
obviously most repugnant to Isabella's natural disposition and must be
admitted to leave a stain on her memory, which no colouring of history can
conceal. It may find some palliation, however, in the bigotry of the age, the
more excusable in a woman, whom education, general example, and natural
distrust of herself, accustomed to rely, in matters of conscience, on the spiritual
guides, whose piety and professional learning seemed to qualify them for the
trust. Even in this very transaction, she fell far short of the suggestions of some
of her counsellors, who urged her to put every inhabitant without exception to
the sword; which, they affirmed, would be a just requital of their obstinate
rebellion, and would prove a wholesome warning to others! We are not told who
the advisers of this precious measure were; but the whole experience of this
reign shows, that we shall scarcely wrong the clergy much by imputing it to
them. That their arguments could warp so enlightened a mind, as that of
Isabella, from the natural principles of justice and humanity, furnishes a
remarkable proof of the ascendancy which the priesthood usurped over the
most gifted intellects, and of their gross abuse of it, before the Reformation, by
breaking the seals set on the sacred volume, opened to mankind the uncorrupted channel of divine truth.[31]

The fate of Málaga may be said to have decided that of Granada. The latter
was now shut out from the most important ports along her coast; and she was
environed on every point of her territory by her warlike foe, so that she could
hardly hope more from subsequent efforts, however strenuous and united,than
to postpone the inevitable hour of dissolution. The cruel treatment of Málaga
was the prelude to the long series of persecutions, which awaited the wretched
Muslims in the land of their ancestors; in that land, over which the star of
Islamism, to borrow their own metaphor, had shone in full brightness for nearly
eight centuries, but where it was now fast descending amid clouds and tempests
to the horizon.

The first care of the sovereigns was directed toward repeopling the
depopulated city with their own subjects. Houses and lands were freely
granted to such as would settle there. Numerous towns and villages with a
wide circuit of territory were placed under its civil jurisdiction, and it was
made the head of a diocese embracing most of the recent conquests in the
south and west of Granada. These inducements, combined with the natural
advantages of position and climate, soon caused the tide of Christian population to flow into the deserted city; but it was very long before it again

reached the degree of commercial consequence to which it had been raised by the Spanish Muslims.

After these salutary arrangements, the Spanish sovereigns led back their victorious legions in triumph to Córdoba, whence dispersing to their various homes they prepared, by a winter's repose, for new campaigns and more brilliant conquests.

NOTES

1. Vedmar, *Antiguedad y Grandezas de la Ciudad de Velez*, (Granada, 1652) fol.148. – Mariana, *Hist. de España*, tom.ii, lib.25, cap.10. – Pulgar, *Reyes Católicos*, part iii, cap.70. – Carbajal, *Anales*, MS., año 1487. – Bleda, Corónica, lib.5, cap.14.

2. Cardonne, *Hist. d'Afrique et d'Espagne*, tom.iii, pp.292–4. – Pulgar, *Reyes Católicos, ubi supra*. – Vedmar, *Antiguedad Velez*, fol.150, 151.

3. L. Marineo, *Cosas Memorables*, fol.175. – Vedmar, *Antiguedad Velez*, fol.150.151. – Marmol, *Rebelion de Moriscos*, lib.1, cap.14.

   In commemoration of this event, the city incorporated into its escutcheon the figure of a king on horseback in the act of piercing a Moor with his javelin. Vedmar, *Antiguedad Velez*, fol.12.

4. Bernaldez, *Reyes Católicos*, MS, cap.52. – Marmol, *Rebelion de Moriscos*, lib.1, cap.14.

5. Condé doubts whether the name Málaga is derived from the Greek μαλακη, signifying 'agreeable', or the Arabic *malka*, meaning 'royal'. Either etymology is sufficiently pertinent. (See El Nubiense, *Descripcion de España*, p.186. not.) For notices of sovereigns who swayed the sceptre of Málaga, see Casiri, *Bibliotheca Escurialensis*, tom.ii, pp.41, 56, 99, *et alibi*.

6. Condé, *Dominacion de los Arabes*, tom.iii, p.237. – Pulgar, *Reyes Católicos*, cap.74. – El Nubiense, *Descripcion de España*, not p.144.

7. Bernaldez, *Reyes Católicos*, MS., cap.82. – Vedmar, *Antiguedad Velez*, fol.154. – Pulgar, *Reyes Católicos*, cap.74.

8. This cavalier, who took a conspicuous part both in the military and civil transactions of this reign, was descended from one of the most ancient and honourable houses in Castile. – Hyta, (*Guerras Civiles de Granada*, tom.i, p.399) with more effrontery than usual, has imputed to him a chivalrous encounter with a Saracen, which is recorded of an ancestor, in the ancient Chronicle of Alonso XI:

   'Garcilasso de la Vega
   desde alli se ha intitulado,
   porque en la Vega heciera
   campo con aquel pagano.'

   Oviedo, however, with good reason, distrusts the etymology and the story, as he traces both the cognomen and the peculiar device of the family to a much older date than the period assigned in the Chronicle. *Quincuagenas*, MS., bat.1, quinc.3, dial.43.

9. Pulgar, *Reyes Católicos*, cap.75. – Salazar de Mendoza, *Crón. del Gran Cardenal*, lib.1, cap.64.

10. Bernaldez, *Reyes Católicos*, MS., cap.76. – Carbajal, *Anales*, MS., año 1487.

11. Pulgar, *Reyes Católicos, ubi supra*. – Bernaldez, *Reyes Católicos*, MS., *ubi supra*.

12. Peter Martyr, *Opus Epist.*, lib.1, epist.63. – Pulgar, *Reyes Católicos*, cap.76. – Bernaldez, *Reyes Católicos*, MS., cap.83. – Oviedo, *Quincuagenas*, MS., bat.1, quinc.1, dial.36.
13. Pulgar, *Reyes Católicos*, cap.76.
14. Salazar de Mendoza, *Crón. del Gran Cardenal*, lib.1, cap.64. – Zurita, *Anales*, tom.iv, cap.70. – Bernaldez, *Reyes Católicos*, MS., cap.83.
15. Bleda, *Corónica*, lib.5, cap.15. – Condé, *Dominacion de los Arabes*, tom.iv, pp.237, 238. – Bernaldez, *Reyes Católicos*, MS., cap.83. – Pulgar, *Reyes Católicos*, cap.79.
16. Pulgar, *Reyes Católicos, ubi supra.*

    During the siege, ambassadors arrived from an African potentate, the king of Tremecen [Tlemcen], bearing a magnificent present to the Castilian sovereigns, interceding for the Málagans, and at the same time asking protection for his subjects from the Spanish cruisers in the Mediterranean. The sovereign graciously complied with the latter request, and complimented the African monarch with a plate of gold, on which the royal arms were curiously embossed, says Bernaldez, *Reyes Católicos*, MS., cap.84.

17. This nobleman, Don Alvaro de Portugal, had fled his native country, and sought an asylum in Castile from the vindictive enmity of João II, who had put to death the Duke of Braganza, his elder brother. He was kindly received by Isabella, to whom he was nearly related, and subsequently preferred to several important offices of state. His son, the Count of Gelves, married a granddaughter of Christopher Columbus. Oviedo, *Quincuagenas*, MS.
18. Oviedo, *Quincuagenas*, MS., bat.1, quinc.1, dial.23. – Peter Martyr, *Opus Epist.*, lib.1, epist.63. – Bernaldez, *Reyes Católicos*, MS., cap.84. – Bleda, *Corónica*, lib.5, cap.15. – L. Marineo, *Cosas Memorables*, fol.175, 176.
19. Pulgar, *Reyes Católicos*, cap.87–89. – Bernaldez, *Reyes Católicos*, MS., cap.84.
20. Bernaldez, *Reyes Católicos*, MS., cap.87. – Pulgar, *Reyes Católicos*, cap.71.
21. Condé, *Dominacion de los Arabes*, tom.iii, pp.237, 238. – Pulgar, *Reyes Católicos*, cap.80. – Caro de Torres, *Ordenes Militares*, fol.82, 83.
22. Pulgar, *Reyes Católicos*, cap.91. – Bernaldez, *Reyes Católicos*, MS., cap.84.
    The honest exclamation of the Curate brings to mind the similar encomium of the old Moorish ballad,

    '*Caballeros Granadinos,*
    Aunque Moros, hijosdalgo.'

                    – Hyta, *Guerras Civiles de Granada*, tom.i, p.257.

23. There is no older well-authenticated account of the employment of gunpowder in mining in European warfare, so far as I am aware, than this by Ramírez. Tiraboschi, indeed, refers, on the authority of another writer, to a work in the library of the Academy of Siena, composed by one Francesco Giorgio, architect of the Duke of Urbino, about 1480, in which that person claims the merit of the invention (*Letteratura Italiana*, tom.vi, p.370). The whole statement is obviously too loose to warrant any such conclusion. The Italian historians notice the use of gunpowder mines at the siege of the little town of Serezanello in Tuscany, by the Genoese, in 1487, precisely contemporaneous with the siege of Málaga. (Machiavelli, *Istorie Fiorentine*, lib.8. – Giocciardini, *Istorie d'Italia* (Milano, 1803) tom.iii, lib.6).

This singular coincidence, in nations having then but little intercourse, would seem to infer some common origin of greater antiquity. However this may be, the writers of both nations are agreed in ascribing the first successful use of such mines on any extended scale to the celebrated Spanish engineer, Pedro Navarro, when serving under Gonzalo of Córdoba, in his Italian campaigns at the beginning of the sixteenth century. Guicciardini, *ubi supra*. – Paolo Giovio, De Vitâ Magni Gonsalvi, (*Vitæ Illustrium Virorum*, Basiliæ, 1578) lib.2. – Aleson, *Annales de Navarra*, tom.v, lib.35, cap.12.

24. Cardonne, *Hist. d'Afrique et d'Espagne*, tom.iii, p.296. – L. Marineo, *Cosas Memorables*, fol.175. – Radesy Andrada, *Las Tres Ordenes*, fol.54. – Pulgar, *Reyes Católicos*, cap.92. – Bernaldez, *Reyes Católicos*, MS., cap.85.

25. Pulgar, *Reyes Católicos*, cap.93. – Cardonne, *Hist. d'Afrique et d'Espagne*, tom.iii, p.296.

The Muslim historians state, that Málaga was betrayed by Ali Dordux, who admitted the Spaniards into the castle, while the citizens were debating on Ferdinand's terms (See Condé, *Dominacion de los Arabes*, tom.iii, cap.39). The letter of the inhabitants, quoted at length by Pulgar, would seem to be a refutation of this. And yet there are good grounds for suspecting false play on the part of the ambassador Dordux, since the Christian writers admit, that he was exempted, with forty of his friends, from the doom of slavery and forfeiture of property, passed upon his fellow-citizens.

26. Bernaldez, *Reyes Católicos*, MS., cap.85.

27. Carbajal, whose meagre annals have scarcely any merit beyond that of a mere chronological table, postpones the surrender till September. *Anales*, año 1487. – Marmol, *Rebelion de Moriscos*, lib.1, cap.14.

28. Bleda, *Corónica*, lib.5, cap.15.

As a counterpart to the above scene, twelve Christian 'renegades', found in the city, were transfixed with canes, *acañavereados*, a barbarous punishment derived from the Moors, which was inflicted by horsemen at full gallop, who discharged pointed reeds at the criminal, until he expired under repeated wounds. A number of relapsed Jews were at the same time condemned to the flames. 'These,' says father Abarca, 'were the *fêtes* and illuminations most grateful to the Catholic piety of our sovereigns!' Abarca, *Reyes de Aragón*, tom.ii, fol.30, cap.3.

29. Pulgar, *Reyes Católicos, ubi supra*. – Bernaldez, *Reyes Católicos*, MS., *ubi supra*. – Peter Martyr, *Opus Epist.*, lib.1, epist.82.

30. Bernaldez, *Reyes Católicos*, MS., cap.87. – Bleda, *Corónica*, lib.5, cap.15.

About four hundred and fifty Moorish Jews were ransomed by a wealthy Israelite of Castile for 27,000 doblas of gold. This suggests the Jewish stock did not significantly suffer amidst persecution.

It is scarcely possible that the circumstantial Pulgar should have omitted to notice so important a fact as the scheme of the Moorish ransom, had it occurred. It is still more improbable, that the honest Curate of Los Palacios should have fabricated it. Any one who attempts to reconcile the discrepancies of contemporary historians even, will have Lord Oxford's exclamation to his son Horace brought to his mind ten times a day: 'Oh! read me not history, for that I know to be false.'

31. Pulgar, *Reyes Católicos*, cap.94. – *Col. de Céd.* tom.vi, no.321.

CHAPTER 6

CONQUEST OF BAZA AND SUBMISSION OF
AL-ZAGAL (1487–89)

The Sovereigns visit Aragón. – The King lays Siege to Baza. – Its great Strength. – Gardens cleared of their Timber. – The Queen raises the Spirits of her Troops. – Her patriotic Sacrifices. – Suspension of Arms. – Baza Surrenders. – Treaty with al-Zagal. – Difficulties of the Campaign. – Isabella's Popularity and Influence.

In the autumn of 1487, Ferdinand and Isabella, accompanied by the younger branches of the royal family, visited Aragón, to obtain the recognition from the cortes, of Prince Juan's succession, now in his tenth year, as well as to repress the disorders into which the country had fallen during the long absence of its sovereigns. To this end, the principal cities and communities of Aragón had recently adopted the institution of the *Hermandad*, organized on similar principles to that of Castile. Ferdinand, on his arrival at Zaragoza in the month of November, gave his royal sanction to the association, extending the term of its duration to five years, a measure extremely unpalatable to the great feudal nobility, whose power, or rather abuse of power, was considerably abridged by this popular military force.[1]

The sovereigns, after accomplishing the objects of their visit, and obtaining an appropriation from the cortes for the Moorish war, passed into Valencia, where measures of like efficiency were adopted for restoring the authority of the law, which was exposed to such perpetual lapses in this turbulent age, even in the best constituted governments, as required for its protection the utmost vigilance, on the part of those intrusted with the supreme executive power. From Valencia the court proceeded to Murcia, where Ferdinand, in the month of June, 1488, assumed the command of an army amounting to less than twenty thousand men, a small force compared with those usually levied on these occasions; it being thought advisable to suffer the nation to breathe a while, after the exhausting efforts in which it had been unintermittingly engaged for so many years.

Ferdinand, crossing the eastern borders of Granada, a no great distance from

Vera, which speedily opened its gates, kept along the southern slant of the coast as far as Almería; whence, after experiencing some rough treatment from a sortie of the garrison, he marched by a northerly circuit on Baza, for the purpose of reconnoitring its position, as his numbers were altogether inadequate to its siege. A division of the army under the Marquis Duke of Cádiz suffered itself to be drawn here into an ambuscade by the wily old monarch al-Zagal, who lay in Baza with a strong force. After extricating his troops with some difficulty and loss from this perilous predicament, Ferdinand retreated on his own dominions by the way of Huéscar, where he disbanded his army, and withdrew to offer up his devotions at the cross of Caravaca. The campaign, though signalized by no brilliant achievement, and indeed clouded with some slight reverses, secured the surrender of a considerable number of fortresses and towns of inferior note.[2]

The Nasrid chief, al-Zagal, elated by his recent success, made frequent forays into the Christian territories, sweeping off the flocks, herds, and growing crops of the husbandmen; while the garrisons of Almería and Salobreña, and the bold inhabitants of the valley of Purchena, poured a similar devastating warfare over the eastern borders of Granada into Murcia. To meet this pressure, the Christian sovereigns reinforced the frontier with additional levies under Juan de Benavides and Garcilasso de la Vega; while Christian knights, whose prowess is attested in many a Moorish lay, flocked there from all quarters, as to the theatre of war.

During the following winter, of 1488, Ferdinand and Isabella occupied themselves with the interior government of Castile, and particularly the administration of justice. A commission was specially appointed to supervise the conduct of the *corregidors* and subordinate magistrates, 'so that every one', says Pulgar, 'was most careful to discharge his duty faithfully, in order to escape the penalty, which was otherwise sure to overtake him'.[3]

While at Valladolid, the sovereigns received an embassy from Maximilian I, son of the Emperor Frederic IV, of Germany, soliciting their cooperation in his designs against France for the restitution of his late wife's rightful inheritance, the Duchy of Burgundy, and engaging in turn to support them in their claims on Rosellon and Cerdaña. The Spanish monarchs had long entertained many causes of discontent with the French court, both with regard to the mortgaged territory of Rosellon, and the Navarra; and they watched with jealous eye the daily increasing authority of their formidable neighbour on their own frontier. They had been induced in the preceding summer, to equip an armament at Biscay and Guipuscoa, to support the Duke of Brittany in his wars with the French regent, the celebrated Anne de Beaujeu. This expedition, which proved disastrous, was followed by another in the spring of the succeeding year.[4] But, notwithstanding these occasional episodes to the great work in which they were engaged, they had little leisure for extended operations; and, although they entered into the proposed treaty of alliance with Maximilian I, they do not seem to have contemplated any movement of importance before the termination of the Granadan war. The Flemish ambassadors, after being entertained for forty days in a style suited to impress them with high ideas of the magnificence of the Castilian court, and of its friendly disposition toward their master, were dismissed with costly presents, and returned to their own country.[5]

These negotiations show the increasing intimacy growing up between the European states, who, as they settled their domestic feuds, had leisure to turn their eyes abroad, and enter into the more extended field of international politics. The tenor of this treaty indicates also the direction, which affairs were to take, when the great powers should be brought into collision with each other on a common theatre of action.

All thoughts were now concentrated on the prosecution of the war with Granada, which, it was determined, should be conducted on a more enlarged scale than it had yet been; notwithstanding the fearful pest which had desolated the country during the past year, and the extreme scarcity of grain, owing to the inundations caused by excessive rains in the fruitful provinces of the south. The great object proposed in this campaign was the reduction of Baza, the capital of that division of the empire, which belonged to al-Zagal. Besides this important City, that monarch's dominions embraced the wealthy seaport of Almería, Guadix, and numerous other towns and villages of less consequence, together with the mountain region of the Alpujarras, rich in mineral wealth; whose inhabitants, famous for the perfection to which they had carried the silk manufacture, were equally known for their enterprise and courage in war, so that al-Zagal's division comprehended the most potent and opulent portion of the empire.[6]

In the spring of 1489, the Castilian court passed to Jaén at which place the Queen was to establish her residence, as presenting the most favourable point of communication with the invading army. Ferdinand advanced as far as Sotogordo, where, on the 27th of May, he put himself at the head of a numerous force, amounting to about fifteen thousand horse and eighty thousand foot, including persons of every description; among whom was gathered, as usual, that chivalrous array of nobility and knighthood, who, with stately and well-appointed retinues, were accustomed to follow the royal standard in these crusades.[7]

The first point, against which operations were directed, was the strong post of Cuxar, two leagues only from Baza, which surrendered after a brief but desperate resistance. The occupation of this place, and some adjacent fortresses, left the approaches open to al-Zagal's capital. As the Castilian army toiled up the heights of the mountain barrier, which towers above Baza on the west, their advance was menaced by clouds of Granadan light troops, who poured down a tempest of musket-balls and arrows on their heads. These however were quickly dispersed by the advancing vanguard; and the Castilians, as they gained the summits of the hills, beheld the lordly city of Baza, reposing in the shadows of the bold sierra that stretches toward the coast, and lying in the bosom of a fruitful valley, extending eight leagues in length, and three in breadth. Through this valley flowed the waters of the Guadalentin and the Guadalquiton, whose streams were conducted by a thousand canals over the surface of the vega. In the midst of the plain, adjoining the suburbs, might be descried the orchard or garden, as it was termed, of Baza, a league in length, covered with a thick growth of wood, and with numerous villas and pleasure-houses of the wealthy citizens, now converted into garrisoned fortresses. The suburbs were encompassed by a low mud wall; but the fortifications of the city were of uncommon strength. The place, in addition to ten thousand troops of its own, was garrisoned by an equal number from Almería; picked men, under the command of the Nasrid Prince Cidi Yahye, a relative of al-Zagal, who lay at this time in Guadix, prepared to cover his own dominions against any hostile movement of his rival in Granada. These veterans were commissioned to defend the place to the last extremity; and, as due time had been given for preparation, the town was victualled with fifteen months' provisions, and even the crops growing in the vega had been garnered before their prime, to save them from the hands of the enemy.[8]

The first operation, after the Christian army had encamped before the walls of Baza, was to get possession of the garden, without which it would be impossible to enforce a thorough blockade, since its labyrinth of avenues afforded the inhabitants abundant facilities of communication with the surrounding country. The assault was intrusted to the Grand Master of Santiago, supported by the principal cavaliers, and the King in person. Their reception by the enemy was such as gave them a foretaste of the perils and desperate daring they were to encounter in the present siege. The broken surface of the ground, bewildered with intricate passes, and thickly studded with trees and edifices, was peculiarly favourable to the desultory and illusory tactics of the Muslims. The Castilian cavalry was brought at once to a stand; the ground proving impracticable for it, it was dismounted, and led to the charge by its officers on foot. The men, however, were soon scattered far asunder from their banners and their leaders. Ferdinand, who from a central position endeavoured to overlook the field, with the design of supporting the attack on the points most requiring it, soon lost sight of his columns amid the precipitous ravines, and the dense masses of foliage which everywhere intercepted the view. The combat was carried on, hand to hand, in the utmost confusion. Still the Castilians pressed forward, and, after a desperate struggle for twelve hours, in which many of the bravest on both sides fell, and the Muslim chief Reduan Zafarga had four horses successively killed under him, the enemy were beaten back behind the entrenchments that covered the suburbs, and the Christians, hastily constructing a defence of palisades, pitched their tents on the field of battle.[9]

The following morning Ferdinand had the mortification to observe, that the ground was too much broken, and obstructed with wood, to afford a suitable place for a general encampment. To evacuate his position, however, in the face of the enemy, was a delicate manoeuvre, and must necessarily expose him to severe loss. This he obviated, in a great measure, by a fortunate stratagem. He commanded the tents nearest the town to be left standing, and thus succeeded in drawing off the greater part of his forces, before the enemy was aware of his intention.

After regaining his former position, a council of war was summoned to deliberate on the course next to be pursued. The chiefs were filled with despondency, as they revolved the difficulties of their situation. They almost despaired enforcing the blockade of a place, whose peculiar situation gave it such advantages. Even could this be effected, the camp would be exposed, they argued, to the assaults of a desperate garrison on the one hand, and of the populous city of Guadix, hardly twenty miles distant, on the other; while the good faith of Granada could scarcely be expected to outlive a single reverse of fortune; so that, instead of besieging, they might be more properly regarded as themselves besieged. In addition to these evils, the winter frequently set in with much rigour in this quarter; and the torrents, descending from the mountains, and mingling with the waters of the valley, might overwhelm the camp with an inundation, which, if it did not sweep it away at once, would expose it to the perils of famine by cutting off all external communication. Under these gloomy impressions, many of the council urged Ferdinand to break up his position at once, and postpone all operations on Baza, until the reduction of the surrounding country should make it comparatively easy. Even the Marquis of Cádiz gave in to this opinion; and Gutierre de Cárdenas, Commander of León, a cavalier deservedly high in the confidence of the King, was almost the only person of consideration decidedly opposed to it. In this perplexity, Ferdinand, as usual in similar exigencies, resolved to take counsel of the Queen.[10]

Isabella received her husband's despatches a few hours after they were written, by means of the regular line of posts maintained between the camp and her station at Jaén. She was filled with chagrin at their import, from which she plainly saw, that all her mighty preparations were about to vanish into air. Without assuming the responsibility of deciding the proposed question, however, she besought her husband not to distrust the providence of God, which had conducted them through so many perils toward the consummation of their wishes. She reminded him, that the Spanish Muslims' fortunes were never at so low an ebb as at present, and that their own operations could probably never be resumed on such a formidable scale or under so favourable auspices as now, when their arms had not been stained with a single important reverse. She concluded with the assurance, that, if his soldiers would be true to their duty, they might rely on her for the faithful discharge of hers in furnishing them with all the requisite supplies.

The exhilarating tone of this letter had an instantaneous effect, silencing the scruples of the most timid, and confirming the confidence of the others. The soldiers, in particular, who had received with dissatisfaction some intimation of what was passing in the council, welcomed it with general enthusiasm; and every heart seemed now intent on furthering the wishes of their heroic Queen by prosecuting the siege with the utmost vigour.

The army was accordingly distributed into two encampments; one under the Marquis Duke of Cádiz, supported by the artillery, the other under king Ferdinand on the opposite side of the city. Between the two, lay the garden or orchard before mentioned, extending a league in length; so that, in order to connect the works of the two camps, it became necessary to get possession of this contested ground, and to clear it of the heavy timber with which it was covered.

This laborious operation was intrusted to the Commander of León, and the work was covered by a detachment of seven thousand troops, posted in such a manner as to check the sallies of the garrison. Notwithstanding four thousand *taladores*, or pioneers, were employed in the task, the forest was so dense, and the sorties from the city so annoying, that the work of devastation did not advance more than ten paces a day, and was not completed before the expiration of seven weeks. When the ancient groves, so long the ornament and protection of the city, were levelled to the ground, preparations were made for connecting the two camps, by a deep trench, through which the mountain waters were made to flow; while the borders were fortified with palisades, constructed of the timber lately hewn, together with strong towers of mud or clay, arranged at regular intervals. In this manner, the investment of the city was complete on the side of the vega.[11]

As means of communication still remained open, however, by the opposite sierra, defences of similar strength, consisting of two stone walls separated by a deep trench, were made to run along the rocky heights and ravines of the mountains until they touched the extremities of the fortifications on the plain; and thus Baza was encompassed by an unbroken line of circumvallation.

In the progress of the laborious work, which occupied ten thousand men, under the indefatigable Commander of León, for the space of two months, it would have been easy for the people of Guadix, or of Granada, by cooperation with the sallies of the besieged, to place the Christian army in great peril. Some feeble demonstration of such a movement was made at Guadix, but it was easily disconcerted. Indeed, al-Zagal was kept in check by the fear of leaving his own territory open to his rival, should he march against the Christians. Boabdil, in the meanwhile, lay inactive in Granada, incurring the odium and contempt of his people, who stigmatized him as a Christian in heart, and a pensioner of the

Christian sovereigns. Their discontent gradually swelled in a rebellion, which was suppressed by him with a severity that at length induced a sullen acquiescence in a rule, which, however inglorious, was at least attended with temporary security.[12]

While the camp lay before Baza, a singular mission was received from the Sultan of Egypt, who had been solicited by the Muslims of Granada to interpose in their behalf with the Christian sovereigns. Two Franciscan friars, members of a religious community in Palestine, were bearers of despatches; which, after remonstrating with the sovereigns on their persecution of the Spanish Muslims, contrasted it with the protection uniformly extended by the Sultan to the Christians in his dominions. The communication concluded with menacing a retaliation of similar severities on these latter, unless the sovereigns desisted from their hostilities toward Granada.

From the camp, the two ambassadors proceeded to Jaén, where they were received by the Queen with all the deference due to their holy profession, which seemed to derive additional sanctity from the spot in which it was exercised. The menacing import of the Sultan's communication, however, had no power to shake the purposes of Ferdinand and Isabella, who made answer, that they had uniformly observed the same policy in regard to their Muslim, as to their Christian subjects; but that they could no longer submit to see their ancient and rightful inheritance in the hands of strangers; and that, if these latter would consent to live under their rule, as true and loyal subjects, they should experience the same paternal indulgence which had been shown to their brethren. With this answer the reverend emissaries returned to the Holy Land, accompanied by substantial marks of the royal favour, in a yearly pension of one thousand ducats, which the Queen settled in perpetuity on their monastery, together with a richly embroidered veil, the work of her own fair hands, to be suspended over the Holy Sepulchre. The sovereigns subsequently despatched the learned Peter Martyr as their envoy to the Muslim court, in order to explain their proceedings more at length, and avert any disastrous consequences from the Christian residents.[13]

In the meanwhile, the siege went forward with spirit; skirmishes and single encounters taking place every day between the high-mettled cavaliers on both sides. These chivalrous combats, however, were discouraged by Ferdinand, who would have confined his operations to strict blockade, and avoided the unnecessary effusion of blood; especially as the advantage was most commonly on the side of the enemy, from the peculiar adaptation of their tactics to this desultory warfare. Although some months had elapsed, the besieged rejected with scorn every summons to surrender; relying on their own resources, and still more on the tempestuous season of autumn, now fast advancing, which, if it did not break up the encampment at once, would at least, by demolishing the roads, cut off all external communication.

In order to guard against these impending evils, Ferdinand caused more than a thousand houses, or rather huts, to be erected, with walls of earth or clay, and roofs made of timber and tiles; while the common soldiers constructed cabins by means of palisades loosely thatched with the branches of trees. The whole work was accomplished in four days; and the inhabitants of Baza beheld with amazement a city of solid edifices, with all its streets and squares in regular order, springing as it were by magic out of the ground, which had before been covered with the light and airy pavilions of the camp. The new city was well supplied, owing to the providence of the Queen, not merely with the necessaries, but the luxuries of life. Traders flocked there as to a fair, from Aragón, Valencia, Catalonia, and even Sicily, freighted with costly merchandise, and with jewelry and other articles of luxury; such as, in the indignant lament of an old chronicler, 'too often corrupt the souls of the soldiery, and bring waste and dissipation into a camp'.

That this was not the result, however, in the present instance, is attested by more than one historian. Among others, Peter Martyr, the Italian scholar before mentioned, who was present at this siege, dwells with astonishment on the severe decorum and military discipline, which everywhere obtained among this motley congregation of soldiers. 'Who would have believed,' says he, 'that the Galician, the fierce Asturian, and the rude inhabitant of the Pyrenees, men accustomed to deeds of atrocious violence, and to brawl and battle on the lightest occasions at home, should mingle amicably, not only with one another, but with the Toledans, La Manchans, and the wily and jealous Andalusian; all living together in harmonious subordination to authority, like members of one family, speaking one tongue, and nurtured under a common discipline; so that the camp seemed like a community modelled on the principles of Plato's republic!' In another part of this letter, which was addressed to a Milanese prelate, he panegyrizes the camp hospital of the Queen, then a novelty in war; which, he says, 'is so profusely supplied with medical attendants, apparatus, and whatever may contribute to the restoration or solace of the sick, that it is scarcely surpassed in these respects by the magnificent establishments of Milan'.[14]

During the five months which the siege had now lasted, the weather had proved uncommonly propitious to the Castilians, being for the most part of a bland and equal temperature, while the sultry heats of midsummer were mitigated by cool and moderate showers. As the autumnal season advanced, however, the clouds began to settle heavily around the mountains; and at length one of those storms, predicted by the people of Baza, burst forth with incredible fury, pouring a volume of waters down the rocky sides of the sierra, which, mingling with those of the vega, inundated the camp of the besiegers, and swept away most of the frail edifices constructed for the use of the common soldiery. A still greater calamity befell them in the dilapidation of the roads, which, broken up or worn into deep gullies by the force of the waters, were rendered perfectly impassable. All communication was of course suspended with Jaén, and a temporary interruption of the convoys filled the camp with consternation. This disaster, however, was speedily repaired by the Queen, who, with an energy always equal to the occasion, caused six thousand pioneers to be at once employed in reconstructing the roads; the rivers were bridged over, causeways new laid, and two separate passes opened through the mountains, by which the convoys might visit the camp, and return without interrupting each other. At the same time, the Queen bought up immense quantities of grain from all parts of Andalusia, which she caused to be ground in her own mills; and when the roads, which extended more than seven leagues in length, were completed, fourteen thousand mules might be seen daily traversing the sierra, laden with supplies, which from that time forward were poured abundantly, and with the most perfect regularity, into the camp.[15]

Isabella's next care was to assemble new levies of troops, to relieve or reinforce those now in the camp; and the alacrity with which all orders of men from every quarter of the kingdom answered her summons is worthy of remark. But her chief solicitude was to devise expedients for meeting the enormous expenditures incurred by the protracted operations of the year. For this purpose, she had recourse to loans from individuals and religious corporations, which were obtained without much difficulty, from the general confidence in her good faith. As the sum thus raised, although exceedingly large for that period, proved inadequate to the expenses, further supplies were obtained from wealthy individuals, whose loans were secured by mortgage of the royal demesne; and, as a deficiency still remained in the treasury, the Queen as a last resource, pawned the crown jewels and her own personal ornaments to the merchants of Barcelona and Valencia, for such sums as they were willing to advance on them.[16] Such were the efforts made by this high-spirited woman, for the furtherance of her patriotic enterprise. The extraordinary results, which she was enabled to effect, are less to be ascribed to the authority of her station, than to that perfect confidence in her wisdom and virtue, with which she had inspired the whole nation, and which secured their earnest cooperation in all her undertakings. The empire, which she thus exercised, indeed, was far more extended than any station however exalted, or any authority however despotic, can confer; for it was over the hearts of her people.

Notwithstanding the vigour with which the siege was pressed, Baza made no demonstration of submission. The garrison was indeed greatly reduced in number; the ammunition was nearly expended; yet there still remained abundant supplies of provisions in the town, and no signs of despondency appeared among the people. Even the women of the place, with a spirit emulating that of the dames of ancient Carthage, freely gave up their jewels, bracelets, necklaces, and other personal ornaments, of which the Granadan ladies were exceedingly fond, in order to defray the charges of the mercenaries.

The camp of the besiegers, in the meanwhile, was also greatly wasted both by sickness and the sword. Many, desponding under perils and fatigues, which seemed to have no end, would even at this late hour have abandoned the siege; and they earnestly solicited the Queen's appearance in the camp, in the hope that she would herself countenance this measure, on witnessing their sufferings. Others, and by far the larger part, anxiously desired the Queen's visit, as likely to quicken the operations of the siege, and bring it to a favourable issue. There seemed to be a virtue in her presence, which, on some account or other, made it earnestly desired by all.

Isabella yielded to the general wish, and on the 7th of November arrived before the camp, attended by the Infanta Isabella, the Cardinal of Spain, her friend the Marchioness of Moya, and other ladies of the royal household. The inhabitants of Baza, says Bernaldez, lined the battlements and housetops, to gaze at the glittering cavalcade as it emerged from the depths of the mountains, amidst flaunting banners and strains of martial music, while the Spanish cavaliers thronged forth in a body from the camp to receive their beloved mistress, and gave her the most animated welcome. 'She came,' says Martyr, 'surrounded by a choir of nymphs, as if to celebrate the nuptials of her child; and her presence seemed at once to gladden and reanimate our spirits, drooping under long vigils, dangers, and fatigue.' Another writer, also present, remarks, that, from the moment of her appearance, a change seemed to come over the scene. No more of the cruel skirmishes, which had before occurred every day; no report of artillery, or clashing of arms, or any of the rude sounds of war, was to be heard, but all seemed disposed to reconciliation and peace.[17]

The Muslims probably interpreted Isabella's visit into an assurance, that the Christian army would never rise from before the place until its surrender. Whatever hopes they had once entertained of wearying out the besiegers, were therefore now dispelled. Accordingly, a few days after the Queen's arrival, we find them proposing a parley for arranging terms of capitulation.

On the third day after her arrival, Isabella reviewed her army, stretched out in order of battle along the slope of the western hills; after which, she proceeded to reconnoitre the beleaguered city, accompanied by the King and the Cardinal of Spain, together with a brilliant escort of the Spanish chivalry. On the same day, a conference was opened with the enemy through the *comendador* of León; and an armistice arranged, to continue until the old monarch, al-Zagal, who then lay at Guadix, could be informed of the real condition of the besieged, and his instructions be received, determining the course to be adopted.

The *alcaide* of Baza represented to his master the low state to which the garrison was reduced by the loss of lives and the failure of ammunition. Still, he expressed such confidence in the spirit of his people, that he undertook to make good his defence some time longer, provided any reasonable expectation of succour could be afforded; otherwise, it would be a mere waste of life, and must deprive him of such vantage ground as he now possessed, for enforcing an honourable capitulation. The Muslim prince acquiesced in the reasonableness of these representations. He paid a just tribute to his brave kinsman Cidi Yahye's loyalty, and the gallantry of his defence; but, confessing at the same time his own inability to relieve him, authorized him to negotiate the best terms of surrender which he could, for himself and garrison.[18]

A mutual desire of terminating the protracted hostilities infused a spirit of moderation into both parties, which greatly facilitated the adjustment of the articles. Ferdinand showed none of the arrogant bearing, which marked his conduct toward the unfortunate people of Málaga, whether from a conviction of its impolicy, or, as is more probable, because the city of Baza was itself in a condition to assume a more imposing attitude. The principal stipulations of the treaty were, that the foreign mercenaries employed in the defence of the place should be allowed to march out with the honours of war; that the city should be delivered up to the Christians; but that the natives might have the choice of retiring with their personal effects where they listed; or of occupying the suburbs, as subjects of the Castilian crown, liable only to the same tribute which they paid to their Muslim rulers, and secured in the enjoyment of their property, religion, laws, and usages.[19]

On the fourth day of December, 1489, Ferdinand and Isabella took possession of Baza, at the head of their legions, amid the ringing of bells, the peals of artillery, and all the other usual accompaniments of this triumphant ceremony; while the standard of the Cross, floating from the ancient battlements of the city, proclaimed the triumph of the Christian arms. The brave *alcayde*, Cidi Yahye, experienced a reception from the sovereigns very different from that of the bold defender of Málaga. He was loaded with civilities and presents; and these acts of courtesy so won upon his heart, that he expressed a willingness to enter into their service. 'Isabella's compliments,' says the Arabian historian, drily, 'were repaid in more substantial coin.'

Cidi Yahye was soon prevailed on to visit his royal kinsman al-Zagal, at Guadix, for the purpose of urging his submission to the Christian sovereigns. In his interview with that prince, he represented the fruitlessness of any attempt to withstand the accumulated forces of the Spanish monarchies; that he would only see town after town pared away from his territory, until no ground was left for him to stand on, and make terms with the victor. He reminded him that the baleful horoscope of Boabdil had predicted the downfall of Granada, and that experience had abundantly shown how vain it was to struggle against the tide of destiny. The unfortunate monarch listened, says the Muslim annalist, without so much as moving an eyelid; and, after a long and deep meditation, replied with the resignation characteristic of the Moors, 'What Allah wills, he brings to pass in his own way. Had he not decreed the fall of Granada, this good sword might have saved it; but his will be done!' It was then arranged, that the principal cities of Almería, Guadix, and their dependencies, constituting the domain of al-Zagal, should be formally surrendered by that prince to Ferdinand and Isabella, who should instantly proceed at the head of their army to take possession of them.[20]

On the seventh day of December, therefore, the Spanish sovereigns, without allowing themselves or their jaded troops any time for repose, marched out of the gates of Baza, King Ferdinand occupying the centre, and the Queen the rear of the army. Their route lay across the most savage district of the long sierra, which stretches toward Almería; leading through many a narrow pass, which a handful of resolute Muslims, says an eyewitness, might have made good against the whole Christian army, over mountains whose peaks were lost in clouds, and valleys whose depths were never warmed by a sun. The winds were exceedingly bleak, and the weather inclement; so that men, as well as horses, exhausted by the fatigues of previous service, were benumbed by the intense cold, and many of them frozen to death. Many more, losing their way in the intricacies of the sierra, would have experienced the same miserable fate, had it not been for the Marquis of Cádiz, whose tent was pitched on one of the loftiest hills, and who caused beacon fires to be lighted around it, in order to guide the stragglers back to their quarters.

At no great distance from Almería, Ferdinand was met, conformably to the previous arrangement, by al-Zagal, escorted by a numerous body of Muslim cavaliers. Ferdinand commanded his nobles to ride forward and receive the Nasrid prince. 'His appearance,' says Martyr, who was in the royal retinue, 'touched my soul with compassion; for, although a lawless barbarian, he was a king, and had given signal proofs of heroism.' Al-Zagal, without waiting to receive the courtesies of the Spanish nobles, threw himself from his horse, and advanced toward Ferdinand with the design of kissing his hand; but the latter, rebuking his followers for their 'rusticity', in allowing such an act of humiliation in the unfortunate monarch, prevailed on him to remount, and then rode by his side toward Almería.[21]

This City was one of the most precious jewels in the diadem of Granada. It had amassed great wealth by its extensive commerce with Syria, Egypt, and Africa; and its corsairs had for ages been the terror of the Catalan and Pisan marine. It might have stood a siege as long as that of Baza, but it was now surrendered without a blow, on conditions similar to those granted to the former city. After allowing some days for the refreshment of their wearied forces in this pleasant region, which, sheltered from the bleak winds of the north by the sierra they had lately traversed, and fanned by the gentle breezes of the Mediterranean, is compared by Martyr to the gardens of the Hesperides, the sovereigns established a strong garrison there, under the Commander of León, and then, striking again into the recesses of the mountains, marched on Guadix, which, after some opposition on the part of the populace, threw open its gates to them. The surrender of these principal cities was followed by that of all the subordinate dependencies belonging to al-Zagal's territory, comprehending a multitude of hamlets scattered along the green sides of the mountain chain that stretched from Granada to the coast. To all these places the same liberal terms, in regard to personal rights and property, were secured, as to Baza.

As an equivalent for these broad domains, the Nasrid chief was placed in possession of the *taha*, or district, of Andaraz, the vale of Alhaurin, and half the salt-pits of Maleha, together with a considerable revenue in money. He was, moreover, to receive the title of King of Andaraz, and to render homage for his estates to the crown of Castile.

This shadow of royalty could not long amuse the mind of the unfortunate prince. Al-Zagal pined away amid the scenes of his ancient empire; and, after experiencing some insubordination on the part of his new vassals, he determined to relinquish his petty principality, and withdraw forever from his native land. Having received a large sum of money, as an indemnification for the entire cession of his territorial rights and possessions to the Castilian crown, he passed over to Africa, where, it is reported, he was plundered of his property by the barbarians, and condemned to starve out the remainder of his days in miserable indigence.[22]

The suspicious circumstances attending this prince's accession to the throne, threw a dark cloud over his fame, which would otherwise seem, at least as far as his public life is concerned, to be unstained by any opprobrious act. Al-Zagal possessed such energy, talent, and military science, as, had he been fortunate enough to unite the Spanish Muslim nation under him by an undisputed title, might have postponed the fall of Granada for many years. As it was, these very talents, by dividing the state in his favour, served only to precipitate its ruin.

The Spanish sovereigns, having accomplished the object of the campaign, after stationing part of their forces on such points as would secure the permanence of their conquests, returned with the remainder to Jaén, where they disbanded the army on the 4th of January, 1490. The losses sustained by the troops, during the whole period of their prolonged service, greatly exceeded those of any former year, amounting to not less than twenty thousand men, by far the larger portion of whom are said to have fallen victims to diseases incident to severe and long-continued hardships and exposure.[23]

Thus terminated the eighth year of the War of Granada; a year more glorious to the Christian arms, and more important in its results, than any of the preceding. During this period an army of eighty thousand men had kept the field, amid all the inclemencies of winter, for more than seven months; an effort scarcely paralleled in these times, when both the amount of levies, and period of service, were on the limited scale adapted to the exigencies of feudal warfare.[24] Supplies for this immense host, notwithstanding the severe famine of the preceding year, were punctually furnished, in spite of every embarrassment presented by the want of navigable rivers, and the interposition of a precipitous and pathless sierra.

The history of this campaign is, indeed, most honourable to the courage, constancy, and thorough discipline of the Castilian soldier, and to the patriotism and general resources of the nation; but most of all to Isabella. She it was, who fortified the timid councils of the leaders, after the disasters of the garden, and encouraged them to persevere in the siege. She procured all the supplies, constructed the roads, took charge of the sick, and furnished, at no little personal sacrifice, the immense sums demanded for carrying on the war; and, when at last the hearts of the soldiers were fainting under long-protracted sufferings, she appeared among them, like some celestial visitant, to cheer their faltering spirits, and inspire them with her own energy. The attachment to Isabella seemed to be a pervading principle, which animated the whole nation by one common pulse, impressing a unity of design on all its movements. This attachment was imputable to her sex as well as character. The sympathy and tender care, with which she regarded her people, naturally raised a reciprocal sentiment in their bosoms. But, when they beheld her directing their counsels, sharing their fatigues and dangers, and displaying all the comprehensive intellectual powers of the other sex, they looked up to her as to some superior being, with feelings far more exalted than those of mere loyalty. The chivalrous heart of the Christian Spaniard did homage to her, as to his tutelar saint; and she held a control over her people, such as no man could have acquired in any age, – and probably no woman, in an age and country less romantic.

*   *   *   *   *

AUTHOR'S CHAPTER COMMENTS

Pietro Martire, or, as he is called in English, Peter Martyr, so often quoted in the present chapter, and who will constitute one of our best authorities during the remainder of the history, was a native of Arona (not of Anghiera, as commonly supposed), a place situated on the borders of Lake Maggiore, in Italy (Mazzuchelli, *Scrittori d'Italia*, Brescia, 1753–63, tom.ii, *voce* Anghiera). He was of noble Milanese extraction. In 1477, at twenty-two years of age, he was sent to complete his education at Rome, where he continued ten years, and formed an intimacy with the most distinguished literary characters of that cultivated capital. In 1487, he was persuaded by the Castilian ambassador, the Count of Tendilla, to accompany him to Spain, where he was received with marked distinction by the Queen, who would have at once engaged him in the tuition of the young nobility of the court, but, Martyr having expressed a preference of a military life, she, with her usual delicacy, declined to press him on the point. He was present, as we have seen, at the siege of Baza, and continued with the army during the subsequent campaigns of the Moorish war. Many passages of his correspondence, at this period, show a whimsical mixture of self-complacency with a consciousness of the ludicrous figure which he made in 'exchanging the Muses for Mars'.

At the close of the war, he entered the ecclesiastical profession, for which he had been originally destined, and was persuaded to resume his literary vocation. He opened his school at Valladolid, Zaragoza, Barcelona, Alcalá de Henares, and other places; and it was thronged with the principal young nobility from all parts of Spain, who, as he boasts in one of his letters, drew their literary nourishment from him. '*Suxerunt mea literalia ubera Castellæ principes fere omnes.*' His important services were fully estimated by the Queen, and, after her death, by Ferdinand and Charles V, and he was recompensed with high ecclesiastical preferment as well as civil dignities. He died about the year 1525, at the age of seventy, and his remains were interred beneath a monument in the cathedral church of Granada, of which he was prior.

Among Martyr's principal works is a treatise *De Legatione Babylonica*, being an account of a visit to the Sultan of Egypt, in 1501, for the purpose of deprecating the retaliation with which he had menaced the Christian residents in Palestine, for the injuries inflicted on the Spanish Muslims. Peter Martyr conducted his negotiations with such address, that he not only appeased the Sultan's resentment, but obtained several important immunities for his Christian subjects, in addition to those previously enjoyed by them.

He also wrote an account of the discoveries of the new world, entitled *De Rebus Oceanicis et Novo Orbe* (Coloniae, 1574), a book largely consulted and commended by subsequent historians. But the work of principal value in our researches is his *Opus Epistolarum*, being a collection of his multifarious correspondence with the most considerable persons of his time, whether in political or literary life. The letters are in Latin, and extend from the year 1488 to the time of his death. Although not conspicuous for elegance of diction, they are most valuable to the historian, from the fidelity and general accuracy of the details, as well as for the intelligent criticism in which they abound, for all which, uncommon facilities were afforded by the writer's intimacy with the leading actors, and the most recondite sources of information of the period.

This high character is fully authorized by the judgment of those best qualified to pronounce on their merits, – Martyr's own contemporaries. Among these, Dr. Galindez de Carbajal, a counsellor of King Ferdinand and constantly employed in the highest concerns of state, commends these epistles as 'the work of a learned and upright man, well calculated to throw light on the transactions of the period' (*Anals*, MS., prólogo). Alvaro Gomez, another contemporary who survived Martyr, in the *Life of Ximenes*, which he was selected to write by the University of Alcalá, declares, that 'Martyr's *Letters* abundantly compensate by their fidelity for the unpolished style in which they were written' (*De Rebus Gestis*, fol. 6). And Juan de Vergara, a name of the highest celebrity in the literary annals of the period, expresses himself in the following emphatic terms: 'I know no record of the time more accurate and valuable. I myself have often witnessed the promptness with which he put down things the moment they occurred. I have sometimes seen him write one or two letters, while they were setting the table. For, as he did not pay much attention to style and mere finish of expression, his composition required but little time, and experienced no interruption from his ordinary avocations' (see his letter to Florian de Ocampo apud Quintanilla y Mendoza, Archetypo de Virtudes, Espejo de Prelados, el Venerable Padre y siervo de Dios, F. Francisco Ximenez [Jimenez] de Cisneros (Palmero, 1653), Archivo, p.4). This account of precipitate manner in which the epistles were composed, may help to explain the cause of the occasional inconsistencies and anachronisms, that are to be found in them; and which their author, had he been more patient of the labour of revision, would doubtless have corrected. But he seems to have had little relish for this, even in his more elaborate works, composed with a view to publication (see his own honest confession in his book *De Rebus Oceanicis*, dec.8, cap.8, 9). After all, the errors, such as they are, in his *Epistles*, may probably be chiefly charged on the publisher. The first edition appeared at Alcalá de Henares, in 1530, about four years after the author's death. It had now become exceedingly rare. The second and last, being the one used in the present history, came out in a more beautiful form from the Elzevir press, Amsterdam, in 1670, folio. Of this also but a small number of copies were struck off. The learned editor takes much credit to himself for having purified the work from many errors, which had flowed from the heedlessness of his predecessor. It will not be difficult to detect several yet remaining. Such, for example, as a memorable letter on the *lues veneres* (No. 68.) obviously misplaced, even according to its own date; and that numbered 168, in which two letters are evidently blended into one. But it is unnecessary to multiply examples. It is very desirable that an edition of this valuable correspondence should be published, under the care of some one qualified to illustrate it by his intimacy with the history of the period, as well as to correct the various inaccuracies which have crept into it, whether through the carelessness of the author or of his editors.

I have been led into this length of remark by some strictures which met my eye in the recent work of Mr. Hallam; who intimates his belief, that the *Epistles* of Martyr, instead of being written at their respective dates, were produced by him at some later period (*Introduction to the Literature of Europe*, London, 1837, vol.i, pp.439–441), a conclusion which I suspect this acute and candid critic would have been slow to adopt, had he perused the correspondence in connection with the history of the times, or weighed the unqualified testimony borne by contemporaries to its minute accuracy.

NOTES

1. Zurita, *Anales*, tom.iv, fol.351, 352, 356. – Mariana, *Hist. de España*, tom.ii, lib.25, cap.12. – Pulgar, *Reyes Católicos*, part 3, cap.95.

2. Ferreras, *Hist. d'Espagne*, tom.viii, p.76. – Pulgar, *Reyes Católicos*, cap.98. – Zuñiga, *Annales de Sevilla*, p.402. – Cardonne, *Hist. d'Afrique et d'Espagne*, tom.iii, pp.298, 299. – Carbajal, *Anales*, MS., año 1488.

3. Condé, *Dominacion de los Arabes*, tom.iii, pp.239, 240. – Pulgar, *Reyes Católicos*, cap.100, 101. – During the preceding year, while the court was at Murcia, we find one of the examples of prompt and severe exercise of justice, which sometimes occur in this reign. One of the royal collectors having been resisted and personally maltreated by the alcayde of Salvatierra, a place belonging to the crown, and by the *alcalde* of a territorial court of the Duke of Alva, the Queen caused one of the royal judges privately to enter into the place, and take cognizance of the affair. The latter, after a brief investigation, commanded the *alcayde* to be hung up over his fortress, and the *alcalde* to be delivered over to the court of chancery at Valladolid, who ordered his right hand to be amputated, and banished him from the realm. This summary justice was perhaps necessary in a community, that might be said to be in transition from a state of barbarism to that of civilization, and had a salutary effect in proving to the people, that no rank was elevated enough to raise the offender above the law. Pulgar, cap.99.

4. Ialigny, *Hist. de Charles VIII*, pp.92, 94. – Sismondi, *Hist. des Français*, tom.xv, pp.77. – Aleson, *Annales de Navarra*, tom.v, p.61. – *Histoire du Royaume de Navarre*, pp.578, 579. – Pulgar, *Reyes Católicos*, cap.102.

In the first of these expeditions, more than a thousand Spaniards were slain or taken at the disastrous Battle of St. Aubin, in 1488, being the same in which Edward Woodville, the Englishman who made such a gallant figure at the siege of Loja, lost his life. In the spring of 1489, the levies sent into France amounted to two thousand in number. These efforts abroad, simultaneous with the great operations of the Moorish war, show the resources as well as energy of the sovereigns.

5. Pulgar, *Reyes Católicos, ubi supra*.

6. Bernaldez, *Reyes Católicos*, MS., cap.91. – Zurita, *Anales*, tom.iv, fol.354. – Bleda, *Corónica*, fol.607. – Abarca, *Reyes de Aragón*, tom.ii, fol.307.

Such was the scarcity of grain that the prices in 1489, quoted by Bernaldez, are double those of the preceding year. Both Abarca and Zurita mention the report, that four fifths of the whole population were swept away by the pestilence of 1488. Zurita finds more difficulty in swallowing this monstrous statement than father Abarca, whose appetite for the marvellous appears to have been fully equal to that of most of his calling in Spain.

7. Peter Martyr, *Opus Epist.*, lib.2, epist.70. – Pulgar, *Reyes Católicos*, cap.104.

It may not be amiss to specify the names of the most distinguished cavaliers who usually attended the King in these Moorish wars; the heroic ancestors of many a noble still extant in Spain.

Alonso de Cárdenas, Master of Santiago.
Juan de Zuñiga, Master of Alcantara.
Juan Garcia de Padilla, Master of Calatrava.
Rodrigo Ponce de León, Marquis Duke of Cádiz.
Enríque de Guzmán, Duke of Medina Sidonia.
Pedro Manrique, Duke of Nájera.
Juan Pacheco, Duke of Escalona, Marquis of Villena.
Juan Pimentel, Count of Benavente.
Fadrique de Toledo, son of the Duke of Alva.
Diego, Fernández de Córdoba, Count of Cabra. [Uncle to individual of the same name, below –Ed]
Gomez Alvarez de Figueroa, Count of Feria.
Alvaro Tellez Girón, Count of Ureña.
Juan de Silva, Count of Cifuentes.
Fadrique Enriquez, Adelantado of Andalusia.
Alonso Fernandez de Córdoba, Lord of Aguilar [brother of Gonzalo de Córdoba].
Gonzalo de Córdoba, afterwards known as the Great Captain.
Luis Porto-Carrero, Lord of Palma.
Gutierre de Cárdenas, First Commander of León.
Pedro Fernández de Velasco, Count of Haro, Constable of Castile.
Beltrán de la Cueva, Duke of Alburquerque.
Diego Fernández de Córdoba, *alcaide* of the royal pages, afterwards Marquis of Comaras.
Alvaro de Zuñiga, Duke of Bejar.

Iñigo López de Mendoza, Count of Tendilla, afterwards Marquis of Mondejar.
Luis de Cerda, Duke of Medina Celi.
Iñigo López de Mendoza, Marquis of Santillana, Second Duke of Infantado.
Garcilasso de la Vega, Lord of Batras.

8. Zurita, *Anales*, tom.iv, fol.360. – Condé, *Dominacion de los Arabes*, tom.iii, p.241. – Peter Martyr, *Opus Epist.*, lib.2, epist.70. – Estrada, *Problacion de España*, tom.ii, fol.239. – Marmol, *Rebelion de Moriscos*, lib.1, cap.16.

9. Pulgar, *Reyes Católicos*, cap.106, 107. – Condé, *Dominacion de los Arabes*, tom.iii, cap.40. – Peter Martyr, *Opus Epist.*, lib.1, epist.71. – Pulgar relates these particulars with a perspicuity very different from his entangled narrative of some of the preceding operations in this war. Both he and Martyr were present during the whole siege of Baza.

10. Bernaldez, *Reyes Católicos*, MS., cap.92. – Cardonne, *Hist. d'Afrique et d'Espagne*, tom.iii, pp.299, 300. – Bleda, *Corónica*, p.611. – Garibay, *Compendio*, tom.ii, p.664.

   Don Gutierre de Cárdenas, who possessed so high a place in the confidence of the sovereigns, occupied a station in the Queen's household at the time of her marriage with Ferdinand. His discretion and general ability enabled him to retain the influence which he had early acquired, as is shown by a popular distich of that time:

> 'Cardenas, y el Cardenal, y Chacon, y
>   Fray Mortero,
> Traen la Corte al retortero.'

Fray Mortero was Don Alonso de Burgos, Bishop of Palencia, confessor of the sovereigns. Don Juan Chacon, was the son of Gonzalo, who had the care of Don Alfonso and the Queen during her minority, when he was induced by the liberal largesses of Juan II, of Aragón, to promote her marriage with his son Ferdinand. The elder Chacon was treated by the sovereigns with the greatest deference and respect, being usually called by them 'father'. After his death, they continued to manifest a similar regard towards Don Juan, his eldest son, and heir of his ample honours and estates. Salazar de Mendoza, *Dignidades*, lib.4, cap.1. – Oviedo, *Quincuagenas*, MS., bat.1, quinc.2, dial.1, 2.

11. Cardonne, *Hist. d'Afrique et d'Espagne*, tom.iii, p.304. – Pulgar, *Reyes Católicos*, cap.109. – Peter Martyr, *Opus Epist.*, lib.2, epist.73. – Bernaldez, *Reyes Católicos*, MS., cap.92.

12. Condé, *Dominacion de los Arabes*, tom.iii, cap.40. – Mariana, *Hist. de España*, tom.ii, lib.25, cap.12. – Pulgar, *Reyes Católicos*, cap.111.

13. Pulgar, *Reyes Católicos*, cap.112. – Ferreras, *Hist. d'Espagne*, tom.viii, p.86.

14. Bernaldez, *Reyes Católicos*, MS. – Peter Martyr, *Opus Epist.*, lib.2, epist.79, 80. – Pulgar, *Reyes Católicos*, cap.113, 114, 117. – Garibay, *Compendio*, tom.ii, p.667. – Bieda, *Corónica*, p.64.

   The plague which fell heavily this year on some parts of Andalusia, does not appear to have attacked the camp, which Bleda imputes to the healing influence of the Spanish sovereigns, 'whose good faith, religion, and virtue, banished the contagion from their army, where it must otherwise have prevailed'. Personal comforts and cleanliness of the soldiers, though not quite so miraculous a cause, may be considered perhaps full as efficacious.

15. Peter Martyr, *Opus Epist.*, lib.2, epist.73. – Pulgar, *Reyes Católicos*, cap.116.
16. Pulgar, Reyes Católicos, cap.118 – Archivo de Simancas, *Mem. de la Acad. de Hist.*, tom.vi, p.311.

   The city of Valencia loaned 35,000 florins on the crown and 29,000 on a collar of rubies. They were not wholly redeemed till 1495. Señor Clemencin has given a catalogue of the royal jewels (see *Mem. de la Acad. de Hist.*, tom.vi, illustracion 6), which appear to have been extremely rich and numerous, for a period anterior to the discovery of those countries, whose mines have since furnished Europe with its *bijouterie.* Isabella, however, set so little value on them, that she divested herself of them in favour of her daughters.

17. Bernaldez, *Reyes Católicos*, MS., cap.92. – Pulgar, *Reyes Católicos*, cap.120, 121. – Ferreras, *Hist. d'Espagne*, tom.vii, p.93. – Peter Martyr, *Opus Epist.*, lib.3, epist.80.
18. Peter Martyr, *Opus Epist.*, lib.3, epist.80. – Condé, *Dominacion de los Arabes*, tom.iii, p.242. – Carbajal, *Anales*, MS., año 1489. – Cardonne, *Hist. d'Afrique et d'Espagne*, tom.iii, p.305.
19. Pulgar, *Reyes Católicos*, cap.124. – Marmol, *Rebelion de Moriscos*, lib.1, cap.16.
20. Condé, *Dominacion de los Arabes*, tom.iii, cap.40. – Bieda, *Corónica*, p.612. – Bernaldez, *Reyes Católicos*, MS., cap.92. – Marmol, *Rebelion de Moriscos*, lib.1, cap.16.
21. Peter Martyr, *Opus Epist.*, lib.3, epist.81. – Cardonne, *Hist d'Afrique et d'Afrique et d'Espagne*, tom.iii, p.340. – Pulgar, *Reyes Católicos, loc. cit.* – Condé, *Dominacion de los Arabes*, tom.iii, cap.40.
22. El Nubiense, *Descripcion de España*, p.160, not. – Carbajal, *Anales*, MS., año 1488. - Cardonne, *Hist. d'Afrique et d'Espagne*, tom.iii, p.304. – Peter Martyr, *Opus Epist.*, lib.3, epist.81. – Condé, *Dominacion de los Arabes*, tom.iii, p.245, 246. – Bernaldez, *Reyes Católicos*, MS., cap.93.
23. Zurita, *Anales*, tom.iv, fol.360. – Abarca, *Reyes de Aragón*, tom.ii, fol.308.
24. The city of Sevilla alone maintained 600 horses and 8,000 foot under the Count of Cifuentes, for the space of eight months during the siege. See Zuñiga, *Annales de Sevilla*, p.404.

CHAPTER 7

SIEGE AND SURRENDER OF THE CITY OF GRANADA (1490–92)

The Infanta Isabella affianced to the Prince of Portugal. – Isabella deposes Judges at Valladolid. – Encampment before Granada. – The Queen surveys the City. – Muslim and Christian Chivalry. – Conflagration of the Christian Camp. – Erection of Santa Fé. – Capitulation of Granada. – Results of the War. – Its Moral Influence. – Its Military Influence. – Fate of the Spanish Muslims. – Death and Character of the Marquis of Cádiz.

In the spring of 1490, ambassadors arrived from Lisbon for the purpose of carrying into effect the treaty of marriage, which had been arranged between Affonso, heir of the Portuguese monarchy, and Isabella, Infanta of Castile. An alliance with this kingdom, which from its contiguity possessed such ready means of annoyance to Castile, and which had shown such willingness to employ them in enforcing the pretensions of Juana 'Beltraneja', was an object of importance to Ferdinand and Isabella. No inferior consideration could have reconciled the Queen to a separation from this beloved daughter, her eldest child, whose gentle and uncommonly amiable disposition seems to have endeared her beyond their other children to her parents.

The ceremony of the affiancing took place at Sevilla, in the month of April, Don Fernando de Silveira appearing as the representative of the Prince of Portugal; and it was followed by a succession of splendid *fêtes* and tourneys. Lists were enclosed, at some distance from the city on the shores of the Guadalquivir, and surrounded with galleries hung with silk and cloth of gold, and protected from the noontide heat by canopies or awnings, richly embroidered with the armorial bearings of the ancient houses of Castile. The spectacle was graced by all the rank and beauty of the court, with the Infanta Isabella in the midst, attended by seventy noble ladies, and a hundred pages of the royal household. The cavaliers of Spain, young and old, thronged to the tournament, as eager to win laurels on the mimic theatre of war, in the presence of so brilliant an assemblage, as they had shown themselves in the sterner contests with the

234

Spanish Muslims. King Ferdinand, who broke several lances on the occasion, was among the most distinguished of the combatants for personal dexterity and horsemanship. The martial exercises of the day were relieved by the more effeminate recreations of dancing and music in the evening; and every one seemed willing to welcome the season of hilarity, after the long-protracted fatigues of war.[1]

In the following autumn, the Infanta was escorted into Portugal by the Cardinal of Spain, the Grand Master of Santiago, and a numerous and magnificent retinue. Her dowry exceeded that usually assigned to the infantas of Castile, by five hundred marks of gold and a thousand of silver; and her wardrobe was estimated at one hundred and twenty thousand gold florins. The contemporary chroniclers dwell with much complacency on these evidences of the stateliness and splendour of the Castilian court. Unfortunately, these fair auspices were destined to be clouded too soon by the death of the prince, her husband.[2]

No sooner had the Campaign of the preceding year been brought to a close, than Ferdinand and Isabella sent an embassy to the King of Granada, requiring a surrender of his capital, conformably to his stipulations at Loja, which guaranteed this, on the capitulation of Baza, Almería, and Guadix. That time had now arrived; King Boabdil, however, excused himself from obeying the summons of the Spanish sovereigns, replying that he was no longer his own master, and that, although he had all the inclination to keep his engagements, he was prevented by the inhabitants of the city, now swollen much beyond its natural population, who resolutely insisted on its defence.[3]

It is not probable that the Nasrid king did any great violence to his feelings, in this evasion of a promise extorted from him in captivity. At least, it would seem so from the hostile movements which immediately succeeded. The people of Granada resumed all at once their ancient activity, foraying into the Christian territories, surprising Alhendin and some other places of less importance, and stirring up the spirit of revolt in Guadix and other conquered cities. Granada, which had slept through the heat of the struggle, seemed to revive at the very moment when exertion became hopeless.

Ferdinand was not slow in retaliating these acts of aggression. In the spring of 1490, he marched with a strong force into the cultivated plain of Granada, sweeping off, as usual, the crops and cattle, and rolling the tide of devastation up to the very walls of the city. In this campaign he conferred the honour of knighthood on his son, Prince Juan, then only twelve years of age, whom he had brought with him, after the ancient usage of the Castilian nobles, of training up their children from very tender years in the Moorish wars. The ceremony was performed on the banks of the grand canal under the battlements almost of the beleaguered city. The dukes of Cádiz and Medina Sidonia were Prince Juan's sponsors; and, after the completion of the ceremony, the new knight conferred the honours of chivalry in like manner on several of his young companions in arms.[4]

In the following autumn, Ferdinand repeated his ravages in the vega, and, at the same time appearing before the disaffected city of Guadix with a force large enough to awe it into submission, proposed an immediate investigation of the conspiracy. He promised to inflict summary justice on all who had been in any degree concerned in it; at the same time offering permission to the inhabitants, in the abundance of his clemency, to depart with all their personal effects wherever they would, provided they should prefer this to a judicial investigation of their conduct. This politic proffer had its effect. There were few, if any, of the citizens, who had not been either directly concerned in the conspiracy, or privy to it. With one accord, therefore, they preferred exile to trusting to the tender mercies of their judges. In this way, says the Curate of Los Palacios, by the mystery of our Lord, was the ancient city of Guadix brought again within the Christian fold; the mosques converted into Christian temples, filled with the harmonies of Catholic worship, and the pleasant places, which for nearly eight centuries had been trampled under the foot of the infidel, were once more restored to the followers of the Cross.

A similar policy produced similar results in the cities of Almería and Baza, whose inhabitants, evacuating their ancient homes, transported themselves, with such personal effects as they could carry, to the city of Granada, or the coast of Africa. The space thus opened by the fugitive population was quickly filled by the rushing tide of Christian Spaniards.[5]

It is impossible at this day, to contemplate these events with the triumphant swell of exultation, with which they are recorded by contemporary chroniclers. That the Granadans were guilty (though not so generally as pretended) of the alleged conspiracy, is not in itself improbable, and is corroborated indeed by some Muslim documents. But the punishment was altogether disproportionate to the offence. Justice might surely have been satisfied by a selection of the authors and principal agents of the meditated insurrection, – for no overt act appears to have occurred. But avarice was too strong for justice; and this act, which is in perfect conformity to the policy systematically pursued by the Spanish crown for more than a century afterward, may be considered as one of the first links in the long chain of persecution, which terminated in the expulsion of the Moriscoes.

During the following year, 1491, a circumstance occurred illustrative of the policy of the present government in reference to ecclesiastical matters. The chancery of Valladolid having appealed to the Pope in a case coming within its own exclusive jurisdiction, the Queen commanded Alonso de Valdivieso, Bishop of León, the president of the court, together with all the auditors to be removed from their respective offices, which she delivered to a new board, having the Bishop of Oviedo at its head. This is one among many examples of the constancy with which Isabella, notwithstanding her reverence for religion, and respect for its ministers, refused to compromise the national independence by recognizing in any degree the usurpations of Rome. From this dignified attitude, so often abandoned by her successors, she never swerved for a moment during the course of her long reign.[6]

The winter of 1490 was busily occupied with preparations for the closing campaign against Granada. Ferdinand took command of the army in the month of April, 1491, with the purpose of sitting down before the Nasrid capital, not to rise until its final surrender. The troops, which mustered in the Val de Velillos, are computed by most historians at fifty thousand horse and foot, although Martyr, who served as a volunteer, swells the number to eighty thousand. They were drawn from the different cities, chiefly, as usual, from Andalusia, which had been stimulated to truly gigantic efforts throughout this protracted war,[7] and from the nobility of every quarter, many of whom, wearied out with the contest, contented themselves with sending their quotas, while many others, as the marquises of Cádiz, Villena, the counts of Tendilla, Cabra, Ureña, and Alonso de Aguilar, appeared in person, eager, as they had borne the brunt of so many hard campaigns, to share in the closing scene of triumph.

On the 26th of the month, the army encamped near the fountain of Ojos de Huéscar, in the vega, about two leagues distant from Granada. Ferdinand's first movement was to detach a considerable force, under the Marquis of Villena, which he subsequently supported in person with the remainder of the army, for the purpose of scouring the fruitful regions of the Alpujarras, which served as the granary of the capital. This service was performed with such unsparing rigour, that no less than twenty-four towns and hamlets in the mountains were ransacked, and razed to the ground. After this, Ferdinand returned loaded with spoil to his former position on the banks of the Genil, in full view of the Granadan metropolis, which seemed to stand alone, like some sturdy oak, the last of the forest, bidding defiance to the storm which had prostrated all its brethren.

Notwithstanding the failure of all external resources, Granada was still formidable from its local position and its defences. On the east it was fenced in by a wild mountain barrier, the *Sierra Nevada*, whose snow-clad summits diffused a grateful coolness over the city through the sultry heats of summer. The side toward the vega, facing the Christian encampment, was encircled by walls and towers of massive strength and solidity. The population, swelled to two hundred thousand by the immigration from the surrounding country, was likely, indeed, to be a burden in a protracted siege; but among them were twenty thousand, the flower of the Muslim chivalry, who had escaped the edge of the Christian sword. In front of the city, for an extent of nearly ten leagues, lay unrolled, the magnificent vega,

'*Fresca y regalada vega,*
Dulce recreacion de damas
Y de hombres gloria immensa'

whose prolific beauties could scarcely be exaggerated in the most florid strains
of the Moorish minstrel, and which still bloomed luxuriant, notwithstanding
the repeated ravages of the preceding season.[8]

The inhabitants of Granada were filled with indignation at the sight of their
enemy, thus encamped under the shadow, as it were, of their battlements. They
sallied forth in small bodies, or singly, challenging the Castilians to equal
encounter. Numerous were the combats which took place between the high-
mettled cavaliers on both sides, who met on the level arena, as on a tilting-
ground, where they might display their prowess in the presence of the
assembled beauty and chivalry of their respective nations; for the Spanish camp
was graced, as usual, by the presence of Queen Isabella and the infantas with
the courtly train of ladies, who had accompanied their royal mistress from
Alcalá la Real. The Spanish ballads glow with picturesque details of these
knightly tourneys, forming the most attractive portion of this romantic minstrelsy, which, celebrating the prowess of Muslim, as well as Christian warriors,
sheds a dying glory round the last hours of Granada.[9]

The festivity, which reigned throughout the camp on the arrival of Isabella,
did not divert her attention from the stern business of war. She superintended
the military preparations, and personally inspected every part of the encampment. She appeared on the field superbly mounted, and dressed in complete
armour; and, as she visited the different quarters and reviewed her troops, she
administered words of commendation or sympathy, suited to the condition of
the soldier.[10]

On one occasion, she expressed a desire to take a nearer survey of the city. For
this purpose, a house was selected, affording the best point of view, in the little
village of Zubia, at no great distance from Granada. The King and Queen
stationed themselves before a window, which commanded an unbroken prospect of the Alhambra, and the most beautiful quarter of the town. In the
meanwhile, a considerable force, under the Marquis Duke of Cádiz, had been
ordered, for the protection of the royal persons, to take up a position between
the village and the city of Granada, with strict injunctions on no account to
engage the enemy, as Isabella was unwilling to stain the pleasures of the day
with unnecessary effusion of blood.

The people of Granada, however, were too impatient long to endure the
presence, and as they deemed it, the bravado of their enemy. They burst forth
from the gates of the capital, dragging along with them several pieces of
ordnance, and commenced a brisk assault on the Spanish lines. The latter
sustained the shock with firmness, till the Marquis of Cádiz, seeing them

thrown into some disorder, found it necessary to assume the offensive, and, mustering his followers around him, made one of those desperate charges, which had so often broken the enemy. The Granadan cavalry faltered; but might have disputed the ground, had it not been for the infantry, which, composed of the rabble population of the city, was easily thrown into confusion, and hurried the horse along with it. The rout now became general. The Castilian cavaliers, whose blood was up, pursued to the very gates of Granada, 'and not a lance,' says Bernaldez, 'that day, but was dyed in the blood of the infidel'. Two thousand of the enemy were slain and taken in the engagement, which lasted only a short time; and the slaughter was stopped only by the escape of the fugitives within the walls of the city.[11]

About the middle of July, an accident occurred in the camp, which had like to have been attended with fatal consequences. The Queen was lodged in a superb pavilion, belonging to the Marquis of Cádiz, and always used by him in the Granadan war. By the carelessness of one of her attendants, a lamp was placed in such a situation, that during the night, perhaps owing to a gust of wind, it set fire to the drapery or loose hangings of the pavilion, which was instantly in a blaze. The flame communicated with fearful rapidity to the neighbouring tents, made of light, combustible materials, and the camp was menaced with general conflagration. This occurred at the dead of night, when all but the sentinels were buried in sleep. The Queen, and her children, whose apartments were near hers, were in great peril, and escaped with difficulty, though fortunately without injury. The alarm soon spread. The trumpets sounded to arms, for it was supposed to be some night attack of the enemy. Ferdinand snatching up his arms hastily, put himself at the head of his troops; but, soon ascertaining the nature of the disaster, contented himself with posting the Marquis of Cádiz, with a strong body of horse, over against the city, in order to repel any sally from that quarter. None, however, was attempted, and the fire was at length extinguished without personal injury, though not without loss of much valuable property, in jewels, plate, brocade, and other costly decorations of the tents of the nobility.[12]

In order to guard against a similar disaster, as well as to provide comfortable winter quarters for the army, should the siege be so long protracted as to require it, it was resolved to build a town of substantial edifices on the place of the present encampment. The plan was immediately put in execution. The work was distributed in due proportions among the troops of the several cities and of the great nobility; the soldier was on a sudden converted into an artisan, and, instead of war, the camp echoed with the sounds of peaceful labour.

In less than three months, this stupendous task was accomplished. The spot so recently occupied by light, fluttering pavilions, was thickly covered with solid structures of stone and mortar, comprehending, besides dwelling houses, stables for a thousand horses. The town was thrown into a quadrangular form, traversed by two spacious avenues, intersecting each other at right angles in the centre, in the form of a cross, with stately portals at each of the four extremities. Inscriptions on blocks of marble in the various quarters, recorded the respective shares of the several cities in the execution of the work. When it was completed, the whole army was desirous that the new city should bear the name of their illustrious Queen; but Isabella modestly declined this tribute, and bestowed on the place the title of *Santa Fé*, in token of the unshaken trust, manifested by her people throughout this war, in Divine Providence. With this name it still stands as it was erected in 1491, a monument of the constancy and enduring patience of the Christian Spaniards 'the only city in Spain,' in the words of a Castilian writer, 'that has never been contaminated by the Muslim heresy'.[13]

The erection of Sante Fé by the Christians struck a greater damp into the people of Granada, than the most successful military achievement could have done. They beheld the enemy setting foot on their soil, with a resolution never more to resign it. They already began to suffer from the rigorous blockade, which effectually excluded supplies from their own territories, while all communication with Africa was jealously intercepted. Symptoms of insubordination had begun to show themselves among the overgrown population of the city, as it felt more and more the pressure of famine. In this crisis, the unfortunate Boabdil and his principal counsellors became convinced, that the place could not be maintained much longer; and at length, in the month of October, propositions were made through the Vizier Abul Cazim Abdelmalic, to open a negotiation for the surrender of the place. The affair was to be conducted with the utmost caution; since the people of Granada, notwithstanding their precarious condition, and their disquietude, were buoyed up by indefinite expectations of relief from Africa, or some other quarter.

The Spanish sovereigns intrusted the negotiation to their secretary Fernando de Zafra, and to Gonzalo de Córdoba, the latter of whom was selected for this delicate business, from his uncommon address, and his familiarity with the Moorish habits and language. Thus the capitulation of Granada was referred to the man, who acquired in her long wars the military science, which enabled him, at a later period, to foil the most distinguished generals of Europe.

The conferences were conducted by night with the utmost secrecy, sometimes within the walls of Granada, and at others; in the little hamlet of Churriana, about a league distant from it. At length, after large discussion on both sides, the terms of capitulation were definitively settled, and ratified by the respective monarchs on the 25th of November, 1491.[14]

The conditions were of similar, though somewhat more liberal import, than those granted to Baza. The inhabitants of Granada were to retain possession of their mosques, with the free exercise of their religion, with all its peculiar rites and ceremonies; they were to be judged by their own laws, under their own *cadis* or magistrates, subject to the general control of the Castilian governor; they were to be unmolested in their ancient usages, manners, language, and dress; to be protected in the full enjoyment of their property, with the right of disposing of it on their own account, and of migrating when and where they would; and to be furnished with vessels for the conveyance of such as chose within three years to pass into Africa. No heavier taxes were to be imposed than those customarily paid to their Muslim sovereigns, and none whatever before the expiration of three years. King Boabdil was to reign over a specified territory in the Alpujarras, for which he was to do homage to the Castilian crown. The artillery and the fortifications were to be delivered into the hands of the Christians, and the city was to be surrendered in sixty days from the date of the capitulation. Such were the principal terms of the surrender of Granada as authenticated by the most accredited Castilian and Muslim authorities; which I have stated the more precisely, as affording the best data for estimating the extent of Spanish perfidy in later times.[15]

The conferences could not be conducted so secretly, but that some report of them got air among the populace of the city, who now regarded Boabdil with an evil eye for his connection with the Christians. When the fact of the capitulation became known, the agitation speedily mounted into an open insurrection, which menaced the safety of the city, as well as of Boabdil's person. In this alarming state of things, it was thought best by that monarch's counsellors, to anticipate the appointed day of surrender; and the 2nd of January, 1492, was accordingly fixed on for that purpose.

Every preparation was made by the Christians for performing this last act of the drama with suitable pomp and effect. The mourning which the court had put on for the death of Prince Affonso of Portugal, occasioned by a fall from his horse a few months after his marriage with the Infanta Isabella, was exchanged for gay and magnificent apparel. On the morning of the 2nd, the whole Christian camp exhibited a scene of the most animating bustle. The Grand Cardinal Mendoza was sent forward at the head of a large detachment, comprehending his household troops, and the veteran infantry grown grey in the Granadan wars, to occupy the Alhambra preparatory to the entrance of the sovereigns.[16] Ferdinand stationed himself at some distance in the rear, near a Muslim mosque, since consecrated as the hermitage of St. Sebastian. He was surrounded by his courtiers, with their stately retinues, glittering in gorgeous panoply, and proudly displaying the armorial bearings of their ancient houses. The Queen halted still farther in the rear, at the village of Armilla.[17]

As the column under the Grand Cardinal advanced up the Hill of Martyrs, over which a road had been constructed for the passage of the artillery, he was met by the Nasrid King Boabdil, attended by fifty cavaliers, who descending the hill, rode up to the position occupied by Ferdinand on the banks of the Genil. As the Nasrid approached the Castilian King; he would have thrown

himself from his horse, and saluted his hand in token of homage, but Ferdinand
hastily prevented him, embracing him with every mark of sympathy and
regard. Boabdil then delivered up the keys of the Alhambra to his conqueror
saying, 'They are thine, O king, since Allah so decrees it; use thy success with
clemency and moderation.' Ferdinand would have uttered some words of
consolation to the unfortunate prince, but he moved forward with dejected air
to the spot occupied by Isabella, and, after similar acts of obeisance, passed on
to join his family, who had preceded him with his most valuable effects on the
route to the Alpujarras.[18]

The sovereigns during this time waited with impatience the signal of the
occupation of the city by the cardinal's troops, which, winding slowly along the
outer circuit of the walls, as previously arranged, in order to spare the feelings of
the citizens as far as possible, entered by what is now called the Gate of Los
Molinos. In a short time, the large silver cross, borne by Ferdinand throughout
the crusade, was seen sparkling in the sunbeams, while the standards of Castile
and Santiago waved triumphantly from the red towers of the Alhambra. At this
glorious spectacle, the choir of the royal chapel broke forth into the solemn
anthem of *Te Deum*, and the whole army, penetrated with deep emotion,
prostrated themselves on their knees in adoration of the Lord of Hosts, who had
at length granted the consummation of their wishes, in this last and glorious
triumph of the Cross.[19] The grandees who surrounded Ferdinand then
advanced toward the Queen, and kneeling down saluted her hand in token of
homage to her as sovereign of Granada. The procession took up its march
toward the City, 'the King and Queen moving in the midst,' says an historian,
'emblazoned with royal magnificence; and, as they were in the prime of life, and
had now achieved the completion of this glorious conquest, they seemed to
represent even more than their wonted majesty. Equal with each other, they
were raised far above the rest of the world. They appeared, indeed, more than
mortal, and as if sent by Heaven for the salvation of Spain.'[20]

In the meanwhile the Nasrid King, traversing the route of the Alpujarras,
reached a rocky eminence which commanded a last view of Granada. He
checked his horse, and, as his eye for the last time wandered over the scenes of
his departed greatness, his heart swelled, and he burst into tears. 'You do well,'
said his more masculine mother, 'to weep like a woman, for what you could not
defend like a man!' 'Alas,' exclaimed the unhappy exile, 'when were woes ever
equal to mine!' The scene of this event is still pointed out to the traveller by the
people of the district; and the rocky height, from which the Nasrid chief took
his sad farewell of the princely abodes of his youth, is commemorated by the
poetical title of *El Ultimo Suspiro del Moro*, 'The Last Sigh of the Moor'.

The sequel of Boabdil's history is soon told. Like his uncle, al-Zagal, he pined
away in his barren domain of the Alpujarras, under the shadow, as it were, of his
ancient palaces. In the following year, he passed over to Fez with his family,

having commuted his petty sovereignty for a considerable sum of money paid him by Ferdinand and Isabella, and soon after fell in battle in the service of an African prince, his kinsman. 'Wretched man,' exclaims a caustic chronicler of his nation, 'who could lose his life in another's cause, though he did not dare to die in his own. Such,' continues the Muslim chronicler, with characteristic resignation, 'was the immutable decree of destiny. Blessed be Allah, who exalteth and debaseth the kings of the earth, according to his divine will, in whose fulfilment consists that eternal justice, which regulates all human affairs.' The portal, through which King Boabdil for the last time issued from his capital, was at his request walled up, that none other might again pass through it. In this condition it remains to this day, a memorial of the sad destiny of the last of the kings of Granada.[21]

The fall of Granada excited general sensation throughout Christendom, where it was received as counterbalancing, in a manner, the loss of Constantinople, nearly half a century before. At Rome, the event was commemorated by a solemn procession of the Pope and cardinals to St. Peter's, where high mass was celebrated, and the public rejoicing continued for several days.[22] The intelligence was welcomed with no less satisfaction in England, where Henry VII was seated on the throne. The circumstances attending it, as related by Lord Bacon, will not be devoid of interest for the reader.[23]

Thus ended the War of Granada, which is often compared by the Castilian chroniclers to that of Troy in its duration, and which certainly fully equalled the latter in variety of picturesque and romantic incidents, and in circumstances of poetical interest. With the surrender of its capital, terminated the Islamic empire in the Peninsula, after an existence of seven hundred and forty-one years from the date of the original conquest. The consequences of this closing war were of the highest moment to Spain. The most obvious, was the recovery of an extensive territory, hitherto held by a people, whose difference of religion, language, and general habits, made them not only incapable of assimilating with their Christian neighbours, but almost their natural enemies; while their local position was a matter of just concern, as interposed between the great divisions of the Spanish monarchy, and opening an obvious avenue to invasion from Africa. By the new conquest, moreover, the Spaniards gained a large extent of country, possessing the highest capacities for production, in its natural fruitfulness of soil, temperature of climate, and in the state of cultivation to which it had been brought by its ancient occupants; while its shores were lined with commodious havens, that afforded every facility for commerce. The scattered fragments of the ancient Visigothic empire were now again, with the exception of the little state of Navarra, combined into one great monarchy, as originally destined by nature; and Christian Spain gradually rose by means of her new acquisitions from a subordinate situation, to the level of a first-rate European power.

The moral influence of the Granadan war, its influence on the Spanish character, was highly important. The inhabitants of the great divisions of the country, as in most countries during the feudal ages, had been brought too frequently into collision with each other to allow the existence of a pervading national feeling. This was particularly the case in Spain, where independent states insensibly grew out of the detached fragments of territory recovered at different times from the Nasrid monarchy. The War of Granada subjected all the various sections of the country to one common action, under the influence of common motives of the most exciting interest; while it brought them in conflict with a race, the extreme repugnance of whose institutions and character to their own, served greatly to nourish the nationality of sentiment. In this way, the spark of patriotism was kindled throughout the whole nation, and the most distant provinces of the Peninsula were knit together by a bond of union, which has remained indissoluble.

The consequences of these wars in a military aspect are also worthy of notice. Up to this period, war had been carried on by irregular levies, extremely limited in numerical amount and in period of service; under little subordination, except to their own immediate chiefs, and wholly unprovided with the apparatus required for extended operations. The Spaniards were even lower than most of the European nations in military science, as is apparent from the infinite pains of Isabella to avail herself of all foreign resources for their improvement. In the war of Granada, masses of men were brought together, far greater than had hitherto been known in modern warfare. They were kept in the field not only through long campaigns, but far into the winter; a thing altogether unprecedented. They were made to act in concert, and the numerous petty chiefs brought in complete subject to one common head, whose personal character enforced the authority of station. Lastly, they were provided with all the requisite munitions, through the providence of Isabella, who introduced into the service the most skilful engineers from other countries, and kept in pay bodies of mercenaries, as the Swiss for example, reputed the best disciplined troops of that day. In this admirable school, the Spanish soldier was gradually trained to patient endurance, fortitude, and thorough subordination; and those celebrated captains were formed, with that invincible infantry, which in the beginning of the sixteenth century spread the military fame of their country over all Christendom.

But, with all our sympathy with the conquerors, it is impossible, without a deep feeling of regret, to contemplate the decay and final extinction of a race, who had made such high advances in civilization as the Spanish Muslims; to see them driven from the stately palaces reared by their own hands, wandering as exiles over the lands, which still blossomed with the fruits of their industry, and wasting away under persecution, until their very name as a nation was blotted out from the map of history.[24] It must be admitted, however, that they had long since reached their utmost limit of advancement as a people. The light shed over their history shines from distant ages; for, during the later period of their existence, they appear to have reposed in a state of torpid, luxurious indulgence, which would seem to argue, that, when causes of external excitement were withdrawn, the inherent vices of their social institutions had incapacitated them for the further production of excellence. In this impotent condition, it was wisely ordered, that their territory should be occupied by a people, whose religion and more liberal form of government, however frequently misunderstood or perverted, qualified them for advancing still higher the interests of humanity.

It will not be amiss to terminate the narrative of the War of Granada, with some notice of the fate of Rodrigo Ponce de León, Marquis Duke of Cádiz; for he may be regarded in a peculiar manner as the hero of it, having struck the first stroke by the surprise of Alhama, and witnessed every campaign till the surrender of Granada. A circumstantial account of his last moments is afforded by the pen of his worthy countryman, the Andalusian Curate of Los Palacios. The gallant marquis survived the close of the war only a short time, terminating his days at his mansion in Sevilla, on the 28th of August, 1492, with a disorder brought on by fatigue and incessant exposure. He had reached the forty-ninth year of his age, and, although twice married, left no legitimate issue. In his person, he was of about the middle stature, of a compact, symmetrical frame, a fair complexion, with light hair inclining to red. He was an excellent horseman, and well skilled indeed in most of the exercises of chivalry. He had the rare merit of combining sagacity with intrepidity in action. Though somewhat impatient, and slow to forgive, he was frank and generous, a warm friend, and a kind master to his vassals.[25]

He was strict in his observance of the Catholic worship, punctilious in keeping all the church festivals and in enforcing their observance throughout his domains; and, in war, he was a most devout champion of the Virgin. He was ambitious of acquisitions, but lavish of expenditure, especially in the embellishment and fortification of his towns and castles; spending on Alcalá de Guadaira, Jerez, and Alanis, the enormous sum of seventeen million maravedies. To the ladies he was courteous as became a true knight. At his death, the King and Queen with the whole court went into mourning; 'for he was a much loved cavalier,' says the Curate, 'and was esteemed, like the Cid, both by friend and foe; and no Moor durst abide in that quarter of the field where his banner was displayed'.

His body, after lying in state for several days in his palace at Sevilla, with his trusty sword by his side, with which he had fought all his battles, was borne in solemn procession by night through the streets of the city, which was everywhere filled with the deepest lamentation; and was finally deposited in the great chapel of the Augustine church, in the tomb of his ancestors. Ten Muslim banners, which he had taken in battle with the infidel, before the war of

Granada, were borne along at his funeral, 'and still wave over his sepulchre,' says Bernaldez, 'keeping alive the memory of his exploits, as undying as his soul'. The banners have long since mouldered into dust; the very tomb which contained his ashes has been sacrilegiously demolished; but the fame of the hero will survive as long as anything like respect for valour, courtesy, unblemished honour, or any other attribute of chivalry, shall be found in Spain.[26]

*   *   *   *   *

AUTHOR'S CHAPTER COMMENTS

One of the chief authorities on which the account of the Granadan War rests, is Andres Bernaldez, Curate of Los Palacios. He was a native of Fuente in León, and appears to have received his early education under the care of his grandfather, a notary of that place, whose commendations of a juvenile essay in historical writing led him later in life according to his own account, to record the events of his time in the extended and regular form of a chronicle. After admission to orders, he was made chaplain to Deza, Archbishop of Sevilla, and Curate of Los Palacios, an Andalusian town not far from Sevilla, where he discharged his ecclesiastical functions with credit, from 1488 to 1513, at which time, as we find no later mention of him, he probably closed his life with his labours.

Bernaldez had ample opportunities for accurate information relative to the Granadan War, since he lived, as it were, in the theatre of action, and was personally intimate with the most considerable men of Andalusia, especially the Marquis of Cádiz, whom he has made the Achilles of his epic, assigning him a much more important part in the principal transactions, than is always warranted by other authorities. His *Chronicle* is just such as might have been anticipated from a person of lively imagination, and competent scholarship for the time, deeply dyed with the bigotry and superstition of the Spanish clergy in that century. There is no great discrimination apparent in the work of the worthy curate, who dwells with goggle-eyed credulity on the most absurd marvels, and expends more pages on an empty court show, than on the most important schemes of policy. But if he is no philosopher, he has, perhaps for that very reason, succeeded in making us completely master of the popular feelings and prejudices of the time; while he gives a most vivid portraiture of the principal scenes and actors in this stirring war, with all their chivalrous exploit, and rich theatrical accompaniment. His credulity and fanaticism, moreover, are well compensated by a simplicity and loyalty of purpose, which secure much more credit to his narrative than attaches to those of more ambitious writers, whose judgment is perpetually swayed by personal or party interests. The chronicle descends as late as 1513, although, as might be expected from the author's character, it is entitled to much less confidence in the discussion of events which fell without the scope of his personal observation. Notwithstanding its historical value is fully recognized by the Castilian critics, it has never been admitted to the press, but still remains, ingulfed in the ocean of manuscripts, with which the Spanish libraries are deluged.

It is remarkable that the War of Granada, which is so admirably suited in all its circumstances to poetical purposes, should not have been more frequently commemorated by the epic muse. The only successful attempt in this way, with which I am acquainted, is the '*Conquisto di Granata*', by the Florentine Girolamo Gratiani, Modena, 1650. The author has taken the licence, independently of his machinery, of deviating very freely from the historic track; among other things, introducing Columbus and the Great Captain as principal actors in the drama, in which they played at most but a very subordinate part. The poem, which swells into twenty-six cantos, is in such repute with the Italian critics, that Quadrio does not hesitate to rank it 'among the best epical productions of the age'. A translation of this work has recently appeared at Nuremberg, from the pen of C.M. Winterling, which is much commended by the German critics.

Mr. Irving's late publication, the *Chronicle of the Conquest of Granada*, has superseded all further necessity for poetry, and unfortunately for me, for history. He has fully availed himself of all the picturesque and animating movements of this romantic era; and the reader, who will take the trouble to compare his Chronicle with the present more prosaic and literal narrative, will see how little he has been seduced from historic accuracy by the poetical aspect of his subject. The fictitious and romantic dress of his work has enabled him to make it the medium for reflecting more vividly the floating opinions and chimerical fancies of the age, while he has illuminated the picture with the dramatic brilliancy of colouring denied to sober history.

NOTES

1. Carbajal, *Anales*, MS., año 1490. Bernaldez, Reyes Católicos, MS., cap.95. – Zuñiga, *Annales de Sevilla*, pp.404, 405. – Pulgar, *Reyes Católicos*, part 3, cap.127. – La Clède, *Hist. de Portugal*, tom.iv. p.19. – Faria y Sousa, *Europe Portuguesa*, tom.ii, p.452.
2. Faria y Sousa, *Europa Portuguesa*, tom.ii, p.452–6. – Florez, *Reynas Católicas*, p.845. – Pulgar, *Reyes Católicos*, cap.129. – Oviedo, *Quincuagenas*, MS., bat.1, quinc.2, dial.3.
3. Condé, *Dominacion de los Arabes*, tom.iii, cap.41. – Bernaldez, *Reyes Católicos*, MS., cap.90.

    Neither the Muslim nor Castilian authorities impeach the justice of the summons made by the Spanish sovereigns. I do not, however, find any other foundation for the obligation imputed to Boabdil in them, than that monarch's agreement during his captivity at Loja, in 1486, to surrender his capital in exchange for Guadix, provided the latter should be conquered within six months. Pulgar, *Reyes Católicos*, p.275. – Garibay, *Compendio*, tom.iv, p.418.
4. L. Marineo, *Cosas Memorables*, fol.176. – Pulgar, *Reyes Católicos*, cap.130. – Zurita, *Anales*, tom.iv, cap.85. – Cardonne, *Hist. d'Afrique et d'Espagne*, tom.iii, p.309.
5. Pulgar, *Reyes Católicos*, cap.131, 132. – Bernaldez, *Reyes Católicos*, MS., cap.97. – Condé, *Dominacion de los Arabes*, tom.iii, cap.41 – Peter Martyr, *Opus Epist.*, lib.3, epist.84. – Garibay, *Compendio*, tom.iv, p.424. – Cardonne, *Hist. d'Afrique et d'Espagne*, tom.iii, pp.309, 310.
6. Carbajal, *Anales*, MS, año 1491.
7. According to Zuñiga, the quota furnished by Seville this season amounted to 6,000 foot and 500 horse, who were recruited by fresh reinforcements no less than five times during the campaign. *Annales de Sevilla*, p.406. – See also *Col. de Cédulas*, tom.iii, no.3. [Today, Ladero Quesada's *Castilla y La Conquista del Reino de Granada*

(1967) is probably the best authority on the size of various forces raised during the War of Granada. – ED}

8. Condé, *Dominacion de los Arabes*, tom.iii, cap.42. – Bernaldez, *Reyes Católicos*, MS., cap.100. – Peter Martyr, *Opus Epist.*, lib.3, epist.89. – Marmol, *Rebelion de Moriscos*, lib.1, cap.18. – L. Marineo, *Cosas Memorables*, fol.177.

Martyr remarks, that the Genoese merchants, 'voyagers to every clime, declare this to be the largest fortified city in the world'. Casiri had collected a body of interesting particulars respecting the wealth, population, and social habits of Granada, from various Arabic authorities. *Bibliotheca Escurialensis*, tom.ii, pp.247–60.

The French work of *Laborde, Voyage Pittoresque* (Paris, 1807), and the English one of Murphy, *Engravings of Arabian Antiquities of Spain* (London, 1816), do ample justice in their finished designs to the general topography and architectural magnificence of Granada. [Twentieth-century pictorial books on Granada and Muslim Spain abound, an ever futile quest to capture the un-reproducible visual experience of a personal visit. Miraculously, much remains. – ED}

9. On one occasion, a Christian knight having discomfited with a handful of men a much superior body of Muslim chivalry, King Boabdil testified his admiration of his prowess by sending him on the following day a magnificent present, together with his own sword superbly mounted. (*Mem. de la Acad. de Hist.*, tom.vi, p.178). The Moorish ballad beginning '*Al Rey Chico de Granada,*' describes the panic occasioned in the city by the Christian encampment on the Xenil:

'*Por ese fresco Genil*
un campo viene marchando,
todo de lucida gente,
las armas van relumbrando.
 '*Las vanderas traen tendidas,*
y un estandarte dorado;
el General de esta gente,
es el invicto Fernando,
la qua anima a qualquier soldado.'

10. Bernaldez, *Reyes Católicos*, MS., cap.101.
11. Bernaldez, *Reyes Católicos*, MS., cap.101. – Condé, *Dominacion de los Arabes*, tom.iii, cap.42. – Peter Martyr, *Opus Epist.*, lib.4, epist.90. – Pulgar, *Reyes Católicos*, cap.133. – Zurita, *Anales*, tom.iv, cap.88.

Isabella afterwards caused a Franciscan monastery to be built in commemoration of this event at Zubia, where, according to Mr. Irving, the house from which she witnessed the action is to be seen today. See *Conquest of Granada*, chap.90, note.

12. Peter Martyr, *Opus Epist.*, lib.4, epist.91. – Bernaldez, *Reyes Católicos*, MS., cap.101. – Garibay, *Compendio*, tom.ii, p.673. – Bleda, *Corónica*, p.619. – Marmol, *Rebelion de Moriscos*, lib.1, cap.18.
13. Estrada, *Poblacion de España*, tom.ii, pp.344. – Peter Martyr, *Opus Epist.*, lib.4, epist.91. – Marmol, *Rebelion de Moriscos*, lib.1, cap.18.

Hyta, who embellishes his florid prose with occasional extracts from the beautiful ballad poetry of Spain, gives one commemorating the erection of Santa Fé.

'Cercada esta Santa Fe
con muxho lienzo encerado
al rededor muchas tiendas
de seda, oro, y brocado.
       'Donde estan Duques, y Condes,
Señores de gran estado,', etc.
              – Guerras de Granada, p.515.

14. Pedraza, *Antiguedad de Granada*, fol.74. – Giovio, *De Vitâ Gonsalvi, apud Vitæ Illust. Virorum*, pp.211, 212. – Salazar de Mendoza, *Crón. del Gran Cardenal*, p.236. – Cardonne, *Hist. d'Afrique et d'Espagne*, tom.iii, pp.316, 317. – Condé, *Dominacion de los Arabes*, tom.iii, cap.42. – L. Marineo, *Cosas Memorables*, fol.178. – Marmol, however, assigns the date in the text to a separate capitulation respecting Boabdil, dating that made in behalf of the city three days later, (*Rebelion de Moriscos*, lib.1, cap.19). This author had given the articles of the treaty greater fullness and precision than any other Spanish historian. [Antonio de la Torre's *Los Reyes Católicos y Granada*, (1946), Part II covers considerable detail on the 1483–89 agreements between Boabdil and the Spanish Sovereigns. – ED]

15. Marmol, *Rebelion de Moriscos*, lib.1, cap.19. – Condé, *Dominacion de los Arabes*, tom.iii, cap.42. – Zurita, *Anales*, tom.ii, cap.90. – Cardonne, *Hist. d'Afrique et d'Espagne*, tom.iii, pp.317, 318. – Oviedo, *Quincuagenas*, MS., bat.1, quinc.1, dial.28.

    Martyr adds that the principal Moorish nobility were to be removed from the city (*Opus Epist.*, lib.4, epist.92). Pedraza, who had devoted a volume to the history of Granada, does not seem to think the capitulation worth specifying. Most modern Castilians pass very lightly over them. They furnish so bitter a comment on the conduct of subsequent Spanish monarchs. Marmol and the judicious Zurita agree in every substantial particular with Condé, and this coincidence may be considered as establishing the actual terms of the treaty.

16. Oviedo, whose narrative exhibits many discrepancies with those of other contemporaries, assigns this part to the Count Tendilla, the first Captain-General of Granada (*Quincuagenas*, MS., bat.1, quinc.1, dial.28). But, as this writer, though an eyewitness, was but thirteen or fourteen years of age at the time of the capture, and wrote some sixty years later from his early recollections, his authority cannot be considered of equal weight with that of persons, who like Martyr, described events as they were passing before them.

17. Pedraza, *Antiguedad de Granada*, fol.75. – Salazar de Mendoza, *Crón. del Gran Cardenal*, p.238. – Zurita, *Anales*, tom.iv, cap.90. – Peter Martyr, *Opus Epist.*, lib.4, epist.92. – Abarca, *Reyes de Aragon*, tom.ii, fol.309. – Marmol, *Rebelion de Moriscos*, lib.1, cap.20.

18. Marmol, *Rebelion de Moriscos, ubi supra.* – Condé, *Dominacion de los Arabes*, tom.iii, cap.43. – Pedraza, *Antiguedad de Granada*, fol.76. – Bernaldez, *Reyes Católicos*, MS., cap.102. – Zurita, *Anales*, tom.iv, cap.90. – Oviedo, *Quincuagenas*, MS., bat.1, quinc.1, dial.28.

19. Oviedo, *Quincuagenas*, MS., *ubi supra.* – One is reminded of Tasso's description of the somewhat similar feelings exhibited by the crusaders on their entrance into Jerusalem.

'*Ecco apparir Gerusalem si vede,*
Ecco additar Gerusalem si scorge;
Ecco da mille voci unitamente
Gerusalemme salutar si sente.

* * *

'*Al gran piacer che quella prima vista*
Dolcemente spiro nell' altrui petto,
Alta contrizion successe, mista
Di timoroso e riverente affetto.
Osano appena d'innalzar la vista
Ver la città.'

– *Gerusalemme Liberata*, Cant.iii, st.3, 5.

20. Mariana, *Hist. de España*, tom.ii, p.397. –Pedraza, *Antiguedad de Granada*, fol.76. – Carbajal, *Anales*, MS., año 1492. – Condé, *Dominacion de los Arabes*, tom.iii, cap.43. – Bleda, *Corónica*, pp.621, 622. – Zurita, *Anales*, tom.iv, cap.90. – Marmol, *Rebelion de Moriscos*, lib.1, cap.20. – L. Marineo, and indeed most of the Spanish authorities, represent the sovereigns as having postponed their entrance into the city until the 5th or 6th of January. A letter transcribed by Pedraza, addressed by the Queen to the Prior of Guadalupe, one of her council, dated from the city of Granada on the 2nd of January, 1492, shows the inaccuracy of this statement. See folio 76.

In Mr. Lockhart's picturesque version of the Moorish ballads, the reader may find an animated description of the triumphant entry of the Christian army into Granada.

'There was crying in Granada
        when the sun was going down,
Some calling on the Trinity, some calling
        on Mahoun;
Here passed away the Koran, there in
        the cross was borne,
And here was heard the Christian bell,
        and there the Moorish horn;
Te Deum laudamus was up the Alcala
        sung,
Down from the Alhambra's minarets
        were all the crescents flung;
The arms thereon of Aragon and Castile
        they display
One king comes in triumph, one
        weeping goes away.'

21. Condé, *Dominacion de los Arabes*, tom.iii, cap.90. – Cardonne, *Hist. d'Afrique et d'Espagne*, tom.iii, pp.319, 320. – Garibay, *Compendio*, tom.iv, lib.40, cap.42. – Marmol, *Rebelion de Moriscos*, lib.1, cap.20.

Mr. Irving, in his beautiful Spanish Sketch book, *The Alhambra*, devotes a chapter to mementos of Boabdil, in which he traces minutely the route of the deposed monarch after quitting the gates of his capital. The same author, in the Appendix to his *Chronicle of Granada*, concludes a notice of Boabdil's fate with the following description of his person. 'A portrait of Boabdil el Chico is to be seen in the picture gallery of the Generalife. He is represented with a mild, handsome face, a fair complexion, and yellow hair. His dress is of yellow brocade, relieved with black velvet; and he has a black velvet cap, surmounted with a crown. In the armory of Madrid are two suits of armor said to have belonged to him, one of solid steel, with very little ornament; the morion closed. From the proportions of these suits of armor, he must have been of full stature and vigorous form.'

[The sealed portal through which Boabdil departed the city of Granada was in the tower of the *Siete Suelos* (Seven Floors), and was destroyed during the Peninsular War (1809–14). It has been rebuilt in recent restoration of the Alhambra. See Enrique Sordo, *Moorish Spain*, (New York, 1963) p.124. – ED]

22. Senarega, *Commentaril de Rebus Genuensibus, apud Muratori, Rerum Italicarum Scriptores*, (Mediolani, 1723–51), tom.xxiv, p.531. – It formed the subject of a theatrical representation before the court of Naples, in the same year. This drama, or *Farsa*, as it is called by its distinguished author, Sannazaro, is an allegorical medley, in which Faith, Joy, and the false prophet Muhammad play principal parts. The difficulty of a precise classification of this piece, has given rise to warmer discussion among the Italian critics than the subject may be thought to warrant. See Signorelli, *Vicende della Coltura nelle due Sicilie* (Napoli, 1810), tom.iii, pp.543 *et seq.*

23. 'Somewhat about this time, came letters from Ferdinando and Isabella, king and queen of Spain; signifying the final conquest of Granada from the Moors; which action, in itself so worthy, King Ferdinando, whose manner was never to lose any virtue for the showing, had expressed and displayed in his letters, at large, with all the particularities and religious punctos and ceremonies, that were observed in the reception of that city and kingdom; showing amongst other things, that the king would not by any means in person enter the city until he had first seen the Cross set up upon the great tower of Granada, whereby it became Christian ground. That likewise, before he would enter, he did homage to God, pronouncing by an herald from the height of that tower, that he did acknowledge to have recovered that kingdom by the held of God Almighty, and the glorious Virgin, and the virtuous apostle St. James, and the holy father Innocent VIII, together with the aids and services of his prelates, nobles, and commons. That yet he stirred not from his camp, till he had seen a little army of martyrs to the number of seven hundred and more Christians that had lived in bonds and servitude, as slaves to the Moors, pass before his eyes, singing a psalm for their redemption; and that he had given tribute unto God, by alms and relief extended to them all, for his admission into the city. These things were in the letters, with many more ceremonies of a kind of holy ostentation.

'The king, ever willing to put himself into the consort or quire of all religious actions, and naturally affecting much the king of Spain, as far as one king can affect another, partly for his virtues, and partly for a counterpoise to France; upon the receipt of these letters, sent all his nobles and prelates that were about the court, together with the mayor and aldermen of London, in great solemnity to the church of Paul; there to hear a declaration from the lord chancellor, now cardinal. When they were assembled, the cardinal, standing upon the upper most step, or halfpace, before the quire and all the nobles, prelates, and governors of the city at the foot of the stairs, made a speech to them; letting them know that they were assembled in that consecrated place to sing unto God a new song. For that, said he, these many years the Christians have not gained new ground or territory upon the infidels, nor enlarged and set farther the bounds of the Christian world. But this is now done by the prowess and devotion of Ferdinando and Isabella, kings of Spain; who have, to their immortal honour, recovered the great and rich kingdom of Granada, and the populous and mighty city of the same name from the Moors, having been in possession thereof by the space of seven hundred years, and more; for which this assembly and all Christians are to render laud and thanks to God, and to celebrate this noble act of the king of Spain; who in this is not only victorious but apostolical, in the gaining of new provinces to the Christian faith. And the rather for that this victory and conquest is obtained without much effusion of blood. Whereby it is to be hoped, that there shall be gained not only new territory, but infinite souls to the Church of Christ, whom the Almighty, as it seems, would have lived to be converted. Herewithal he did relate some of the most memorable particulars of the war and victory. And after his speech ended, the whole assembly went solemnly in procession, and Te Deum was sung.' Lord Bacon, *History of the Reign of King Henry VII, in his Works* (ed. London, 1819), vol.v, pp.85, 86. – See also Hall, *Chronicle*, p.453.

24. The African descendants of the Spanish Muslims, unable wholly to relinquish the hope of restoration of the delicious abodes of their ancestors, continued for many generations, and perhaps still continue, to put up a petition to that effect in their mosques every Friday. Pedraza, *Antiguedad de Granada*, fol.7.

25. Carbajal, *Anales*, MS., año 1492. Don Enríque de Guzmán, Duke of Medina Sidonia, the ancient enemy, and since the commencement of the Granadan War, the firm friend of the Marquis of Cádiz, died the 28th of August, on the same day with the latter.

26. Zuñiga, *Annales de Sevilla*, p.411. – Berenaldez, *Reyes Católicos*, MS., cap.104.

The Marquis left three illegitimate daughters by a noble Spanish lady, who all formed high connections. He was succeeded in his titles and estates, by the permission of Ferdinand and Isabella, by Don Rodrigo Ponce de León, the son of his eldest daughter, who had married with one of her kinsmen. Cádiz was subsequently annexed by the Spanish Sovereigns to the crown, from which it had been detached in Enríque IV's time, and considerable estates were given as an equivalent, together with the title of Duke of Arcos, to the family of Ponce de León.

EDITOR'S NOTE

With the completion of the war of conquest, the Catholic Sovereigns gave some serious attention to the scheme of the Genoese navigator, Christopher Columbus (Cristoforo Colombo). Since 1486, Columbus had been proposing to conquer new trade routes to the Far East by sailing west. However, the War of Granada strained Castile's resources and restricted the sovereigns' deliberation of further risky ventures. Columbus followed the court in the campaigns of 1487, and was present at the August surrender of Málaga. Following the surrender of Granada in January 1492, Columbus met with Isabella and Ferdinand at the siege camp, Santa Fé. His request was almost rejected, but on 17 April at Santa Fé the Catholic Sovereigns and Columbus signed their agreement. Columbus sailed from Palos on 3 August and anchored off an Island in the Bahamas on 12 October 1492.

Prescott and his Work
Editor's Commentary

I Prescott's Work

William Hickling Prescott was born at Salem, Massachusetts, 14 May 1796, and graduated from Harvard College in 1814. While at college, he had an accident which destroyed the sight in his left eye. The incident later led to an infection in his other eye, and left him almost blind. Prescott abandoned his study of law and travelled in Europe for a time. Returning to Boston, he contemplated writing a history of the Italian Renaissance, but in 1826, a friend who was a scholar of Spanish literature suggested that he write about the reign of Ferdinand and Isabella.

Prescott knew that he would be breaking new ground with such a work in English. However, the Peninsular War (1808–14) had awakened the English-reading public's interest in Spain. Prescott soon recognized that the reign of these sovereigns had had an impact on Western history, far beyond its significance in Spain alone. In this reign, Prescott discerned the drama of a medieval kingdom exploding into a modern world empire. Prescott found the research an arduous and expensive task. Fortunately, his father, who was well established financially, supported Prescott in the effort. Due to his failing eyesight, Prescott eventually had to have material read to him. He drafted his text in large script, which was later re-transcribed by full-time secretaries. Prescott arranged to have imported from Europe vast amounts of copied research materials on European and Spanish Muslim history. He spent seven-and-a-half years writing *The History of the Reign of Ferdinand and Isabella, the Catholic*, which was published in December, 1837. The publisher cautioned Prescott not to expect a profit, and that he would be lucky to break even. At best, it was expected that only 500 books would be purchased over a five-year period. The first 500 sold immediately and 17,000 sold within a few years. Many in the English-reading world appreciated Prescott's 'uncovering' this slighted moment of history, and were impressed with his masterful scholarship on such a vast epic.

In 1850, Prescott travelled to England, France, and Italy to receive many accolades. He was elected a member of Madrid's Royal Academy of History. His work on the Spanish sovereigns was translated into German, Spanish, and Italian by 1848, and made him the first American historian to acquire an international reputation for historical scholarship. According to a study of Prescott's major works by the Library of Congress and the Hispanic Foundation in 1958 (commemorating the centenary of his death), *Ferdinand and Isabella* had been published in fifteen editions (not counting numerous reprintings) and had been translated into nine languages.

The success encouraged Prescott to write on the *conquistadors* in the Americas. His *History of the Conquest of Mexico* (1843), and *History of the Conquest of Peru* (1847) were the result. These works were translated into many more languages than his initial work. These histories of the conquests of Latin and Central America were republished (often in abridged format) during the mid-twentieth century, and became his best-known works. Prescott began writing *The History of the Reign of Philip II, King of Spain*, and published three volumes in 1847–58. He did not finish the project before his death, in Boston, 28 January 1859. This last work on Spain, like his work on the Spanish sovereigns, has not been republished unabridged in this century.

An interesting aside to Prescott's writing of the histories on the Spanish conquests in America is that the most celebrated American author of the time, Washington Irving, withdrew his plans to publish on the same subject. Irving had published his *Chronicle of the Conquest of Granada* in 1829, before Prescott published his work on Ferdinand and Isabella. While Irving would remain the most popular author for the general reading public, he was well aware of Prescott's superior scholarship. In a revision of his work, Irving attempted to support his narrative with references to Prescott's work, as well as proudly quoting Prescott's endorsement of Irving's 'dramatic brilliancy'.

II PRESCOTT'S REPUTATION AND STYLE

No single work can satisfy all the various interests and scholarly pursuits of all the many historians. Certainly over a period of time, even accurate historical works can become 'dated' in that ensuing research and fresh perspectives have been uncovered or more adequately examined by different researchers and writers. The reading public's interests, values (or persuasions) and literary preferences also change with time. It is only fair, in part, to judge Prescott's style and analyses in the context of his time. A number of laudatory appraisals of Prescott's *The Reign of Ferdinand and Isabella*, are given in *The Library of Literary Criticism of English and American Authors, Volume VI, 1855–1874*, edited by C.W. Moulton (Gloucester, Mass., 1959), pp.181–5. A half-century after the first publication of his history of the Catholic Sovereigns, Prescott continued to elicit praise typified by the following:

'Though this history was the first written by Prescott, it has scarcely been excelled in merit by any of its successors.... Prescott's writings are conspicuous for thoroughness of research, keenness of insight, impartiality of judgment, picturesqueness of narration, exclusion of irrelevant matter, and correctness and elegance of style.' [Charles K. Adams, *A Manual of Historical Literature* (1882), p.407.]

There was also some early criticism of Prescott reported in Roger Howell's Introduction to his edited and abridged *Prescott, The Conquest of Mexico, The Conquest of Peru and other Selections* (New York, 1966), p.xvii: 'Prescott became a famous historian, though not without some resentment of European intellectual snobbishness. Though this was mild compared to some American circles who thought he was not hard enough on Spanish Catholicism, and some who thought that (in his later works on Mexico) he credited the Aztecs with too much cultivation.... A contemporary English critic, Richard Ford criticized Prescott for his "tendency to sneer at monarchies, courts, and chivalry".' These charges are ironic, for with the passage of time, the pendulum of criticism has almost swung in reverse on each account. Most of the early criticism of Prescott did not attack his scholarship but, rather, his treatment of social issues.

Historiography in the Western world has evolved since Prescott's time. Almost concurrent with Prescott's publishing his works, 'the scientific school' was emerging as a conceptual approach to history, and by the early twentieth century it was regarded as the fundamental measure by most professional historians. Prescott's careful scepticism and attention to documentation should have earned him acceptance in such a group. Articulating the view of the early 'scientific school' toward Prescott, Henry Steele Commager stated: 'His [Prescott's] history was narrative rather than analytical, descriptive rather than philosophical, and the brilliance of the coloring conceals a lack of depth. His concern was with politics, war and diplomacy rather than with social or economic institutions....' However, Commager continues by qualifying his criticism of Prescott and honestly admits what many of the later school chose to ignore: 'Although he was essentially a literary historian, Prescott's reliance upon source material, conscientious research and critical acumen established standards of scholarship which justify the claim that he was the first American scientific historian.' Going further, Commager added, '[Prescott's] observance of the most rigid standards did much to raise the level of historical scholarship in the United States.' [Henry Steel Commager, 'William Hickling Prescott', ed. Edwin R.A. Seligman *et al.*, *Encyclopedia of the Social Sciences*, vol. xii (1930–35), p.324].

Prescott has been examined most extensively by the mid twentieth-century American scholar, Clinton H. Harvey Gardiner, who wrote several works on William Prescott (note bibliography to this work). Gardiner's *William Hickling Prescott: a Bibliography* (Austin, Texas, 1969) contains several observations in Prescott's defence. Gardiner's response to the earlier recorded remarks by Henry Commager was that such criticism derives 'in part, from history's changing nature' (p.145). Gardiner finds it unjust that Prescott should be held to criteria not yet established. Further, Gardiner states that the most thoughtful proponents of the 'scientific' persuasion have to admit that Prescott adhered to much of the tenets of the school even before its broad incorporation into academia, regardless of Prescott's reputation as a 'narrative' historian.

The 'scientific' approach to history gave rise to an array of sub-methodologies, each emphasizing a more restricted discipline of study. Twentieth-century Western historians have placed importance on assessing social and economic conditions of the past, collecting quantitative data, examining and interpreting contemporary art images and archeological findings. The list of specialized areas to explore continues to expand, but the trend generally de-emphasizes literary sources (chronicles) which were the core of Prescott's research. While some extreme positions may find it fashionable to dismiss outright histories which are not garnished with statistics and lengthy postulations of human behavioural theories, the most coherent historical studies are held together by the 'glue' that narrative history provides. Narrative history constructs the framework that gives meaning to what would otherwise be a chaos of 'data'.

Repeated criticisms of Prescott cite his emphasis on wars and grand politics, and the insufficient attention he gave to economics and the general society. These charges and Prescott's 'literary' or 'romantic' reputation do not deny him the esteem of later and highly respected historians of late medieval and Renaissance Spain. Among such historians are Roger Bigelow Merriman, Jocelyn N. Hillgarth, Jean H. Mariéjol, and Joseph F. O'Callaghan, to name but a few, who attest to the value of Prescott's pioneering work. While some of the more recently published works in the English language on medieval Spain seem to omit direct reference to Prescott, they usually include one or more of the authors just listed. Merriman and Mariéjol, in particular, avow an indebtedness to Prescott that goes beyond mere deferential formality among authors. The editor and translator of a mid-twentieth-century publication of Mariéjol's work provides an eloquent assessment of Prescott:

'More than one hundred and twenty years ago a distinguished American, William Hickling Prescott, wrote, *The Reign of Ferdinand and Isabella the Catholic* (1838). His book was so well conceived and so surely executed that it remains a standard work. The themes of war, court intrigue, and diplomacy, however, were most congenial to Prescott's romantic bent; he did not neglect social and economic developments, but he relegated them to background of his picturesque canvas.' [Benjamin Keen's introduction to Jean Hippolyte Mariéjol's *The Spain of Ferdinand and Isabella*, trans. and ed. by Benjamin Keen, (1961), p.ix.]

Anyone who reads Prescott and researches in the same field cannot help but agree with Keen's observation that Prescott did acknowledge the social and economic influences on the heroic and dramatic events he describes. Had there been in his time more developed disciplines in these narrower topics as they pertained to the late fifteenth-century Iberian Peninsula, Prescott would certainly have included such in his work. The new disciplines enhance our understanding of medieval Spain and are valuable additions to Prescott's original examination of the epic of Ferdinand and Isabella. They certainly do not 'date' or diminish the main thrust and general accuracy of Prescott's work that related the military decisions and operations of the War of Granada.

Prescott's mastery of the prevailing knowledge of Western European history at his time remains solid today in the areas that he addressed. He was primarily interested in the political developments, and grasped the distinctive, central and dramatic theme surrounding the reign of Ferdinand and Isabella. His observation and thorough presentation of this theme remains the bedrock of all subsequent interpretations. In a letter, Prescott explained his motive to undertake the work:

'The subject brings me to the point whence [modern] English history had started, is untried ground, & in my opinion a rich one. The age of Ferdinand is most important as containing the germs of the modern system of European politics, & the three sovereigns Henry VII, Louis XI, & Ferdinand were important engines in the overturning the old system. It is in every aspect an interesting and momentous period of history. The materials authentic, ample.' [*The Literary Memoranda of William Hickling Prescott*, ed. C. Harvey Gardiner (Oklahoma, 1961), p.66–7.]

Irwin R. Blacker, editor of *The Portable Prescott, The Essence of Ferdinand and Isabella, The Conquest of Mexico, The Conquest of Peru* (New York, 1963, 1966) assesses Prescott as giving only cursory treatment of manners and customs, that he neglected the day-to-day life of the ordinary citizens of Spain and he rarely dealt with matters below the court. 'What he did capture were the personalities of those who fought and governed. He traced the development of the peninsula into a single great nation. He followed the internal conflicts, the conquest of the Moors, border campaigns with the French, and more central European wars in Italy ... as well as the beginnings of the overseas empire which was to help thrust the newly formed country [state] into the first rank of nations.' Blacker concludes that Prescott 'Relates history as an engrossing story. He wrote well [of] battles, diplomacy, and biography.... His portraits of the two Catholic monarchs, of Cardinal Ximenes [Jiménez] and Captain General Gonsalvo were among the best portions of his three volumes and have not been surpassed' (p.6).

While Prescott may not serve some modern social or economic agendas, his focus on political leadership and military events certainly profits the study of military history. Since Prescott's time, our knowledge has been considerably enhanced about the Spanish Muslims and on the broader aspects of changes in Western military warfare (particularly gunpowder weaponry) that occurred during the latter part of the fifteenth century. These themes have been addressed in the Introduction. It should be noted that no other scholars during Prescott's time – nor for many years after – thoroughly grasped these facets. The valuable contributions of the social and economic studies by modern social scientists cannot be ignored in relation to military matters. Such historical perspectives have improved our understanding of the underlying vitality of the Castilian society and provided a greater appreciation for the administrative actions initiated by the Catholic Sovereigns. The Arabists and Orientalists have unlocked a wealth of knowledge about the Hispano-Maghribi community and uncovered much of the enigmatic actions of the Nasrid leaders of the Granadan kingdom. The exciting part is that there is more to be learned.

In his coverage of the War of Granada, Prescott provided a disciplined assessment of and attention to his sources, and he exhibited an educated awareness of the broader historical context of Western European history. His weaknesses were a lack of sufficient information about Muslim history and an inadequate examination of the impact late fifteenth-century French and Burgundian warfare developments had on the Granadan war.

Prescott's writing style, though in vogue among scholars during his time, might be considered too decorative for modern readers. His lengthy descriptions can be distracting. On the other hand, he produces a rich narrative that is often missing in the terse accounts of modern writers. Prescott paints his scenes with descriptive narrative for dramatic effect. After all, his world did not have the profusion of pictorial aids provided by today's media, and visualization with words was appreciated.

Traces of ethnic and religious bias prevalent in Prescott's time and society can be detected in portions of his writings. He made an effort to be objective. His notes and chapter comments are full of circumspect assessments of both his sources and his observations. However, by today's standards, such self-assured confidence in Western Eurocentric perceptions compromises his analyses of social aspects. This weakness is fortunately minimized by his rather even scepticism.

Prescott's reporting of various legends evidently justifies placing him in the 'romantic school' of historians. The expression is frequently used to place his work on a par with that of Washington Irving. Though his writing manner is similar (indeed, he tried to emulate Irving's manner in the belief that it was preferred by the reading public), Prescott approached legends quite differently. It is obvious from his accompanying, qualifying – often openly sceptical – statements that Prescott reported a legend primarily to ensure full presentation of the 'evidence'.

III EDITORIAL APPROACH TO KNOWN ERRORS, STYLE AND OUTDATED OBSERVATIONS IN PRESCOTT'S TEXT

Prescott's rendition of the Spanish Muslims' War of Granada contains a few minor errors due to a lack of competent translations of the few Arabic works known to exist. Further difficulty is caused by the manner in which Muslim scholars recorded their history. Muslim political, as well as social, traditions encouraged generalizations and excessive tributes to monarchs. Translators of the Arabic writing of the period noted that the style employed by the Muslim authors was as important, if not more so, than the content. The fragmented remains of Spanish Muslim records has been a problem which has only recently been overcome.

A few errors in Condé's text (a central source for Prescott) misidentify some of the Muslims in the story. To eliminate confusion and distraction, the correct names are substituted in the text. Other minor errors induced by Condé are addressed as adjuncts to Prescott's original notes, or are inserted as editorial remarks within brackets at appropriate places in the text.

Comparison of Prescott's account of the War of Granada with the versions of later writers makes it obvious that only a few corrections are necessary. The most important editing has entailed adding significant findings of modern researchers, who have had much broader access to the Spanish archives. It is to Prescott's credit that even the latest Spanish scholars do not cite any primary chroniclers of whom Prescott was not aware. In this respect, nothing has changed since Charles Julian Bishko reported in a 1961 edition of *The American Historical Association's Guide to Historical Literature* (New York, 1961, p.509) the following: 'Despite the recent spate of studies on one or the other of the Catholic Kings (see bibliographies in Aguado Bleye, *Manuael de Historia de España*, v.2) no comprehensive work based on fresh archival exploration had appeared to replace Prescott's now over a century old classic as a general picture of this crucial reign.'

The challenge for historians of Prescott's time, and one which has only recently been alleviated, was obtaining knowledge of the military organization and operations of the Granadan military. Since Prescott was careful not to relate what he could not support, new understanding of the Granadan military does not require adjustments to his narrative. Instead, this material has been presented in the Introduction on military aspects. The same course of action has been taken in the matters of artillery and infantry developments just prior to the War of Granada.

Rather than attempt to rewrite Prescott's work – amounting to abridgment – it is better to let it remain as it is. Readers will value differently Prescott's scholarly expressions (or academic embellishments, depending on one's perspective). There are only a few lengthy sentences and paragraphs that have been editorially broken into separate parts for greater clarity.

The spelling of names defies simple rules. Some principal names have been standardized, rather than follow Prescott's occasional reference to the same individual by substituting an alternative appellation. Some alternative names, if used by one or more prominent historical source, have been indicated in brackets. Spanish and Portuguese name spellings are followed for the native individuals. Select exceptions have been made for the most famous persons, namely Ferdinand [Fernando] and Isabella [Isabel]. The spelling of 'Muslim' has been an arbitrary choice by the editor from among many transliteration versions that seem to inundate the subject. The words 'Spanish Muslims', 'Muslims', and 'Granadan' have been substituted in many instances where the word 'Moor' was used. Likewise, 'Christian Spanish' or 'Castilian' has been substituted in many cases where merely 'Spanish' was used. These substitutions were made to bring the narrative more in line with conventions followed by recent studies of the era which attempt an even treatment of both sides in the War of Granada.

No attempt is made to expand upon nor to explain Prescott's several literary references. No translations are given beyond what Prescott provided. There is no attempt to verify all of Prescott's references or update them to more modern editions. Prescott's notes refer to pages and volumes of many chronicles which are difficult, if not impossible in some cases, to obtain in the exact version he used. However, his citations remain useful guides to use with later editions of the documents, almost all of which are in the bibliography to this work.

Prescott's assessment of the economic situation of Arabia, originally part of the text that is now Chapter I of this work, has been omitted. This assessment was correct for the nineteenth century (though reflecting Western bias), but contrasts markedly with the economic conditions in Arabia today. Like several authors who describe the Arab world prior to mid twentieth-century oil kingdoms of the Arabian Peninsula, Prescott lamented the conditions of poor, tribal bedouins in Arabia. Such observations, directed toward Prescott's nineteenth-century audience, would be unnecessary and distracting in this book.

In his original work, Prescott included a chapter on the Inquisition among those that dealt with the war. The chapter had nothing to do with the war and has been left out of this work.

IV Prescott's Sources

In the 'author's chapter comments', at the end of some of the chapters, Prescott provides better identification and analysis of his primary sources than one finds in the works of many later historians on the same subject. He made extensive use of the Spanish chroniclers who were either contemporary with, or wrote soon after, the events.

Prescott blazed into worlds not well known to the English reading public or casual scholar of his time. In preparing for his work, Prescott noted 'that the reign of Ferdinand and Isabella was little known to the English reader, though the French writers had treated the subject well.' [*The Literary Memoranda of William Hickling Prescott*, ed. C. Harvey Gardiner (Oklahoma, 1961), p.96.] Prescott was able to build upon Spanish historians of the seventeenth and early eighteenth centuries. Not content with these, Prescott went further. With the assistance of Americans in Spain, and backed by the financial support of his father, Prescott obtained copies of the early Christian Spanish chronicles. Prescott was aided immeasurably by a close friend, George Ticknor, professor of modern languages at Harvard and author of *History of Spanish Literature* (Boston, 1963). Ticknor was primarily responsible for interesting Prescott in the project, and provided the necessary language skills and contacts in Spain to enable Prescott to work with the early Spanish documents.

For much of his knowledge of the Muslims, Prescott relied on a limited selection of published works by Spanish and French orientalists who rendered loose translations of Arabic texts found in Western libraries and private collections: Denis Dominique Cardonne (1720–83), *Histoire d'Afrique et d'Espagne sous la domination des Arabes* (Paris, 1765), and José Antonio Condé (1765–1820), *Historia de la dominacion de los Arabes en España* (1820), translated by Mrs Jonathan Foster as *History of the Dominion of the Arabs in Spain* (London, 1854). In addition, there were some unreliable translations of Arabic documents included in some of the chronicles and literary accounts by Christian Spanish chroniclers. Ticknor was familiar with Condé's work and recognized the potential to include material of Muslim authors. In later editions of his *History of Ferdinand and Isabella*, Prescott benefited from the advice of a Spanish scholar, Pascual de Gayangos, who worked in the British Library. Pascual de Gayangos y Arce (1809–1897) later wrote *The History of the Mohammedan dynasties in Spain* (London, 1840–1843) based in a loose translation of Ahmad ibn Muhammad al-Maqqari (d.1631/2?), a renowned Muslim historian from North Africa. Although the two never met, Prescott and Gayangos corresponded extensively. Gayangos was able to furnish Prescott with copies of some Spanish archival documents, which supplemented the predominant reliance on the early chronicles.

Prescott never visited Spain. His research was literary. However, at the time and for many years to follow, even the Spanish historians largely confined their examination to the early chronicles. For his expansive description of Spanish landscape and structures, Prescott obviously relied on others, not the least of whom was Washington Irving, who spent three years in Spain recording elaborate verbal landscapes and imagery.

V SELECTIVE REVIEW OF HISTORICAL SOURCES SINCE THE MIDDLE OF THE NINETEENTH CENTURY

Since Prescott's time scholarship has continued to enrich our understanding of aspects of the War of Granada. The following is a brief summary of the significant role played by several of the authors mentioned in the bibliography.

A professional military historian's examination of the War of Granada is presented in volume II of Serafín María de Soto, Condé de Clonard's *Historia orgánica de la armas de infantería y caballería españolas desde la creación del ejército permanente hasta el día* (1851–59). However, the work emphasizes the Christian Spanish army and not the Muslim forces. José Arántegui y Sanz's *Apuntes Históricos sobre la artillería española en los siglos xiv y xv* (Madrid, 1887) [not in the bibliography] provided a basis for the Spanish military historian Jorge Vigón's *Historia de la artillería Española* (1947), which describes the artillery of the Catholic Sovereigns in the fifteenth century along with photos of some of the pieces at the *Museo del Ejército*, Madrid's Army museum. Vigón's *El Ejército de los Reyes Católicos* (1968) is a study of the full development of the Spanish army under the sovereigns including the important developments after the War of Granada.

The French historian Jean Hippolyte Mariéjol's *L'Espagne sous Ferdinand et Isabelle: Le Gouvernement, les Institutions et les Moeurs* (1892) is one of the first to address economic and social facets, which Prescott and other early historians were accused of slighting. On military matters, Mariéjol deferred to Prescott.

Twentieth-century scholars continued to explore the Granadan history. Al-Bustani and Carlos Quiros made a Spanish translation of an anonymous and contemporary Muslim account of the Nasrids, generally known as *Nubdhat al-Asr fi akhbar muluk Bani Nasr* ('*The Nubdhat*'), published in 1940. Louis Mercier translated writings of the late-fourteenth-century Arabic historian Ibn Hudhayl al-Andalusi, Ali ibn abd al-Rahman (d. c.1405) as *L'Ornement des âmes et la devise des habitents de l'Andalus* (Paris, 1924), and *La Parure des cavaliers et l'insigne des preux* (Paris, 1939). In his *L'Art Militaire et les Armées au Moyen Age en Europe et dans le Proche Orient* (1946), Ferdinand Lot provided considerable attention to *La Reconquista*, which had been slighted in many non-Spanish histories of the medieval era. Évariste Lévi-Provençal's *Histoire de l'Espagne musulmane* (1950–53) and Ambrosio Huici Miranda's Spanish translation of many Arabic authors continued to expand Western knowledge of the Muslims in Spain. However, Luis Seco de Lucena Paredes' extensive work on the Nasrids of Granada aided scholars with invaluable 'decoding' of the array of fragmented (and evidently vaguely written) Arabic texts relating to the Nasrids. He is treated as the authority on the Granadans by two of the finest scholars on the war between Castile and the Nasrid kingdoms in 1481–92, Rachel Arié and Miguel Angel Ladero Quesada. For English texts, the military aspects have been the focus of the works by Paul Stewart and Weston F. Cook, Jr., as frequently referenced in earlier portions of this book.

Weaponry and technical aspects have been recently examined by Ada Bruhn Hoffmeyer and David Nicolle, in particular, with necessary attention to the Muslim side. Mention must be made of some works dealing with early gunpowder artillery. Though they do not deal with the War of Granada, Carlo M. Cipolla, John F. Guilmartin and Clifford J. Rogers provide valuable insight into the development of artillery and firearms at the end of the medieval era with a broader geographic perspective than do earlier English-language examinations of the introduction of gunpowder weapons into Western warfare. This summary is certainly not an exhaustive tally of the available material on warfare applicable to examining the War of Granada. Most of the works in the bibliography offer a deeper well of further sources.

GLOSSARY

acostamiento: Spanish noble who fought as a vassal in return for a fief or pay.

adalid/adalide: Scout (generally Muslim guide in al-Andulus mountains). Prescott (ch.2 note 14) associates the term with an old Spanish expression, *renegadoes*, for scouts used by Christians and perceived as Spanish Muslim deserters. Some chroniclers use *adalide* for leader of the medieval military force, or host.

adelantado: Spanish governor of a province; sometimes called '*mayor*', had military authority.

al-Andalus: The region of the Iberian Peninsula ruled by the Muslims.

alcadie: Military scout, sometimes leader of a minor raid or of a town militia.

alcaide/alcayde: Governor of a fortress, leader of a city militia.

alcalde: Mayor; leader.

alcázaba: Main fortress in a Spanish Muslim city, usually an integral part of the town's ramparts.

alcázar: The citadel of Spanish Muslim cities; term remained under Spanish Christian rule. It was surrounded by walled fortifications, within which were the alcazaba (the main fortress) and the residences of the senior officials and nobles of the city.

alfaki/alfaquí: In the late fifteenth century, a religious and civic leader in Muslim communities, revered for his prophecies and interpretation of omens.

alferez/alferes: Military leader of a Muslim or Christian Spanish army host; the figurative 'standard-bearer' of the host if a king or sultan were present.

arquebus: The term is used by many historians to refer to fifteenth-century handguns which had match-holding and trigger devices (*serpentines*). Contemporary fifteenth-century chroniclers identified such 'matchlock' firearms by various terms: *serpentinas*, *escopeta* (Italian), *espingarda* (Spanish), and *arquebuse* (French) to name but a few. The *arquebus* of the fifteenth century should not be confused with the French '*arquebuse*' developed late in the sixteenth century, which was a more advanced firing mechanism and was used by mounted troops.

artillery: Crew-operated and generally large weapons used in ancient and medieval eras mostly for sieges – both offensively and defensively. In the fifteenth century, the term still could include non-gunpowder siege engines as the *trébuchet*, *catapult*, etc. See *bombard*, *cannon*, *culverin*, *mortar*, *pasavolante* and *war machine*.

arubda/arrobda: Entailed: siege, pitched battle, frontier guard, or garrison work.

atalaya: Watch-tower, many were scattered throughout the mountains of Andalusia.

atalayero: Militia auxiliary who performed as a scout.

ballesta: Hand-held crossbow. [French: *arbalest*; German: *Armbrust*]

ballestero: Crossbowman. [French: *arbalétrier*]

ballista: Large crossbow [*balista* (Sp), *balliste* (Fr)], mounted on a stand and manned by a crew, that shot large darts or small rocks. As a direct-line shooting weapon, it was usually employed as a fixed-position anti-personnel weapon. It could usually be pivoted on its mount and angled slightly to fire against attackers advancing along confined approaches. An Arabic term for this weapon was *gaws al-ziyar*.

battle: The English term has two distinct meanings [which is shared with the Spanish and French: *batalla* (Sp), *bataille* (Fr)]. (1) Combat between armies. (2) Describes a tactical grouping of medieval armies. Generally there were three or more 'battles' on the battlefield, or when marching toward a possible engagement. The basic three 'battles' were: the 'main battle', 'forward van' (also: 'van', or 'vanguard'), and 'rear van'. The French terms (which are used in many English texts) are, respectively: *bataille, avant-garde, arriere-garde*. Spanish terms are: *batalla, vanguardia, rezaga*. Generally, when forming for combat, the three 'battles' deployed in line; the forward van and the rear van becoming 'wings' on either side of the main 'battle'. See *khamis* and *route*.

boca de fuego: Medieval Spanish expression for a gun tube, literally, 'mouth of fire' [*bouche à feu* (Fr)]. The term generally applied to a gunpowder artillery piece.

bombard: Early, large gunpowder artillery piece, employed primarily for siege operations. While some chroniclers and later writers use the term to apply to all the gunpowder artilley, '*bombard*' came more specifically to describe the very large-bore guns. This would distinguish them from the smaller bore and longer tubes of the *culverin* or *pasavolante* categories, and the *mortar*, which had a very large bore and much shorter tube.

buckler: Small round shield [*rodelas* or *escudo* (Sp)], used in close infantry fighting to parry an opponent's thrusting weapon, and complementing the use of a short sword, dagger, or thrusting spear.

caballera: Cavalry, or cavalry troop; also newly enobled knight.

caballero: Knight.

caballero armado: Mounted man-at-arms (*hombre de armas*).

caballero hidalgo: Noble who was paid man-at-arms.

caballero villano: Non-noble (or 'lesser noble') man-at-arms, or 'commoner knight' who had privileges similar to those of a noble (particularly tax exemptions) by possessing a horse and body protection suitable for military service.

cadi: State secretary in Muslim domains.

cannon: Gunpowder artillery weapon. Used generally to apply to all artillery guns. In the late fifteenth and sixteenth centuries the term identified categories of guns which were long-barrelled and had much smaller bore diameters than did either bombards or mortars.

capitanía: Military unit, a 'company', commanded by a *capitán* (captain); broadly applied to many types of units, as did *'capitán'* in referring to military leaders. The terms began to be associated with more specifically defined unit structures as the *Hermandad* and the *guardas viejas* developed.

captain-general: This became an increasingly useful title for monarchs of the late medieval era to use in designating senior military commanders with the explicit understanding that the title and implied position were not hereditary, as had become common in many cases for the titles of 'constable' and 'marshal'.

caravel: The *caravel* [*carabela* (Sp)] appeared in mid thirteenth century as a Portuguese fishing vessel. Early configurations were rigged with two or three lateen sails, typical of the Mediterranean ships. It was used for Portuguese expeditions around the coasts of Africa. Some fifteenth-century pictures show the caravel with a quarter-deck or castle in the stern and partial square sails, most likely for venturing further into the Atlantic Ocean. Columbus' *Niña* and *Pinta* were caravels.

carrack: The *carrack* [from Arabic *qaraqir*, meaning 'merchant ship'] had bulging round hull and square-rigged masts. It was built in the beginning of the fifteenth century. Designs were first noted in the Low Countries of Europe [Flemish *'kraeck'*]. It was capable of being a well-armed merchant ship, with guns on both sides, on a quarter-deck in the aft section, and on a forecastle over the bow. Columbus' *Santa Maria* is believed to have been a carrack.

catapult: A war machine (engine). The term has been used by many writers to refer to all machines that hurled projectiles. Some writers limit its application to the medium-size machines that operate by a swinging beam under torsion, generally, more specifically referred to as a *mangonel*.

cavalgada: Raid, armed foray (similar to *chevauchée* of the Hundred Years' War); can refer either to the marauding party or the booty itself. [See Prescott's note 11 in Chapter 4.]

cerbatana: Category of fifteenth-century Spanish cannon.

chevauchée: An expeditionary raid. Expression used often to describe large military forays of the Hundred Years' War. See *cavalgada*.

chorta: Militia formed to maintain internal order in the Umayyad Caliphate at Córdoba.

compagnie d'ordonnance: In the late medieval era, the standing army created by the French King, Charles VII, soon after the 1444 truce in the Hundred Years' War. Royal *ordonnances* described the company structures; the captains were appointed by the king; and the soldiers were paid on a regular basis from the royal treasury. The basic unit was the feudal *lance*, which eventually was formalized to be of 100 *lances* per *compagnie*. See *lance*. In 1471, the Duke of Burgundy, Charles 'the Rash', developed a more structured *compagnie d'ordonnance* and incorporated infantry spearmen into his formations.

company: In medieval times, the term described mercenary units. In 1351, a French chronicler, Philip Mouskés, used the term to describe a fraternity of warriors. The Flemish chronicler, Froissart, used the expression 'free companies' for the bands that prowled France and occasionally wandered into Spain during the Hundred Years' War. 'Grand, or great, companies' describe large (containing more than one mercenary company) bands of men-at-arms that operated mainly in Italy as *condottieri*, around the fourteenth and fifteenth centuries. When these forces began to wear a noticeable portion of shiny plate metal for body protection, around the fifteenth century, they were also called 'white companies'.

condotta: Contract by an Italian city-state for services of mercenary companies, led by captains. See *condottiere*.

condottiere: Professional military leader (freely translated as 'captain') who contracted to lead fourteenth and fifteenth century mercenary armies in the service of various Italian states. [*condottieri* (pl)].

constable: Adopted early in the medieval era by France as a senior military command position directly under the king. Juan I introduced the office of constable into Castile. During the War of Granada, Ferdinand's presence in the field effectively usurped the constable's role and it became a hereditary title without significant military command rank.

corregidor: Magistrate, royal official sent to oversee Castilian municipal councils.

cuadrilla: Various meanings: (1) Spanish for *route*, a grouping of about 50 men-at-arms under a knight in medieval cavalry. (2) Leader of an *escuadra* (squadron) which was a sub-unit of one of the *capitanías* (companies) formed by Ferdinand the Catholic.

culverin: Various meanings: (1) French term that became widely used for a category of late fifteenth century cannon which was different from the earlier gunpowder *bombards* in that it had a much smaller bore diameter, and was quite long. Many were relatively 'portable', in that they could be manhandled and positioned for aiming by several men. (2) The term was sometimes used by early chroniclers to refer to hand-held small cannon. However, the expression had wide and very imprecise use by contemporary fifteenth century chroniclers.

daraga: Small, leather, kidney-shaped shield used by Moorish and Spanish *jinete* cavalry.

dobla: Gold Spanish coin.

escaladore: Scaler (of fortress walls in siege operations).

escopeta: Early Italian hand-held gun, usually with a matchlock; an arquebuse.

escudo: Buckler (small, usually round, shield). The term was used to describe an infantry soldier so equipped [*lanza y escudo*, spear and buckler].

espada jinéta: Hispano-Moresque straight sword with a distinctive hilt.

espingarda: Spanish for the handgun used by Christian and Muslim forces in the fifteenth century. It corresponded to the contemporary French *arquebuse* or Italian *escopeta*. By the late fifteenth century, the Iberian Peninsula armies had a large number of *espingardas* with matchlock firing mechanisims.

espingardero: Christian or Muslim Spanish handgunner.

extranjero: Foreign auxiliary in Christian Spanish army.

falchion: In French, *fauchon*; a slightly curved, broad-bladed sword of the Middle Ages. The falchion used in the late fifteenth century appears to be of Eastern [Muslim] origin. It was too wide to be used other than as an infantry weapon, and related more to a 'cutlass' than a scimitar.

faris: Arabic term for a warrior with a horse and roughly equivalent to the European 'knight', suggesting aristocratic social status. See *ghazi.*

ghazi: An Arabic term roughly equivalent to the European 'man-at-arms' or 'knight', a professional (experienced) warrior. Plural is *ghuzat.* The term appears to have been used to emphasize a warrior who fought to defend the Faith, on *jihad.* Although broadly used by many Western authors to describe elite Muslim warriors, it is doubtful that it had this meaning in the late fifteenth-century Hispano-Maghribi domains.

gomere/ghumarah: Member of the Gomara Berber tribe which had a reputation as fierce warriors.

guardas viejas: 'Old guard', the Royal Bodyguard that existed as a small cavalry of the Castilian kings before the reign of Isabella. It was not formally re-established until 1493. Later, under the command of Gonzalo de Ayora, the guard became a focus of military standardization in the Spanish army.

hagib: Prime minister, or chief, in Spanish Muslim government. Equivalent to Turkish vizier.

hermandad: 'Brotherhood': armed bands, originally formed by early medieval Christian communities to maintain civil order and to provide regional defence. The institution was revived by Ferdinand and Isabella as the *Santa Hermandad* ('Holy Brotherhood') in 1474. In the course of the War of Granada, the organization came under Royal direction and was used to impose some standardization on the large levies of manpower. It was disbanded after the war, but many of the organizational patterns adopted during the war formed the basis for Ferdinand's new standing army that followed.

hidalgo: Christian Spanish noble whose ancestor was enobled from 1464, or earlier.

hombre de armas: See *man-at-arms.*

jinete: Castilian for light cavalryman (*genete*) of a Maghribi tradition, originally armed with a small shield (*daraga*) and throwing spears or javelins. Later they employed short lances. Jinetes wore little or no body protection, relied on manoeuvrability and tactical speed for defence, and were accomplished in hit-and-run tactics. They were excellent for ambushes and mountain-pass skirmishes, but they were weak in open battle against heavily armed cavalry.

khamis: The term designated a battle formation of the Granadan-Maghrib armies. It was similar to the medieval European '*battle*'. There were five 'khamis' formations (vanguard, centre, left-wing, right-wing, reserve/rear-guard/baggage-train) in the overall deployment of an army (called a '*tabiya*').

lance: French and English term for the smallest medieval cavalry unit. German term was *gleve*. French and Burgundian *lances* were composed of a man-at-arms, accompanied by a squire, mounted archers, and light cavalrymen; the size of such contingents varied from four to eight in Central European armies, possibly as high as nine in the English. See *lanza*.

lancero: Spanish for pikeman, lancer, or infantry arm with pole weapons.

lanza: Various meanings: (1) Spanish for '*lance*', described their smallest medieval cavalry unit. In northeastern Spain, the cavalry generally followed the French custom. However, in Castile the *lanza* was normally one *hombre de armas*, or *jinete*, sometimes accompanied by an attendant. (2) A weapon such as a lance or spear. (3) An infantryman armed with a *lanza* weapon.

league: About three English statute miles. A marine length of three geographic miles or 1/20 of an equatorial degree. Land length varies at latitudes between 12,750 to 24,250 feet.

lombarda: Used by many Spanish writers for '*bombard*'.

man-at-arms: Originally vassal to a king or nobleman, who maintained himself (and possibly a small contingent under him) ready with armour, weapons, and horse to serve as a warrior in service of his feudal master. In instances where mounted combat was not practical (e.g., narrow mountain passes) or when forces did not have access to sufficient war-horses, the term was applied to well armed and trained warriors. If mounted, his horse usually had some body protection and he could be known as a *caballero armado*. Not all men-at-arms had the social status of a knight, even though some authors use the terms interchangeably. See *caballero*.

mangonel: Some writers consider this to be a generic name, and synonymous with '*catapult*', for all medium-size war machines [engines] throwing large stones and darts. Others associate it more specifically with the machine that operated by a swinging arm under torsion, like the ancient Roman *onager*. Some suggest a further distinction that the *mangonel* has a sling at the throwing end, rather than a cup; the latter being used by the *catapult*. The Arabic for '*mangonel*' was '*arrada*', or the more generic *manjanik/manganiq*.

maravedi: Originally coin money used by both Christians and Spanish Muslims until the early thirteenth century. Became the Castilian standard money of account.

marche: French frontier province, like the one established in the northeastern region of the Iberian Peninsula early in the Middle Ages.

marshal: A military supervisory role. If neither king nor constable were present, the senior marshal commanded the army.

mexuar: Arab council of state

mitcales: Arab gold money

Morisco: Spanish Muslim living under Christian Spanish rule. Generally referring to one who professed acceptance of the Christian faith. Since most were forced to accept Christianity, their belief and loyalty to the Christian monarchy were suspect. The term was used by many chroniclers to connote disloyal Spanish subjects who had some Muslim background.

mortar: In the medieval era, the mortar was an artillery weapon that shot heavy projectiles in a high trajectory, but over a shorter range than did cannon. They were especially used to lob large destructive loads over fortress walls at the defenders. Compared to cannon, the mortar had a much shorter tube and wider mouth. They were usually bell-shaped, or conical, and looked like a small bombard.

moschetto: (1) Italian small cannon (similar to a small *culverin*) of the late fifteenth century. (2) The more powerful long-barrelled firearm (*mosquete*) developed by the Spanish in the sixteenth century.

mozarab: Christian who did not convert to Islam while living in Islamic territories, but accepted Muslim ways and Arabic speech.

mudéjar: Muslim subject under Christian dominions.

musket: (1) Initially derived from the sixteenth-century Italian *moschetto*, and made into a heavy individual firearm (*mosquete*) by the Spanish in the sixteenth century. In French, *mousquet*. The long barrel and thick stock required a supporting 'rest'. Being more powerful, the heavy musket replaced the arquebus. (2) In the late seventeenth century, it became the generic English term for most infantry smooth-bore firearms that had become lighter and no longer required support rests.

muwallad: Muslim of Iberian Peninsula origin; or a convert to Islam who lived in al-Andalus. The term distinguished such persons from Spanish Muslims with North African (Berber), Persian, or Arabian ancestry. Sometimes spelled *muladí*, particularly referring to a Christian who converted.

naft: Arabic term for various flammable substances (in the modern world it is 'petroleum'). The term was used by very early Arabic chroniclers for 'Greek fire', or similar flame-throwing war engines. In the fifteenth century, Arabic writers were known to use it for 'cannon'.

pasavolante: A category of *culverin*-type cannon, gunpowder artillery weapon.

pedone: Urban infantryman who fought for privileges. They were led by a *juez* who was appointed by the king. City sections were led by their own *alcadie*.

pedrero: (1) Spanish for stone worker, among the high-paid cutters of the stone balls for the bombards and cannons; as such, many cutters became part of the siege artillery train and assumed broader duties as gunner assistants. The term assumed, as did other expressions, the meaning of artilleryman in general. (2) The term also was used for an early artillery mortar.

peón: Infantryman, foot soldier.

petard: Explosive device placed upon a gate or wall in order to blast a hole.

pole-arm: A long-stave thrusting weapon [pole-, staff-, or shaft-weapon] which had many configurations derived from ancient times. Although the basic spear and lance were technically 'pole-arms', the term, in context of medieval warfare, referred to poles/shafts with metal points and blades of various designs to permit thrusting and/ or slashing at an opponent. Such weapons were the easiest to acquire for rural or urban mobs and militias. Pole-arms were most effective in battle when used by a well disciplined infantry formation, as shown in the phalanxes of the ancient Greeks and, later, mid-medieval era Swiss.

ribadoquine: Multi-barrelled gun (small calibre) on wheeled carriage. Sometimes referred to as an 'organ gun'. In the late fourteenth and fifteenth centuries they were used as an anti-personnel weapon to defend gates and passageways, and (very rarely) in the field.

ribat: Arabic for frontier area where there was a struggle to defend the Muslim faith, or fortress area.

route: French term for a contingent of mounted men-at-arms, a sub-group of a *battle*, loosely described as a 'squadron', generally numbered 50, who rallied about a knight permitted to fly a pennon. See *battles* and *cuadrillas*.

saif/sayf: Generic Arabic word for sword. Early Muslim swords generally had straight blades. The curved blades began in Eastern Muslim societies and were not common, especially in the Maghrib, until the sixteenth century.

serpentina: See *arquebus*.

serpentine: Various meanings associated with early gunpowder weapons: (1) a category of smaller French and Burgundian cannon, (2) loosly mixed dry components of gunpowder, (3) the Z- or S-shaped device which provided a lever (trigger) to ensure controlled joining of the lit match to the touchhole on early hand-held guns. See *arquebus*.

stradiot: Light cavalryman from Albania, introduced into the Italian Wars of the late fifteenth century as Venetian auxiliaries.

taifa: One of the 'petty' (small) states formed as Spanish Muslim kingdoms after the breakup of the Umayyad Iberian dynasty, and again after the domination of the Almoravides.

Tanto Monta: The motto of the Catholic Sovereigns. It appears on the *Pennon Real* (Royal Banner) of King Ferdinand V and Queen Isabella I of Castile. The banner is perserved at *Musée del Ejército*, Madrid. The motto roughly translates to mean 'as much to one as to the other', signifying their unusual dual monarchial authority. Often accompanying the motto were the individual symbols of the two sovereigns, shown as a double oxen-yoke and a sheaf of arrows. There are two versions as to which monarch each of the symbols represent. (1) The yoke is for Isabella, the Y (for *yugo*, meaning yoke) is the equivalent in Spanish for the letter I, in Isabella's name. The arrows (*feches*, meaning arrows) is the F in Ferdinand's name. (2) The other interpetation is that the symbols are matched the other way around, and the cipher letters are to honour the other's partner. [See José Luis Calvo y Luis Grávalos González, *Banderas de España* (Madrid, 1983), pp.42–3, and Calvert, *Musée del Ejército* (Madrid, 1907), p.61].

thughur: A military frontier zone of the Cordoban Caliphate. The concept continued throughout the course of the reduction of Muslim domains on the Iberian Peninsula.

trébuchet: Non-gunpowder war machine that lobbed various projectiles in high trajectory, over fortress walls. The early versions, originating in the orient, operated by traction: many men pulling on long cords to hoist the opposite, longer end of the pole. They were of medium to very large size. The late medieval *trébuchet* operated on a counter-weight [counterpoise] principal and was popular for siege and fortress defence until gunpowder artillery became fully established. Nations that were slow in developing their gunpowder artillery had such weapons into the sixteenth century.

trueno: Spanish term for 'thunderclap' like early English 'thunder', to generally describe fourteenth- and early fifteenth-century gunpowder weapons.

vega: Spanish Muslim agricultural area. The 'Vega of Granada' was the fertile land to the immediate southwest of the city of Granada.

wali: Muslim governor.

war machine: Non-gunpowder artillery device, sometimes referred to as a 'war-engine'. Used mostly in sieges – both in offence and defence of fortifications – and continued to be employed along with gunpowder weapons well past the fifteenth century. War machines generally hurled stones, naphtha, and various large objects; or they shot directly large arrows or medium sized stones. There is considerable difficulty in matching specific names to precise descriptions. The Arabic writers often used *manjanik (manganiq)* as a generic term for the the artillery machine. An early English term was *'gyns'*. See *ballista, catapult, mangonel, trébuchet.*

BIBLIOGRAPHY

Abun-Nasr, Jamil. *A History of the Maghrib in the Islamic Period*, Cambridge University Press, Cambridge, 1987.

Allmand, Christopher T. *The Hundred Years' War: England and France at War, c.1300–c.1450*, Cambridge University Press, Cambridge, 1988.

anonymous Arabic author. *Nubdhat al-Asr fi akhbar muluk Bani Nasr* [the *Nubdhat*], translated into Spanish by al-Bustani and Carlos Quiros as *Fragmento de la época sobre noticias de los reyes Nazaritas o capitulación de Grandado*, Larache: Institute General Franco, Madrid, 1940.

Arié, Rachel. *L'Espagne musulmane au temps des Nasrides (1232–1492)*, Editions E. de Boccard, Paris, 1973.

Ayalon, D. *Gunpowder and Firearms in the Mamlūk Kingdom, A Challenge to Medieval Society*, Vallentine, Mitchell, London, 1956.

Bachrach, Bernard S. 'Medieval Siege Warfare: A Reconnaissance, *Journal of Military History*, vol.58, no.1 (January), Society for Military History, Lexington, Virginia, 1994.

Balaguer, Victor. *Los Reyes Católicos*, tomo II, Libero Tercero, *Las guerras de Granada*, Real Academia de la Historia, Madrid, 1898.

Basin, Thomas. *Histoire de Charles VII*, translated from Latin to French by Charles Samaran, Société d'Edition «Les Belles Lettres», Paris, 1964.

Beeler, John. *Warfare in Feudal Europe, 730–1200*, Cornell University Press, Ithaca and London, 1971.

Benavides, Antonio. *Memoria sobre la guerra del reino de Granada, y los tratos y conciertos que precedieron a las capitulaciones de la Ciudad*, [*Memoria*], Madrid, 1845.

Bernáldez, Andréas. *Memorias del reinado de los Reyes Católicos*, eds. M: Gómez-Moreno and J. de la Mata Carriazo, Real Academia de la Historia, Madrid, 1962.

Bishko, Charles H. 'The Castilian as Plainsman: The Medieval Ranching Frontier in La Mancha and Extremadura', *The New World Looks at Its History*, eds. A.R. Lewis and T.F. McGann, Austin, Texas, 1963.

_____. 'The Spanish and Portuguese Reconquest, 1095–1492', in *A History of the Crusades*, eds. H.W. Hazard and Kenneth Sutton, 3 vols, University of Wisconsin, Madison, 1975, vol. 3, pp.396–456.

Blacker, Irwin R., ed., *The Portable Prescott: The Essence of Ferdinand and Isabella, The Conquest of Mexico, The Conquest of Peru,* edited sections of the original works, with a biographical introduction; Viking Press, New York, 1963, 1966.

Bradbury, Jim. *The Medieval Siege*, Boydell, Woodbridge, 1992.

Buehr, Walter. *Firearms*, Thomas Y. Crowell, New York, 1967.

Burne, Alfred H. *The Agincourt War*, Eyre & Spottiswoode, London, 1956; Greenwood Press, Westport, Connecticut, 1967; Greenhill, London, 1991.

Burns, Robert I. *Moors and Crusaders in Mediterranean Spain*, Collected Studies, Variorum, London, 1878.

Calvert, Albert F. *Spanish Arms and Armour, being a historical and descriptive account of the Royal Armoury of Madrid*, John Lane, London, 1907.

Calvo Perez, Jose Luis and Luis Gravalos Gonzalez. *Banderas de Espagna*, Silex, Madrid, 1983.

Cantwell, Robert. 'William Hickling Prescott', *Famous American Men of Letters*, Dodd, Mead, New York, 1961.

Cipolla, Carlo M. *Guns, Sails, and Empires: Technological Innovation and the Early Phases of European Expansion 1400–1700*, Pantheon Books and Minerva Press, London and New York, 1965.

Circourt, Anne Marie Joseph Albert, comte de. *Histoire des Mores mudejares et des Morisques*, G.A. Dentu, Paris, 1846.

Clephan, Robert C. 'The Ordnance of the Fourteenth and Fifteenth Centuries', *The Archaeological Society*, 68, London, 1911.

Clonard, Serafín María de Soto y Abbach, conde de. *Historia orgánica de la armas de infantería y caballería españolas desde la creación del ejército permanente hasta el día*, vol.2 (of 16), D.B. Gonzalez, Madrid, 1851–59.

Colin, G.S. 'The Maghrib' in *Encyclopaedia of Islam*, 2nd edition, vol.I, E.J. Brill, Leiden, Luzac and London, 1960.

Commager, Henry Steele, 'Prescott, William Hickling (1796–1859)', *Encyclopedia of the Social Sciences*, vol.xii, Macmillan, New York, 1930–35.

Condé, José A. *History of the Dominion of the Arabs in Spain (Historia de la Dominacion de los Arabes en España)*, translated from the Spanish by Mrs Jonathan Foster, 3 vols, Henry G. Bohn, London, 1854.

Contamine, Philippe. *La Guerre au Moyen âge*, Presses Universitaires de France, Paris, 1980. English translation *War in the Middle Ages* by Michael Jones, Basil Blackwell, Oxford, 1984.

Cook, Weston F., Jr. 'The Cannon Conquest of Nasrid Spain and the End of the Reconquista', *Journal of Military History*, vol.57, no.1 (January), Society for Military History, Lexington, Virginia, 1993.

_____ . *The Hundred Years War for Morocco: Gunpowder and the Military Revolution in the Early Modern Muslim World*, Westview Press, Boulder, Colorado, 1994.

_____ . 'Warfare and Firearms in Fifteenth Century Morocco, 1400–

1492', *War & Society*, vol.11, no.1, October, Australian Defence Force Academy, Canberra, 1993.

De Amezüa, A.G. and Mayo. *La battalla de Lucena y el redadero ratrato de Boabdil*, Imprenta Clásica Española, Madrid, 1915.

Delbrück, Hans. *Medieval Warfare*, vol.III of *History of the Art of War* series, translated by Walter J. Renfroe, Jr., University of Nebraska Press, Lincoln, 1990.

_____. *The Dawn of Modern Warfare*, vol.IV of *History of the Art of War* series, translated by Walter J. Renfroe, Jr., University of Nebraska Press, Lincoln, 1990.

Descola, Jean. *Histoire d'Espagne*, Fayard, Paris, 1959, 1967, 1979, translated by Elaine P. Halperin as *A History of Spain*, Alfred A. Knopf, New York, 1963.

De Vries, Kelly Robert. *Medieval Military Technology*, Broadview Press, Peterborough, Ontario, 1992.

Díez de Games, Gutierre. *El Victorial: Crónica de don Pero Niño, Conde de Buelna*, ed. Juan de Mata Carriazo, Madrid, 1940. English translation by Joan Evans of sections published as '*The Unconquered Knight*', *The Chronicle of Don Pero Niño, Count of Buelna*, Routledge, London, 1928.

Dozy, Reinhart. *Histoire des Musulmans d'Espagne jusqu'à la Conquête de l'Andalousie par les Almoravides*, 4 vols, Leiden, 1861. A second edition, edited by É. Lévi-Provençal, 3 vols, was published in Leiden, 1932. An English translation by Francis Griffin Stokes was published as *Spanish Islam*, Frank Cass, London, 1972.

Duffy, Christopher. *Siege Warfare: The Fortress in the Early Modern World, 1494–1660*, Routledge and Kegan Paul, London and Henley, 1979.

Dupuy, R. Ernest and Trevor N. *The Encyclopedia of Military History from 3500 BC to the Present*, Harper & Row, New York, 1964, 1977, 1993.

Duro, Fernandez Cesáreo. *La marina de Castilla*, El Progreso Editorial, Madrid, 1894.

Egg, Eric. 'From the Beginning to the Battle of Marignano – 1515', in *Guns: An Illustrated History of Artillery*, ed. Joseph Jobé, Crescent, New York, 1971.

Elliott, J.H. *Imperial Spain 1469–1716*, Edward Arnold, London, 1963; St. Martin's Press, New York, 1964.

Firoozye, B.H. 'Warfare in Fifteenth Century Castile', PhD dissertation, University of California, 1974.

Fletcher, Richard. *Moorish Spain*, Weidenfeld & Nicolson, London, 1992; Henry Holt, New York, 1993.

Fuentes Cervera, Eduardo de. *El Ejército y las armas en la época de los Reyes Católicos*, Madrid, 1951.

Fuller, J.F.C. *The Decisive Battles of the Western World, 480 BC–1757*, vol.1 (of 3), Eyre & Spottiswoode, London, and Funk & Wagnalls, New York, 1954; Chapter 18, 'The Reconquest and Unification of Spain', and Chapter 19, 'The Siege of Málaga, 1487, and the Conquest of Granada, 1492'.

Gardiner, Clinton Harvey. *Hickling Prescott – An Annotated bibliography of Published Works*, Washington, DC, 1958.

_____. *The Literary Memoranda of William Hickling Prescott*, 2 vols, University of Oklahoma, Norman, Oklahoma, 1961.

_____. *Prescott and His Publishers*, South Illinois University Press, Carbondale, 1959.

_____. *William Hickling Prescott: a Bibliography*, University of Texas Press, Austin, Texas, 1969.

Gayangos, Pascual de. *The History of the Mohammedan Dynasties in Spain*, a free translation of the work of Ahmad ibn Muhammad Maqqari (d.1631), extracted from the *Nafhu-t-tib min qhosni-l-Andalusi-r-rattib wa tarikh lisanu-d-din Ibni-l-Khattib* annotated with many historical notes; 2 vols., W.H. Allen, London, 1840–43. A Spanish version, *Historia de los dinastias mahometanas de España*, was reportedly published in 1843; publisher is unknown.

Gibb, H.A.R., J.H. Kramers, E. Lévi-Provençal, and J. Schacht, eds. *The Encyclopedia of Islam*, 2nd edition, 8 vols, E.J. Brill, Leiden, Luzac and London, 1960–93.

Guilmartin, John F. *Gunpowder and Galleys: Changing Technology and Mediterranean Warfare at Sea in the Sixteenth Century*, Cambridge University Press, Cambridge, 1974.

Hale, John Rigby. 'Early Development of the Bastion: an Italian Chronology 1450–1534', in *Europe in the Late Middle Ages*, eds. J.R. Hale, J.R.L. Highfield, and B. Smalley, Northwestern University Press, Evanston, 1955.

_____. 'Gunpowder and the Renaissance: an Essay in the History of Ideas', in *From Renaissance to the Counter Reformation*, Jonathan Cape, London, 1966.

Harvey, Leonard P. *Islamic Spain, 1250 to 1500*, The University of Chicago Press, Chicago, 1990.

Hassan, Ahmad Y. al-, and Donald R. Hill. *Islamic Technology – an Illustrated History*. Cambridge University, Cambridge, 1986.

Heath, Ian. *Armies of the Middle Ages*, vol.I, Wargames Research Group, Sussex, 1982.

Hess, Andrew Christie. 'The Evolution of the Ottoman Seaborne Empire in the Age of Oceanic Discoveries, 1453–1525', *American Historical Review*, 75 (December), American Historical Association, Washington, DC, 1970.

_____. 'Firearms and the Decline of Ibn Khaldun's Military Elite', *Archivum Ottomanicum*, 5, Mouton, The Hague, 1972.

Hewitt, H.J. 'The Organization of War', in *The Hundred Years War*, ed. Kenneth Fowler, Macmillan and Saint Martin's Press, New York, 1971.

Heymann, F.G. *John Zizka and the Hussite Revolution*, Princeton University Press, Princeton, New Jersey, 1955.

Highfield, R. ed. *Spain in the Fifteenth Century, 1369–1516, Essays and Extracts by Historians of Spain*, translations by Frances M. López-Morillas; Macmillan, London; Harper & Row, New York, 1972.

Hillgarth, Jocelyn N. *The Spanish Kingdoms 1250–1516*, 2 vols, Clarendon Press, Oxford, 1976–78.

Hime, H.W.L. *The Origin of Artillery*, Longmans, Green, London, 1915.

Hoffmeyer, Ada Bruhn. *Arms and Armour in Spain: A Short Survey*, 2 vols, Instituto de Estudios Sobre Armas Antiguas Consejo Superior de Investigaciones Cientificas, Patronato Menendez y Pelayo, Madrid, 1972–82.

Hogg, Oliver F.G. *Artillery: Its Origin, Heyday and Decline*, Hurst, London, 1969; Archon Books, Connecticut, 1970.

_____. *Clubs to Cannon*, Gerald Duckworth, London, 1968.

Holt, P.M., A.K.S. Lambton and B. Lewis, eds. *The Cambridge History of Islam*, 2 vols, Cambridge University Press, Cambridge, 1970.

Howell, Roger, ed. *Prescott, The Conquest of Mexico, The Conquest of Peru and other Selections*, abridged, Twayne, New York, 1966.

Huici Miranda, Ambroxio. *Las grandes batallas de la Reconquista*, Instituto de Estudios Africanos, Madrid, 1956.

_____. 'The Iberian Peninsula and Sicily', *The Cambridge History of Islam*, vol.2, part VII, 'Africa and the Muslim West', Chapter 7, Cambridge University Press, Cambridge, 1970.

Ibáñez de Ibero, Carlos. *Historia de la marina de guerra española desde el siglo XIII hasta nuestros días*, Espasa Calpe, Madrid, 1939.

Irving, Washington. *Chronicle of the Conquest of Granada*, 2 vols, author's revised edition (Agapida Edition), G.P. Putnam, New York, 1893. First published: AMS Press, New York, 1829; recent publication: *A Chronicle of the Conquest of Granada*, 'by Fray Antonio Agapa' with introduction by editor Miriam J. Shillingsburg, Twayne, Boston, 1988.

Johnson, Curt. 'Lanza Gineta: Spanish Light Cavalry of the Early Italian Wars, Toward Cerignola, No.1', *Scenarios for Wargamers*, vol.1, no.1 (November), Chevy Chase, Maryland, 1992.

Kamen, Henry. *Spain 1469–1714: a Society in Conflict*, Longman, New York, 1983.

Ladero Quesada, Miguel Angel. *Castilla y la Conquista del Reino de Granada*, Editorial Gredos, Valladolid, 1967.

_____. *Granada: Historia de un país Islámico (1232–1571)*, Editorial Gredos, Madrid, 1969.

Landström, Björn. *The Ship, An Illustrated History*, Doubleday, New York, 1961.

Lane-Poole, Stanley. *The Moors in Spain*, Putnam, New York, 1899.

Lavin, James D. *A History of Spanish Firearms*, Herbert Jenkins, London, and Arco, New York, 1965.

Lévi-Provençal, Évariste. *Histoire de l'Espagne musulmane*, 3 vols, Leiden, Paris, 1950–53.

Liss, Peggy K. *Isabel the Queen, Life and Times*, Oxford University Press, New York, and Oxford, England, 1992.

Lomax, Derek W. *The Reconquest of Spain*, Longman, London, 1978.

Lot, Ferdinand. *L'Art Militaire et les Armées au Moyen Age en Europe et dans le Proche Orient*, 2 vols, Payot, Paris, 1946.

Lunenfeld, Marvin. *The Council of the Santa Hermandad; a study of the pacification forces of Ferdinand and Isabella*, University of Miami Press, Coral Gables, Flordia, 1970.

_____. *Keepers of the City: the corregidores of Isabella I of Castile, 1474–1504*, Cambridge University Press, Cambridge, 1987.

Lynn, John A. *Tools of War: Instruments, Ideas, and Institutions of Warfare*, 1445–1871, University of Illinois Press, Urbana, 1990.

MacDonald, Ian A. *Don Fernando de Antequerra*, Oxford University Press, Oxford, 1948.

MacKay, Angus. *Spain in the Middle Ages, From Frontier to Empire, 1000–1500*, Macmillan, London, 1977, 1993.

Mallett, Michael. *Mercenaries and Their Master: Warfare in Renaissance Italy*, The Bodley Head, London, 1974.

Mann, James Gow, ed. *Wallace Collection Catalogues. European Arms and Armour*, 2 vols, Clowes, London, 1962.

Mann, James Gow. 'Notes on the Armour worn in Spain from the Tenth to the Fifteenth Century', *Archaeologia*, LXXXIII, 1933.

Maqqari, Ahmad ibn Muhammad [al-] (d. 1631), *Nafhu-t-tib min qhosni-l-Andalusi-r-rattib wa tarikh lisanu-d-din Ibni-l-Khattib*, translated in to English and Spanish and edited by Pascual de Gayangos. See Gayangos' *History of the Mohammedan Dynasties in Spain*.

Mariéjol, Jean Hippolyte. *L'Espagne sous Ferdinand et Isabelle*, May et Motteroz, Paris, 1892; translated and edited by Benjamin Keen as *The Spain of Ferdinand and Isabella*, Rutgers University, New Jersey, 1961.

Mata Carriazo, Juan de. *La España de los Reyes Católicos*, vol.17, *Historia de España*, ed. R. Menéndez Pidal, Espasa Calpe, Madrid, 1969.

_____. *Los Relieves de la Guerra de Granada en la Silleria del Coro de la Catedral de Toledo*, Universidad de Granada, Granada, 1985.

Mata Carriazo, Juan de, ed. *Crónica de los Reyes Católicos*, 2 vols, Madrid, 1927, 1943.

Mercier, Louis. *L'Ornement des âmes et la devise des habitants de l'Andalus (un traité de guerre sainte islamique)*; loose translation of the late fourteenth-century Arabic historian Ibn Hudhayl's *Tuhfat al-Anfus wa Shaar Sukkan al-Andalus*; Libraire Orientaliste, Paul Geuthner, Paris, 1924.

_____. *La Parure des cavaliers et l'insigne des preux* [The dress of Knights and Insignias of Valiant Warriors], partial translation of Hudhayl's *Hilyat al-Fursan wa Shiar ash-Shujan*, believed to have been written thirty years after *Tuhfat al-Anfus*, Libraire Orientaliste, Paul Geuthner, Paris, 1939.

Merriman, Roger Bigelow. *The Rise of the Spanish Empire in the Old and in the New*, 4 vols (vol. 2: *The Catholic Kings*), Macmillan, New York, 1918–34, 1962.

Montagne, Robert. *Les Berbères et la Makhzan dans le Sud du Maroc*, Comté de l'Afrique Française, Paris, 1930; translated with annotations by David Seddon as *The Berbers: Their Social and Political Organization*, Frank Cass, London, 1973.

Morrison, Sean. *Armor*, Thomas Y. Crowell, New York, 1963.

Moulton, Charles W., ed. *The Library of Literary Criticism of English and American Authors, Volume VI, 1855–1874*, Peter Smith, Gloucester, Mass., 1959.

Needham, Joseph. *Gunpowder as the Fourth Power*, Hong Kong University Press, Hong Kong, 1985.

Nicolle, David. 'Abu Abdullah Muhammad XI Boabdil of Granada', *Military Illustrated*, no.43 (December) 1991.

_____. *Early Medieval Islamic Arms and Armour*, Instituto de Estudios Sobre Armas Antiguas Consejo Superior de Investigaciones Cientificas, Patronato Menendez y Pelayo, Madrid, 1976.

_____. *El Cid and the Reconquista 1050–1492*, illustrations by Angus McBride, Osprey Men-at-Arms Series, Osprey, London, 1988.

_____. 'Fernando El Catolico', *Military Illustrated*, no.44 (January) 1992.

Oakeshott, R. Ewart. *The Archaeology of Weapons*, Frederick A. Praeger, New York, 1960, 1963.

O'Callaghan, Joseph F. *A History of Medieval Spain*, Cornell University Press, Ithaca, New York, 1975.

Oman, Charles. *A History of the Art of War in the Middle Ages*, 2 vols, Methuen, London, 1924; Greenhill, London, 1991.

_____. *A History of the the Art of War in the Sixteenth Century (1495–1606)*, Methuen, London, 1937; Greenhill, London, 1989.

Palencia, Alonso de. *Guerra de Granada*. Translated by A. Paz y Mélia from original Latin work: *Narrato Belli Adversus Granatenses*, reprinted as *Crónica de Enríque IV*, 3 vols, Bibliotheca de Autores Españoles, Madrid, 1975.

Partington, J.R. *A History of Greek Fire and Gunpowder*, W. Heffer, Cambridge, 1960.

Pérez, José Luis Calvo y Luis Grávalos González. *Banderas de España*, Silex, Madrid, 1983.

Pipes, Daniel. *Slave Soldiers and Islam, the Genesis of a Military System*, Yale University Press, New Haven, 1981.

Powers, James F. *A Society Organized for War*, University of California, Berkeley and Los Angeles, 1988.

Pratt, Fletcher. *The Battles That Changed History*, Doubleday, New York, 1956.

Prescott, William Hickling. *History of the Reign of Ferdinand and Isabella, the Catholic*, 3 vols, Stationers, Boston, 1837; 3rd edition in 2 vols, John B. Alden, New York, 1838; 15th edition with all of author's final revisions and edited by John Foster Kirk, J.B. Lippincott, Philadelphia, 1892.

_____. *History of the Reign of Ferdinand*, abridged and edited by C. Harvey Gardiner, Allen and Unwin, London, 1962; reprinted with illustrations, Limited Editions Club of New York, 1967.

_____. *The Portable Prescott: The Essence of Ferdinand and Isabella, The Conquest of Mexico, The Conquest of Peru,* selected and edited portions of the works, with a Biographical Introduction by Irwin R.Blacker, The Viking Press, New York, 1963, 1966.

_____. *Prescott, The Conquest of Mexico, The Conquest of Peru and other Selections,* edited and abridged, and with an Introduction by Roger Howell, Twayne, New York, 1966.

_____. *Prescott: Unpublished Letters to Gayangos in the Library of the Hispanic Society of America,* edited by Clara Louisa Penney, Hispanic Society of America, New York, 1927.

_____. *The History of the Conquest of Mexico,* 3 vols, Harper and Brothers, New York, 1843; edited and abridged in 1 vol. with introduction by C.H. Gardiner, The University of Chicago Press, Chicago, 1966.

Pulgar, Fernando del. *Crónica de los reyes católicos,* 2 vols, Espasa Calpe, Madrid, 1943.

Rodgers, William L. *Naval Warfare Under Oars: Fourth through Sixteenth Centuries,* Naval Institute Press, Annapolis, 1940, 1967.

Rogers, Clifford J. 'The Military Revolutions of the Hundred Years' War', *The Journal of Military History,* vol.57, no.2 (April), Lexington, Virginia, 1993.

Ronart, Stephan and Nandy. *Concise Encyclopedia of Arabic Civilization, the Arab West,* Djambatan, Amsterdam, 1959, 1966.

Ropp, Theodore. *War in the Modern World,* Collier Books, New York, 1962.

Runciman, Steven. *The Fall of Constantinople 1453,* Cambridge University Press, Cambridge, 1965, 1992.

Russell, P. E. *The English Intervention in Spain and Portugal in the Time of Edward III and Richard II,* Clarendon Press, Oxford, 1955.

Seco de Lucena Paredes, Luis. *The Book of the Alhambra, A History of the Sultans of Granada,* Editorial Everest, León, 1990.

Sherborne, J. 'The Battle of La Rochelle and the War at Sea, 1368–1389', *Bulletin of the Institute of Historical Research,* vol.42 (May), Athlone Press, London, 1969.

Shestack, Alan. *Fifteenth Century Engravings of Northern Europe,* National Gallery of Art, Washington, DC, 1967.

Sordo, Enrique. *Moorish Spain,* Crown, New York, 1963.

Stewart, Paul J., Jr. *The Army of the Catholic Kings: Spanish Military Organization and Administration in the Reign of Ferdinand and Isabella, 1474–1516,* PhD dissertation, University of Illinois Press, Urbana, 1961.

_____. 'Military Command and the Development of the Viceroyalty under Ferdinand and Isabella', *The Journal of Medieval and Renaissance Studies,* vol.5, no.2 (Fall), 1975.

_____. 'The *Santa Hermandad* and the First Italian Campaign of Gonzalo de Córdoba, 1495–1498', *Renaissance Quarterly,* vol.28, no.1 (Spring), 1975.

_____. 'The Soldier, the Bureaucrat, and Fiscal Records in the Army of Ferdinand and Isabella', *The Hispanic American Historical Review*, vol.49, no.2 (May), 1969.

Stone, George C. *A Glossary of the Construction, Decoration and Use of Arms and Armor, in All Countries and in All Times*, Jack Brussel, New York, 1934.

Suárez Fernández, Luis. *Los Reyes Católicos: el tiempo de la guerra de Granada*, Ediciones Rialp, Madrid, 1989.

_____. 'The Atlantic and the Mediterranean Among the Objectives of the House of Trastámara', and 'The Kingdom of Castile in the Fifteenth Century', in *Spain in the Fifteenth Century, 1369–1516, Essays and Extracts by Historians of Spain*, ed. R. Highfield, translations by Frances M. López-Morillas; Harper & Row, New York, and Macmillan, London, 1972.

Tarassuk, Leonid and Claude Blair, eds. *The Complete Encyclopedia of Arms & Weapons*, Country Life, London, and Simon and Schuster, New York, 1982.

Taylor, F.L. *The Art of War in Italy, 1494–1529*, Cambridge University Press, Cambridge, 1921; Greenhill, London, 1993.

Terrasse, H. 'Military architecture in the Muslim West' in *Encyclopaedia of Islam*, 2nd edition, vol.I, E.J. Brill, Leiden, Luzac and London, 1960.

Torre, A. de la. *Los reyes católicos y Granada*, Institut Jerónimo Zurita, Madrid, 1946.

Vale, Malcolm G.A. *War and Chivalry*, Duckworth, London, 1981.

Valera, Mosén Diego de. *Crónica de los Reyes Católicos*. ed. Juan de Mata Carriazo, Jose Molina, Madrid, 1927.

Verbruggen, J.F. *The Art of War in Western Europe during the Middle Ages*, translated by S. Willard & S.C.M. Southern, North-Holland, Amsterdam, New York, Oxford, 1977.

Vicens Vives, Jaime. *Approaches to the History of Spain*, translated and edited by Joan Connelly Ullman from *Aproximación a la historia de España* (Editorial Vicens-Vives, Barcelona, 1952, 1960), University of California Press, Berkeley, California, 1967.

Vigón Suero-Díaz, Jorge. *El Ejército de los Reyes Católicos*, Editoral Nacional, Madrid, 1968.

_____. *Historia de la artillería Española*, 3 vols, Institut Jerónimo Zurita, Madrid, 1947.

Vogt, John. *Los Ejercitos de la Reconquista*, Servicio Historico Militar, Madrid, 1984.

_____. 'Saint Barbara's Legion: Portuguese Artillery in the Struggle for Morocco, 1415–1578', *Military Affairs*, 41 (December), American Military Institute, Ft. Leavenworth, Kansas, 1977.

INDEX

282